Two Decades of Legislative Politics and Governance in Nigeria's National Assembly

Fatai Ayinde Aremu · Adebola Rafiu Bakare
Editors

Two Decades of Legislative Politics and Governance in Nigeria's National Assembly

Issues, Achievements, Challenges and Prospects

palgrave
macmillan

Editors
Fatai Ayinde Aremu
Department of Political Science
University of Ilorin
Ilorin, Nigeria

Adebola Rafiu Bakare
Department of Political Science
University of Ilorin
Ilorin, Nigeria

ISBN 978-981-33-4454-9 ISBN 978-981-33-4455-6 (eBook)
https://doi.org/10.1007/978-981-33-4455-6

This Palgrave Macmillan imprint is published by the registered company Springer Nature Singapore Pte Ltd.
The registered company address is: 152 Beach Road, #21-01/04 Gateway East, Singapore 189721, Singapore

Dedicated to all victims of the COVID-19 Pandemic and all frontline health workers worldwide

Foreword

Not too long ago, *The Economist* asked a profound question, "What's Gone Wrong with Democracy?" The essay, an intense global review of how democracy is floundering in Europe, North and South America, Asia and Africa, emphatically surmised that democracy is under stress worldwide. It is noted that in some countries, no sooner than dictators are displaced, the euphoria dissipates as successor regimes failed to enthrone viable democratic alternatives. The flaws inherent in the operation of democratic institutions and processes begin to manifest in entrenched polarization and endless squabbles among competing elite factions and power blocs. In Egypt, the Morsi-led government that followed the toppling of decades-long reign of Hosni Mubarak in Cairo was short-lived as a result of irreconcilable ideological and sectarian interests. Its southern neighbour, Sudan, is still grappling with the aftermath of the dethronement of President Omar Al-Bashir who held sway in Khartoum for thirty years.

Indeed, democracy is going through difficult times. The very institutions that are designed to make democracy work sometimes fail to swiftly and sufficiently meet the aspirations of the citizens. In particular, the Legislature which constitutionally is the custodian of people's mandate is often mired in intractable partisan intrigues and aimlessly endless debates leading to unnecessary paralysis. Between 2018 and 2019, the United States experienced its longest government shutdown in history because the Congress failed to pass appropriation bill due to disagreement with

President Donald Trump over the latter's insistence on $5.7 billion federal funds for the construction of US–Mexico border wall. While millions of Americans reel under the excruciating pain of economic hardship caused by COVD-19 Pandemic, the Congress refused to approve President Trump's $300 billion economic relief package that would pay unemployment benefits, protect citizens from eviction and offer student loan relief. As Capitol Hill lock horns with the White House over ideological and partisan interests, public confidence in democratic institutions especially the legislature continue to suffer even in the United States.

As the saying goes, if gold rusts, what will iron do? In Nigeria, public confidence and trust in the National Assembly is low. The results of 2017 Afrobarometer survey Round 7 revealed that 88% of respondents never contacted the National Assembly to air their views on important problems confronting the nation and 65% believed members of National Assembly never listened to what they have to say. When asked how much they trust the National Assembly, 43% said "not at all," 32% chose "just a little" while 16% said they "somewhat" trusted the National Assembly. Only 8% said they trusted the National Assembly "a lot."The trust deficit is massive and public confidence in the legislature as an accountable and democratic institution is not getting stronger largely because of unfavourable image, which in itself derives from self-inflicted harm by operators of the institution. The National Assembly is a major news item when it comes to the jumbo pay of legislators adjudged to be among the highest in the world, legislature–executive confrontations which usually paralyzed the system, delays in the passage of the appropriation bill sometimes spilling over to second quarter of the fiscal year, shady implementation of constituency development fund, perversion of oversight and public hearings, allegations of legislation for the highest bidder, among others. All these contribute to poor public perception of the National Assembly.

It is possible to infer that there is poor public knowledge of the workings of the National Assembly which is complicated by a flawed media coverage that is borne by the failure of the National Assembly to effectively connect the people through the media. In each episode of legislative–executive conflict, the legislature is often seen as the guilty one largely because it lacks the resources and technical reach of the executive. Unlike the executive, turn-over rate in the National Assembly is around 70%. Each legislative session witnesses massive new entrants with limited knowledge of parliamentary procedures. The technical support available each legislator, in terms of quantity and quality, is grossly insufficient to match the extensive bureaucratic strength of the executive. Therefore, each duel with the executive brings additional damage to the reputation and public image of the National Assembly. Yet, the National Assembly is often desirous of exercising its constitutional mandate of holding the executive accountable. This dilemma is a continuous decimal in the annals of legislative history in Nigeria, especially in the Fourth Republic which has recorded the longest unbroken period of legislative experience.

This book, *Two Decades of Legislative Politics and Governance in Nigeria's National Assembly: Issues, Achievements, Challenges and Prospects*, is a timely interrogation of the salient issues concerning the National Assembly. Its unique assemblage of chapters produced by a blend of seasoned researchers and embedded frontline parliamentary staff invites readers to a nuanced engagement of the contours of the National Assembly and how it has fared in Nigeria's thorny political ecosystem in the last two decades.

Professor Habu S. Galadima
Director General
National Institute for Policy and Strategic Studies (NIPSS)
Kuru, Nigeria

About This Book

This book provides a detailed narrative introduction to legislative politics and governance in Nigeria. It evaluates the performance of the Nigerian National Assembly following the country's first ever experience of twenty years of uninterrupted democratic rule between 1999 and 2019. The book contains 15 chapters written by seasoned scholars and edited by experts in legislative studies. While the editors admit that no single piece could comprehensively cover all issues relating to the twenty years experience of the Nigerian national legislature, the book successfully covers the salient issues that are germaine to the understanding of legislative politics and evaluation of the legislative performance of the National Assembly. The well articulated writing and analytical styles adopted make the book to be handy and very useful to fresh learners, lawmakers, analysts, legislative aides and all other stakeholders.

Contents

Editors and Contributors

About the Editors

Fatai Ayinde Aremu is a Professor of Political Science, University of Ilorin, Nigeria. He obtained B.Sc. Political Science in University of Jos, M.Sc. Political Science in Usmanu Dan Fodio University, Sokoto and Ph.D. Asia Pacific Studies at the Ritsumeikan Asia Pacific University in Japan where he was awarded certificate of excellence for outstanding quality of research.

He was a Senior Technical Advisor on Policy and Legislative Advocacy at a Bill and Melinda Gates Foundation funded advocacy and social accountability project, Partnership for Advocacy in Child and Family Health (PACFaH), a project anchored by development Research and Projects Centre (dRPC), Abuja, Nigeria. In that position, he coordinated and conducted a number of studies, training programmes and top-notch policy engagement on health sector budget, health policy and legislation. Before joining dRPC, he was the Head of Socio-Political Unit at the National Institute for Legislative and Democratic Studies, National Assembly, Abuja where he conducted policy research and training activities on policy engaged research, bill analysis and budget tracking for Legislators, Legislative Aides and Parliamentary Staff.

Professor Aremu has developed, organized and facilitated a number of policy engagement activities and conducted training programmes in policy oriented research. These include Critical Policy Engaged Research (CPER) and Informed Research Consumers (IRC) modules which address the peculiar needs of demand and supply sides of research evidence. The modules have been piloted and delivered successfully across African countries. The training programmes which take place twice a year is delivered to cohorts of researchers and policy actors from different African policy institutions, universities, research institutes, CSOs and think-tanks. It is funded and organized by the Partnership for Social and Governance Research (PASGR) and Institute for Development Studies (IDS), University of Sussex, UK, in Nairobi, Kenya with the support of DFID.

He organized and facilitated the Utafiti Sera Policy Forumon Inclusive Growth and Employment Creation in Agriculture and Agro processing in Nigeria at National Institute for Legislative and Democratic Studies (NILDS) in collaboration with the Partnership for African Social and Governance Research (PASGR). He facilitated a policy training retreat for Members of Senate and House Committees on Health, Primary Healthcare, Health Institutions and Appropriation. The Retreat which took place in Pan African

Parliament, Midrand also involved interactive sessions with the South African Parliamentary Committees on Health and Appropriation in Cape Town, South Africa.

He is presently a Directing Staff at the National Institute for Policy and Strategic Studies (NIPSS), Nigeria's apex policy think-tank.

He is the author of *Asymmetrical Foreign Policy Behaviour of Japan and China* (2011) and co-editor of *Introduction to International Relations* (2012). His works have appeared in *Africa Today*, *African and Asian Studies*, *Ritsumeikan Journal of Asia Pacific Studies*, *Asia Pacific World*, etc.

Adebola Rafiu Bakare (Ph.D.) teaches in the Department of Political Science, University of Ilorin, Nigeria. His research interest is on legislative studies, governance institutions, psephology and security studies. He has published widely on legislative issues and has developed a model (ILES) for legislative assessment which is suitable for assessing institutional lawmaking effectiveness in both developed and developing democracies across the world. He recently participated in a European Union Agency for Fundamental Rights-(FRA) funded research with Eticas Research and Consulting (Barcelona, Spain) on *Biometric Data in Large EU: IT-Systems in the Areas of Borders, Visa and Asylum—Fundamental Rights Implications.* He is a member of several professional bodies including Nigerian Political Science Association (NPSA), West African Political Science Association (WAPSA), Nigerian Society of International Affairs (NSIA) and Nigeria Institute of Management (Chartered), among others. He has published in several reputable national and international journals and has contributed chapters in edited books. He is currently the Managing Editor of "*Political Science Review* (PSR)," the official journal of the Department of Political Science and the Editorial Secretary of *Ilorin Journal of Business and Social Sciences* (IJBSS), the official journal of Faculty of Social Sciences, both of the University of Ilorin. He is the founder and Executive Director of Centre for Legislative Research, Documentation and Training (CLRD&T).

Contributors

Terfa W. Abraham National Institute for Legislative and Democratic Studies (NILDS), Abuja, Nigeria

Oluwashina Moruf Adebiyi Department of Political Science, Faculty of Social Sciences, University of Ilorin, Ilorin, Nigeria

Angela Ajodo-Adebanjoko Department of Political Science, Federal University Lafia, Lafia, Nigeria

Fatima Omotayo Aliu Department of Political Science, Faculty of Social Sciences, University of Ilorin, Ilorin, Nigeria

Opeyemi Idowu Aluko Department of Political Science, Ajayi Crowther University, Oyo, Nigeria

Adekunle Mojeed Animashaun Department of Political Science, Fountain University, Osogbo, Nigeria

Fatai Ayinde Aremu Department of Political Science, University of Ilorin, Ilorin, Nigeria

Gafar Idowu Ayodeji Department of Political Science, Tai Solarin University of Education, Ijagun, Ogun State, Nigeria

Victoria N. Azu Department of Political/Administrative Studies, University of Port Harcourt, Port Harcourt, Nigeria

Adebola Rafiu Bakare Department of Political Science, University of Ilorin, Ilorin, Nigeria

Chigozie Francis Chilaka Department of Political Science, Federal University Otuoke, Bayelsa State, Nigeria

Michael C. Egwu Department of Political Science, Federal University of Lafia, Lafia, Nasarawa State, Nigeria

Muritala Babatunde Hassan Department of Political Science, Federal University Dutse, Dutse, Jigawa, Nigeria

Adewale Harrison Idowu Department of Political Science and Public Administration, Adekunle Ajasin University, Akungba-Akoko, Nigeria

Onyebuchi Ugochukwu Obianua Department of International Relations & Strategic Studies, Adamawa Sate Polytechnic, Yola, Jimeta, Nigeria

Boris Happy Odalonu Department of Political Science, Federal College of Education, Eha-Amufu, Enugu State, Nigeria

Okpanachi Linus Odiji Department of Political Science, Kogi State University, Anyigba, Nigeria

Andrew Ariyo Tobi Department of Public Administration, Olabisi Onabanjo University, Ago-Iwoye, Ogun State, Nigeria

Patrick Nnadozie Udefuna Department of Democratic Studies, National Assembly, National Institute for Legislative Studies (NILS), Abuja, Nigeria

Korikiye Wenibowei Department of Political Science, Isaac Jasper Boro College of Education, Sagbama, Nigeria

Abbreviations

ACN	Action Congress of Nigeria
AFRC	Armed Forces Ruling Council
ANPP	All Nigerian Peoples Party
APC	All Progressive Congress
APGA	All Progressives Grand Alliance
BPE	Bureau for Public Enterprise
CDC	Constitution Drafting Committee
CNA	Clerk of the National Assembly
CPA	Commonwealth Parliamentary Association
CPC	Congress for Progressive Change
CSOs	Civil Society Organisations
DSS	Directorate of Security Service
EFCC	Economic and Financial Crimes Commission
FCT	Federal Capital Territory
FGN	Federal Government of Nigeria
FOIA	Freedom of Information Act
FRA	Fiscal Responsibility Act
FRN	Federal Republic of Nigeria
ICPC	Independent Corrupt Practices and other related offences Commission
ILES	Institutional Legislative Effectiveness Score
INEC	Independent National Electoral Commission
IPU	Inter-Parliamentary Union
LES	Legislative Effectiveness Score
LGAs	Local Government Areas
MDAs	Ministries, Departments and Agencies

MP	Members of Parliament
NASS	National Assembly
NCAA	Nigeria Civil Aviation Authority
NDI	National Democratic Institute
NDP	National Democratic Party
NDSC	National Defence and Security Council
NILDS	National Institute of Legislative and Democratic Studies
PAC	Public Accounts Committee
PARP	Policy Analysis and Research Project
PC	Parliamentary Centre
PDP	Peoples' Democratic Party
PILDAT	Pakistan Institute of Legislative Development and Transparency
PLAC	Policy and Legal Advocacy Centre
PRC	Provisional Ruling Council
PRP	People's Redemption Party
RMFAC	Revenue Mobilisation Allocation and Fiscal Commission
SMC	Supreme Military Council
UNPP	United Nigeria People's Party
USAID	United States' Agency for International Development
WBI	World Bank Institute

List of Figures

List of Tables

CHAPTER 1

The Place of Legislature in Democratic Governance: An Introduction

Fatai Ayinde Aremu and Adebola Rafiu Bakare

Introduction

Parliamentary democracy in Nigeria dates back to colonial era when the British government established the Lagos Legislative Council in 1862. Subsequently, the legislature has witnessed several transformations in terms of its powers, institutional design, composition and procedures. Indeed, Nigeria has had a history in legislative practice that was periodically truncated by military intervention only to resurface with modifications. In the First Republic, the National Assembly lasted three years, from 1963 when the country became a Republic to 1966 when the country witnessed her first military coup. After thirteen years of military rule, democratic governance was restored in 1979 marking the emergence of the Second Republic. During the Second Republic, the National Assembly lasted for four years between 1979 and 1983. It was suspended for the second time in the wake of the General Muhammadu Buhari-led military coup. The National Assembly of the Third Republic was

F. A. Aremu · A. R. Bakare (✉)
Department of Political Science, University of Ilorin, Ilorin, Nigeria

F. A. Aremu and A. R. Bakare (eds.), *Two Decades of Legislative Politics and Governance in Nigeria's National Assembly*,
https://doi.org/10.1007/978-981-33-4455-6_1

a hybrid institution which operated under a military President, General Ibrahim Babangida, who convened the Assembly on 5 December 1992, with restricted legislative powers. During this period, Bills passed by the National Assembly are subjected to the approval of the National Defense and Security Council before the assent of the military President (National Assembly 2010). The tenure of the Third Republic's National Assembly was terminated in November 1993. After six years of another round of military rule, the country transited to civil rule in 29 May 1999, heralding the emergence of the Fourth Republic. For the first time in Nigeria's political history, the national parliament has witnessed twenty years of uninterrupted legislative practice. While this appears to excite advocates of democratic rule, the National Assembly has continued to attract attention among scholars of Nigerian politics. On the one hand, the excitement stems out of the fact that Nigeria could be said to have overcome the challenge of frequent military's forceful takeover of political space. On the other hand, there is anxiety over how the behaviour of legislators could be posing a threat to the sustenance of the legislature as an institution.

This contradictory trajectory necessitated the need to interrogate the performance of the institution in the country. While previous attempts to assess the effectiveness and efficiency level of the Nigerian National Assembly are appreciated, especially those of Staddon (2013), Ojo and Omotola (2014), Tyoden (2014), and Fashagba et al. (2019), evidence abound that the process is still evolving, as there is dearth of literature on the study of the Nigerian legislature. This could be majorly attributed to the fact that legislative studies as a sub-discipline itself is still evolving across the world and especially in Africa. To this end, this book readily comes to the rescue in bridging the literature gap and contributing to the expansion of the knowledge frontier on legislative studies and political science in general.

On our part, we observed that it is more nuance to interrogate the issues and developments that characterized the twenty years experience of legislative politics and governance in the country, if one aims to achieve a more robust evaluation and analysis. It is pertinent to note that analysing all the issues and developments in a single volume is practically impossible, thus, the book is dedicated to the salient ones. While some of these salient issues and developments have helped strengthened Nigeria's democracy, others seem inimical to democratic survival to the extent that some people out of frustration are beginning to suggest a return to military rule. Since inception of the Fourth Republic, the issues on the National Assembly have always been topical in the news headlines. Sometimes, its internal controversial issues are been made public and at other times, the excessive confrontations with the executive mostly end up heating the polity. Most of these issues end up projecting the legislature as an institution of self-centred persons. The first issue which served as the first litmus test faced by the National Assembly was the challenges of electing, selecting and appointing its leaders, both Principal Officers and Committee Chairmen. The process became worrisome when it heightened political tension in the country. At a point, it pitches the Governors against the President and at another point; it almost resulted into ethno-religious quagmire. Ever since the institution took-off on the note of disordered selection of its leaders, it has become a norm synonymous with its traditions which makes a study into the trend inevitable and as such discussed in Chapter 10.

As mentioned earlier, the issue of excessive confrontation with the executive is also identified as a defining character and nature of the National Assembly in the last twenty years. The first of its kind was the House of Representatives' attempt under the leadership of Rt. Hon. Ghali Umar Na'Abah to impeach President Olusegun Obasanjo on 13 August 2002. The House requested Obasanjo to resign in two weeks or face impeachment for committing seventeen constitutional infractions ranging from unconstitutional military deployment to against the inhabitants of Zaki Biam and Odi; to his withholding of the 13% derivation to deserving States, among others (*The Punch*, December 23, 2002). The action led to a situation that could be termed as 'political cold war' which eventually re-defined the political landscape of the country. During this period, the Senate stood aloof as the upper chamber was battling its internal leadership crisis that resulted in the emergence of three Senate Presidents in four years. The leadership crisis was believed to be instigated by President Obasanjo in order to have his puppet installed as the Senate President to check the relentless power intoxication of the House of Representatives. However, the confrontation was politically settled with dire consequences for the major actors in the House, as they never returned for sophomore term. This impeachment attempt became a milestone in the history of Nigerian politics as the potency of the legislature to check the excesses of the executive became evident, especially under a formidable leadership (Na'Abba 2016). This scenario was repeated between 2015 and 2019 (8th National Assembly) between the Senator Bukola Saraki-led Senate and the Muhammadu Buhari-led executive (though not to the extent of impeaching the President) that also saw the Senate President and his loyalists in the chamber lost their re-election bids in the 2019 election. In view of this, it becomes expedient to explore this trajectory for the twenty years under review. Chapter 2 of the book examined the nature and dynamics of the relationship between the legislature and other arms of government and the extent by which the legislature wielded its powers on the executive in response to the domineering attempt of the executive.

The National Assembly has been under criticism and condemnations owing to the wide allegations of corruption related activities. The instances of alleged corruption activities seem too enormous that the institution has become synonymous to house of corruption. Several people perceive the National Assembly to be an abode for self-centred politicians. An instance was the celebrated allegation by the then President Olusegun Obasanjo in 2016 that the National Assembly is 'an assemblage of thieves and rogues'. In the same vein, the Nigerian legislators were referred to as 'legislathieves' (Olaoye 2015). It is pertinent to note that the corrupt tendency in the National Assembly could be traced to the period of self-appropriation of fishy allowances which include but not limited to furniture, newspaper, wardrobe and constituency office maintenance, all with outrageous amount not published for public knowledge. This was heightened by the 2010 official vehicle purchase scandal of the Rt. Hon. Dimeji Bankole-led House of Representatives. To date, the National Assembly continuously engages in vehicle purchase scandals. The one that seems to caught public attention most, was the buying of Toyota Land Cruiser Sport Utility Vehicles (SUVs) for all the 109 Senators at the unit rate of N35 million and Peugeot cars for the 360 members of the House in deviant to public opposition. This happened when the country was grappling with the harsh effects of economic recession (*This Day*, April 28, 2016). In addition, the National Assembly is condemned as a result of the institution's failure to resolve most of the corruption cases before it. Prominent among these are: the Maina and Senator Aloysius Etuk's pension scam, the popular fuel subsidy scam of Honourable Farouk Lawan's $620,000 bribe allegedly taken from Femi Otedola, the police pension fraud involving Senators, and most importantly, the Senator Stalla Oduah's alleged N255million-worth armoured car scandal (Adams 2015). To this end, it may not be out of place to interrogate the issues and challenges to the transparency and accountability responsibility of the National Assembly which was thoroughly examined in Chapter 7.

The National Assembly's negative public perception (as discussed in Chapter 10) is one that refused to abate in recent times. The institution is perceived as a channel through which public resources are siphoned under the guise of constituency project. This is coupled with huge salaries and allowances which the National Assembly has refused to make public. While the legislators are much aware of the challenge (of negative public perception) and identified it as the most worrisome of the legislative challenges (Umoru 2016), it is disturbing to note that the national legislators are not taking appropriate actions to address it. On the contrary, the National Assembly seems preoccupied with actions that are inimical to the survival of the democratic project such as irresponsiveness and insensitivity to people's plights, refusal or failure to pass important Bills, and frustrating the efforts of the executive especially in the fight against corruption through non-passage of Whistle Blowers Protection Bill and Special Criminal Courts Bill, among others (Nnamdi 2017). In addition, the incessant physical brawls by the legislators over personal interests which mostly culminated into habitual releases of the videos by Senator Dino Melaye mocking the punishment meted out on dissenting lawmakers, especially in the case of Senator Ali Ndume, who was suspended as a result of his position on the alleged N300 million SUV car purchased by the then Senate President Bukola Saraki and the certificate scandal against Senator Dino Melaye.

Other major development/issues that rocked the National Assembly in its twenty years experience under the Fourth Republic that were interrogated in the book include: unsatisfactory oversight on the executive (Chapter 8), frosty legislative-executive relations, effectiveness and efficiency debate (Chapter 6), poor legislative-constituency relations (Chapter 10), the challenges of women legislators amidst a male-dominated institution (Chapter 13), emerging norm of defection politics in the legislature (Chapter 14), and scandalous salaries and allowances, among others.

It is against this backdrop that this book examines the journey so far by interrogating the major issues and developments that characterized the twenty years of legislative practice by assessing the National Assembly's effectiveness in the Fourth Republic. In doing this, the book is divided into sixteen chapters. On the one hand, Chapter 1 serves as the introduction setting the template for the discourse of other chapters. Chapter 2 traces the origin of the legislature in Nigeria and also interrogated its relationship with the executive and the judiciary. Chapter 3 engages the nature of legislative politics and governance as witnessed in Nigeria over the twenty years of unbroken democracy. Chapter 4 interrogates the voting patterns in Nigeria's successive legislative elections. Chapter 5 of the book explores the committee system in the National Assembly, highlighting the issues and challenges hindering the efficiency and effectiveness of the committees in both chambers. Chapter 6 evaluates the lawmaking output of the institution in terms of the analysis of number and content of Bills and the implications for legislative effectiveness. In Chapter 7, the accountability bargain of the National Assembly is interrogated in the attempt to identify the issues, challenges and prospects of the institution's responsibility to engender transparency and accountability in the country.

On the other hand, Chapter 8 of the book assesses the oversight role of the National Assembly; and the leadership crisis and its implications for institutional efficiency and stability is examined in Chapter 9. Chapter 10 explores the legislative-constituency relations in Nigeria. Chapters 11 and 12 assess the overall performances of the National Assembly with each chapter dedicated to the House of Representatives and Senate respectively. Chapter 13 discusses the challenges of women legislators in Nigeria, as Chapter 14 examines the paradox of defection politics in the national legislature. Chapter 15 of the book wraps up discourse by taking summary inventory of the arguments and submissions of the various chapters and presenting the overall submission of the book in terms of how well the National Assembly fairs in twenty years of uninterrupted legislative practice.

References

Adams, D. (2015). *Top 10 Corruption Scandals Nigeria's National Assembly Hasn't Resolved*. Available online at http://omojuwa.com/2015/04/top-10-corruption-scandals-nigerias-national-assembly-hasnt-resolved-report/. Accessed on November 10, 2016.

Fashagba, J. Y., Ajayi, O. M., & Nwankwor, C. (2019). *The Nigerian National Assembly*. Switzerland: Springer.

Na'Abba, G. U. (2016). *Beware of Obasanjo, All He Wants Is to Install a Puppet—Na'Abba Warns Buhari in an Interview*. Available online at https://adelove.com/2016/01/03/beware-of-obasanjo/. Accessed on November 11, 2016.

National Assembly. (2010). *Nigeria Legislature: 1861-2011*. Abuja: Department of Information and Publications, National Assembly.

Nnamdi, C. (2017). *National Assembly: The Nigeria Number One Enemy*. Available online at http://www.nairaland.com/3625827/national-assembly-nigeria-number-one. Accessed April 12, 2017.

Ojo, E. O., & Omotola, J. S. (2014). *The Legislature and Governance in Nigeria* (Vol. 1). Ibadan: John Archers Publishers Ltd.

Olaoye, W. (2015, June 29). Legislathief Wars. *DailyTrust*. Available online at https://www.dailytrust.com.ng/daily/index.php/opinion/58469-legislathief-wars. Accessed on November 12, 2016.

Staddon, A. (2013). Benchmarking and Self-Assessment Frameworks for Democratic Parliaments. *Nigerian Journal of Legislative Studies, 5*(2), 125–138.

The Punch. (2002, December 23). *As the House of Reps Revisits the Impeachment Clause*. http://pacetv.ng/en_news/as-the-house-of-reps-revisits-the-impeachment-clause/. Accessed on November 11, 2016.

This Day. (2016, April 28). *The National Assembly Vehicle Scandal*. Available online at https://www.thisdaylive.com/index.php/2016/04/28/the-national-assembly-vehicle-scandal/. Accessed on November 12, 2016.

Tyoden, S. G. (2014). *Legislators and the Legislature: A Guide for Legislators in Nigeria*. Kuru: National Institute for Policy and Strategic Studies (NIPSS).

Umoru, H. (2016, August 30). Negative Perception about us by the Public Worrisome— Senate. *Vanguard*. Available online at http://www.vanguardngr.com/2016/08/negative-perception-us-public-worrisome-senate/. Accessed on November 12, 2016.

CHAPTER 2

The Legislature in Nigeria: Origin, Significance and Relationship with Other Arms of Government

Chigozie Francis Chilaka, Onyebuchi Ugochukwu Obianua, and Adewale Harrison Idowu

Introduction

The Nigerian state operates a presidential system of government, and one of the cardinal attributes of the presidential system of government is the

C. F. Chilaka (✉)
Department of Political Science, Federal University Otuoke, Bayelsa State, Nigeria
e-mail: chilakafc@fuotuoke.edu.ng

O. U. Obianua
Department of International Relations & Strategic Studies, Adamawa Sate Polytechnic, Yola, Jimeta, Nigeria

A. H. Idowu
Department of Political Science and Public Administration, Adekunle Ajasin University, Akungba-Akoko, Nigeria

F. A. Aremu and A. R. Bakare (eds.), *Two Decades of Legislative Politics and Governance in Nigeria's National Assembly*,
https://doi.org/10.1007/978-981-33-4455-6_2

distribution of power among three arms or organs of government. The legislature is one of the three main organs of government, the others being the executive and the judiciary. The legislature as an organ of government is very unique in nature because of its representative nature that factors into consideration all the sections of a country. One of its main functions is to make laws for a country. Hence, it is saddled with the responsibility of enacting laws that will not only lead to orderly society but also assist and provide the other arms of government with enabling authority to carry out its functions.

The legislature is either unicameral or bicameral as the case may be in some countries. On the one hand, countries that adopt bicameral legislature, have upper and lower chambers in form of the Senate and the House of Representatives as practiced at the Federal level in Nigeria and the USA; which is also called the House of Lords and Commons in the United Kingdom. On the other hand, the countries that use unicameral legislature only have one legislative House empowered to make laws. Examples of such countries include Spain, New Zealand and Bulgaria among others. Sometimes, a country may adopt the combination of the two types especially in different tiers of government. For instance, Nigeria operates bicameral legislature at the federal and unicameral at the state and local government levels.

The type of legislature a country operates depends on several factors such as the historical origin of the legislature in the country; the history of constitutional making; socio-economic and class structures and religious considerations among others. Despite these factors, it is how the legislature performs its functions and conducts its affairs that determine the survival democracy. As aptly noted by Ademola (1988), though there may be differences in the modus operandi of legislatures, however the ability of the institution to effectively and efficiently perform its functions determine to a large extent how viable any democracy could be. In other words, the legislature must be capable of representing the will of the people. The laws they enact must be capable of safeguarding the people's will and forestalling arbitrariness on the part of the executive. For this to be possible the institution entrusted to make laws for the state, need to have a balance in terms of representation, competent and dispassionate in judgement, altruistic, be responsible to the people, discharge its functions effectively, careful in exercising its powers, and more importantly, above board (Ogunna 1983).

Apart from the law making function of the legislature in Nigeria, it is also saddled with the responsibilities of approving budget and monitoring its implementation, confirming important appointments made by the executive, initiating constitutional amendments if stipulated, investigating complaints of public concern, oversight function of government agencies and impeaching an executive when necessary. For instance, the National Assembly of Nigeria has its oversight function contained in Section 88 of the constitution which provides that the legislature has the power through its resolution published in its official Gazette to direct an investigation into the activities of the executive arm of the government.

In other to safeguard democracy, the executive arm is charged with implementing legislative laws and other functions vested on it by the constitution such as maintenance of law and order, conducting international relations, initiation of bills for public good and appointment and removal of public officials among others. In the same vein, the judiciary is charged with the interpretation of the constitution, and the interpretation and adjudication of laws by resolving disputes and punishing offenders. Based on this, it is clear that there is trinity in government. Government sits on a tripod substantially expressed through rule making, rule application and rule adjudication.

The basic premise and objective of this chapter is to examine the origin and significance of the legislature in Nigeria and also factor into analysis its relationship with others arms of government in Nigeria. To achieve the foregoing objectives, the chapter is divided into seven sections with this brief introduction as section one. Section two explores the origin and evolution of the legislature in Nigeria. Section three explains the structure of the legislature in Nigeria. Section four attempts a theoretical explanation of the relationship between the various organs of government. Section five spotlights the importance of the legislature. Section six examines the relationship or synergy between the legislature and other organs of government while section seven is devoted to conclusion and recommendations.

Definition, Origin and Evolution of the Legislature in Nigeria

A plethora of definitions exists for the term 'legislature'. It is in the simplest term, the body charged with the responsibility of law making for the general citizenry of the state, for the preservation of human rights, protection of citizen's interest and towards the delivery of good governance to the people. It is that arm of government which performs the function of law making through deliberations. Legislature has also been described as the body 'empowered to make, amend or repeal laws for a nation' (Oyediran 1998, p. 30). This body mostly consists of elected representatives. For, legislature refers to that arm of government whose membership is either constituted or elected to make laws, monitor/regulate the activities of the executives, while also protecting the general interest of the people. Also, Okoosi-Simbine (2010) avers that legislature is a body in a given political system whose point of duty is law making and policy influencing. Legislature is thus, the representative and projector of the will of the people. It is the embodiment of the sovereignty of the people in any democratic setting (Olufemi 2010, p. 45).

For Loewenberg (1995, p. 736), legislature refers to 'assemblies of elected representatives from geographically defined constituencies, with law making functions in the government process'. It is the 'eyes of the people…expected to do for the people what the citizenry could not do for themselves as a result of perceived hindrances of population, coordination and resources' (Arowolo 2015, p. 2).

Two distinct features have been identified with legislature, which differentiate it from other arms of government. The first is the fact that legislature has the constitutional authority to pass laws; secondly, its members are often elected to represent the interest of the general citizenry (Jewell 1997). Legislature has also been conceived as a medium through which the people seek to articulate their interest and ensure that the government is run according to their wishes (Macey 1993). What this implies is that the legislature provides the platform for the people to have a say in their own affairs as it is being run by the government. Hence, Carey's (2006) submission that legislature, owing to its large membership, offers the possibility for a more accurate representation of a highly diverse people, while also creating more cordial relations between the representatives (legislators) and the voters (the people).

The origin and development of the legislature in Nigeria can be traced to 1861. It was the year the colonial government officially annexed Lagos as a Colony. For the effective governance of Lagos to meet colonial political and economic needs, the Colonial Governor established a Legislative Council to oversee the affairs of the Colony. For the effective governance of Lagos to meet colonial political and economic needs, a legislative council was established to superintend the colony. Members of the legislative council, selected by the colonial powers, were ten in number of which two were indigenous people. Ironically, this law-making arm lacked the power to perform law making function but served only as an advisory body to the colonial governor (Ademola 1988).

Later, the colony of Lagos became part of the Southern Protectorate, the colonial government amalgamated the Southern and Northern Protectorates, which birthed the Colony and Protectorate of Nigeria, in 1914. It appointed Frederick Lugard as the First Governor General of the amalgamated colonies. For efficient administration of the amalgamated colonies with British interest as the motivating factor, Lugard established a Legislative Council comprised of thirty-six (36) members arbitrarily selected and handpicked by the colonial government to represent contending interests. Only six were Nigerians. The Council, like the Lagos Council that preceded it had no legislative power and performed no legislative function. It only performed advisory and ratificatory function.

However, in 1922, a major constitutional development that impacted positively on legislative development in Nigeria occurred, with the enactment of the Clifford Constitution which provided for the election of four Nigerians in a forty-six membership Council. The other forty-two members were handpicked to represent other interests (Agi 1983). As a result of nationalists' struggles in Nigeria, the elective principle that was introduced by the Clifford Constitution was replicated in the 1946 Richard's and the 1951 Macpherson Constitution respectively as they tried to increase the number of elected Nigerians into the Colonial Legislative Councils. McPherson constitution, created bicameral regional legislatures known as the House of Chiefs and the House of Assembly in the Northern and Western regions.

However, according to Mojeed (2009) present day rule-making institutions in Africa were an outcome of protest against non-inclusion of Africans in managing the political affairs of their respective countries. Before World War I, colonial powers felt it was a waste of resources to provide separate legislative bodies for the colonies they consider an extension of their countries. Hence, Ademola (1988, p. 87) noted that; through a series of constitutional conferences and developments in 1954, 1957 and 1958, Nigeria became an independent nation on 1 October 1960, and adopted the Westminster Parliamentary system of government. Since it was modeled after the British system, the Nigerian Federal Legislature was bicameral. It had two legislative Houses—the senate and House representatives which had 44 members selected for the senate and 312 members elected to the House to serve for five years from various parts of the country.

From the foregoing discussion, it must be noted that the legislature in Nigeria is an offshoot of colonialism and appendage of colonial powers meant to ratify the functions of the Colonial Governor. Hence, the Nigerian legislature was not privileged to develop as an autonomous institution with all the attributes of a law making body in modern democracies as a result of its post-colonial character. Borrowing from the 1951 McPherson constitution, independence constitution of 1960 adopted bicameral legislature in both the federal and regional levels. However, the ratificatory function of the legislature bequeathed by the colonial power was inherited unmistakably. More fundamentally, parliamentarians in the First Republic were divided along ethnic lines.

Ademola (1988, p. 88) observed that the attainment of independence did not alter the ratificatory function and non-deliberative role of the Nigerian legislature. Before independence, the Nigerian legislature had been stripped of all the liberal democratic functions and attributes of a legislature in a liberal democratic state. The post-independent political arrangements that emerged did not favour the development of these attributes and of a democratic political culture that was germane to the development of representative liberal democracy. This made the legislature in the First Republic to become a rubber stamp for the executive branch. Many Nigerians elected into the parliament between 1960 and 1966, took time to come to terms with what their responsibilities are. Agi (1983, p. 102), observed that:

> In post-independence Nigeria until 1966, comparatively few people-electors and elected-seemed to have comprehended the role of the representative sent to a legislature...Representatives often did not understand their obligation to their constituents in an elective political system, beyond vague awareness that they should work to gain amenities for them. Few members ever came to know their constituents or encouraged their constituents to bring forward their problems and grievances.

Hence, the legislature became not the pantheon of law making body in the real sense of it but a body tailored for ratificatory function. This was the nature of the legislature in Nigeria until the First Republic was terminated through a military coup d' etat on 15 January 1966, which lasted for 13 years in the first instance. The tragedy of military rule is that the legislature is the arm of government that is most affected because in a military regime it is non-existent unlike the executive and judiciary.

On 1 October 1979, a new constitution was promulgated which birthed the Second Republic and adopted the American styled presidential system of government. The 1979 constitution made provision for the legislature at the federal and state levels. Hence, the evolution of the legislature in Nigeria continued with the Second Republic. The legislative powers of the Nigerian state were vested in the National Assembly. The National Assembly was divided into two Houses—a Senate and House of Representatives. Elections to the Senate and House of Representatives were conducted on July 8 and 15, 1979 respectively. In the Second Republic, the Senate was composed of 95 Senators elected on equal representation of five senators from each of the 19 states in the country as at then, while the House of Representatives was made up of 445 members elected from 19 states on the basis of population (The Constitution of Federal Republic of Nigeria 1979). At the state levels, a unicameral legislative system was established and its composition was determined by population of respective states.

The evolution and development of the legislature in Nigeria was stifled in 1983 when the General Muhammadu Buhari-led military staged a comeback to power. It was not until May 1999 that the legislature was re-instituted into the political firmament of Nigeria in what is generally referred to as the Fourth Republic till date. The 1999 Constitution (as amended) was in many ways a replication of the 1979 Constitution with few modifications. It recognized both the Senate and House of Representatives as part of the National Assembly. It equally approves a unicameral legislative system at state levels. In terms of membership, the Senate is made up of 109 Senators with 3 from each state and 1 representing the Federal Capital Territory in the country, while the House of Representatives is composed of 306 members distributed based on population size.

Structure of Nigerian Legislature

The structure of the legislature in Nigeria consists of political and administrative frameworks that have been put in place to enable it achieve its legislative mandate. According to Policy and Legal Advocacy Centre (2015), the National Assembly is made up of the Senate and House of

Representatives respectively. The composition of each House is contained in the constitution and rules governing the day-to-day operation of the Houses.

There is a hierarchical arrangement of legislatures in Nigeria. The National Assembly legislates at the federal level. The State House of Assembly legislates for the states while Local Government Council Legislatures make laws for local government councils. The affairs of both chambers of the National Assembly are directed by the principal officers.

The Senate is presided by a Senate President also known as the President and Chairman of the National Assembly. The Deputy Senate President (DSP) acts in the capacity of the Senate President when he is absent. However, there are other functions of the DSP. The Leader of the majority party, is regarded as the Senate Majority Leader, with the Majority Whip try to speed up government business by ensuring cooperation of members. In their absence, they are assisted by the Deputy Majority Leader and Deputy Whip. On the other hand, the Minority Leader and their Whips equally try to stall government business so as to earn the sympathy of the electorates.

The structure of the Senate is also replicated in the House of Representatives except that the Presiding Officer of the House of Representative is called the Speaker and his Deputy-the Deputy Speaker. In addition, the National Assembly creates Standing Committees headed by a Chairman to function. Presently there are 54 and 84 Standing Committees in the Senate and House of Representatives respectively. This is also the way it is at the state and local government levels in Nigeria.

The structure of the National Assembly (Senate and House of Representatives), in what can be called its administrative arm is manned by a Clerk of House, who is also an accounting officer of the House. He is assisted by a Deputy Clerk. The departments in both Houses are manned by separates the Clerks respectively. They execute decisions emanating from both Houses. They are all responsible to the Presiding Officers (Policy and Legal Advocacy Centre 2015).

This structural arrangement is also replicated in the states Houses of Assembly across the country. The Presiding Officer, the Senate President or Speaker as the case may be is usually seated at the head of the Chamber, in front of the Presiding Officer is the clerk of the Assembly and his Assistants. Other elected representatives sit at designated places within the Chamber as assigned to them by the Senate President or Speaker. At the middle of the Chamber is a Table, big enough to play billiards on, which holds the mace-the symbol of legislative authority. For a legislature to sit without the mace is like New York without the Statue of Liberty (Ede 2002).

The Nigerian Legislature in the First, Second and Third Republics (1960–1999)

The Nigerian legislature in the First, Second and Third Republics which spanned between the periods of 1960 to 1999 were not so much different from one another in composition and function. Owing to independence in 1960, the country adopted the Westminster Parliamentary system of government. The First Republic legislature created by the independence and the Republican constitutions of 1960 and 1963 respectively was a bicameral legislature. It had the Senate and the House of Representatives for the federation; and the House of Assembly for regions (Tom and Attai 2014). While the Senate served as the upper chamber for the federation, the House of Chiefs was the upper chamber at the regional level. House of Representatives was made up of 312 members, elected for a period of 5 years; and the Senate had 56 nominated members from the various regions (East, West, North and Mid-West) of the country (Adebo 1988; Asobie 1998). Each of the 4 regions had 12 members each, while 4 were from the Federal capital, Lagos, the remaining 4 were appointed by the president on the advice of the Prime Minister (Asobie 1998). While the presidents of Senate of the First Republic were Nnamdi Azikiwe (1960), Dennis Osadebay (1960–1963) and Nwafor Orizu (1963–1966), the House of Representatives had Ibrahim Jalo Waziri as its speaker throughout the First Republic. The two Houses (Senate and Representatives) had the sole responsibility of making laws for the entire country.

At the regional level, the House of Assembly and House of Chiefs performed similar functions as those at the federal level. Thus, implying a share of legislative powers between federal and regional Assemblies (Nwaubani 2014). While the federal took care of issues on the exclusive list (such as defence, external affairs, currency, etc.), issues on the concurrent list (such as education, Police, Agriculture, etc.) were taken care of by both the federal and regional Assemblies. Issues on the residual list were left in the hands of regional Assemblies (Nwaubani 2014). The legislature in the First Republic has been criticized as highly ineffective, not able to perform its sacrosanct function of legislation effectively (Oyediran 1998).

The First Republic was brought to an abrupt end by military intervention on 15 January 1966. This period of military interregnum lasted till 1979, which thus, meant that the country had no legislature for 12 years. With the advent of the Second Republic in 1979, the 1979 constitution provided and made room for a bicameral legislature for the country. The legislature was this time, made up of 450 members of the House of Representatives and 96 members of the Senate. Both Houses were, for the first time, jointly referred to as the National Assembly (Banjo 2013). Abegunde (2016) observed that the Senate was made up of one elected member from each of the 5 territorial constituencies into which the existing 19 states were divided and one from the Federal Capital territory. While the Second Republic Senate was led by Senate President Joseph Wayas, the House of Representatives was led by Speakers Edwin Ume-Ezeoke (1979–1983) and ChahaBiam (1983). At the state level, the bicameral of the First Republic was replaced with a unicameral legislature, with the nomenclature; House of Assembly.

In 1983, the legislative process in Nigeria was once again interrupted by another military intervention, dealing a blow to the Second Republic legislature. The military period lasted between 1983 and 1993, where the Third Republic came into limelight. As build up to the Third Republic and in preparations for same, Banjo (2013) observed that General Babaginda, the military President, set up a 17-member Political Bureau in 1986 and another 46-member Constitutional Review Committee in 1987 to review both the 1963 and 1979 constitutions. Furthermore, the regime constituted a 452 member Constituent Assembly in 1988 to scrutinize the work of the Constitution Review Committee. All of these gave birth to the 1989 constitution which was to guide the Third Republic. The 1989 constitution yet again, provided for a bicameral legislature at the federal level and a unicameral legislature at state level. The same legislative arrangements were in operation for both the Second Republic and aborted Third Republic of Nigeria (Tom and Attai 2014; Abegunde 2016). While Senate Presidents Iyorchia Ayu (1992–1993) and Ameh Ebute (1993) provided leadership for the Senate, the House of Representatives was yet to get any leadership before the Republic was brought to an abrupt end.

The Nigerian Legislature in the Fourth Republic

The democratic dispensation Nigeria since 1999 has been the longest ever experienced in the country's democratic history, currently spanning over19 years. Under this dispensation, the legislature has witnessed a total of five Assemblies, viz: the 4th Assembly (1999–2003); the 5th Assembly (2003–2007); the 6th Assembly (2007–2011); the 7th Assembly (2011–2015); and the 8th Assembly (2015–2019). The exclusive, concurrent and residual legislative structure of the First, Second and Third Republics were retained in the Fourth Republic. It is also worth mentioning that the structures of all the Fourth Republic Assemblies have been similar in terms of composition and function. Table 2.1 presents the general composition of legislature of the Fourth Republic in terms of membership composition.

The Nigerian 4th Assembly (1999–2003)

Following the cancellation of the 1993 general elections, the Third Republic came to an abrupt end, resulting in the suspension of legislature for a period of 6 years from 1993 to 1999. Civil democratic rule was however restored in 1999 when General Abdulsalami Abubakar signed the 1999 constitution into law (*The Guardian*, 16 May 2005). The 1999 constitution thus, ushered in the Fourth Republic and the 4th Assembly, retaining a bicameral at federal level and a unicameral legislature at state level. The 4th National Assembly was inaugurated on 29 May 1999. Chapter five of the 1999 constitution separates legislature into two Houses of Federal House of Representatives and the Senate, with both Houses sitting in different chambers.

The House of Representatives was made up of 360 members who were elected from the 360 federal constituencies across the country (Banjo 2013). The Senate was made up of 109 members representing the 109 Senatorial Districts across the country. It is pertinent to note that while membership of the House of Representatives from each state was based on the numerical strength of each state, it was however not based on the same for the Senate (Abegunde 2016). The House of Representatives under the 4th Assembly was headed by a speaker of the House, SalisuBuhari (1999–2000) and Ghali Umar Na'Abba, while the Senate was headed by the Senate President. The 4th Senate had three different presidents. At inception, it was headed by Evan Enwerem, who was later

Table 2.1 State distribution of members in the legislature of Nigeria's 4th Republic

S/N	*State*	*Senators*	*Federal constituencies (House of Representatives)*
1.	Abia	3	8
2.	Adamawa	3	8
3.	AkwaIbom	3	10
4.	Anambra	3	11
5.	Bauchi	3	12
6.	Bayelsa	3	5
7.	Benue	3	11
8.	Borno	3	10
9.	Cross River	3	8
10.	Delta	3	10
11.	Ebonyi	3	6
12.	Edo	3	9
13.	Ekiti	3	6
14.	Enugu	3	8
15.	Gombe	3	6
16.	Imo	3	10
17.	Jigawa	3	11
18.	Kaduna	3	16
19.	Kano	3	24
20.	Katsina	3	15
21.	Kebbi	3	8
22.	Kogi	3	9
23.	Kwara	3	6
24.	Lagos	3	24
25.	Nasarawa	3	5
26.	Niger	3	10
27.	Ogun	3	9
28.	Ondo	3	9
29.	Osun	3	9
30.	Oyo	3	14
31.	Plateau	3	8
32.	Rivers	3	13
33.	Sokoto	3	11
34.	Taraba	3	6
35.	Yobe	3	6
36.	Zamfara	3	7
37.	FCT	1	2
	Total	**109**	**360**

Source Authors' Compilation

removed from office on 18 November 1999, and was replaced by Chuba Okadigbo. Okadigbo was impeached on 8 August 2000, and was replaced by Anyim Pius Anyim, who saw the 4th Senate through to the end. Both the President of the Senate and the speaker of the House of Representatives were supported by a deputy and a clerk. The Senate President and the speaker of the House of Representatives were the third and fourth respectively (after the president and vice president) in the hierarchical order of the federal system of government Nigeria operated during the period. This structure has since been retained till date. It is also worth mentioning that all subsequent Assemblies in the 4th Republic of Nigeria have all taken the shape, in terms of composition, structure and function, of the 4th Assembly, with difference only in members and leadership.

The Nigerian 5th Assembly (2003–2007)

The Nigerian 5th Assembly also took after the pattern of the 4th assembly, retaining the bicameral legislature. Following the general elections of 2003, the Nigerian 5th Assembly was inaugurated on 3 June 2003. Just as its predecessor, the 5th Assembly was made up of 109 elected Senators in the Senate and 360 elected representatives in the House of Representatives. The Senate was led by Senate President Adolphus Wabara, who was later resigned as the president in April 2005, following bribery allegations levelled against him. He was succeeded by Senator Ken Nnamani. The House of Representatives was headed by speaker of the House, Aminu Bello Masari. The Nigerian 5th Assembly, like every other previous Assemblies, was tasked with the responsibility of legislation, oversight and representation. The Assembly passed a total of 129 bills during the period it lasted (Saraki, as cited in *Vanguard* Online, March 29, 2018). The Assembly ran until 5 June 2007, when another general election was held in the country.

The Nigerian 6th Assembly (2007–2011)

The 6th Assembly also took after the 5th Assembly in structure, membership and function. It was therefore, a bicameral legislature with the House of Representatives and the Senate. Following the general election of 2007, the Nigerian 6th Assembly was inaugurated on 5 June 2007. While the House of Representatives consisted 360 members, the Senate consisted of 109 members, all elected from across the country. The 6th Senate was led by Senate President David Mark and the House of Representatives was initially headed by the speaker, Patricia Etteh, who was later forced to resign on the ground of alleged mismanagement of funds. She was succeeded by DimejiBankole. The 6thAssembly was able to pass a total of 82 bills in the period of four years it lasted (Saraki, as cited in *Vanguard* Online, March 29, 2018). The Assembly came to a close on 6 June 2011, following the conduct of the 2011 general election.

The Nigerian 7th Assembly (2011–2015)

The Nigerian 7th Assembly was also structured in terms of composition, membership and function, after the 6th Assembly. It was a bicameral legislature with the House of Representatives and the Senate. Following the general election of 2011, the Nigerian 7th Assembly was inaugurated on 6 June 2011. While the House of Representatives consisted of 360 elected members from across the 360 federal constituencies in the country, the Senate was made up of 109 elected members from across the 109 Senatorial Districts in the country. Again, David Mark was re-elected the Senate President for the second consecutive time in the 7th Senate. For the House of Representatives, Aminu Waziri Tambuwal succeeded DimejiBankole as speaker of the 7th Assembly. The 7th Assembly passed a total of 128 bills during the period it lasted (Saraki, as cited in *Vanguard* Online, March 29, 2018). The Assembly came to a close on 6 June 2015, following the conduct of the 2015 general election.

The Nigerian 8th Assembly (2015–2019)

The Nigerian 8th Assembly replicates the structure of the 7th Assembly in terms of composition, membership and function. It retains a bicameral legislature with the Senate and the House of Representatives. Following the general election of 2015, the Nigerian 8th Assembly was inaugurated on 9 June 2015. It is composed of 360 members of the House of Representatives and 109 members of the Senate, all elected from across the respective federal constituencies and Senatorial Districts in the country. While the Senate is being led by Senate President BukolaSaraki, the House of Representatives is led by Speaker YakubuDogara, both of the opposition party, the Peoples Democratic Party (PDP). The Nigerian 8th Assembly is thus, unique in this regard, as it marks the first time in the history of Nigerian legislature, where both legislative chambers are being

Table 2.2 Speakers of Nigerian House of Representatives from Inception to Date

S/N	*Name*	*Date*	*Political Party*
1.	Sir Frederic Metcalfe	1955–1959	–
2.	JajaWachucku	1959–1960	NCNC
3.	Ibrahim Jalo Waziri	1960–1966	NPC
4.	Edwin Ume-Ezeoke	1979–1983	NPN
5.	Chaha Biam	1983	NPN
6.	Salisu Buhari	1999–2000	PDP
7.	Ghali Umar Na'Abba	2000–2003	PDP
8.	Aminu Bello Masari	2003–2007	PDP
9.	Patricia Etteh	2007	PDP
10.	DimejiBankole	2007–2011	PDP
11.	Aminu Waziri Tambuwal	2011–2015	APC
12.	YakubuDogara	2015–2019	PDP

Source Authors' Compilation

led by the opposition party. As of 29 March 2018, exactly 33 months into its inauguration, the 8th Assembly had passed a total of 200 bills (Saraki, as cited in *Vanguard* Online, March 29, 2018). The Nigerian 8th Assembly is expected to run until 9 June 2019, after the 2019 general election to usher in new members.

Tables 2.2 and 2.3 provide information on the leadership of the Nigerian Assemblies since inception to date.

The Legislature and Other Arms of Government: A Theoretical Explanation

To understand the relationship between the legislature and other arms of government, the principle and theory of separation of power comes to mind. The theory is not just regarded as one of the most fundamental tenets of liberal democracy; it is also geared towards efficiency and most fundamentally, towards guarding against the abuse of authority (Spindler 2006).

Table 2.3 Presidents of Nigerian Senate from inception to date

S/N	*Name*	*Date*	*Political Party*
1.	Nnamdi Azikiwe	1960	NCNC
2.	Dennis Osadebay	1960–1963	NCNC
3.	Nwafor Orizu	1963–1966	NPC
4.	Joseph Wayas	1979–1983	NPN
5.	Iyorchia Ayu	1992–1993	SDP
6.	Ameh Ebute	1993	SDP
7.	Evan Enwerem	1999	PDP
8.	Chuba Okadigbo	1999–2000	PDP
9.	Anyim Pius Anyim	2000–2003	PDP
10.	Adolphus Wabara	2003–2005	PDP
11.	Ken Nnamani	2005–2007	PDP
12.	David Mark	2007–2015	PDP
13.	Bukola Saraki	2015–2019	PDP

Source Authors' Compilation

Political thinkers such as Baron De Montesquieu, supported the idea that organs of government would be arbitrary and undermine individual freedom if their powers are not separated. Hence, in 1748 he developed the theory of Separation of Power, in his book entitled, *The Spirit of Laws*. It was an attempt to safeguard individual liberty and avoid despotism and arbitrariness in governance.

The idea of tripod division of state functions may be traced back to the writings of Plato, Aristotle, Cicero and Machiavelli. According to Aristotle, a state should have three functions—deliberative, magisterial and judicial (cited in Nwaogu 2013). Bodin, a French philosopher, further emphasized the necessity of separation of these three powers in his work, *The Republic* (1576). He was especially in favour of separation of the judicial functions from the other two arms of government. For example, he frowned at government officials being the judge and legislature at the same time (Igwe 2002).

Absolutism may have been extolled and supported by some leaders but scholars are not indifferent to the dangers inherent and the eventuality of tyranny occasioned by the concentration of power in the firm hands of one institution, body of persons or one man. According to Oraegbunam (2005), if the legislative and executive powers are concentrated in same person or persons, the danger of the legislature making repressive laws which the executive will implement would be high. Little wonder, Montesquieu (1748) outlined a tripod division of political powers among the arms of government because the concentration of these powers in the hands of the Monarch led to tyranny and despotism in France.

Since Montesquieu, mooted the idea of separation of power, many countries have adopted the theory in practice to suit their peculiar circumstances. Hence, Separation of power is the placement of the three arms of government in three separate but identifiable groups of people. At the same time, the constitution, the constitution provides the opposite theory of Checks and Balances, so that the various arms can reconcile with each other while checking each other's excesses.

The principle of separation of power is very relevant to many constitutional democracies because it makes each branch of government directly responsible to the people and ensures that tyranny and arbitrariness are checked at all levels of government. Hence its codification in modern state system and its practice constitutionally is a triumph of democracy over tyranny.

Despite the restraint brought about by the principles of separation of powers, it has most times proved inadequate in exorcizing the inherent wicked instinct of man to subvert institutions of government. Particularly, members of the executive and legislature arms of government have been more culpable in implementing this principle in the breach. For instance, in December 2006, President Olusegun Obasanjo without recourse to constitutional provisions, unilaterally declared the office of the Vice President, occupied by AlhajiAtikuAbubakar, vacant due to the fact that the Vice President left Peoples Democratic Party (PDP), to Action Congress (AC). The President or the Vice, can only be removed from office through impeachment which is the responsibility of the National Assembly.

Perhaps, this is the reason why Sir John Dalberg-Acton (1834–1902) postulated that Power tends to corrupt, and absolute power corrupts absolutely. Nevertheless, the theory adequately explains the whole gamut of the relationship between the three arms of government as it applies in all democracies. The Legislature is authorized to make laws; the executive implements government laws in the form of policies and programmes;

and the judiciary tries all breaches of the laws. The powers and functions of each are independent but coordinate. No arm can have absolute authority. This prevents abuse of power as usually seen in a monarchical system where all powers are concentrated in a single authority.

Within the context of this chapter, the Nigerian Constitution (as amended) recognizes separation of powers as a vital principle of the constitution. The basis powers of government are found in relevant sections of the constitution. Sections, 4, 5 and 6 of the Nigerian constitution deals with the powers of the three arms of government. Most fundamentally, the Constitution clearly explains the role of the Legislature and the Executive in law making and oversight functions, especially with regards to budgetary and fiscal issues. Thus, while the executive prepares the budget, the Legislature scrutinizes and approves the budget. The Legislature also has the responsibility of performing oversight on the executive to ensure that financial expenditure complies with budgetary provisions. While the judiciary interprets and adjudicate on any contradiction arising therefrom.

However, to have a complete separation of powers amongst the three arms of government is difficult if not impossible. On this basis, Wade (1955) noted that convenient though it is to divide the main organs of government into three, the doctrine in its application to modern government does not mean that a rigid threefold classification of their functions is possible. It is meaningful to checkmate the excesses of arms of government.

Hence, what are often obtainable in practical sense are checks and balances underlining the competitive and cooperative form of relationship inherent in the theory of separation of powers. For instance, the fact that the bill passed by the legislature is required to be assented to by the executive before it becomes law means that the executive arm is involved in law making. Also, the interpretations of laws made by the legislature, by the judiciary which can render it intra vires or ultra vires suggest that the judiciary is involved in law making (Laski 1952). Hence Aniche (2009, p. 45) noted that 'the principle of checks and balances recognizes the imperative of the three arms of government posing as watchdogs to one another in their discharge of constitutional roles in ensuring that they operate within the confines of their political space'. Based on this, the three arms of government relate on issues of governance for the welfare of the people.

Significance of Legislature in Nigeria

Given the doctrine of separation of powers in presidential system, the legislature is very crucial in enforcing transparency, responsiveness and accountability in any democratic setting. Given this importance, the cruciality of the legislature for the survival of democracy cannot be overemphasized.

The powers to make laws for the peace, order and good governance of the Nigerian federation or any part thereof, is vested on the National Assembly. In fact, the matters for which the legislature is empowered by the constitution to legislate on are many and touches virtually all facets of a state's life. If we examine matters in the exclusive and concurrent legislative list, there is no aspect of our national life that the legislature is not empowered to legislate on. Hence it is saddled with the responsibility of making laws for the safeguard and general welfare of the people.

Apart from the primary function of law making, the legislature performs the function of proper representation of the people. Before being law makers, members of the legislature are representatives of their people. They ensure that they pursue strategies that can improve services in their constituents by setting up Constituency Office to enhance accessibility; sponsoring Bills on the floor of the House; meeting with their constituents; presenting petitions on behalf of their constituents to ensure that their grievances are addressed; consulting their constituents on certain legislative issues that borders them among others. Members of the legislature are expected to attend the sittings of the House and make contributions to debate to ensure that laws or government policies embody the interest of their people.

Another fundamental role the legislature plays in Nigeria is the approval of budgets. It is this power of the purse, that gives the legislature the exclusive right to determine and approve all appropriation of funds. Issues touching on this are called 'money Bills'. The Nigerian constitution defines money Bills as the payment, issue or withdrawal from the Consolidated Revenue Fund. For money Bills to be operational, the constitution grants the National Assembly the power to authorize withdrawal from the Consolidated Revenue Fund. The implication therefore, is that government can only spend money approved and authorized by the legislature. The legislature performs this function and exercises this power through the budget process.

As a corollary to the above, the legislature also scrutinizes, evaluates and supervises government performance and implementation of the budget. The power to do this is contained in the constitution and the Standing Orders and Rules of the legislature. This is called oversight function. The oversight function of the legislature is very crucial for the survival of democracy. Oversight is the mechanism by which the legislature monitors and evaluates the activities of ministries, departments and parastatals to ensure that laid down rules are followed in the implementation and execution of projects. The genesis of oversight function of the legislature starts with the annual budget hearing known as budget defence. At this stage, each ministry or department appear before the appropriate committee of the House to defend their budget. When the budget gets to the implementation stage the legislative committee in charge of the ministry or department would continue to monitor the progress made in the implementation in relation to funds approved for the ministry or department. This is a form of check on the activities of the executive arm. According to Ede (2002, p. 127); 'this is a form of performance appraisal. They also act as watchdog to ensure that the executive does not practice any improper act'. In the same vein, the Policy and Legal Advocacy Centre (2015) reiterated that based on legislative oversight, the legislature needs to ensure that appropriation bills are implemented in the manner it is approved.

Furthermore, the legislature is important because it helps to ensure that people of proven integrity are appointed into positions of authority. Many appointments made by the executive arm need the confirmation of the legislature. Ambassadors, Ministers, Chairmen and Members of Boards, Judges, among others need the confirmation of the legislature. In some cases, foreign treaties entered into by the country need the confirmation of the legislature. The Nigerian constitution explicitly shows that no treaty can be enforced without the consent of the National Assembly. Any treaty not ratified by the National Assembly is of no effect. Again, the constitution shows the President cannot make some appointments without the approval of such appointments by the National Assembly. The President also requires their approval to remove some of his appointees from office.

The legislature also plays the role of educating and informing the public, approval of declaration of wars and determination of state of emergency, and checkmating other arms of government especially the executive. No doubt, the legislature is one public institution whose role is vital for the survival of democracy not just in Nigeria but the world at large.

Relationship with Other Arms of Government

Governmental powers are usually shared by three important institutions of government known as arms or organs of government. They are the legislature, executive and judiciary saddled with the constitutional responsibility to enact, apply and interpret laws. Many attempts have been made to establish a proper balance between the three arms to ensure that they work independently but coordinate to safeguard liberty and vitiate absolutism. After all one vital ingredient of constitutionalism is to avoid tyranny which is usually enthroned when leaders pursue interests at the expense of the state (Charles 2005).

It is on this basis that many countries have adapted the principle of separation of power and checks and balances to suite the peculiar political circumstances. Today, in Nigeria for example, the arms of government that are saddled with the power to make laws are distinct from the arm to execute the laws as well as that of interpretation of laws. Hence, the three important arms of government operate with distinct and identifiable groups of people. However, to avoid a big gulf between the arms of government, the principle of checks and balances is used to checkmate and reconcile one arm with the others.

The legislature is the branch of government constitutionally empowered to make laws at the federal, state and local government levels in Nigeria. Despite this, the use of such law making powers is limited by interpretation of the judiciary. As noted by Ede (2002, p. 83);

> Although the National Assembly and the State Houses of Assembly have power to make laws for the Federation and States, respectively, the exercise of such powers are subject to jurisdiction of the courts as well as the judicial tribunals established by law. Neither the National Assembly nor a State House of Assembly has power to make law to oust or purport to oust the jurisdiction of a court of law or a judicial tribunal established by law. Also, with regard to criminal wrongs, they have no power to make any law that shall have retrospective effect.

The constitution has fixed the limits of power for each of the three organs of government. But the same constitution, mindful of the danger of operating three parallel governments, also provided for a spill-over of function between one arm and another. No arms of government can function effectively and efficiently without the assistance of the other.

The judges who are appointed by the President are subject to confirmation by the National Assembly. The judiciary on its part does not waste time to declare any law made by the National Assembly that conflicts with the constitution as null and void. In the same vein, illegal actions taken by the executive are declared unconstitutional and of no effect. For instance, in 2001, the National Assembly passed a law purporting to extend the tenure of office of Local Government Chairmen and Councillors from three to four years. The Supreme Court did not waste time to declare the law null and void since the National Assembly has no power to legislate on that as contained in the 1999 Constitution as amended.

Though the power to make laws is vested in the National Assembly, the separation of power that exist between the arms on one hand ensured that bills passed by the National Assembly need the assent of the President to become a law in the real sense of it. The President reserves the right to veto such a Billby withholding his assent. In this situation, the President is said to have exercises 'Executive or Presidential Veto'. On the other hand, the legislature can check the executive veto by overriding it to become law through two-third majority of members of the National Assembly. This situation is referred to 'Legislative Veto'

> The use of veto by the President has dealt a devastating blow to the concept of separation of powers because it tends to widen the executive powers to include that of legislation. The executive equally exercise legislative function by initiating much of the items that form the subject of discussion in the legislature, such as bills and other messages. Equally, the President performs legislative function because of his exclusive right to summon the national Assembly, by a proclamation, after the election. The President also performs some judicial functions by the exercise of the prerogative of mercy, and through the use of administrative tribunals. (Ede 2002, p. 105)

Similarly, the President cannot except on invitation participate in the affairs of the National Assembly. However, the constitution empowers the President to deliver his annual budget speech to a joint session of the National Assembly. He may as well, be permitted to address the Assembly on other issues of national importance from time to time. The relationship between the President and the legislature is lubricated through the President's Liaison Officer on National Assembly Matters. He ensures that no communication gap exists between the executive and the legislation which helps to diffuse tension that may arise between them.

Relatedly, the power to appropriate and approve expenditures of money lies with the National Assembly, but the actual release of the approved money is the sole responsibility of the executive. This is one major area of legislative-executive friction especially as it relates to budget implementation. The legislature most times makes changes to estimates submitted to it by the executive which the executive most times frowns at. The legislature usually invites Ministers and top government officials who are part of the executive to defend the budget of their ministries and most times the outcome is not usually palatable. This is why it is pertinent that the legislature and the executive must have a cordial working relationship. Apart from this, through its legislative oversight functions officials of the executive are invited to answer questions about the actions of their ministries and departments.

Again, some appointments made by the President such as Ministers, Judges, Ambassadors, Chairmen and members of Boards and Commissions, among others need the confirmation of the National Assembly. More fundamentally, the legislature has the constitutional right to impeach the president if it is established that he has abused his office or committed other gross misconduct. In addition, when heads of government agencies set up committees and panels to investigate official misconduct and mete out appropriate punishments without judicial input, they are inadvertently performing judicial functions.

The foregoing is some of the ways the legislature relates with the other arms of government. Hence this complex web of interaction between the three arms makes it impossible to have a complete separation of power. However, that is not to say that one can effectively operate without the other. As clearly observed by Ede (2002, p. 107);

> It is pertinent to note that without the legislature and the judiciary, the executive would have provided an administration of some sort. That is why the executive is sometimes erroneously referred to as the Government. The legislature and judiciary have come to temper the harshness and rigidity of one-man rule. However, while the legislature and judiciary may complement the executive, the existence of either of them without the executive is unimaginable.

That the functions of the three arms overlaps should not be a barrier to the three arms in checkmating one another. The legislature should not be a rubber stamp of the executive neither should the judiciary be used to advance the interest of the executive. However, the spirit of partnership between the three arms is expected to eclipse or suppress the impasse often observed among the three.

It is a well-known fact that in all democracies the judiciary plays a key role in upholding rule of law. Section 4(8) of the 1999 Constitution (as amended) stipulates that 'the National Assembly shall not enact any law that ousts or purports to oust the jurisdiction of a court of law or of a judicial tribunal otherwise the courts shall declare such laws null and void'. The doctrine of checks and balances, vests in the judiciary the power to keep a check on the executive and legislature. The judiciary does this through Judicial Review by which the judiciary checkmates any form of executive or legislative abuse of power. Judicial review helps to interpret the constitution and laws enacted by the legislature and implemented by the executive. Based on Section 4(8), of the 1999 Constitution (as amended), judicial review is the authority of the court to review the constitutionality or otherwise of legislative acts. The judiciary creates a level playing ground for the smooth functioning of the other arms of government.

Conclusion

The foregoing discussion shows the trajectory of the legislature in Nigeria from pre-independence to post-colonial era. Specifically, the chapter showed that the structure of the legislature makes it a well lubricated machine that enables it to carry out its functions. Also the chapter tried to show how the doctrine of separation of power and checks and balances enhances the independence and cordiality of the legislature and other arms of government. More importantly, the role of the legislature as one of the pillars of democracy was adequately examined in relation with other arms of government.

From the above it can be observed that the legislature all over the world is an institution that can play an important and fundamental role for the survival and consolidation of democracy. The legislative efforts and powers are usually channelled into making laws for the wellbeing of the country and checkmating the excesses of other arms of government through its oversight function. As a body that embodies the will and aspirations of the people, the legislature essentially but not exclusively represents a solution to the myriad of problems confronting many democracies in the world.

Hence, to sustain and strengthen the evolving robust and cordial working relationship between the legislature and other arms of government in Nigeria, there is a need to strengthen the instruments of governance to ensure the independence of the various arms of government both at the federal, state and local government levels. Finally, the legislature and other arms of government must respect and adhere strictly to the tenets of the principles of separation of powers as is explicitly expressed in the 1999 Constitution of the Federal Republic of Nigeria (as amended).

References

Abegunde, O. (2016). Legislature and Democratic Sustainability in Nigeria. *International Journal of Humanities and Social Studies (IJHSS), III*(III), 226–235.

Adebo, A. (1988). The Legislature: Overview and Performance in Nigerian Second Republic. In V. Ayeri & K. Soremekun (Eds.), *Apapa*. Daily Times Press.

Ademola, A. (1988). The Legislature: Overview and Performance. In V. Ayeni & K. Soremekun (Eds.), *Nigeria's Second Republic* (pp. 85–97). Lagos: Daily Times Publications.

Agi, S. P. I. (1983). The Nigerian Legislature in Theory and Practice. In *Democracy and National Development: 1983 and Beyond*. Proceedings of the 10th Annual Conference of Nigerian Political Science Association (pp. 94–122). Nsukka: University of Nigeria Nsukka.

Aniche, E. T. (2009). *A Modern Introduction to Political Science*. Onitsha: Desvic Publishing.

Arowolo, D. E. (2015). Democracy and Bicameralism in Nigeria: Issues, Challenges and the Way Forward. *Review of Public Administration and Management, 3*(7), 1–11.

Asobie, A. S. (1998). Centralizing Trends in Nigerian Federalism. In Babawale, et al. (Eds.), *Re-Inventing Federalism in Nigeria: Issues and Perspective*. Lagos: Malthouse Press Ltd.

Banjo, A. (2013). Leadership Crisis in the Parliament of Nigeria: The Case of the Senate in the Fourth Republic. *Journal of African Studies and Development, 5*(6), 135–144.

Carey, J. M. (2006). Legislative Organization. In R. A. W. Rhodes, A. B. Sarah, & B. A. Rockman (Eds.), *The Oxford Handbook of Political Institutions* (pp. 431–454). Oxford: Oxford University Press.

Charles, M. F. (2005). The Separation of Powers and Constitutionalism in Africa: The Case of Botswana. *Boston College Third World Law Journal, 25*(2), 301–342.

Ede, D. I. (2002). *Nigerian Legislature: Practices and Politics*. Enugu: Mekanand Publications.

Federal Republic of Nigeria. (1979). *The Constitution of Federal Republic of Nigeria, 1979*. Lagos.

Federal Republic of Nigeria. (1999). *The Constitution of the Federal Republic of Nigeria, 1999* (as amended). Abuja.

Igwe, O. (2002). *Politics and Globe Dictionary*. Enugu: Jamoe Enterprises.

Jewell, M. E. (1997). The Legislative. In *The Encyclopaedia American International* (Vol. 17, p. 172). Danbury, CT: Grolier Incorporated.

Laski, H. (1952). *A Grammar of Politics*. London: George Allen and Unwin.

Loewenberg, G. (1995). Legislatures and Parliaments. In S. M. Lipset (Ed.), *Encyclopaedia of Democracy* (Vol. III). London: Rutledge.

Macey, J. R. (1993). Representative Democracy. *Harvard Journal of Law and Public Policy, 16*, 49–54.

Mojeed, O. A. A. (2009). The Legislatures in Africa: A Trajectory of Weakness. *African Journal of Political Science and International Relations, 3*(5), 233–241.

Montesquieu, C.-L. d. (1748). *Spirit of the Laws*. Paris: Garnier Frères.

Nwaogu, N. J. (2013, June 5). *Executive-Legislative Relations and the Challenges of National Security*. Lecture Delivered at the Annual Public Lecture Organized by the Faculty of Social Sciences of the University of Nigeria, Nsukka, at the Princess Alexandra Auditorium.

Nwaubani, O. O. (2014). The Legislature and Democracy in Nigeria, (1960-2003): History, Constitutional Role and Prospects. *Research in Humanities and Social Sciences, 4*(15), 81–90.

Ogunna, A. E. (1983). The Nigerian Legislature: An Appraisal of the Imo State Legislature. In *Democracy and National Development: 1983 and Beyond* (pp. 123–155). Proceedings of the 10th Annual Conference of Nigerian Political Science Association. University of Nigeria Nsukka.

Okoosi-Simbine, A. (2010). Understanding the Role and Challenges of the Legislature in the Fourth Republic: The Case of Oyo State House of Assembly. *Nigeria Journal of Legislative Affairs, 3*(1 and 2), 1–27.

Olufemi, A. C. (2010). *The Task of Democratic Consolidation in Nigeria*. Ibadan: Ilesanmi Press.

Oraegbunam, I. K. E. (2005). *Separation of Powers and Nigerian Constitutional Democracy*. Available at http://www.dawodu.com/oraegbunam1.htm. Retrieved from 9 March 2005.

Oyediran, O. (1998). *Introduction to Political Science*. Ibadan: Oyediran Consult International.

Policy and Legal Advocacy Centre. (2015). *A Guide to the Nigerian National Assembly*. Abuja: PLAC.

Spindler, G. (2006). *Separation of Powers: Doctrine and practice. Parliament of New South Wales*. Retrieved from www.parliament.snw.gov.au/prod...nsf/SeparationofPower.

The Guardian. (2005, May 16). *TokunboAfikuyomi- Legislative Issues: A Critique*.

Tom, E. J., & Attai, A. J. (2014). The Legislature and National Development: The Nigerian Experience. *Global Journal of Arts and Humanities and Social Sciences, 2*(9), 63–78.

Vanguard. (2018). *As of Today, the Senate Has Passed 201 Bills-Saraki*. Retrieved from http://www.vanguardngr.com/2018/03/today-senate-passed-201-bills-saraki/. Accessed 29 December 2018.

Wade, E. C. S. (1955). *Constitutional Law*. London: Green and Coy.

CHAPTER 3

Legislative Politics and Governance in Nigeria's Fourth Republic

Okpanachi Linus Odiji and Victoria N. Azu

Introduction

It was Aristotle Nichomachus (384–322 BCE) who actually captured the omniparience of politics when he described it as the *master science*—meaning no one can escape from the parameters set by politics (Simpson 1997). There is hardly any aspect of human endeavour which is not influenced by politics. The use for instance and popularisation of so many scientific discoveries such as those of nuclear and genetic sciences are subject to the approval and censorship of the governing elite. Though defined as the government of the majority where the minority have a say, democracy is adopted by many human societies to check the excesses of this ruling minority (Odiji 2015; Law Teacher 2013).

O. L. Odiji (✉)
Department of Political Science, Kogi State University, Anyigba, Nigeria

V. N. Azu
Department of Political/Administrative Studies, University of Port Harcourt, Port Harcourt, Nigeria

F. A. Aremu and A. R. Bakare (eds.), *Two Decades of Legislative Politics and Governance in Nigeria's National Assembly*,
https://doi.org/10.1007/978-981-33-4455-6_3

As a system of government, democracy is said to be consolidated only when the various organs of government—legislature, executive and judiciary existing in a state channel their activities towards socio-economic and political advancement of the system (Nwanolue and Iwuoha 2012). While some countries like Britain, France and Russia practice parliamentary system of government which fuses power among these arms of government, others like Nigeria and United States adopt the presidential system which separates power for the purpose of checks and balances. The primary reason for adopting this system is to guide against abuse by any arm of government. In the case of the legislature, it relies on its rules and procedures to carry out its functions which include: representation, lawmaking and oversights. But, this is not always without challenges.

One of such issues is the hullabaloos which occasioned the constitutional amendment process during the Fifth (5th) Assembly which the then President Olusegun Obasanjo purportedly sought a third term. Finding itself almost in the mud water of this politics, the legislators had to throw away the baby with the bathwater. Another scenario was the constitutional crisis which the nation was to be plunged into following President Umaru Yar'Adua's inability to adequately transmit power to Vice President Goodluck Jonathan but for the historic Doctrine of Necessity explored by David Mark the then president of the Nigerian Senate (Mudashir 2018). This discourse, discusses the impact on the governance of actions and inactions which were purportedly carried out to influence the legislature in Nigeria. It is structured as follows: this introduction is followed by a conceptual and contextual explication and an elucidation of the role of the legislature. The work then moves straight to highlight some of the major issues which shaped the legislative period under review. The consequences of the politics in the National Assembly are explanatorily unveiled before proceeding to the summary and recommendations.

Conceptual and Contextual Explication

Etymologically, the word politics has its roots in the Greek politika which was used to refer to the affairs of the polis—that is the state. Over time the meaning of the term got extended to encompass the process of making decisions which apply to members of any group, community or society (Hague and Harrop 2013; Merriam Webster 2019). It is equally used to denote any act aimed at achieving and exercising positions of control over governmental organs and the civil society (Odiji 2013). Various means ranging from peaceful negotiations to militarised violence have been employed over the centuries to achieve political ends. Some of the most common methods of pursuing political interests include the promotion of individual or group's views, negotiation with other interest groups, lawmaking and the exertion of force such as warfare against perceived or identified adversaries (Brady 2017; Hawkesworth and Kogan 2013; Taylor 2012; Blanton and Kegley 2016).

It is within this premise that politics is variously conceived negatively as any unhealthy competition for spheres of power, as war, or war without the shedding of blood (Birkland 2015; Joseph 2014; Johnston and Woodburn 1903). The British national anthem as published in the eighteenth century which asks God to confound the politics of the adversaries and Wendell Philip's profession of not playing politics are some samples of negative connotation of politics (Johnston and Woodburn 1903). Within the contexts elucidated above, political activities can manifest either in positive or negative form.

It is in an effort to guide against the negative aspects of politics particularly at the national level that safeguards such as the principles of separation of powers and checks and balances between the organs of government are adopted by independent states like Nigeria. In consonance with these noble principles as practiced by the old Roman Republic and promoted by Baron de Montesquieu, the Nigerian state just like the United States, Brazil and Kenya is jointly administered by three organs of government—the executive, the legislature and the judiciary. These three arms respectively make laws, administer as well as interpret them whenever each need arises (Lloyd 1998; Price 2011; Schindler 2013). While the president is the head of the executive arm, the senate president and chief justice of the federation are respectively presiding over the affairs of the legislature and the judiciary arms of government in Nigeria. But despite this guiding rule of equality laid down by the principle of separation of power, the executive arm of government is constitutionally mandated to coordinate the day to day running of the affairs of the state.

Whether conceived within the perspective of Laswell as who gets what how and when, or Eastonian notion as the authoritative allocation of values (Olaniyi 2001) and even from the understanding of Mao Tse Tung that it is war without the shedding of blood, one thing is sure about politics: the interest of the active participants within the system is foremostly considered before those of others (Gbadegesin 2016). Legislative politics therefore would be construed in this work as any scheme concerning lawmakers which is aimed at influencing their acts, actions and inactions in order to promote or sustain any particular interest. Some of the most recent scenarios which qualify as legislative politics are the events which unfolded before, during and after President Buhari's presentation of the 2019 Appropriation Bill to the National Assembly. Before this epochal event, reports had gone viral that some members of the parliament particularly those in the opposition had resolved and vowed to boycott the occasion (Nwachukwu 2018; Oyeyipo 2018). Even when they U-turned and were present at the venue, they booed and jeered at the president just to signal that the president enjoys no more the goodwill and support of the people whom they represent (Nwabughiogu 2018; Ayitogo 2018).

Legislative politics such as the one exemplified above is not peculiar to Nigeria. Instances abound in many polities of parliamentary members either antagonising themselves or cooperating as a group to antagonise others. The Brazilian Congress is said for instance to be made up of legislators who rather than being representatives for the good of the country, vote for particularistic benefits they can deliver to constituents. For Kurtz (1997) who focused on the Kenyan legislature, the exercise of informal powers which involves the provision of legitimacy to governmental activities makes the state a bit stable when compared with other categorical states whose legislative politics is negatively affecting governance and development. According to the author, this role by the Kenyan parliament promotes support among the populace for the administration. This legitimising role is important in view of the revolts and bouts of instability that have plagued other nations in the region. By accommodating cultural and historical realities, the Kenyan Assembly allows for opposition and dissent within the system, yet it provides stability. As a result of this, the populace is satisfied with the strength and legitimacy of the system; at the same time, it feels it has some say in the political process (Ornstein 1992 in Kurtz 1997)

In the case of Nigeria, the National Assembly of the country is a bicameral legislature established under Section 4 of the Nigerian Constitution. It consists of a Senate with 109 members and a 360-member House of Representatives. The body, modelled after the federal Congress of the United States, is supposed to guarantee equal representation of the 36 states irrespective of size in the Senate and proportional representation of population in the House. The National Assembly, like many other organs of the Nigerian government, is domiciled in the Federal Capital Territory, Abuja. While the Senate is chaired by a senate president, the house is presided over by the Speaker of the House of Representatives. At any joint session of the Assembly, the President of the Senate presides and in his absence the Speaker of the House presides. The constitution saddles this assembly of people with the responsibility of making laws for the smooth running of the state as well as carrying out oversight functions on the activities of the other organs of the state. The effect of the above is that the respective levels of government are empowered to legislate on a broad range of issues that if effectively utilised through quality legislation and diligent exercise of the legislative oversight functions, will translate into good governance (Jimoh 2015).

Governance itself is defined in the Cambridge Dictionary (2019) as the way organisations and countries are managed at the highest level, and the systems for doing this. It entails all the processes of administering a social system through the laws, norms, power or language of an organised society (Bevir 2012). It is said to relate to the processes of interaction and decision-making among the actors involved in a collective problem that leads to the creation, reinforcement, or reproduction of social norms and institutions (Hufty 2011). From these definitions, it is clear that the concept centres on the responsibility of those in authority to meet the needs of the masses as opposed to select groups in the political system. For the sake of this analysis, the prerequisites for good governance as captured by Tinubu (2008) in Odeh (2015) shall be of immense benefit. They are: popular participation, rule of law, equity, transparency, accountability, responsiveness, consensuses, inclusiveness, effectiveness and efficiency.

A critical appraisal of the performance of the national assembly since 1999 as carried out by Jimoh shows that the legislators did well in terms of passing some bills into law. However, so many other bills whose passage into law are supposed to impact positively on the livelihood of the people were yet to get their nod. Some of them are: The Petroleum Industrial Bill (PIB), Gender and Equal Opportunity Bill, Protection of Persons with Disabilities Bill and the Electoral Act Amendment Bill (Jimoh 2015). This particular work is focused on how legislative politics impact on governance in the Fourth Nigerian Republic which started counting on 29 May 1999. It is from this time that the country became governed according to the fourth republican constitution. It was in many ways a revival of the Second Republic (Ayoade and Akinsanya 2012) which was in place between 1979 and 1983 and suffers many of the same problems—if not more, such as multiple ministries which made governance and administration difficult particularly with respect to the powers conferred on the national assembly to scrutinise not only those who head the ministries, but their policies, programmes and activities.

Role of the Legislative Arm of Government

A survey of legislative practices across the globe particularly of countries with three arms of government which adopt the principles of separation of powers and checks and balances shows that the parliament performs three primary functions which are representation, lawmaking and oversighting (Zvoma 2010; Johnson 2005). A brief description of each of these activities would help in making the analysis ahead easily comprehensible.

Representation

The first among these core functions as observed in democratic countries which Nigeria rejoined on 29th May 1999 is to represent the people who gave them the mandate through the ballot to do so. Because it is extremely difficult for instance for 193,392,500 Nigerians (NPC Projected 2016) to gather and collectively deliberate on matters of national importance akin to the ancient Greek democracy, it obviously becomes imperative to select and mandate a sizeable number of people to represent an entire population of a delineated constituency. In the case of Nigeria, the National Assembly of the country is a bicameral legislature established under Section 4 of the Nigerian Constitution. It consists of a Senate with 109 member and a 360-member House of Representatives. The body, modelled after the federal Congress of the United States, is supposed to guarantee equal representation of the 36 states irrespective of size in the Senate and proportional representation of population in the House. Like many other organs of the Nigerian government, the National Assembly is domiciled in the Federal Capital Territory, Abuja.

Lawmaking

Whether in the United States, France, Brazil or South Africa, the legislative arm of government is bestowed with the task of enacting the most crucial laws which are implemented for the good health of the society (Okoosi-Simbine 2010). In order words, these laws or policies are implemented to promote both public good and societal order. Detailed functions of the legislature are usually documented in the constitution of the land. Article 48 of the Brazilian constitution of 5 October 1988, for instance, stipulates that the National Congress has the power to regulate all matters within the federal government's jurisdiction, particularly on tax, budgets, armed forces, currency, development plans, territorial matters, wages and judicial organisation. The constitutions of the United States, French and South African republics are not so different in terms of basic powers assigned to the parliament (Goitom 2017).

In the case of Nigeria, the legislative arm of the state which consists of the Senate and House of Representatives, is vested according to Section 4 (1) of the constitution of the country, with the legislative powers of the Federation. The commonest understanding of what legislation entails is to pass laws as well as amend and repeal existing laws where and when necessary. This is why it states categorically in Section 4(2) that 'The National Assembly shall have power to make laws for the peace, order and good government of the federation. It is line with this provision that such bills as the National Health Act, Violence against Person Prohibition Act, Economic and Financial Crime Commission (EFCC) Act and the Niger Delta Development Commission (NDDC) Act were passed into law (Jimoh 2015). It is equally within this context that the legislators deemed it necessary to repeal some draconian decrees such as the state security detention of person's decree' (Okocha 2001).

The areas within which the legislature is expected to perform their lawmaking functions for the good governance of the nation are specifically highlighted in Parts I and II of the second schedule to the constitution of the Federal Republic of Nigeria. These items fall within the exclusive and concurrent lists of lawmaking. The Exclusive List, as contained in Part I of the Second Schedule deals with items which only the National Assembly has the sole prerogative to legislate upon, to the exclusion of the States and Local Governments. 68 in number, these items encompass: citizenship, defence, currency, aviation, customs and excise duties, drugs and poisons, copyright, insurance, meteorology and foreign affairs. For items which are contained in the Concurrent List, they appear under the Part II of the Second Schedule to the same Constitution. They include 30 items among which are: public funds at state and local government levels, antiquities and monuments, collection of taxes, stamp duties, voter registration in the local government councils, agriculture, education, cadastral and topographical surveys. It is tagged Concurrent List because the Constitution allows both the National Assembly and the State Houses of Assembly to legislate on the items so specified. These two sets of items are distinguished from the residual list which falls strictly within the purview of the federating states to legislate upon (see Section 4 (7a) of the 1999 Constitution).

Oversight

A major role which distinguishes the legislative arm of government from other state institutions is the task of oversighting the activities of all other organisations operating in the country (Griffith 2005). It keeps watch on both the activities of the executive, judiciary and even private organisations which deals with the populace. Starting with how the lawmakers checkmates the executives, before any bill becomes law, there must be an agreement by both the House of representatives and the Senate and should the President delay or refuse to assent the bill so as to have the force of law, the lawmakers may pass the bill into law by two-thirds of both chambers and overrule the veto and the President's consent will not be required.

Another important function of the legislators within this arena is what has been termed the power of the purse (Okpala 2013). Except in areas and instances where the constitution specifies otherwise, the spending of any public funds requires the approval of the National Assembly.The Nigerian Constitution specifically provides that:

> No moneys shall be withdrawn from any public fund of the Federation, other than the Consolidated Revenue Fund of the Federation, unless the issue of those moneys has been authorized by an Act of the National Assembly...No moneys shall be withdrawn from the Consolidated Revenue Fund or any other public fund of the Federation, except in the manner prescribed by the National Assembly. (CFRN 1999)

The parliament in Nigeria exercises this power in various ways among which are vetting of proposals of the executive branch for funding various activities (mainly through the appropriations process); through audits of public accounts by the Auditor-General (who reports to the National Assembly); and through investigations of the conduct of persons, both natural and juridical, charged with implementation of laws or disbursement of any appropriated funds (Guobadia 2000). Another function in this regard which is akin to the U. S. model is the role the senate plays in screening and confirming the nominees of the president for key statutory positions. This role mandates that names of persons nominated as ministers, ambassadors, and Commissioners (of state agencies like INEC and NPC) be sent to the senate for scrutiny and attendant advice to the president on relevant action (CFRN 1999). Further, the National Assembly exercises oversight over the power of the executive to enter into a treaty of any kind; before it can be implemented in Nigeria, a treaty must first be enacted into law by the National Assembly. Also, a key oversight role of the National Assembly is the power to remove chief executives, including the President, the Vice-President, a Governor and a Deputy Governor, for 'gross misconduct'. However, in exercising this power, the Constitution requires some input from the judiciary.

Like the old Roman Republic whose legislative assemblies had the final decision on the election of magistrates and the execution of capital punishments (Abbott 1901; Byrd 1995), the Nigerian Senate is equally empowered by the provisions of Sections 231 (1) (2) and 238 (1) of the 1999 constitution to confirm the appointment of the chief justice of Nigeria, justices of the supreme court and president of the court of appeal. The parliament also has the power to impeach judges just like other high officials of the executive like the Auditor-General and members of the electoral management body if the President who initially sent their names for confirmation so requested. It is on this note that U.S. supreme court justice Samuel Chase was impeached by the American House of representatives in 1804 before later been acquitted by the senate the following year (Dylan 2018; Humphrey 1899).

Legislative Politics in Fourth Republic's National Assembly

Based on our earlier conception of Legislative Politics as any scheme involving lawmakers which is aimed at influencing the acts, actions and activities of the legislators in order to promote or sustain group interest, may we now unveil in this section some of the major instances of legislative politics which have overtly or covertly affected governance in Nigeria from 1999 to 2019. These would however be grouped and sub-sectionalised into three viz—1999–2007, 2007–2015 and 2015–2019 representing the three major periods in which the Fourth Nigerian Republic can be administratively segmented based on the scope of this work.

Fourth and Fifth Assembly (1999–2007)

The actual politics which transmogrified into a serious challenge which would later affect the activities of the 5th national assembly and in fact impact greatly on governance became obvious on the eve of the election of principal officers of the parliament. The election which was scheduled to hold on 5 June 1999 was preceded by an underground scheming by the newly sworn-in President Olusegun Obasanjo (who sought a parliament tha the would control in view of his military antecedent) to influence the emergence of a level-headed leadership that would promote a cordial executive-legislative working relationship. While the choice of the president was Chief Evans Enwerem and Alhaji Salisu Buhari as Senate president and Speaker of the House of Representatives, respectively, this ran contrary to popular expectation which then was that Dr. Chuba Okadigbo was better fit for the job in view of his academic qualification and political sagacity. At the end of those elections, Chief Obasanjo through an alliance with the south-west-dominated Alliance for Democracy (AD) (Aziken 2009) had his way as his preferred candidates emerged victorious (Ojeifo 2007). This was the origin of the frosty executive–legislative relationship which would later characterise the Fourth Nigerian Republic.

While Enwerem openly served the cause of the executive as he was always in the villa and hardly had time to preside over the national assembly he was to lead (Aziken 2009), senators and other top party members who were opposed to this disposition continued the plot and schemes to unseat him as the leader of the national assembly. Loopholes ranging from allegations of perjury, mismanagement, corruption and ineptitude were all levelled just to sack him from the exalted office. By November 18, 1999, Enwerem became a victim of the legislative politics that occasioned his emergence as well as trailed his reign as the President of the Senate. Expectedly, Dr. Chuba Okadigbo emerged as the new senate president in this resolve to free the national assembly from being a puppet of the executive.

Dr. Okadigbo would no doubt be nostalgically remembered for bringing valour to the senate as he strove to maintain the independence of the legislature against President Obasanjo's desire to work with a legislature which will always genuflect at the table of the executive for handouts. This development, however, did not tally with his highhandedness which manifested in a dictatorial styled leadership in a senate that was composed of egoistical moneybag politicians.

It was not surprising therefore that the transition to Okadigbo's ouster began not too long from when he assumed office. One glaring instance of Okadigbo's highhandedness is his refusal to acknowledge the anniversary of the return to civilian rule on May 29, 2000—known today as democracy day. This was a major signal to the executive that an adversary has emerged in the senate on whom a decisive action had to be taken. Sensing equally that the presidency was unhappy with his antagonistic posture towards it, and aware of possible plot to use members of the senate to unseat him, Okadigbo adjourned the senate till July same year taking with him the mace to his country home Ogbunnike in Anambra state.

By Friday 2 June 2000, policemen acting under the directive of the Inspector-General visited the official residence of the Senate President to retrieve the mace. Reports had it that the cops harassed Okadigbo's family members who were met at the residence. Huge amount of money was allegedly wasted by the presidency to induce senators to impeach Chuba Okadigbo. After a protracted war of attrition between the duo, President Obasanjo and his deputy began to pull apart while Okadigbo was eventually removed following the enmity he created for himself as a result of his unpopular leadership style. A new chapter was yet opened in August 2000 as Anyim Pius Anyim emerged as the third senate president within 14 months.

While all these were taking place in the senate, the then speaker of the house of representatives was engulfed in a certificate and age forgery scandal whose news was published by an investigative weekly news magazine (Suleiman 1999). Despite being assisted to power by the new ruling elite, Buhari resigned from that elated seat as it became obvious that he would not survive the heat generated by this outrageous incident (The News 1999; BBC 1999). Hon. Ghali Umar Na'Abba was elected speaker as a result of the leadership vacuum that would be created. Like Okadigbo, Na'Abba refused to compromise the integrity and independence of the lower chamber despite various inducements and threats allegedly masterminded by the executive arm of government. With the support of majority of the members he survived the onslaughts to remove him.

Like Na'Abba, Anyim Pius Anyim who replaced Okadigbo experienced early enough how his survival and that of the senate was dependent on their collective independence from executive manipulations and vituperation. He resultantly stood firm and unperturbed in the face of executive–legislative cacophony which erupted under his watch. Uncomfortable with this recalcitrant posture of senator Anyim, he was obviously prevented from returning into the senate during the elections of 2003. It would be recalled that it was during this period that election results and victories were principally if not single-headedly decided by the ruling elite instead of the electorate. The Independent National Electoral Commission was then largely reported to be far from enjoying the independence which its name connotes.

After the 2003 elections, Adolphus Wabara emerged the president of the 5th senate and led the national assembly up-till 2005 when he was replaced by Ken Nnamani following allegations of corruption levelled against him. It would be recalled that Wabara initially lost the very election that ushered him into the 5th senate to D.C. Imo—candidate of the All Nigeria People's Party (ANPP) but was later to be declared by a court in June 2003 as elected.

In May 2004 and April 2005, senators with the support of President Obasanjo moved to investigate Wabara over alleged financial misdeeds and gross misuse of office (*Thisday* 2004; *New African* 2005). The senators accused Wabara among others of exceeding his authority by handing out various contracts without the knowledge or approval of the requisite Senate committee (Omunu and Sanusi 2004), and taking a bribe of 400,000 Dollars bribe from the then education minister—Fabian Osuji to facilitate the passage of his ministry's annual budget. Although Wabara had pointed out these allegations were mere politics orchestrated by Igbo senators who wanted his seat (Utomwen and Orilade 2004), he however threw in the towel by resigning in April 2005. The charges against Wabara were dropped in 2010 grounds that the allegations against him were bogus and that the actions of the federal government were most embarrassing, barbaric and uncivilised because the accused had not made statements to any security agents before the broadcast trial and finally pronounced guilty. Hence Wabara and the other accused persons in relation to his case were freed by Justice Odili (*Thisday* 2010). Senator Ken Nnamani stepped in as senate president after Wabara resignation.

Still determined to continue the strive for control of power in the national assembly, Obasanjo's presidency made several attempts at influencing its activities. For instance, while a committee mandated with the task of investigating an allegation of public funds' diversion for personal use initially indicted President Obasanjo, the president rejected the outcome of this investigation and influenced the constitution of another committee instead (*Vanguard* 2007). The new panel after its own inquiry found the Vice President—Atiku Abubakar guilty and recommended that he should be impeached (Ihemeje et al. 2016 citing Fasagba 2009). This was the height of the rift between the president and his deputy mentioned earlier. Despite various stratagems employed by the execute to allow Obasanjo have a third term through the back door, the 5thassembly under the leadership of Senator Ken Nnamani and Hon. Aminu Bello Masari would be fondly remembered for resisting this third term bid.

Sixth and Seventh Assembly (2007–2015)

As Lewis (2011) rightly observed, the change of leadership baton both at the presidency and in the national assembly in 2007 opened a new page to executive–legislative relationship in the fourth Nigerian republic. This is particularly as President Umaru Musa Yar'Adua's commitment to democratic mode of governance contrasted with Obasanjo's dictatorial disposition to running a state. For instance, the 'politicking' which led to the emergence of Senator David Mark as senate president and Hon. (Mrs.) Patricia Etteh as Speaker was obviously devoid of the kind of executive interference which occasioned the election of principal officers of the fourth and fifth Assembly. This notwithstanding, two major issues which transpired within this period exposed how some politicians place politics above governance.

First is the politics which trailed the petroleum industry bill which was an executive bill transmitted twice to the national assembly for consideration. Despite the benefits which this bill would have accrued to the people, it failed to see the light of the day throughout the sixth and seventh assembly. According to the Environmental Rights Action/Friends of the Earth, the lawmakers politicised the bill when many of them became the mouthpiece of Shell and other oil companies which threatened to pull out of Nigeria's oil and gas operations if the PIB was passed (Ezeamalu 2015).

The second issue which accentuated the primordial politics inherent in the sixth and seventh Assembly was the crisis which emanated from the deliberate refusal of President Yar'Adua to transmit a written declaration to the National Assembly to inform it that it was proceeding on health vacation (Fashagba 2010). Although, this quagmire was caused majorly by the ambiguous Section 145 of the 1999 Constitution which provides that whenever the President transmits to the President of the Senate and the Speaker of the House of Representatives, a written declaration that he is proceeding on vacation or unable to discharge the functions of his office, until he transmits to them a written declaration to the contrary, such functions shall be discharged by the Vice President as Acting President (CFRN 1999), it did not provide for the manner by which the President should transmit the written declaration (Sagay 2010). More compounding was the fact that the Constitution did not fix a time limit within which the letter should be transmitted.

For over three months, the legislators failed to arrive at any definite decision on the matter as they were divided into groups. While some explored the inadequacies of the constitution to pursue their selfish interest at the detriment of the country, others sought possible amendments of the relevant provision of the law to create room for Vice President Goodluck Jonathan to substantially wield full presidential powers. But for the doctrine of necessity invoked by senate president David Mark which enabled Dr. Goodluck Jonathan to take over the mantle of leadership, the constitutional crisis would have degenerated to a catastrophic dimension.

Save for the leadership style of senator David Mark who strove to maintain harmonious relationship among the legislators as well as between legislators and the executive, a whole lot of politics ensued in the sixth and seventh Assembly which obviously impacted in no small measure on governance and national development. Apart from the emergence of Hon. Aminu Tambuwal as the Speaker of the House of Representatives against the wishes of the president and some top officials of the peoples' Democratic party created a protracted conflict between and among politicians in the entire governance system, there was a legal battle between President Jonathan and the legislators on the validity of the amendment of the 1999 Constitution without the president's assent. They both disagreed when on 1st January 2012 the president increased the pump price of PMS otherwise called petrol from 65 Naira to 141 Naira per litre (Akpan 2012) to the rift between Rt. Hon. Tambuwal—Speaker of the house of representatives and the president leading to the withdrawal of the speaker's security details, his lockout of the national assembly and his eventual decamp from the peoples' Democratic Party, the sixth House of representatives presided over by Hon. DimejiBankole was characterised by numerous crises one of which saw legislators like Dino Melaye being brutally brandished and bundled out of the plenary for accusing the leadership of the house of misappropriating funds (Utomwen, 2010).

Another manifestation of legislature–executive rivalry was on the removal of fuel subsidy by President Jonathan, on 1 January 2012 leading to an increase in the pump price of PMS (petrol) from N65.00 to N142.00 per litre. Having observed the public outcry and nationwide demonstration against this unusual 'new year gift', the House of Representatives conveyed an extraordinary session on Sunday, 8 January 2012 and passed a motion there and then asking the Jonathan led presidency to reverse the policy. Even though the Senate was reported not to have adopted a formal resolution on the matter, they allegedly mandated their head—Senator David Mark during a closed-door session on 10th January 2012 to convey the position of the members that the price hike should be rescinded (Agande et al. 2012). Both the house and the senate posited that their decision was anchored on the fact that the state of the economy particularly as it affects the living standard of the masses would not permit such an increase at the moment. The president of the senate even went further to mediate between the government and the organised labour which was at the forefront of the mass protests (Umoru 2012). A middle ground was reached at the end of the crisis when both parties settled for 97 Naira pump price.

Following the crises which characterised the sixth and seventh Assembly, whole lots of unfinished legislative businesses were observably left unattended to. A study carried out by CISLAC as cited by Jimoh (2015) reveals for instance several unresolved high-profile cases of corruption which the legislators had denied exhaustive investigation or prosecution. Among these notable cases are: N195 billion Pension Scam, attributed to Abdulrasheed Maina, the Chairman of Pension Reform Task Team; Kerosene subsidy scam by NNPC; Police Pension Fund Fraud; Former Aviation Minister, Stella Oduah's N255 million armoured car scandal; Missing N20 billion Naira oil money; $9.3 million private jet/arms scandal; Abba Morro Immigration job Scandal; Malabu Oil's $1.1 million scandal; Ekiti state Election scandal; Farouk Lawan's $620,000 scandal. All these have impacted overtly or covertly on the living standard of the Nigerian people (Odisu 2016).

Eighth Assembly (2015–2019)

Just like the late President Umaru Musa Yar'Adua, who from the onset of his administration never showed interest in the election of principal officers of the national assembly. President Muhammadu Buhari maintained a disposition of non-interference in legislative politics. It was not surprising therefore that Senator Bukola Saraki and Hon. Yakubu Dogara, despite being aware of their party's (All Progressive Congress) zoning arrangement for key positions in the national assembly, they renegade and conspire with the opposition Peoples Democratic Party to emerge senate president and speaker of the house of representatives, respectively (Mudashir 2015). In the deal which particularly brought the senate president to power, the Saraki group had to trade the position of the Deputy President of the Senate to Senator Ike Ekweremadu in order to get the support of the opposition.

While some praise the president for being non-partisan on legislative affairs, this very disposition became the undoing of the president (also the party leader) as the repercussion which ensued not only denied the ruling party the cohesion and harmony it needed to work as a team to deliver democratic dividends to the Nigerian people, it has equally brought disrepute to the Nigerian state as the world watched the ochlocracy in the National Assembly on a day the president presented the 2019 budget to senators and representatives who were supposed to listen and react distinguishably and honourably (Olowolagba 2018; Nwabughiogu 2018). They instead embarrassingly and uncontrollably jeered and cheered the president of the federal republic of Nigeria. Consequently, embarrassed and uncomfortable by these unruly behaviours, the president cautioned the lawmakers to be mindful of the fact that the world is watching their deeds (*Thisday* 2018). Although, legislative politics manifesting in such ochlocratic actions against top state officials are not peculiar to Nigeria, as instances of such behaviours abound in Britain, Sri Lanka, India, South Africa and Japan, the concern with the Nigerian case and particularly the eighth assembly, is how the foundation of executive–legislative relationship was laid on a gully and muddy arrangement. Adisa et al. (2017) succinctly corroborated this position when they noted that:

> The Executive and Legislature are always engaged in cat and mouse relations in most democracies. And the Nigerian situation has never really been different, even when the ruling party maintains an overwhelming control

> of the chambers. The story of the 8th National Assembly has however been peculiar. Its journey in 2015 took off on an acrimonious note, as the ruling All Progressives Congress (APC) was pitted against members of the National Assembly who were bent on choosing their own leaders.

The actual war between the leadership of the National Assembly and the ruling APC became apparent when in September 2015, the Federal Government of Nigeria dragged the Senate President, Dr. Bukola Saraki—who doubled as chairman of the National Assembly, to the Code of Conduct Tribunal on the allegation of false asset declaration. This was to be followed by several other acts and actions which were believed to have been orchestrated by the ruling elite and/or those sympathetic to it in the national assembly. Notable among these actions are the docking of Saraki's wife over allegation of corruption, the raising of case of certificate forgery against senator Dino Melaye—an ally of Dr. Bukola, suspension of Sen. Ali Ndume, stealing of the senate mace by thugs believed to be loyal to Senator OvieOmo-Agege—a staunch supporter of President Buhari. Retaliatorily, the national assembly have on their own part deliberately padded and delayed the budgets sent to it for consideration, refused to confirm for appointment some nominees of the president among whom is Mr. Ibrahim Magu as substantive chairman of the Economic and Financial Crimes Commission (EFCC), suspensions of Ali Ndume and Omo-Agege for calling for the investigation of allegations against Bukola Saraki and Dino Melaye and for unapologetically professing to be a pro-Buhari right in the senate chambers (Omaga 2017).

Effects of Legislative Politics on Governance in Nigeria

Having conceptualised and contextualised legislative politics as well as exemplified some instances of legislative politics within the purview of this discourse, it is now apt to sieve out and explain how legislative politics impacts on governance in Nigeria. This shall be discussed within five problematic themes drown out from events which unfolded in the fourth to eight National Assembly as highlighted in the preceding section above: we would see how these problems (Waste of time and resources; pursuit and promotion of selfish interests; lawbreaking instead of lawmaking; denial of quality leadership and governance; and denial of quality representation and participation) have affected governance.

Waste of Time and Resources

The first major challenge posed by legislative politics to governance particularly in view of the way and manner it is conducted in Nigeria is the delay in passing laws and carrying out quality oversights which impacts on the livelihood of the citizenry. Apart from the stages involved in lawmaking and oversight activities, the senate had five presidents between 1999 and May 2007 as a result of the fierce contestation and rivalry among those who sought the highest position of the National Assembly. In the unhealthy competitions and resultant scandals which ensued, huge amount of money generally believed to be public funds was allegedly wasted to induce senators to unseat Chuba Okadigbo who appeared too radical and recalcitrant for the presidency to control. Equally documented in a vanguard report of 2009 was a very large amount of taxpayers' money allegedly misappropriated to pacify rebellious senators in order to suppress the call for the removal of Adolphus Wabara when he was senate president. Similarly, several stratagems were employed to unseat Ghali Umar Na' Abba when he was the speaker of the House of Representatives.The discovery of Ghana Must Go bags purportedly laid on the floor of the national assembly to induce members, the procurement of exotic cars for Senators and Representatives at the exorbitant price of N35 million each (*Sugar Daily*, April 10, 2016) despite public outcry against it, and the revelation of the former CBN governor—Sanusi Lamido that the national assembly alone spends 25% of the national budget would all not be forgotten in a hurry. In all of these, ample time which could have been utilised to carry out quality representation, lawmaking and oversights were instead used to pursue and promote selfish and parochial interests.

Pursuit and Promotion of Selfish Interests

The second challenge posed by the politicking in the National Assembly is the outright pursuit and promotion of selfish interests by individuals and groups. Lawmakers have observably created unnecessary caucuses, power blocs and alliances based on individual or group interests to sabotage either themselves or the other organs of governments. The politics surrounding the various issues leading to agitations to unseat Chuba Okadigbo, Adolphus Wabara, Ghali Na'Abba and Patricia Etteh mentioned earlier, have their roots in the intention of individuals and groups to pursue and promote their selfish interest at the expense of that of the people of Nigeria. The suspension of Abdulmumin Jibrin for exposing the role of the hierarchy of the house on the budget padding scenario (Anofi 2016), and those of Ali Ndume and Ovie Omo-Agege which courts at different points declared ultra vires show how the tyrannical pursuit of selfish interest have denied some constituencies the rights of representation and participation in governance.

Lawbreaking Instead of Lawmaking

The fact that the law courts have reversed some of the decisions of the lawmakers as exemplified above is an indication that the lawmakers have not lived up to their responsibilities. Even the obvious fact derivable from the empty seats of the National Assembly during proceedings, shows that most senators and representatives do not attend plenaries. Yet Nigerian citizens are yet to hear of any senator or house of representative members who have been queried or punished for not attending plenary. Attendance in the two chambers is still very poor despite not being on part-time. As Odisu (2016) have already noted, this is in sharp contrast with the scintillating debates in the well-attended British Parliament and the US Congress that we watch on international broadcast media like the Cable News Network (CNN).

Lack of Quality Representation and Participation

The waste of time and resources, pursuit and promotion of selfish interest and the violation of laws by those who were ordinarily supposed to be prudent, altruistic, law abiders, is a manifestation that quality representation and participation are lacking in the Nigerian polity. While these(quality representation and participation) continue to constitute some the major parameters for assessing good governance anywhere in the world, their near absence as occasioned by inability of many lawmakers to interact with their constituencies before making decisions shows the dearth of quality representation and participation in Nigeria. Constituency offices of legislators which served as the meeting point between elected representatives and members of their constituencies no longer serve that purpose. Hence decisions are made and vote are cast without consulting community members. The case of Senator Ayo Akinyelure who wept and apologised to his constituency for supporting girl child marriage exemplifies the lack of quality representation which is being stressed (Badejo 2013; Sahara Reporters 2013).

Lack of Quality Leadership and Governance

When legislative duties and matters such as lawmaking and oversights are politicised to favour individuals or groups without recourse to the people whom the mandate to legislate is drawn from, it would certainly impact negatively on overall leadership and governance of the affected community. While consistent accountability, political cohesiveness and citizens' right to decision making—which are the hallmark of good governance are through public hearing which are largely lacking in the conduct of lawmaking in Nigeria, these have to a very large extent denied the citizens the so much-desired dividends of democracy which are supposed to accrue to them.

Conclusion and Recommendations

The saying that time wasted can never be regained is equally true of resources. A great deal of legislative time and national resources have been expended since June 1999 when vested interests compete over who and who should run the affairs of the lawmaking institution in Nigeria. Starting with the entitlement which have been claimed by individuals and groups who were erroneously elected or appointed to positions of authority in the legislature to public funds which were used to induce parliamentarians to act in particular ways, the Nigerian masses cannot but be said to have been cheated by the political elite. While members of this group pursue and promote their selfish interests, thoughts of the common good are most often relegated to the background. This for instance is the reason the much-applauded PetroleumIndustry Bill (PIB) could not be passed in 10 years. While laws have in the legislative period under review been flagrantly abused by some parliamentarians, only selective justice has been seen to be meted on violators. In this respect, one may be bold to decry the poor level of representation and participation in the Nigerian polity. Also, in the absence of quality representation and participation especially in the act of lawmaking, any argument in favour of good governance cannot hold water.

To correct these anomalies in order for the populace to substantially enjoy the dividends of democracy whose hallmark is accountability, rule of law, quality representation and participation—which they intuitively vote for, there is need for the electorate to thoroughly engage those who aspire to represent them before they are eventually voted. Equally, there is a need for the citizens to be conscious always with the activities of their representatives in the National Assembly. Like Senator Ayo Akinyelure was made to apologise to his constituency and promise not to betray their thrust anymore, if other parliamentarians are mindful that they would definitely face their constituencies when they return home, they would be careful with the ways their activities are carried out. Hence, there is a need for the establishment and operationalisation of a publicly owned constituency office for every senatorial and house of representatives' constituency. Finally, the laws, its enforcement agencies as well as the courts should be reviewed and strengthened as the case may be to allow for acute separation of powers and checks and balances.

References

Anofi, D. (2016, September 29). Budget Padding: Jibrin Suspended for 180 Legislative Days. *The Nation*. www.thenationonlineng.net. Retrieved January 10, 2019.

Adisa, T., Olatunji, J. S., & Daniel, K. (2017, December 30). Examining Executive—Legislature Relationship in 2017. *Tribune*. www.tribuneonlineng.com. Retrieved January 10, 2019.

Bevir, M. (2012). *Governance: Avery Short Introduction*. Oxford: Oxford University Press.

Abbott, F. F. (1901). *A History and Description of Roman Political Institutions*. Elibron Classics.

Agande, B., Umoru, H., & Shaibu, I. (2012, January 21). Senators, Reps React to Fuel Price Hike. *Vanguard*. p. 1.

Akpan, M. (2012, May 25). The President's Misadvisers. *Newswatch*. Friday.

Ayitogo, N. (2018, December 20). Budget Presentation: Why We Booed Buhari—Law Maker. *Premium Times*. www.premiumtimesng.com. Retrieved January 10, 2019.

Ayoade, J. A., & Akinsanya, A. A. (Eds.). (2012). *Nigeria's Critical Election, 2011*. Lanham, MD: Lexington Books.

Aziken, E. (2009, June 9). The Plots and Scandals of the Senate Since 1999. *Vanguard*. Retrieved February 20, 2018.

Badejo, A. (2013, July 22). Under Age Marriage Law: Ondo Senator Weeps, Says He Voted in Error. *Daily Post*. www.dailypost.ng. Retrieved January 19, 2019.

BBC. (1999, July 22). Nigerian Speaker Quits in Tears. *BBC News*. http://news.bbc.co.uk/2/hi/africa/401123.stm. Retrieved January 5, 2019.

Birkland, T. A. (2015). *Introduction to the Policy Process*. New York: M. E. Sharpe.

Blanton, S. L., & Kegley, C. W. (2016). *World Politics: Trends and Transformation, 2016–2017*. Hampshire: Cengage Learning.

Brady, L. P. (2017). *The Politics of Negotiation: American Dealings with Allies, Adversaries and Friends*. Chapel Hill: University of North Carolina Press.

Byrd, R. (1995). *The Senate of the Roman Republic*. US Government Printing Office Senate Document 103–23.

CFRN. (1999). *Constitution of the Federal Republic of Nigeria*. Lagos: Federal Government Press.

Dylan, M. (2018, October 5). Impeaching a Supreme Court Justice Explained. *Vox Media*. www.vox.com. Retrieved January 12, 2019.

Ezeamalu, B. (2015, September 18). Assembly Refused to Pass Petroleum Industry Bill—Group. *Premium Times*. www.premiumtimesng.com. Retrieved January 12, 2019.

Fashagba, J. Y. (2010). Exploring the Nigeria's Central Legislative Institutions. In J. Y. Fashagba, O. M. Ajayi, & C. Nwankwor (Eds.), *The Nigerian National Assembly* (pp. 1–13). Springer.

Gbadegesin, S. (2016, November 18). Is Politics All About Self-Interest? *The Nation*. thenationolineng.net. Retrieved January 7, 2019.

Goitom, H. (2017). National Parliaments: Nigeria. *Law Library of Congress*. Global Legal Research Centre. www.law.gov. Retrieved January 12, 2019.

Griffith, G. (2005). *Parliaments and Accountability: The Role of Parliamentary Oversight Committees* (NSW Parliamentary Library Research Service, Briefing Paper, Number 12/05).

Guobadia, D. A. (2000). *The Legislature and Good Governance Under the 1999 Constitution* (I. A. Ayua, et al., Eds.). Nigeria: Issues in the 1999 Constitution 43.

Hague, R., & Harrop, M. (2013). *Comparative Government and Politics: An Introduction*. London, UK: Macmillan International Higher Education.

Hawkesworth, M., & Kogan, M. (2013). *Encyclopedia of Government and Politics*. Oxfordshire: Routledge.

Hufty, M. (2011). Investigating Policy Processes: The Governance Model Analytical Framework (GAF). In U. Wiesmann & H. Hurni (Eds.), *Research for Sustainable Development: Foundations, Experiences, and Perspectives* (Vol. 6, pp. 403–424). Bern: Geographica Bernensia.

Humphrey, A. P. (1899). The Impeachment of Alexander Chase. *The Virginia Law Register*, *5*(5), 281–302.

Ihemeje, C. C. G., Zaid, B. A., & Jayum, A. J. (2016). Factors Influencing the Executive and Legislative Conflict in Nigeria Political Development. *IOSR Journal of Humanities and Social Science, 21*(8), Ver. 7.

Jimoh, A. (2015, August 27). Legislative Duties and Democratic Governance in Nigeria: The Mistakes 8th Assembly Should Not Repeat. *CISLAC*. http://cislacnigeria.net/category/articles/.

Johnson, J. K. (2005). *Role of Parliaments in Government*. Washington, DC: World Bank Institute.

Johnston, A., & Woodburn, J. A. (1903). *American Orations: V. The Anti-slavery Struggle*. New York: G.P. Putnam's sons.

Joseph, W. (2014). *Politics in China: An Introduction* (2nd ed.). London: Oxford University Press.

Kurtz, K. (1997). Legislatures and Citizens: Public Participation and Confidence in the Legislature. *Trust for Representative Democracy*. http://www.ncsl.org/legislators. Retrieved January 7, 2019.

Law Teacher. (2013). Democracy Does Not Merely Mean Majority Rule. www.lawteacher.net/freelawessays. Retrieved 14 January, 2019.

Lloyd, M. D. (1998, September 22). *Polybius and the Founding Fathers: The Separation of Powers*. 1999 Donald E. Glover Award, Outstanding Final Project. www.mlloyd.org. Retrieved November 17, 2012.

Merriam-Webster Online. (2019). Definition of Political. Merriam-Webster Inc. Springfield, MA. www.merriam-webster.com. Retrieved January 6, 2019.

Mudashir, I. (2018, March 29). Doctrine of Necessity to the Rescue. *Daily Trust*. www.dailytrust.com.ng. Retrieved January 21, 2019.

Mudashir, I. (2015, August 17). Nigeria: When Will Saraki Visit Villa. *Daily Trust*. www.dailytrust.com.ng. Retrieved January 21, 2019.

New African. (2005, May 01). Adolphus Wabara and Alice Mobolaji Osomo Unseated After Corruption Allegations. Archived from the original on 22 January 2013. Retrieved October 6, 2009.

Nwachukwu, J. O. (2018, December 14). 2019 Budget: Senator Ndume Addresses Lawmakers Threatening Boycott of Buhari's Presentation. *Daily Post*. www.dailypost.ng.

Nwabughiogu, L. (2018, December 19). 2019 Budget: How Senators, Reps Jeered, Cheered President Buhari. *Vanguard*. vanguardngr.com.

Nwanolue, B. O. G., & Iwuoha, V. C. (2012). Democratic Consolidation and Challenges of Legislative Politics in Nigeria: A Political Economy Approach. *Singaporean Journal of Business Economics, and Management Studies, 1*(2), 25–38.

Odeh, A. M. (2015). The Effects of Corruption on Good Governance in Nigeria. *International Journal of Development and Sustainability, 4*(3), 292–307.

Odiji, O. (2013). *Understanding the Career Opportunities in Political Science* (71 pp.). Lokoja: Divine Favour Printing and Publishing.

Odiji, O. (2015). Democracy and National Development in Nigeria, 1999–2015. *International Journal of Governance and Development, 4*(2).

Odisu, T. A. (2016). The Nigerian Legislature and the Crisis of Governance. *Scientific Journal of Review, 5*(9), 453–457.

Ojeifo, S. (2007, August 3). Nigeria: Enwerem, Former Senate President Dies at 71. *Thisday*. Retrieved August 24, 2007.

Olaniyi, J. (2001). *Introduction to Contemporary Political Analysis*. Lagos: Fapsony.

Olowolagba, F. (2018, December 19). 2019 Budget: National Assembly Under Attack as Senators, Reps Boo Buhari. *Daily Post*. www.dailypost.ng. Retrieved January, 2019.

Okpala, K. (2013). Public Accounts Committee and Oversights Function in Nigeria: A Tower Built on Sinking Sand. *International Journal of Business and Management*, 8 (13).

Okocha, C. (2001, July 23). Nigeria: National Assembly to Repeal Draconian Decrees. *Thisday*. www.thisdaylive.com. Retrieved January 15, 2019.

Okoosi-Simbine, A. (2010). Understanding the Role and Challenges of the Legislature in the Fourth Republic: The Case of Oyo State House of Assembly. *Nigeria Journal of Legislative Affairs, 3*(1&2), 1–27.

Omaga, D. (2017, April 11). Rift Between the Executive and the Legislative Arms of Government: A Red Herring. *The Nigerian Voice*. https://www.thenigerianvoice.com. Retrieved January 20, 2019.

Omunu, H. and Sanusi, I. (2004, April 26). Nigeria: Senators Move Against Wabara in Impeachment Motion. *Daily Trust*. https://www.dailytrust.com.ng. Retrieved January 05, 2019.

Oyeyipo, S. (2018, December 14). House Members Threatened to Boycott Buhari's Budget Presentation Wednesday. *Thisday*. www.thisdaylive.com. Retrieved January 10, 2019.

Price, S. (2011, February 22). *The Roman Republic in Montesquieu and Rousseau—Abstract*. Retrieved November 19, 2012.

Sahara Reporters. (2013, July 23). How Protesters Forced Senator Akinyelure to Recant Vote on Child Marriage. www.saharareporters.com. Retrieved January 19, 2019.

Schindler, R. (2013). *Montesquieu's Political Writings*. Retrieved November 19, 2012.

Simpson, P. (1997). *The Politics of Aristotle*. Chapel Hill: University of North Carolina Press.

Suleiman, T. (1999, July 19). Nigeria: Encounter with Salisu Buhari. *Daily Trust*. www.dailytrust.com.ng. Retrieved January 21, 2019.

Taylor, S. L. (2012). *30-Second Politics: The 50 Most Thought Provoking Ideas in Politics, Each Explained in Half a Minute*. London: Icon Books Limited.

The News. (1999, July 19). The face of a Liar. *The News Magazine* (Vol. 13(2), pp. 16–17). Lagos: Independent Communication Network Limited.

Thisday. (2004, May 02). Why Obasanjo Backs Senators Over Probe. https://www.thisdaylive.com. Retrieved January 30, 2019.

Thisday. (2010, June 1). N50m Bribe: Appeal Court Reprimands Obasanjo. https://www.thisdaylive.com. Retrieved January 30, 2019.

Thisday. (2018, December 19). The World Is Watching Us, Buhari Tells Lawmakers. thisdaylive.com.

Tinubu, B. A. (2008, 15 December). *Good Governance, Democracy and Sustainable Development*. A Lecture Delivered at the Centre for Peace and Conflict Studies, University of Ibadan.

Umoru, M. (2012, December 28). Senate's Achievements and Unfinished Business. *Vanguard*. vanguardngr.com. Retrieved January 10, 2019.

Utomwen, D., & Orilade, T. (2004, April 30). I am Ready for Probe - Wabara. *PM News*. https://www.pmnewsnigeria.com. Retrieved January 20, 2019.

Vanguard. (2007, February 28). PTDF: Senate Probe Panel Indicts Atiku. *Obasanjo*. https://www.vanguardngr.com. Retrieved January 10, 2019.

Zvoma, A. M. (2010, March 22). The Role and Function of Parliaments and Mandate of Committees. *LCC/Front Bench Retreat* at Wild Geese Lodge, Harare. www.parlzim.gov.zw.

CHAPTER 4

Interrogating Voting Patterns in Nigeria's Legislative Elections Under the Fourth Republic

Oluwashina Moruf Adebiyi, Fatima Omotayo Aliu, and Opeyemi Idowu Aluko

Introduction

The legislature as a democratic institution plays a crucial and indispensable role in democratic governance. In presidential system of government where government powers are diffused among three organs—executive, legislature and judiciary, the legislature prevents arbitrary use of power by the executive and the judiciary. This gives credence to the notion that any system of government which claims to be democratic and which operates within the confines of the rule of law must be made up of the three organs

O. M. Adebiyi (✉) · F. O. Aliu
Department of Political Science, Faculty of Social Sciences, University of Ilorin, Ilorin, Nigeria

O. I. Aluko
Department of Political Science, Ajayi Crowther University, Oyo, Nigeria

F. A. Aremu and A. R. Bakare (eds.), *Two Decades of Legislative Politics and Governance in Nigeria's National Assembly*,
https://doi.org/10.1007/978-981-33-4455-6_4

performing distinct functions and roles which must be complementary. As posited by Nwabueze (2003) the legislature is the symbol of a country's existence as an independent and supreme entity and the hallmark of its prestige as a state and the source through which the executive derives most of its powers and authority in administering the state. Based on this, it was further noted that the supreme authority of the state is therefore, vested in that organ which possess the power to make laws that are binding on the state (Nwabueze 2003). This must have prompted Polsby (1975) to describe the legislature as the 'nerve ending' of any democratic polity.

What however epitomises the role of the legislature in democratic governance is representation. The legislature in any democratic government represents the voices of the diverse ethno-cultural and religious groupings, particularly in ethnically diverse and heterogeneous societies. By doing this, the legislature serves as a viable connection between those who exercise power and authority and the electorate (Okoosi-Simbine 2010). While the legislature is primarily saddled with the function of making laws, it performs other important roles such as representing the interest of the constituencies from which they emerge. The Policy and Legal Advocacy Centre (PLAC) (2016) noted that one of the basic parameters for measuring the effectiveness of the legislature is the extent to which it responds positively to challenges and issues affecting the general public. In this regard, citizens have the right to feel the impact of their representatives because such legislators represent the interest and aspirations of the various constituencies they represent. Thus, the representation function of the legislative institution is significant to democratic growth and sustainability (PLAC 2016).

One derivative of the above is that much as the legislature occupies a central position in democratic governance, its members are considered men and women of honour. By virtue of the fact that members of the legislature perform the role of representation, they derive their mandate from the people particularly those they represent. In essence, the legislators derive their power, authority and status from the people. This notion is buttressed by Bogdanor (1991) when he observed that membership of the legislature resides with the electorate within a political community. Therefore, legislators are mere representatives of such political community. The power to become a member of the legislature resides with the people and such people exercise the power through elections for their preferred candidates. In Nigeria, elections are held every four years to elect representatives to the National Assembly comprising of the House of Representatives and the Senate. The patterns of such legislative elections have significant effects on democratic sustenance. It is on this premise that, this chapter examines voting patterns in the Nigerian legislative elections in the Fourth Republic. The chapter is structured into four sections. The first section is the introduction. The section dwells on theoretical exposition on periodic election and legislative recruitment. This is followed by an overview of voting patterns and electoral outcomes in Nigeria legislative elections since 1999. The fourth section examines implications of the voting pattern on democratic sustenance in Nigeria and the way forward.

Periodic Elections and Legislative Recruitment: A Theoretical Perspective

The conduct of elections since the emergence of democratic regimes has become one of the major democratic norms in Africa. Since the adoption of democratic system of governance in Africa the conduct of elections has become a significant characteristic of developing democracies most especially those of Africa. Mindful of their transparency and credibility, the fact that elections are held on periodic bases without interruption signifies that the new democracies of Africa are consolidating and developing. Over the years, scholars have demonstrated the importance of elections to democratic consolidation and development (Wojtasik 2013; Dunmoye 2010; Höglund 2009; Sisk 2008; Hughes and May 1988; Cohen 1983).

As noted by Wojtasik (2013) the purposes elections serve are a function of the type of system of government operation in a polity. He argued on the one hand that, in parliamentary systems elections are a way of determining or soliciting political consensus which will at the end translate to a parliamentary majority which have the legitimacy to rule. In presidential systems on the other hand, elections serve as a modicum through which influence can be exerted by elected representatives on the opposition. Other factors which influence the classifications of the functions of elections are the type of electoral system in use in the polity. The electoral system determines the nature of organs which take part in the electoral process and basis on which elections are held and the basis on which winners and losers are determined (Katz 1997).

Generally, elections serve a myriad of purposes in a democratic society. According to Dunmoye (2010) elections help to ensure that those who exercise governmental power emanate from the choices of the electorates. In essence, elections in his perception ensure that the elected representatives are guaranteed legitimate rule. This claim was buttressed by Hughes and May (1988) when they posited that election helps to institutionalise the process of succession by creating a legal administrative framework for handling inter-elite rivalry and providing a modicum for popular backing for the leaders (Hughes and May 1988). To Cohen (1983) elections serve as the basic framework for the workings of the social contract which binds the rulers and the rules. In this regard, he emphasised that the basic utility of elections can be located in educating, entertaining and giving the people a voice and feeling of participation. It was further argued by Cohen (1983) that elections offer electorate freedom of choice, the power to hold elected leaders accountable and provide protection against perpetration of arbitrary rule. Thus, elections serve as the mechanism for converting the consent of the people into government authority.

Elections come in various forms, each being held or conducted according to its purpose. Elections can be categorised as general elections, primary elections, referendum and initiative elections, plebiscites, legislative and recall elections (Encyclopaedia Britannica 2018). General elections are held to determine which political party or candidate will occupy political offices. In primary elections political parties select candidates to represent the party in general elections. The candidates who garner the highest number of votes in the primary election go on to contest the general election on behalf of the party. The referendum and initiative elections are elections in which the preferences and choices of the community as regards a particular issue of public interest is solicited. Referendum and intuitive elections are usually held for voters to vote 'yes' or 'no'. Plebiscites are elections conducted to decide two critical political issues. These are government legitimacy and the nationality of territories contested between governments. Legislative elections are held to elect members of parliaments or the legislature. Recall elections otherwise known as representative recall is a process by which an elected member of parliament can be removed from office by voters through direct vote before the expiration of the term of office of such member (Encyclopaedia Britannica 2018; Yanina 2016).

The importance of elections in recruiting legislators cannot be overemphasised. The fact that elections are conducted to select parliamentarians and legislators to represent people of a particular constituency for a period of time shows that elected legislators are responsible to electorate through whom they derive the mandate to become members of the legislature. In essence, electorate holds the power to 'hire and fire' ineffective legislators. One way through which the electorate exercises this power is through periodic elections. On the one hand, the power to hire a legislator is exercised when the people of a constituency cast their votes for a particular candidate during legislative or parliamentary elections. On the other hand, the people of a constituency can recall a legislator who they consider not representing their interest enough. In this regard, such legislator is considered ineffective and can as well be voted out of office in subsequent legislative election.

In most democracies all over the globe, elections are conducted to determine those who become members of parliament. For instance, in the United States of America, Elections for Senate and Representatives as well as Delegates to the Congress are conducted every six years. The time, place and method of holding such elections are determined in each state by the legislature, although, this can be altered by the Congress. The elections are conducted in each of the states and territories of the United States on every Tuesday after the first Monday in November of every even-numbered year. Elections of the Representatives and Delegates to the Congress are held on the third day of January of the following year (United States Senate 2010). Being an even-numbered year, election to the United States Senate was conducted on 6 November 2018. In the election, 33 of the 100 seats were contested in regular Senate election while two other vacant seats in Minnesota and Mississippi were contested in special elections. The winners in the elections are to occupy the office for six years starting from 3 January 2019 to 3 January 2025 (Aron 2018).

It is important to mention that the Constitution of the United States of America does not make provision for nor does it authorise the recall of Senators and Representatives. This accounts for the reason why no member of Congress has ever been removed from office through recall election (Maskell 2012). Nevertheless, nineteen states in the United States of America have provisions for recall election for state officials and representatives (National Conference of State Legislatures 2016). For instance, Chapter 15 Article 48 of Alaska Statute stipulates that a state official or Representative can be recalled with 25% of the last votes cast for the office being occupied by the official. The grounds on which such officials can be recalled include: lack of fitness, incompetence and neglect of duties or corruption (Encyclopaedia of American Politics 2018).

In Britain, parliamentary elections also known as general election give every part of the United Kingdom the opportunity to have a voice in the selection of the Members of Parliament (MP). MPs represent various Constituencies in the House of Commons for a period of five years. Parliamentary elections in Britain are held after the parliament has been dissolved. The party that wins the majority in the elections forms the government. While it is statutory that parliamentary elections are to be held every five years, there are two conditions under which elections can be held before the expiration of five years. Such elections can occur when: (i) a motion of no confidence is passed on the ruling Government by a simple majority and 14 days elapses without the House passing a confidence motion in any new Government formed and (ii) a motion for a general election is agreed by two-thirds of the total number of seats in the Commons including vacant seats, currently 434 out of 650 (Lynch 2007). British parliamentary elections are conventionally held on a Thursday (Siaroff 2003).

While British voters have the right to vote for individuals who become members of the British Parliament, such voters also have the power to recall non-performing or incompetent parliamentarians. The power of the electorate to remove any member of MP is derived from the Recall of Members of Parliament Act, 2015. The Act stipulates that a recall petition could be instigated if a member is convicted by a competent court of law or he or she is suspended from the Parliament for nothing less than 21 days. If any of these conditions occur, the Speaker of the House would publish a notice to a petition officer, who in turn give notice to the constituency of such member. Following this is a petition that will be made available for signing eight weeks. If at the expiration of eight weeks, 10% of electorate in the constituency of the legislator signed the petition, the seat would be declared vacant, thus, requiring that a by-election be conducted (British Parliament 2015). The rationale behind the adoption of the Act can be found in the long-standing argument in British politics that British voters unlike their American and French counterparts who have two votes each for executive and their legislators, cast one vote for both parliamentarians and executive at the same time, thus given the parliamentarians the burden of double loyalty to their constituency and the political party they represent during elections (*The Economist* 2014).

In South Africa where governance is also based on parliamentary system, elections are held to fill seats in the National Assembly which consists of 400 members who are elected by proportional representation system based on a close list model (Election Guide 2014). Elections into the South African National Assembly are conducted every five years. Elections can be conducted on the order of the President when the Assembly is dissolved. Such elections must be held within 90 days of dissolution of the National Assembly (Election Guide 2014). The last election was conducted on 7th May 2014 the next election therefore is billed to hold on 6th May 2019 provided the National Assembly is not dissolved by the President.

Similarly, in Kenya elections are held to choose members to occupy seats in the National Assembly and the Senate. The National Assembly comprises of 290 members elected from single-member constituencies, forty-seven women representatives elected from the forty-seven counties each forming a single-member constituency and twelve special-interest representatives nominated by political parties in accordance with the proportion of their seats in the National Assembly and a speaker who is an ex-officio member of the Assembly. On the other hand, the Senate comprises of forty-seven members directly elected form each county, sixteen women nominated by the political parties in the Senate on the basis of the proportion of the seats they control; two representatives of the youth (a man and a woman); two representatives of persons with disabilities (also a man and a woman); and the Speaker of the Senate who is also an ex officio member. Parliamentary elections are held every five years precisely on the second Tuesday of August of every five years (The Federal Republic of Kenya 2010).

The significance of periodic elections in recruiting legislators cannot indeed be overemphasised. Elections ensure that elected members of legislatures are accountable to the people of their various constituencies, thus making them act in the interest of the electorate who brought them to power. When elections are conducted for choosing legislators on periodic bases, the fear that a representative who fails to fulfill his or her campaign promises may not be re-elected, thereby, making elected representatives accountable to their constituencies (Fowler 2004). The above position was buttressed by Fowler (2004) when he posited that periodic and democratic elections help in selecting good representatives and incentivising elected representatives to be sensitive to their consistencies, needs and welfare. The accountability of legislators to their constituencies has also been found to be related to the type of electoral system operational in the polity (Matlosa 2003).

For instance, in South Africa, where parliamentary elections are based on proportional representation, voters chose political parties and not individual candidates, thus members of the South African parliament are accountable to their various political parties. This is not to say that the accountability of such representatives is limited to the political parties. The parties in order to ensure that elected representatives are accountable to their constituencies make a list of candidates who will occupy parliamentary seats. When a member of parliament resigns, is expelled, 'cross carpets' to another party or dies the party chooses another person to fill the seat. This indicates that the party is vested with great powers therefore members who ignore party discipline or who reneges on his or her campaign promises loose their seats in parliaments (Matlosa 2003). This position has generated two contending perceptions to the effectiveness of proportional representation in keeping elected parliamentarians effective, responsive and accountable to their various constituencies.

Lodge and Scheidegger (2006) and Sebudubudu and Botlhomilwe (2013) argued that members of parliaments are prone to be more accountable to their respective political parties other than to the electorate from whom they derive their mandate. They further argued that constituency-based model in which electorate in certain geographical zone vote during elections for an individual candidate of their choice engender greater accountability and responsiveness to the electorate because there is a direct connection between the geographical zone and individual Member of Parliament. On the contrary, Matlosa (2003) and Norris (1997) argued that proportional representation system gives room to a fairer representation of political parties in the parliament. They are of the opinion that parliamentarians are not necessarily more accountable in a constituency-based electoral system. They argued that disagreeing with party decisions is not necessarily motivated by issues relating to political principles but may necessarily be motivated by career or other political considerations. In essence, they posited that irrespective of the electoral system, some Members of Parliament will at all times maintain a cordial relationship with their respective constituencies.

Fowler (2004) in a study to determine whether elections help is selecting competent representatives discovered that previously held elections do help in recruiting better representatives which invariably aid incumbents to perform well when they are re-elected. This, according to him, cannot be unconnected with the notion that the electorate always determine the re-election of representatives. In another explanation of the significance of elections in recruiting legislators, Maravall (2007) presented a sequential illustration of how election works. He noted that in the first instance, individual candidates jostle for the votes of the electorate by presenting prospective voters with their intended policies and their ability to initiate the formulation and implementation of such policies. Second, voters during election choose candidates whom they feel possess the ideal policies, initiatives for their development and general welfare. Third, elected representatives after assumption of office put in efforts to set the promised policies in motion. The intended or actual policies under certain political conditions produce outcomes, which shapes the lives of citizens.

By the expiration of the tenure of office of representatives, electorate assesses in retrospect the actual achievement of representatives' vis-à-vis their campaign promises. Before the next election the electorates update their preferences about policies and individual candidates. Lastly, the voters in another election re-elect representatives who they deem had satisfied their desires and aspirations or reject representatives who they perceive as not competent to represent their interest in the legislature. In this regard, elections play the role of selection and assessment in a democratic system (Maravall 2007). This perception of the important role of elections in recruiting and rejecting legislators is shared by Manin et al. (1999, p. 8) when they posited that:

> Mandates are particular kinds of signals that are emitted in elections. They constitute a choice among proposals offered by competing teams of politicians. Once elected, the victorious politicians adopt policies. These policies become transformed into outcomes under the noise of conditions. As the electoral term ends, voters evaluate the outcomes and decide whether or not to retain the incumbent government. (Manin et al. 1999, p. 8)

The significance of elections in recruiting representatives to the legislature can further be explained within the context of the theory of representative democracy. The theory of representative democracy was developed in contrast to the notion of direct democracy as practiced in the Greek-city states (Urbinatil and Warren 2008). According to the authors, representative democracy evolved from two important sources. The first is the expansion of franchise, which transformed liberal and constitutional governments to popular democracies. The second is the creation of a balance between the rulers and the ruled through structured constitutionalism, thus making political parties the main source of representation. Representative democracy is a governance system in which citizens of a country through elections vote for representatives to deliberate on issues related to legislation for the ruling and general welfare of the citizens. It contrasts sharply with autocracy where a dictator has unlimited powers given no room to the people to have a say in the governance process of their country (Gaus and Kukathas 2004).

The theory of representative democracy according to Urbinatil and Warren (2008) has four main assumptions. First, it assumed that representation is a form of relationship between the agents and the principals. In this case, the principals are the constituencies created on a territorial basis and represented by elected agents to represent the interests and aspirations of the people of the constituencies. This clearly separates the source of legitimate power from those who exercise the power. Secondly, the fact that representatives are elected gives credence to the notion that state power and sovereignty resides with the people. Thirdly, the responsiveness of political parties and elected representatives is achievable by elections. Lastly, universal suffrage engenders quality electoral representation and political equality. Thus, elections, responsiveness, guarantee of universal franchise as well as equality are significant concepts to representative democracy. In essence, accountability, quality representation and responsiveness are all derivable through periodic free, fair and credible elections (Esaiasson and Narud 2013).

It is worthy to note that the theory of representative democracy presupposes a form of mutual political relationship between the constituency and the representatives. This political representation, according to Castiglione and Warren (2006, p. 6) can be demonstrated in two distinct ways. First, they noted that: 'political representation involves a representative X being authorized by constituency Y to act with regard to good Z. Authorization means that there are procedures through which Y selects/directs X with respect to Z, and that responsibility over actions/decisions of X rest with Y.' Authorisation further implies the process of selecting representatives through voting in elections. They further noted that: 'political representation involves a representative X being held accountable to constituency Y with regard to good Z. Accountability means that X provides, or could provide, an account of his/her decisions or actions to Y with respect to Z, and that Y has a sanction over X with regard to Z' (Castiglione and Warren

2006, p. 6). This demonstrates that political representation involves a mutual symbiotic relationship between electorates of a constituency and the representative chosen to represent such constituency.

When people of a particular constituency that is, 'Y' vote for individual candidates or parties to represent their interest in the legislature, it is expected that the representatives 'X' after assuming office through the mandate of the people are expected to be accountable to the people in the sense of providing for the general welfare and development of the constituencies. This is what Castiglione and Warren (2006) refer to as good 'Z'. In a situation where 'X' reneges on the expectations of 'Y', then 'Y' sanctions 'X' by voting him or her out in subsequent elections. This illustration can be located within the notion of electoral democracy which Urbinatil and Warren (2008) refer to that aspect of representative relationship in which representatives are given the mandate to represent the people of a constituency to act on behalf of their interests after which they are assessed and re-elected or rejected in future elections. Much as elections are important to recruiting legislators and members of parliament, two important questions are also of equal importance to the study of legislative elections. The first is why do people vote the way they do in a legislative or parliamentary election? Second, what are the implications of the results and voting patterns on democracy? It is therefore critical to know that the most interesting aspects of an electoral process is not always about who wins and who losses but also about explanation and analysis of election results to identify the sources and implications of voting pattern (Merrill and Grofman 1999).

Voting Patterns and Electoral Outcomes: Nigeria's Legislative Elections Since 1999

The Nigerian state operates a bicameral legislature referred to as the National Assembly comprising of the Senate and House of Representatives. The National Assembly (NASS) deriving its powers from the 1999 Constitution is the nation's highest lawmaking body. While the Senate is headed by the President of the Senate and assisted by the Deputy President of the Senate, the House of Representatives is headed by the Speaker and assisted by the Deputy Speaker. The Senate on the one hand consists of 109 members which reflect the 109 Senatorial districts of the country. The Senatorial districts are equally divided among the 36 states which make up the Federal Republic of Nigeria. Each of the states has three senatorial districts while Abuja (the Federal Capital Territory) has one Senatorial district. The House of Representatives on the other hand comprise 360 members representing the 360 Federal Constituencies in which the country is divided. Legislative elections are held every four years to elect the 109 members of the Senate and 360 members of the House of Representatives.

The 1999 National Assembly Elections

Since the restoration of democratic rule in 1999, legislative elections have been conducted on a regular and stable basis. Since that year till date six different elections have been held. These are the legislative elections of 1999, 2003, 2007, 2011, 2015 and 2019. The outcomes of these elections took various patterns and dimensions. The 1999 Senatorial and House of Representative elections were held on the 20th February 1999 and contested by three political parties. These were: the Peoples Democratic Party (PDP), the Alliance for Democracy (AD) and the All Peoples Party (APP). The pre-election period was characterised by campaign promises of the revitalisation of the country after several years of military interregnum. The Inter-parliamentary Union (1999) noted that the three political parties were separated by a narrow margin of ideological differences, thus the campaign period was largely driven by the same vision and appeal to ethnic and regional sentiments to solicit for votes. The conduct of the elections was generally peaceful. It was observed that while the elections were marred by low turnout and 'some serious irregularities' they were generally adjudged to be fair (National Democratic Institute 1999).

The result of the Senatorial election showed that out of a total number of registered voters of 57, 938, 945 voter turnout was 24, 386, 247 approximately 42% of the total number of registered voters. The distribution of the seats indicated that the PDP won majority of the seats in the Senate and the House of Representatives. Table 4.1 shows the number of seats won by each of the three political parties in the National Assembly.

Table 4.1 showed that while the PDP won 66 seats, the APP won 23 and the AD won 19 states. With one vacant seat to be filled it can be observed that while the PDP won approximately 56% of the total valid votes cast for the Senatorial election, the APP won approximately 31% while the AD won approximately 12% of the total valid votes cast for the election. The dominance of the PDP in the 1999 Senatorial election also

Table 4.1 Results of the 1999 National Assembly Elections

Political parties	*Senate*			*House of Representatives*		
	Number of votes	*% of votes*	*Number of seats (109)*	*Number of votes*	*% of votes*	*Number of seats (360)*
PDP	13,753,843	56.4	66	13,924,547	57.1	206
APP	7,608,509	31.2	23	7,046,192	30.6	74
AD	3,023, 895	12.4	19	3,023,895	12.4	68
VACANT SEAT	–	–	1	–	–	12
Total	**24,386,247**	**100**	**109**	**23,994,634**	**100**	**360**

Source African Elections Database (2011)

reflected in the results of the House of Representatives election. The PDP like it did in the Senatorial election won the majority seats in the House of Representatives. With 206 seats the PDP had the majority. The APP was able to win 74 seats while the AD had 68 seats. These results depict the dominance of the PDP both in the Senate and the House of Representatives. In the state by state result of the National Assembly elections it was discovered that the PDP won Senatorial and House of Representatives elections in 21 states including all the states of the South–South, South-East geo-political zone. The party also won in seven states in the northern part of the country. APP won nine states cutting across North-West, North-Central and North-East geo-political zones of Nigeria. The AD on its part won all the Senatorial and House of Representatives seats in the entire South-West geo-political zone.

The 2003 National Assembly Elections

On 12th of April 2003 National Assembly elections were held to elect members of the Senate and House of Representatives on the expiration of the four-year term of office of members. Unlike the 1999 National Assembly elections, about 30 political parties contested the Senate and House of Representative seats (INEC 2003). The conduct of the elections was largely described as not transparent and full of irregularities (European Union Election Observer Mission 2003; International Republican Institute 2003). Though about 30 political parties contested the 2003 National Assembly elections, only seven were able to secure seats in the National Assembly. These were the PDP, AD, All Nigerian Peoples Party (ANPP), United Nigeria People's Party (UNPP), National Democratic Party (NDP), All Progressives Grand Alliance (APGA) and People's Redemption Party (PRP) (International Republican Institute 2003). The PDP, ANPP and the AD were the only parties thatwere able to secure seats in the Senate.

The period leading to the elections was reported to have been characterised by violence which according to reports claimed 100 lives. This was fuelled by a religious riot in the northern part of the country. Election Day violence was said to have claimed about 24 lives (Inter-Parliamentary Union 2003). Out of a total number of registered voters of 60,823,022, turnout was 29,995,171 signifying that 49.3% of the total registered voters participated in the National Assembly Elections. Total valid votes were 29,030,107 (African Election Database 2011). The outcome of the election showed that the PDP won majority seats in the Senate and the House of Representatives. The results of the elections are shown in Table 4.2.

From Table 4.2 it can be observed that the PDP won 76 seats in the Senate, while the ANPP won 27 seats and the AD six seats. This indicated that there was an increase in the number of seats won in the 1999 National Assembly elections from 66 to 76, showing additional 10

Table 4.2 Results of the 2003 National Assembly Elections

Political parties	*Senate*			*House of Representatives*		
	Number of votes	*% of votes*	*Number of seats (109)*	*Number of votes*	*% of votes*	*Number of seats (360)*
PDP	15,585,538	53.69	76	15,927,807	54.49	223
ANPP	8,091,783	27.87	27	8,021,531	27.44	96
AD	2,828,082	9.74	6	2,711,972	9.28	34
UNPP	789,705	2.72	–	803,432	2.75	2
NDP	459,462	1.58	–	561,161	1.92	1
APGA	429,073	1.48	–	397,147	1.36	2
PRP	204,929	0.71	–	222,938	0.76	1
Others	641,535	2.21	–	587,082	2.01	–
Vacant seat	–	–	–	–	–	1
Total	**29,030,107**	**100**	**109**	**29,233,070**	**100**	**360**

Source African Elections Database (2011)

seats won by the party. This also indicated that the PDP garnered more than 50% of the total valid votes cast during the elections. Also, having garnered more than 50% of the total valid votes cast in the House of Representatives election the PDP won 223 seats showing an increase in the number of House of Representatives seats won in 1999 from 206 to 223. The ANPP won 27 Senate seats and 96 House of Representatives seats with approximately 28% of the total valid votes cast for both elections of the National Assembly. The AD won six Senate seats and 34 House of Representatives seats. This shows that in comparison with 1999 National Assembly election the AD lost 13 Senate and 34 House of Representatives seats.

The UNPP and APGA won two House of Representatives each after securing 2.72 and 1.48% of the total valid votes cast for the House of Representatives election, respectively. The NDP and the PRP won one seat each in the House of Representatives election after securing 1.58 and 0.71% of the total valid votes cast in the election respectively. The result showed the continued dominance of the PDP in the National Assembly. The PDP was able to win more seats initially won by other political parties. For instance, the AD lost 13 seats to the PDP signifying that the PDP was able to capture states in the South-West geo-political zone which was formerly the stronghold of the AD. The PDP won 28 states in the 2003 National Assembly Elections including all the states of the South-South and South-East geo-political zone. It was also able to capture five states out of the six states of the South-West geo-political zone formerly in control of the AD. The ANPP won six states while APGA won in 1 state.

The 2007 National Assembly Elections

The 2007 National Assembly elections were held alongside the Presidential election on the 21 of April 2007. Elections were postponed in six Senatorial Districts because of allegations of fraud and malpractices (Inter-Parliamentary Union 2007). 25 political parties participated in the 2007 legislative elections out of which only six were able to secure seats in the National Assembly. While the Independent National Electoral Commission revealed that 35 million voters out of the registered 60 million registered voters turned out for the election, no turnout figures were announced for the National Assembly elections (Inter-Parliamentary Union 2007). Apart from the fact that the elections took place amidst controversies which emanated from the Senate's rejection of a proposed constitutional amendment to enable the then President Chief Olusegun Obasanjo spend a third term in office, the general conduct of the election was described not meeting up to standard. The election was reported to have been characterised by massive fraud, malpractices and violence (International Crisis Group 2007; Transition Monitoring Group 2007).

The result of the elections indicated a higher majority for the PDP. Unlike the 2003 National Assembly elections when the PDP won 76 and 223 seats in the Senate and the House of Representatives, respectively, the PDP in the 2007 National Assembly elections won 260 seats in the House of Representatives and 85 seats in Senate. The number of House of Representatives seats won by the ANPP decreased from 96 in 2003 to 63 in 2007. Similarly, the ANPP in the Senate, unlike in 2003 when it won 27 seats could only manage to win 14 seats in 2007. This showed that the party lost 13 Senate seats in the 2007 National Assembly elections. The Action Congress won was able to win six and 30 seats in the Senate and House of Representatives, respectively. The Progressives People Grand Alliance (PPA) won one Senatorial seat and three House of Representatives seats. The Accord Party and the Labour Party won one Senatorial and House of Representatives seat, respectively (African Election Database 2011). The results of the elections are shown in Table 4.3.

Table 4.3 Results of the 2007 National Assembly Elections

Party	*Senate* *Number of seats (109)*	*House of Representatives* *Number of seats (360)*
People's Democratic Party (PDP)	87	263
All Nigeria People's Party (ANPP)	14	63
Action Congress (AC)	6	30
Progressive People's Alliance (PPA)	1	3
Accord Party (ACCORD)	1	–
Labour Party (LP)	–	1
Total	**109**	**360**

Source African Election Database (2011)

The 2011 National Assembly Elections

The 2011 National Assembly elections were scheduled to hold on the 2nd of April, 2011. Due to logistics reasons most especially the absence of voting materials in many of the polling stations the elections were postponed to the 9th of April 2011 (Independent National Electoral Commission 2011). While 56 political parties fielded candidates for the Senatorial and House of Representatives elections, only political parties were able to secure seats in the Senate and only eight were able to win seats in the House of Representatives. Total turnout for the National Assembly elections was 28,552,140 (Independent National Electoral Commission 2011). The number of seats won by each political party in the elections is shown in Table 4.4.

It can be observed from Table 4.4 that the PDP won 71 and 203 seats in the Senate and House of Representatives elections, respectively. These figures indicated a reduction in the number of seats won by the party in the 2007 National Assembly elections. The Action Congress of Nigeria (ACN) formerly AC won 18 and 69 seats in the Senate and House Representatives elections, respectively. These showed an increase in the number of seats won in 2007 from six to 18 seats in the Senate and 30 to 69 seats in the House of Representatives. The CPC which had not won any seats in the National Assembly won seven seats in the Senate and 38

Table 4.4 Number of seats won by political parties in the 2011 National Assembly elections

Party	*Senate* *Number of seats (109)*	*House of Representatives(HoR)* *Number of seats (360)*
PDP	71	203
CAN	18	69
CPC	7	38
ANPP	7	28
LP	4	8
DPP	1	1
APGA	1	7
Accord Party	1	5
PPN	–	1
Total	**109**	**360**

Source INEC (2011)

seats in the House of Representatives. The ANPP won seven seats in the Senate and 28 seats in the House of Representatives showing a decrease in the number of seats won in 2007 from 14 to seven in the Senate and 63 to 28 in the House of Representatives.

The Labour Party which managed to win one House of Representatives seat in the 2007 elections won four Senate seats and eight House of Representatives seats. The Democratic Peoples' Party (DPP) which also had never won a seat in the National Assembly won one Senate seat and one House of Representatives seat. APGA which has never won a Senate seat won one Senate seat and seven House of Representatives seats in 2011. Similarly, the Accord Party which managed to win one Senate seat in 2007 won one Senate seat and five House of Representatives seats in 2011. The Peoples Party of Nigeria (PPN) managed to win one House of Representatives seat. It is important to note that though the PDP won 71 seats in the Senate and 2003 seats in the House of Representatives, its dominance was reduced in both the Senate and the House of Representatives. For instance, it was not able to win two-thirds of the House of Representatives. The party lost some of its seats to the opposition parties in both Chambers.

The 2015 National Assembly Elections

The 2015 National Assembly elections were initially scheduled to hold on the 14th of February 2015. Citing security reasons and poor distribution of voters' cards, the Independent National Electoral Commission announced the postponement of the elections to 28th of March 2015. Out of a total number of registered voters of 67,422,005, turnout for the National Assembly elections was 29,432,083 (Inter-Parliamentary Union 2015). Though the elections took place amidst spate of insecurity largely brought about by the activities of the deadly Boko Haram insurgent group, the conduct of the elections were generally regarded as peaceful orderly and credible (AUEOM 2015; EUEOM 2015). While 26 political parties contested the 2015 National Assembly elections only two were prominent. These were the All Progressives Congress (APC) and Peoples Democratic Party (PDP).

The APC was formed in February 2013 by four opposition parties. These were the Action Congress of Nigeria (ACN), the Congress for Progressive Change (CPC), the All Nigeria Peoples Party (ANPP) and a faction of the All Progressives Grand Alliance (APGA). It is important to note that before their merger, these political parties separately won 33 seats in the Senate and a total of 132 seats in the House of Representatives (Inter-Parliamentary Union 2015). Similarly, prior to the election there were series of defections from the then ruling party to the then-new opposition party, the APC. Prominent among the defections were the defection of 37 PDP members of the House of Representatives to the APC in December 2013 and the defection of 11 PDP Senators to APC IN January 2014. Also, in October 2014, the then Speaker of the House of Representatives, Aminu Tambuwal defected to the APC. Consequently, shortly before the 2015 National Assembly elections the APC occupied more than 180 seats, 20 seats more than the PDP which held 160 seats (Inter-Parliamentary Union 2015).

The outcome of the elections indicated that the APC won 60 seats in the Senate and won a total number of 225 seats in the House of Representatives. The PDP won 49 seats in the Senate and won 125 seats in the House of Representatives (Inter-Parliamentary Union 2015). The outcome indicated that the APC had a majority in both Chambers outnumbering the PDP who had since 1999 maintained the majority in the National Assembly. Table 4.5 indicates the number of seats won by each political party in the National Assembly elections.

With the outcome of the elections, the PDP which since 1999 retained majority seats in the National Assembly turned the opposition party after the elections. The configuration of the leadership of the Senate after the 2015 elections revealed that it was the first time since 1999 that only two parties out of the registered 28 political parties for the 2015 general elections were represented in the Senate. This also implied that the PDP which has occupied leadership positions in the Senate will have to lose

Table 4.5 Number of seats won by political parties in the 2015 National Assembly elections

Party	*Senate* *Number of seats (109)*	*House of Representatives* *Number of seats (360)*
APC	60	225
PDP	49	125
Others	–	10
Total	**109**	**360**

Source Inter-Parliamentary Union (2015)

Table 4.6 Number of seats won by political parties in the 2019 National Assembly elections

Party	*Senate* *Number of seats (109)*	*House of Representatives* *Number of seats (360)*
APC	62	210
PDP	42	122
YPP	1	10
APGA	–	8
PRP	–	2
AA	–	2
APM	–	1
SDP	–	1
ADP	–	1
LP	–	1
ADC	–	3
PENDING	4	8
Total	**109**	**360**

Source INEC (2019)

such positions to the APC (Osasona 2015). Table 4.6 shows the party affiliation of Senators since 1999.

The 2019 National Assembly Elections

The 2019 National Assembly elections were initially scheduled to hold on 16th of February 2019 alongside the presidential election. Due to logistic challenges the election was later rescheduled to hold on 23rd of February 2019 (Ogundipe 2019). Like in 2015, the 2019 National Assembly elections were held within the context of incessant and persistent violent feud between farmers and herders, kidnappings, armed banditry, cultism and Boko Haram insurgency. Shortly before the elections there was anxiety as to what impact the violent occurrences might have on the elections (Mercy Corps 2015). Many people expressed their feelings that the elections were going to be bloody and violent given the context within which they will be held. Contrary to the notion that the elections will be violent, the 2019 National Assembly elections were generally regarded as peaceful (African Union Election Observation Mission 2019).

The 2019 National Assembly elections were unique in some respect. Firstly, the facts that the elections were contested by 91 political parties make it the first elections to be contested by the highest number of political parties in Nigeria's electoral history. Secondly, with 84,271,832 registered voters, the elections had the highest number of registered voters in the nation's history. Though 91 political parties contested the 2019 National Assembly elections, only 10 were able to secure seats in the House of Representatives, while only three political parties secured seats in the Senate. The elections also recorded the lowest voter turnout since Nigeria's return to multi-party democracy. Out of a total number of registered voters 84,271,832 only 29,364,209 actually came out to cast their votes on the Election Day (Obiejese 2019). Table 4.6 shows the number of seats won by political parties in the Senate and House of Representatives.

From Table 4.7 it can be deduced that the APC won the highest number of seats both in the Senate and House of Representatives, winning 62 and 210 seats, respectively. The PDP came second with 42 Senate seats and 122 House of Representative seats. The Young Progressives Party (YPP) won one Senatorial seat and 10 House of Representative seats. The All Progressives Grand Alliance (APGA) won eight House of Representative seats only. The Peoples Redemption Party won (PRP) and the Action Alliance (AA) won two House of Representative seats each. The African Democratic Congress (ADC) won three House of Representative seats while other parties won one House of Representative seats each. It is important to note that the APC had earlier won 217 seats in the House of Representatives and won 65 seats in the Senate, but a Supreme Court Judgement delivered on the 24th of May 2019 in relation to the appeals relating to the dispute over the validity of the All Progressives Congress' primary elections which produced the candidates fielded by the

Table 4.7 Party affiliations of Senators from 1999 to 2019

Year	*PDP*	*ANPP*	*AD*	*APP*	*APGA*	*LABOUR*	*ACN*	*PPA*	*PRP*	*CPC*	*APC*	*DPP*	*YPP*
1999	71	18	19	1	–	–	–	–	–	–	–	–	–
2003	81	22	6	–	–	–	–	–	–	–	–	–	–
2007	87	14	1	–	–	–	5	1	1	–	–	–	–
2011	70	7	–	–	1	4	18	–	–	8	–	–	–
2015	49	–	–	–	–	– f	–	–	–	–	60	1	–
2019	42	–	–	–	–	–	–	–	–	–	62	–	1

Source Osasona (2015) updated by the Authors

party in the last general elections declared all APC votes in Zamfara state null and void and ruled that candidates with the second highest number of votes won to be declared the winner. On this basis, the APC which had earlier won the three Senatorial seats and seven House of Representative seats in the state lost all to the opposition PDP (Adesomoju 2019).

From the foregoing it can be observed that the PDP had dominated the legislative arm of the Nigerian government since the return to democratic rule. The voting pattern has been such that the PDP had not until 2015 when it lost its dominance to the APC, consistently maintained dominance in the National Assembly. The voting pattern which brings about one-party-dominant parliament does not entail one-party system rather it entails that other parties exist but are not strong enough to wrest parliamentary seats with the dominant party. One-party system is in the least democratic and does not recognise the existence of other parties. While one-party system monopolise power, in one-party-dominant parliament a party wins majority seats through elections to the extent that the outcomes of elections conducted to select parliamentarians is to a large extent a farce (Louise De Jager 2009). Such one-party-dominated National Assembly has detrimental effects on democratic sustenance and consolidation (Kanapyanov and Kaliyev 2015).

Implications of One-Party Dominated Parliament on Democratic Sustenance

The history of legislative elections in Nigeria's Fourth Republic is that of a one-party dominated National Assembly. The PDP until 2015 had won absolute majority of seats both in the Senate and the House of Representatives. From 1999 to 2015 the PDP held a hegemonic power in the National Assembly. In 2015, the APC having won the highest number of seats both in the Senate and House of Representatives was expected to have a firm grip of the Senate, but the intrigues and controversy that surrounded the emergence of the leadership of the upper house gave the PDP edge over the ruling APC in the affairs of the Upper Chamber. The circumstances which led to the emergence of Dr. Olusola Saraki, a former PDP stalwart as the President of the 8th Assembly was totally unacceptable to the leadership of the APC.

Saraki was perceived to have deceived and misled his party's leadership into believing that he will play along in finding solution to the challenge of choice of candidates for top legislative posts in the National Assembly, including those of the President of the Senate and Speaker of the House of Representatives (Sahara Reporters 2015). Saraki was expected to be in a meeting with the party's leadership to find a way out of the leadership crisis instead he held a meeting with PDP and some APC members in the Senate so as to solicit for their support to actualise his aim of becoming the Senate President. The eventual emergence of Saraki as the President of the Senate was seen as blatant disrespect for party rules and wish (Sahara Reporters 2015).

Advocates of one-party-dominated parliament argue that the dominance indicates stability and unanimity (Bowyer 2008; Bimir 2007). They allude to the notion that there is a relationship between party dominance and political stability. They further contend that a dominant political party in legislature fosters hegemony through a well established organisational structure and geographic spread which enables them to carry along people of diverse interests in party activities. This also indicates that the inclusive potentials of a dominant political party in parliament go a long way in stemming the inherent dangers of presidential system. In other words, a one-party dominated parliament can maximise the virtues of parliaments (Oseni 2012).

A one-party dominated parliament has detrimental implications on democratic sustenance. One conspicuous implication is that there is the tendency for dominant political parties in legislature to manage parliaments in the way and manner in which they manage party issues. In such circumstances, the dominant party in the legislature appoints officials to positions without recourse to merit, required qualities and capability (Suttner 2006). A direct consequence of this is that there is no counter force to check the excesses and anomalies of the dominant party in legislative activities and proceedings. In addition this, one-party-dominant parliament breeds impunity and corruption. This is because there is no clear line of distinction between the ruling political, party and the legislature itself. This situation in essence, provides negative motivation for healthy political competition and deliberations among political parties in the legislature. Overall, there is the emergence of a culture of nepotism, corruption and patrimonialism and politics of patronage (Landsberg 2004).

In a one-party dominated parliament, there is the near absence of democratic values, most especially genuine political completion and dynamic legislative electoral outcomes (Giliomee and Simkins 1999). This suggest that dominate parties are maintained in power through dubious electoral competition. This might have led Karume (2004) to aver that one-party domination of the legislature can be achieved by coercion and electoral fraud. In order to maintain its dominance in the legislature, the dominant political party may alter and manipulate electoral processes to the extent that elections to legislative houses remain a mere ritual of democracy. The dominant party is able to achieve this by utilising state resources as well as its dominance in the parliament over issues of public concern. Furthermore, one-party-dominated parliament subjects other fragmented political parties to varying degrees of official embarrassment and harassment. Members of such parties are restricted from airing their views against the dominant parties. The dominant parties utilise official sanctions such as suspensions from legislative proceedings to erring members of smaller parties.

One-party-dominant legislature does not tow the path of a normal or required pattern of electoral competition they rather seek to manipulate electoral contests so as to maintain domination over other smaller and fragmented political parties. This situation is generally inimical to democratic sustenance and consolidation (Doorenspleet and Nijzink 2013). The basic characteristic of one-party-dominated parliament is captured by Pempel (1990, p. 1) when he asserted that:

> In these countries, despite free electoral competition, relatively open information systems, respect for civil liberties, and the right of free political association, a single party has managed to govern alone or as the primary and on-going partner in coalitions, without interruption, for substantial periods of time.

As mentioned earlier, the PDP in Nigeria has maintained a majority in the National Assembly largely through flawed electoral processes particularly those of 2003, 2007 and 2011 (EUEOM 2003; TMG 2007). According to Oseni (2012) opposition parties have remained weak and fragmented specifically from 1999 to 2015. In other words, the dominance of the PDP in Nigeria's National Assembly from 1999 to 2015 has probably been through quasi-legitimate means.

Conclusion

It has been demonstrated in this chapter that the history of legislative elections in Nigeria has been that of a one-sided electoral victory for PDP for four consecutive National Assembly elections held in 1999, 2003, 2007 and 2011. Thus, for the period from 1999 to 2015 the PDP had dominated proceedings in the National Assembly. Even in 2015 when it was expected that the APC will dominate the Senate and the House of Representatives, Saraki's collusion with members of the PDP and some members within the APC to swindle his party to become the Senate President gave the PDP the upper hand in the Senate even before he defected back to PDP. Through this scenario the PDP was able to dominate the Upper Chamber despite having been the minority. While such dominance helps in maintaining stability of the political system, a one-party-dominated parliament has been found to have grievous effects and implications on democracy. Unabated one-party dominance of parliament can imply the establishment of electoral authoritarianism or the entrenchment of it since the dominance is based on hegemony and not healthy party and electoral politics.

References

Aaron, B. (2018, November 7). *Some Democrats Are Complaining About the "Senate popular vote.' It's still not a thing*. Available at https://www.washingtonpost.com/politics/2018/11/07/some-democrats-are-complaining-about-senate-popular-vote-its-still-not.thing/?noredirect=on&utm_term=.1435a513682c. Accessed 23 December 2018.

Adesomoju, A. (2019, May 24). *Supreme Court Delivers Judgment on Zamfara APC Dispute*. Available at https://punchng.com/supreme-court-delivers-judgment-on-zamfara-apc-dispute-may-24/. Accessed 30 May 2019.

African Elections Data Base. (2011). *Elections in Nigeria*. Available at http://africanelections.tripod.com/ng.html#1999_National_Assembly_Election. Accessed 28 December 2018.

African Union Election Observer Mission. (2015). *Release of AUEOM Preliminary Statement on Nigeria Elections*. Available at http://pa.au.int/en/content/release-aueom-preliminary-statement-nigeria-elections. Accessed 3 January 2019.

African Union Election Observation Mission. (2019). *Preliminary Statement: African Union Election Observation Mission (AUEOM) to the Federal Republic of Nigeria 23 February 2019 Presidential and National Assembly Elections*. Available at https://au.int/en/pressreleases/20190225/preliminary-statement-african-union-election-observation-mission-aueom. Accessed 29 May 2019.

Bimir, J. (2007). Divergence in Diversity? The Dissimilar Effects of Cleavages on Electoral Politics in New Democracies. *American Journal of Political Science 51*(3), 602–619.

Bogdanor, V. (1991). *The Blackwell Encyclopaedia of Political Science*. Oxford: Blackwell Publishers.

Bowyer, A. C. (2008). *Parliament and Political Parties in Kazakhstan*. Silk Road Paper, May 2008. Central Asia-Caucasus Institute and Silk Road Studies Program, Johns Hopkins University.

British Parliament. (2015). *Recall of MPs Draft Bill*. Available at www.official-documents.gov.uk. Accessed 24 December 2018.

Castiglione, D., & Warren, M. E. (2006, May 18–19). *Rethinking Democratic Representation: Eight Theoretical Issues*. Prepared for delivery to "Rethinking Democratic Representation" Centre for the Study of Democratic Institutions, University of British Columbia.

Cohen, D. L. (1983). Election and Election Studies in Africa. In O. Y. Barongo (Ed.), *Political Science in Africa. A Critical Review*. London: Zed Books.

Doorenspleet, R., & Nijzink, L. (2013). One-Party Dominance in African Democracies: A Framework for Analysis. In R. Doorenspleet & L. Nijzink (Eds.), *One-Party Dominance in African Democracies*. Boulder: Lynne Rienner Publishers.

Dunmoye, R. A. (2010). Nexus of Democratic Consolidation and Development Imperative in Africa. In K. Mato (Ed.), *Democracy Question and Election Management in Africa*. Ibadan: Daily Graphic Nigeria Limited.

Election Guide. (2014). *Election for South African National Assembly*. Available at http://www.electionguide.org/elections/id/2721/. Accessed 24 December 2018.

Encyclopaedia of American Politics. (2018). *Law Governing Recall*. Available at https://ballotpedia.org/Laws_governing_recall. Accessed 23 December 2018.

European Union Election Observer Mission. (2015). *Nigeria Elections 2015: Arrival Statement by Commonwealth Observer Group*. Available at https://www.thecommonwealth.org/media/news/nigeria-elections-2015-arrival-statement-commonwealth-observer-group. Accessed 4 January 2019.

European Union Election Observer Mission. (2003). *Report: Nigeria's 2003 General Elections*. Available at https://eeas.europa.eu/topics/election-observation-missionseueoms_en/26329/EU%20election%20observation%20mission%20to%20Nigeria%20in%202003. Accessed 2 January 2019.

Esaiasson, P., & Narud, H. M. (2013). *Between Election and Democracy: An Introductory Note*. In P. Esaiasson & H. M. Narud (Eds.), *Between-Election Democracy. The Representative Relationship After Election Day* (pp. 1–14). Colchester: ECPR Press.

Federal Republic of Kenya. (2010). *Constitution of Kenya*. Available at http://www.icla.up.ac.za/images/constitutions/kenya_constitution.pdf. Accessed 24 December 2018.

Fowler, A. (2004). *Do Elections Select for Better Representatives?* Available at https://pdfs.semanticscholar.org/61ef/327937a1d9418ba7997e70676609ed6c5efc.pdf. Accessed 25 December 2018.

Gaus, G. F., & Kukathas, C. (2004). *Handbook of Political Theory*. New York: Sage.

Giliomee, H., & Simkins, C. (1999). *The Awkward Embrace: One-Party Domination and Democracy*. Amsterdam: Harwood Academic Publishers.

Höglund, K. (2009). Electoral Violence in Conflict-Ridden Societies: Concepts, Causes, and Consequences. *Terrorism and Political Violence, 21*(3), 412–427.

Hughes, A., & May, R. (1988). The Politics of Succession in Black Africa. *Third World Quarterly, 10*(1), 20–33.

Inter Parliamentary Union. (1999). *Parliamentary Election Results for Nigeria*. Available at http://archive.ipu.org/parline-e/reports/arc/2364_99.htm. Accessed 26 December 2018.

Inter Parliamentary Union. (2003). *Nigeria's National Assembly Elections*. Available at http://archive.ipu.org/parline-e/reports/arc/2363_03.htm. Accessed 3 January 2019.

Inter Parliamentary Union. (2007). *Nigeria's National Assembly Elections*. Available at http://archive.ipu.org/parline-e/reports/arc/2364_07.htm. Accessed 3 January 2019.

Inter Parliamentary Union. (2015). *Nigeria's National Assembly Elections*. Available at http://archive.ipu.org/parline-e/reports/arc/2364_07.htm. Accessed 3 January 2019.

International Crisis Group. (2007). *2007 Nigerian Failed Elections: Failing State? Report of the ICG on the 2007 Nigeria General Elections*. Brussels: ICG.

International Republican Institute. (2003). *2003 Nigeria Election Observation Report*. Available at www.iri.org/.../Nigeria%27s%202003%20Presidential%20and%20National%20Assem. Accessed 2 January 2019.

Independent National Electoral Commission (2003). *INEC Report of Activities: January 2003–December 2003*. Abuja: INEC.

Independent National Electoral Commission. (2011). *INEC Reschedules 2011 General Elections*. Available at www.inecnigeria.org/?inecarticle=press-release-inec-reschedules-2011...elections. Accessed 3 January 2019.

Independent National Electoral Commission. (2019). *List of Elected Candidates for the 2019 Senatorial Election*. Available at https://www.inecnigeria.org/wp-content/uploads/2019/03/2019-generalelections-list-ofelected-candidates-to-the-senate.pdf. Accessed 28 May 2019.

Kanapyanov, T. Y., & Kaliyev, N. K. (2015). Parliamentary Reforms of 2007 and One Party Dominated Parliament of Kazakhstan (2007–2012). *Mediterranean Journal of Social Sciences, 6*(6), 335–340.

Karume, S. (2004). Party Systems in the SADC Region: In Defence of the Dominant Party System. *Journal of African Elections, 3*(11), 42–61.

Katz, R. S. (1997). *Democracy and Elections*. Oxford: Oxford University Press.

Landsberg, A. (2004). *Prosthetic Memory: The Transformation of American Remembrance in the Age of Mass Culture*. New York: Columbia University Press.

Lodge, T., & Scheidegger, U. (2006). *Political Parties and Democratic Governance in South Africa* (EISA Research Report).

Louise De Jager, N. (2009). *Voice and Accountability in One Party Dominant Systems: A Comparative Case Study of Mexico and South Africa* (Unpublished doctoral thesis). Department of Political Sciences, The University of Pretoria.

Lynch, P. (2007). Party System Change in Britain: Multi-Party Politics in a Multi-Level Polity. *British Politics, 2,* 323–346.

Manin, B., Przeworski, A., & Stokes, S. C. (1999). Elections and Representation. In B. Manin, A. Przeworski, & S. C. Stokes (Eds.), *Democracy, Accountability, and Representation*. Cambridge: Cambridge University Press.

Maravall, J. M. (2007). Accountability and the Survival of Governments. In B. Carles & S. C. Stokes (Eds.), *The Oxford Handbook of Comparative Politics*. Oxford: Oxford University Press.

Maskell, J. (2012). *Recall of Legislators and the Removal of Members of Congress from Office*. USA: Congressional Research Service Report for Congress.

Matlosa, K. (2003). *Electoral Systems and Multiparty Democracy in Southern Africa*. Text of paper presented at the Conference on Elections, Democracy and Governance held in Pretoria, South Africa in April 2003.

Mercy Corps. (2015).*The Economic Costs of Conflict in Nigeria*. Available at https://www.mercycorps.org/research/economic-costs-conflict-nigeria. Accessed 22 April 2019.

Merrill, S., & Grofman, B. (1999). *A Unified Theory of Voting*. Cambridge: Cambridge University Press.

National Conference of State Legislatures. (2016). *Recall of State Officials*. Available at https://eproofing.springer.com/books_v3/mainpage.php?token=Rs8V1ixRqBV-Oyet8I7Ic29lGuso8pxknPifrppVxjv1rHPlGErUwq12infAoYM3. Assessed 30 May 2019.

National Democratic Institute. (1999). *Observing the 1998-99 Nigeria Elections*. Washington, DC: NDI.

Norris, P. (1997). Choosing Electoral Systems: Proportional, Majoritarian and Mixed Systems. *International Political Science Review, 18*(3), 297–312.

Nwabueze, B. (2003). *Constitutional Democracy in Africa*. Ibadan: Spectrum Books Ltd.

Obiejese, K. (2019). *Voter Turnout for Presidential/NASS Election Is Lowest in Recent History, Here Is Why*. Available at https://www.icirnigeria.org/voter-turnout-for-presidential-nass-election-is-lowest-in-recent-history-here-is-why/. Accessed 30 May 2019.

Ogundipe, S. (2019). *It's Official: INEC Postpones all Nigeria's General Elections*. Available at https://www.premiumtimesng.com/news/headlines/313199-its-official-inec-postpones-allnigerias-general-elections.html. Accessed 24 April 2019.

Okoosi-Simbine, A. T. (2010). Understanding the Role of the Legislature in the Fourth Republic: The Case of Oyo State House of Assembly. *Nigeria Journal of Legislative Affairs, 3*(1 & 2), 1–27.

Osasona, T. (2015). *Governance Institutions: Nigeria's 8th Senate*. Available at http://cpparesearch.org/nu-en-pl/a-profile-of-nigerias-8th-senate/. Accessed 15 January 2018.

Oseni, B. A. (2012). *One-Party Dominant Systems and Constitutional Democracy in Africa: A Comparative Study of Nigeria and South Africa* (Unpublished Ph.D. thesis). University of Exeter, Exeter, UK.

Pempel, T. J. (1990). One-Party Dominance and the Creation of Regimes. In T. J. Pempel (Ed.), *Uncommon Democracies: The One-Party Dominant Regimes*. Ithaca, NY: Cornell University Press.

Policy and Legal Advocacy Centre. (2016). *Guide to Effective Representation in the National Assembly*. Abuja: PLAC.

Polsby, N.W. (1975). Legislatures. In F. Greenstein & N.W. Polsby (Eds.), *Handbook of Political Science: Government Institutions and Processes*. Reading, MA: Addison Wesley.

Sahara Reporters. (2015). *How Saraki Deceived Buhari, Outwitted APC to Become "Senate President"*. Available at http://saharareporters.com/2015/06/09/how-saraki-deceived-buhari-outwitted-apc-become-%E2%80%9Csenate-president%E2%80%9D. Accessed 30 May 2019.

Sebudubudu, D., & Botlhomilwe, M. Z. (2013). Interrogating the Dominant Party System in Botswana. In Nicola de Jager and Pierre du Toit (Eds.), *Friend or Foe?: Dominant Party Systems in Southern Africa: Insights from the Developing World* (p. 121). Tokyo, New York, and Cape Town: United Nations University Press.

Suttner, R. (2006). Party Dominance 'Theory': Of What Value? *Politikon, 33*(3), 277–297.

Siaroff, A. (2003). Two-and-a-Half-Party Systems and the Comparative Role of the Half. *Party Politics, 9*(3), 267–290.

Sisk, T. D. (2008, March 24–28). *Elections in Fragile States: Between Voice and Violence*. Paper Prepared for the International Studies Association Annual Meeting, San Francisco, CA.

The Economist. (2014). *Sacking MPs: Recall Recalled*. Available at https://www.economist.com/britain/2014/02/22/recall-recalled. Accessed 24 December 2018.

Transition Monitoring Group. (2007). *An Election Programmed to Fail: Preliminary Report on the Presidential and National Assembly Elections Held on Saturday, April 21, 2007*. Abuja: TMG.

United States Senate. (2010). *Senate Election Law Guidebook*. Washington, DC: US Government Printing Office.

Urbinatil, N., & Warren, M. E. (2008). The Concept of Representation in Contemporary Democracy. *Annual Review of Political Science, 11*, 387–412.

Wojtasik, W. (2013). *Functions of Elections in Democratic System* (Political Preferences, No. 4).

Yanina, W. (2016). Recall Referendums in Peruvian Municipalities: A Political Weapon for Bad Losers or an Instrument of Accountability? *Democratization, 23*(7), 1162–1179.

CHAPTER 5

Committee System in Nigeria's National Assembly: Issues and Challenges

Korikiye Wenibowei

Introduction

There is a growing trend in the general acknowledgement of democracy as the most preferred political administrative system of government in modern society. This makes the study of democratic institutions, their organization, functions and mode of operations inevitable. The large volume of literature on the organization, functions and mode of operations of the Executive, Judiciary, and the Legislative arms of government is a clear indication of intellectual devotion and dedication on the part of democratic scholars and the likes in providing in-depth knowledge on issues concerning these important democratic institutions in society. These intellectual works of scholars have contributed in strengthening democracy and its practice as a form of political administration as well as citizen's appreciation of the internal dynamics concomitant to the system.

K. Wenibowei (✉)
Department of Political Science, Isaac Jasper Boro College of Education, Sagbama, Nigeria

F. A. Aremu and A. R. Bakare (eds.), *Two Decades of Legislative Politics and Governance in Nigeria's National Assembly*,
https://doi.org/10.1007/978-981-33-4455-6_5

However, the maintenance of a stable democratic system has a lot to do with the efficiency and effectiveness of the legislature.

The legislature in all democratic systems remains the platform of the representation of the various diverse interests of the citizens of that nation. It has therefore very enormous task at hand in terms of striking a balance of the divergent demands and expectations of individuals and groups, especially in plural societies. It has also in its onus the responsibility to determine the direction of the country through the formulation of popularly acceptable policies and programs. The performance of these and other responsibilities makes the legislature in modern democracy an indispensable institution and a major study area of scholars of democratic development. Undoubtedly, scholarly contributions that focused on the organization and operations of the legislature have helped broaden appreciation and understanding of the internal mechanisms that promote stability of the institution itself and the continuity of the system in most nations (Akhihiero 2009; Russell et al. 2013). Nevertheless, the whole work of the legislature is organized and evolved around the committee system. It is against this background that the use of the committee system as part of its internal working mechanism has become a major focus among observers and a major area of academic study in most recent times.

The committee system is known and widely practiced among countries with representative democracy. Since its introduction into the legislative process, the committee system has become an integral part of the law making organ and has been responsible for the effectiveness of the legislature in most countries. Vincent (1992) noted in regard to the American Congress that, "the life and operations of American representative government can be seen in congressional committees". The committee system in the American congress has been described as "the nerve ends of congress, the gatherers of information, the sifters of alternatives, and the refiners of legislation" (Vincent 1992). In the same vein, the important role of the committee system is now well acknowledged and accepted, giving the need for the legislature to perform its duties more efficiently and effectively. This position is expatiated by Obiyo (2007) in his words that "the need for overall proficiency in the dispensation of the enormous and myriad legislative duties and responsibilities respectively makes the importance of the committee system within the legislature both important and indispensable".

The committee system may be best described as the engineer room for the contemporary legislature as it makes the processes and procedures of law making a lot easier for the legislators. This chapter is devoted to the understanding of the historical development of the committee system in Nigeria's National Assembly with reference to global perspective of the concept and its practice. It should be noted that, an appreciation of the committee system, its origin and historical evolution is critical to placing the present legislative committee system, particularly in Nigeria, in a proper perspective. The chapter will equally examine the importance of the committee system in Nigeria and this is followed by a discussion on the issues and challenges confronting the committee system in Nigeria's National Assembly.

Origin and Historical Development of the Committee System

The understanding of the origin and development of the committee system in the legislature is important, particularly in appreciating the role the committee system has come to play in the business of law making. The basic reason for this is that, an historical review will throw more light on how and when the committee system originated in some earlier democracies and the import of the system to former colonial territories. Second, it will also help illuminate the complex nature of the organization of the legislature and the processes involved in law making. Therefore, this section focuses on the origin and historical development of the committee system in the legislature.

The committee system is a practice where legislators are divided and distributed into several committees to perform specific responsibilities and report back to the parliament. This arrangement existed in the British House of Commons, under the reign of Queen Elizabeth 1. In the article published in 1894, Franklin Jameson chronicled the origin of the Standing Committee System in American Congress (cited in the Academy of Political Science [APS] 2013), in it, he expressed disappointment of the lack of literature on the historical origin of the committee system in American Congress. Jameson asserts that, "the committee system is one of the most important peculiarities of the American legislative system, perhaps indeed, it's most distinctive peculiarity". However, it is surprising that no "attempt appears to have been made toward tracing completely the history of an institution of such obvious importance" (APS 2013). He further noted that the committee system has "a history extending far back into the past of the Anglo-American people, and to trace that history, from the procedure of the House of Commons under Queen Elizabeth, through that of the colonial legislative assemblies, down to the Revolution and the assembling of the federal congresses".

Equally, Robert Byrd in his history of the American Senate traced the first use of legislative committees to the English Parliament in the fourth century (Roberts 2001). In the same vein, Ralph Harlow's classic study of the legislature dates standing committees in the modern sense to the close of the sixth century in the English Parliament (Richards 1972). Butt (1969) cited in Richards (1972), equally observed that committees with powers including the ability to draft their own bills existed during the reign of Queen Elizabeth the First. In France, the modern legislative committee emerged in the 5th Republic in 1958, but its existence dates back to 1789, when the first legislature was established.

Given this scenario, it is apparent that the legislative committee system may have found its roots in earlier representative democracies in Europe (e.g., Britain, France, Portugal, Spain, Sweden, Australia, etc.) and was later transferred to their respective colonial territories in the Americas, Asia, and Africa. The modern Congressional Committee System in the United States first appeared in its first Continental Congress in 1774 (Vincent 1992; APS 2013; Deering and Smith 1997). However, these initial committees were ad hoc committees who were empowered by Congress to consider legislation only after such bills have been debated and were closely supervised by the parent chamber and were disbanded as soon as the committee completes its task. These ad hoc committees, according to Vincent (1992) "gradually evolved into permanent standing committees, and proposed legislation was referred directly to such committee without initial consideration on the floor of the parent chamber". Robert (2001) asserts that, by 1810, the House had 10 standing committees, each covering a distinct policy area as well as other select committees.

Nevertheless, the modern Congressional Committee System in America may be attributed to the Legislative Reorganization Act of 1946, also known as the LaFollette-Monroney Act (Vincent 1992). This Legislative Act among other things reduced the number of standing committees, codified committee jurisdictions, provided each committee permanent (or statutory staff), and consolidated Congress's oversight powers within the respective committees (Vincent 1992; Deering and Smith 1997). For instance, the act reduced the number of committees to 19 from about

60 in the House of Representatives, and 15 from about 74 in the Senate in 1919 (Vincent 1992).

As legislative business increased over time, the demand for legislative efficiency and effectiveness became more necessary and more expedient. This necessitated the promulgation of "The Legislative Reorganization Act, 1970" by the United States Congress. This Act has been described as a milestone in legislative reforms in the US, as it helped reduce the powers of senior legislators in committees and marked the new beginning of continuous reforms in congress committees in the United States of America (Vincent 1992; Roberts 2001). In essence the committee system started in the US in 1774, but a number of reforms carried out from time to time has enabled the system become more efficient and more effective in discharging legislative responsibilities.

India, a former colonial territory of Great Britain, is another apt example of a representative government with a legislative committee system. The committee system existed in the first Indian Parliament in 1854, when the first committee of four members was appointed to consider what should be its standing order at its first sitting held on May 20, 1854 (Shubhangi 2017; Manikyamba 1995). The legislative committee system in Canada also dates back to the nineteenth century (Russell et al. 2013).

The modern legislature in Africa is one of the superstructures bequeathed to the former colonial territories by their former colonial masters (Alabi 2009; Okechwukwu 2014; Fashagbe 2009). Apart from South Africa, Ethiopia, and Liberia, most of Africa was colonized by one European power or the other. (e.g., Germany, Belgium, Portugal, Spain, Italy, France, Britain), where among European countries whose political and economic interests were greatly and sufficiently represented in Africa. The scramble for and partitioning of the Continent based on the Berlin Conference of 1884 and 1885 gave European countries the right to own, control, and administer their respective territories in Africa. This marked a new beginning in political administration in Africa that led to the imposition on traditional African societies aliened political structures such as the Executive, the Legislature, the Judiciary, the public bureaucracy, and political parties. Colonialism, thus, introduced and produced its own system of political administration and economic control. Therefore, the establishment of the colonial legislature in the former colonial areas in Africa marked the beginning and gradual development of the modern legislative committee system in most of Africa. It must however be noted that, the different European explorers in Africa introduced differing colonial policies aimed at establishing total control of those territories that came under their political and economic whims and caprices.

In British colonial territories, earlier forms of representative government emerged first in Sierra Leone and Gold Coast (Ghana) and later in Nigeria in 1862, where indigenous Africans were either appointed or elected into advisory or deliberative organs of government. In Nigeria, the Lagos Legislative Council was established in 1862 by the British government to oversee the administration of the Lagos area, which was under their control (Alabi 2009; Okechwukwu 2014; Anyebe 2016; Edet and Attai 2014). This was followed by the establishment of the Nigerian Legislative Council in 1914, and the introduction of the "elective principle" in 1923 under the Clifford's Constitution, further strengthened representative government as Nigerians were elected directly by Nigerians into the Legislative Assembly. Though, the elective principle was limited to Lagos and Calabar areas, it however, marked a new beginning and a landmark achievement of the struggle for self-determination by the nationalist at the time. Thus, the origin of the modern legislature in Nigeria dates back to 1862, when the first legislative body was established. However, it should be noted that, like many other former colonial territories in British West Africa, the Nigerian legislature has undergone a series of reforms in the decolonization era and the post-colonial period aimed at enhancing effective performance.

Importance of Committees in the Legislative Process

The Legislature in all democracies is known to perform three very important functions, namely: law making, investigative, and oversight functions (Alabi 2009; Okechwukwu 2014; Anyebe 2016). For example, Richards (1972) put this observation more clearly when he said that, "the main function of the legislature in any democracy is the determination of the will of the people and to formalize it, legislate to make rules and laws for the conduct of the State, society and citizens, then to supervise the Executive to see that the laws are implemented…". In other words, one of the key functions of the legislature is to supervise the Executive arm of government by employing the necessary processes and procedures as prescribed by a country's constitution.

The Nigerian legislature, has strived to ensure the maintenance of stable democratic rule employing its internally established organizational structures and mechanisms available to it. It has equally played significant role in bringing government closer to the people, through engaging the Executive arm of government on policy areas, programs, and projects that is meant to benefit the people they represent. Nevertheless, whatever success achieved by the legislature in performing its statutory responsibilities has been determined by the proficiency of its internal organizational mechanisms, particularly, its committee system. Thus, the committee system is one of the critical aspects of the internal mechanisms that the legislature often employed to get its work done in a professional, efficient, and effective manner. Hence, the importance of the committee system in the modern legislatures in all democracies is well acknowledged by scholars of contemporary democratic studies and the likes (Mezey 1979; More 1960; Tripathi 1980).

Mezey (1979) posits that "the committees are as important as the House itself". Describing the importance of the committee system further, Mezey (1979) stated that, "the committees of Parliament in Britain are called; 'Mini-parliament' and that of the American Congress is described variously as, 'parliament's workshops', 'Laboratories of Congress', the eyes, ears and brain of the Congress". More (1960) asserts that, "no legislature can function effectively without the aid of some committees". Tripathi (1980) writing on the India Parliament noted that "the committee system in Indian parliament has come to stay as an integral part for smooth transaction of the business of the House". Shubhangi (2017) also argued that "without such system, it will almost be impossible for any legislative body to finish the volume of work which is required to handle". Similarly, Richards (1972) noted that the work of the various committees in modern legislature "cannot be ignored by anyone wishing to understand either the legislative process as a whole or a specific piece of legislation". The incumbent Senate President Bukola Saraki in his speech to members of standing committees in the 8th Assembly, specifically referred to the committee system as "a veritable tool that a democratic legislature must rely on for some of its most important works" (Alabi 2017).

From the above assertions, it clearly shows the importance of the committee system in democratic legislatures, whether in Nigeria or elsewhere in the world. However, there is the need for us to understand what roles or functions the committees perform that makes them an integral part of the modern legislature and indispensable in the legislative process.

First, it must be known that, the modern legislature is often faced with a great deal of issues to deal with. Being a representative institution in democratic governance, the legislature is responsible for issues concerning national, political, economic, and social, security, welfare, foreign policy, education, agriculture, science and technology, as well as variety of other national issues. Thus, parliaments usually have to attend to a large number of issues bordering on the nation and its people. In handling these matters, care, thoroughness, efficiency, and effectiveness are needed. The House as a whole usually has no such time to consider bills clause-by-clause, therefore, committees serve as the needed tools for effective consideration of bills. More (1960) asserts that, "discussion of detail is impossible at a large meeting, except debating the broad principles". Equally, Manikyamba (1995) said, "since the House has neither time nor technical expertise in every case, the work load of the House is considerably reduced, because all spade work as well as thorough examination of the point referred to it, is done at the committee stage".

The Senate or the House of Representatives may refer a matter before it to relevant committees for thorough examination, because the parent chamber wants very important information concerning the matter, or because it wants to hear different opinions concerning an issue. In such cases, the use of committees is more relevant, rather than by the Senate sitting as a whole or House of Representatives sitting as a whole. Therefore, the importance of the committee system in modern legislature lies in its onus to be thorough and effective in carrying out its statutory duties. And over the years, the committee system has been very useful and effective in this regards in most democratic legislatures, including the National Assembly in Nigeria.

Second is the investigative role of the modern legislature. Again, this role is being carried out effectively by the relevant committees and subcommittees within the legislature. It is one of the most important non-legislative functions of modern legislatures. Like the efficiency and effectiveness role, the investigative role of House committees is equally very important as it is aimed at ensuring transparency and accountability in governance. In Nigeria, this role may be carried out either by a standing, special, or ad hoc committee of either chambers in relation to the action or actions of any government official suspected to adversely affect the image of the country or may impact negatively on the wellbeing of the general public.

In most democracies the power of the legislature to investigate issues is not expressly enshrined in the constitution. In Nigeria, the Legislature rely on section 88 subsections 1 and 2 of the 1999 Constitution (as amended) for the exercise of this function (FGN 1999). Thus, the power to investigate is recognized and accorded to the legislature, particularly, for the purpose of collecting information from private persons and from governmental agencies when necessary, and to equip legislators more adequately to discharge their legislative functions. The idea is that no modern democratic legislature can legislate wisely or effectively in the absence of adequate information with regard to the conditions which certain legislation is intended to affect or change and where the legislators lack such important information, recourse can be made to access such information.

The third important role of the committee system is its power to carry out oversight functions. Legislative oversight is defined as a process by which the legislative body takes active role in understanding and monitoring the performance of the executive arm and its agencies (PLAC 2016). It is more or less a monitoring mechanism employed by relevant committees of the legislature to ensure the compliance of the executive arm of government as it regards the implementation of a policy or program approved by it. Halchin and Kaiser (2012) refer to oversight "to the review, monitoring, and supervision of federal agencies, programs, activities, and policy implementation". Therefore, legislative oversight involves the asking of questions and probing into the activities of government to ensure accountability and good governance. It is a process carried out after a law has been passed.

The underlying motive is to ensure transparency and accountability in the utilization of public resources on the part of the executive arm. Thus, legislative oversight is a watchdog function performed by the legislature to ascertain the rate of performance of the executive branch of government as regards to implementation of policies and programs.

PLAC (2016) outlined four important functions of oversight role of the legislature to include (i) the identification and avoidance of inefficiency and waste in government such as extravagance, fraud, and misuse of public funds as well as redirection, redistribution, and/or restructuring; (ii) the determination of the extent of government's effectiveness in carrying out public policies as set by the legislature; (iii) the determination of whether responsible parties are administering the law fairly and properly throughout the state; and (iv) increment of knowledge and understanding of governmental programs.

However, the power to exercise oversight function either by the Nigerian National Assembly or by any other democratic legislature is done largely through its committee system. The Nigerian National Assembly and its committees have the powers to summon private individuals, heads of governmental agencies and departments to the floor of the House to give evidence or produce documents containing vital information that may help them in their investigative process. Section 88–89 of the 1999 Constitution of the Federal Republic of Nigeria (as amended), clearly vest in the National Assembly (i.e., Senate and House of Representatives), the power to investigate (a) any matter in, respect of which it has the power to make laws; and (b) the conduct of any parastatal or official responsible for administering and Act of the Nation or in charge of disbursing funds (FGN 1999; Fawole 2018). Section 89 gives the National Assembly the power to obtain or procure evidence, or summon anyone to give evidence or produce documents, and the power to issue a warrant to compel the attendance of any such witness. It is these two provisions of the constitution that empowers the National Assembly to carry out oversight functions. Therefore, oversight as an expression is not stated verbatim in the constitution, but as a function of the legislature, it is derived from the sections 88 and 89 of the 1999 constitution as amended. This is the reason why its application often generates conflict between the Legislature and Executive arm of government.

Ezeani (2010) noted that the exercise of oversight functions by the National Assembly has not only been controversial, but also remained a major source of conflict between the arms of government. Perhaps, those who framed the constitution expected the possible conflict that may arise in the application of the investigative powers of the legislature, and thus, added a caveat on sections 88 and 89, limiting the powers of oversight. Section 88 states that the power to investigate is only exercisable for the purpose of enabling it to (a) make laws on any matter within its legislative competence and correct defects in existing laws; and (b) expose corruption, inefficiency, or waste in execution or administration of laws (FGN 1999). This simply implies that the application of the oversight function is limited only to those areas the legislature can make laws or that will enable it improved on an existing statute (s).

Premised on the foregoing, the importance of the legislative committee system lies in its investigative powers to enable it effectively carry out its law making and watchdog functions. In order to achieve these activities, the legislative committees depend on an important process known as public hearing. Public hearing is an investigative instrument employed by legislative committees to gather valuable information to help them make a new law or to better an existing law. Public hearing enable legislators make informed analysis and decisions (Yamamoto 2007). Public hearing also remains supplementary information source to information and reports obtained from government officials. Information or evidence obtained from this process is usually included in the records of the specific committee carrying out the exercise. Though, public hearing is not the only means through which members of the public can participate in the law making process, other means include interested members of the public attending legislative committee meetings, and broadcast of committee hearings via the electronic media, that will allow citizens to follow up activities. But public hearing remains a vital legislative instrument that provides the platform for the public to participate and contribute to the processes of law making in a democratic regime.

In his study of 88 national parliaments across the world, Yamamoto (2007) posits that "in 19 of 71 national parliaments, permanent committees can take the decision to hold hearings to gather evidence in public or in camera, while in some, permanent committees must obtain authorization to open their hearings to the public".

Category of persons that a legislative committee can invite includes government officials, experts in specific areas, interested parties, and members of the general public. However, persons appearing before a legislative committee are usually protected in some ways. Though, there is no express constitutional provision for this, it is nevertheless, the right of the witness to require of the committee a demonstration of its authority to inquire into his activities and showing that the questions asked of him are pertinent to the committee's area of inquiry alone (More 1960). In order words, the committee is expected to restrict its questions to only areas relevant to the investigation, and it is not expected to probe into the personal life of the witness.

Hearing as an integral part of the committee system has, to a great extent, enabled legislators perform their statutory responsibilities more efficiently and more effectively in most democracies.

Constitution and Institutional Framework of Committee System in the National Assembly

The committee system, as earlier noted, existed in the British House of Commons and most contemporary democracies, particularly, former British colonial territories adopted similar practices from their former colonial powers. Regarded as a critical structure in the legislative process, committee system is now recognized by many constitutions and institutional structure among democratic states in the world. In the United States of America, South Africa, France, India, Jamaica, Honduras, Nigeria, Australia, Canada, and several other democracies recognize the importance of the committee system in their constitutions and an institutional structure in the law making process (Francis 1989; Shubhangi 2017; Vincent 1992). In Nigeria, for example, section 62(1–4), and sections 88, 89 and 103(1–3), of the 1999 constitution (as amended) spell out the nature and powers of committees that can be constituted and for what purpose a committee could be constituted, and the procedures for constituting the committee as well as the limit of the powers the committee may exercise (FGN 1999; Fashagbe 2009).The Senate Rules and the Standing Orders of the House of Representatives are internal documents that are meant to reinforce the institutionalization of the operational mechanisms of the National Assembly. Thus, the proceedings of the National Assembly are governed by provisions of the Constitution of the Federation and the internal operational documents in both chambers of the National Assembly.

For example, section 62 (1) of the 1999 Constitution as amended in 2011 states that,

> the Senate or the House of Representatives may appoint a committee of its members for such special or general purpose as in its opinion would be better regulated and managed by means of such a committee, and may by resolution, regulation or otherwise as it thinks fit, delegate any functions exercisable by it to any such committee. (FGN 1999)

On the other hand, subsection (2) empowers the Senate and the House of Representatives to determine the number its members to be appointed in any of its committees, their term of office and quorum of a committee. Subsection (3) empowers both Senate and the House of Representatives to appoint a joint Committee on Finance consisting of an equal number of persons and may likewise appoint other joint committees to effectively carry out their functions (FGN 1999). Subject to these provisions of the Constitution, the Senate and the House of Representatives are thus empowered not only to set up committees for smooth and orderly conduct of their duties, but are also empowered to "regulate its own procedure, including the procedure for summoning and recess of the House" (FGN 1999).

It is against the above background that the Senate and the House of Representatives set up committees to facilitate their work of law making. However, in setting up the various committees, both chambers of the National Assembly are guided by what their standing orders and other extant rule. The Standing Order is simply a set of rules put together by the members of a particular legislative chamber primarily to provide guide for the conduct of legislative business for that particular chamber both in plenary sessions and in committee sittings. It is the main document that provides the guiding principles that set in motion the daily activities of the chamber as well as direct members on how the business of the chamber can be conducted. The Standing Order or the House Rules have items such as how a motion can be moved, committees can be set up, reports can be laid before the chamber, how interrogations can be conducted, etc. Therefore, it is an important document for the successful operation of the National Assembly. However, it is subject to changes and amendments from time to time.

For instance, Senate House Rules 17–19, prescribe the setting up of the Standing Committees, membership, and procedures of the committees. There are about 57 standing committees in the Senate and about 89 standing committees in the House of Representatives. Standing Committees in the Senate are Senate Committee on Appropriation, Senate Committee on Air Force, Senate Committee on Health, Senate Committee on Environment, Senate Committee on Banking/Insurance, Senate Committee on Marine transport, Senate committee on National planning, Senate Committee on Women Affairs, Senate committee on finance, Senate committee on integration and cooperation, Senate Committee on Education, Senate Committee on National security & Intelligence, Senate Committee on Up Stream Petroleum Sector, Senate Committee on Power, Senate Committee on Federal Capital Territory (FCT), Senate Committee on Defence and Army, Senate Committee on National Population, among others.

Standing Committees in the House of Representatives include among others House Committee on Anti-Corn, National Ethics &Value, House Committee on the Air Force, House Committee on the Army, House Committee on Aviation, House Committee on Banking and Currency, House Committee on the Capital Market, House Committee on Commerce, House Committee on Communication, House Committee on Cooperation, Integration and NEPAD, House Committee on Culture and Tourism, House Committee on Defence, House Committee on Drugs, Narcotics and Financial Crimes, House Committee on Education, House Committee on Electoral Matters, House Committee on Employment and Productivity, House Committee on the Environment, House Committee on Ethics and Privilege, House Committee on the Federal Executive Territory, House Committee on Federal Character, House Committee on Finance, House Committee on Foreign Affairs, House Committee on Gas. There are also four Joint Committees, viz,

- Joint Committee on Agriculture and Rural Development
- Joint Committee on Labour and Productivity, Petroleum Resources and Justice
- Joint Committee on Finance, Appropriation and Electoral Matters
- Joint Committee on Health and Commerce.

Membership of Legislative Committees

Members of the various committees are appointed at the beginning of the life of each of the chambers under their respective rules. An important thing that needs to be mentioned regarding membership of committees in the National Assembly is that members of opposition parties must be appointed into committees as they form minority in the various committees and are usually allowed to invite witnesses in matters of investigations. For example, as a practice in the United States Congress under House Rule 26 (4d) is that whenever any hearing is conducted by a committee (except the Committee on Appropriation) upon any measure or matter, the minority in the committee is entitled, though upon request made by a majority of the minority members to the chairman before the completion of any hearing, to call witnesses selected by the minority to testify with respect to the issue under investigation (Deering and Smith 1997). Thus, committees consist of both members of the ruling party and members of the opposition parties who have been elected into the legislative chamber.

Each committee is made up of the chairman and other members who are also legislators. They are appointed by the selection committee. The selection committee is made up of members of the leadership of both chambers of legislature. The main responsibility of the selection committee is to assign members into the various House committees. The Senate President is the chairman of the selection committee of the Senate, and the Speaker in the case of the House of Representative. Criteria considered for appointment of members into committees include interest, cognate experience of lawmakers, hobby, politics, and prerogative power of the presiding officer.

Membership of committees also includes administrative staff of the National Assembly who serves as secretary to the committee, appointed by the Clerk of the National Assembly in the case of Nigeria.

Workings of the Committee System

The entire work of a committee is done by its members and the final report is presented to the House. Committees carry out oversight functions and scrutinize bills. Since, they carry out these responsibilities on behalf of Parliament, the proceedings of a committee are often recognized and regarded as proceedings of parliament, and thus, it attracts the same privileges and protections as parliament itself. In this regard, witnesses appearing before it to give evidence are widely protected and are immune from been sued or prosecuted for what they say in evidence to the committee. Since committees are created to facilitate the smooth running of the legislature and to ensure the making of good laws, information and information gathering is a major task of the various committees. It is in recognition of this that committees carry out oversight functions and investigative activities. It meant primarily to obtain vital information that will help enhance the law making process. Hence, committees are empowered to conduct inquiry and invite government officials and individuals who, in their opinion, can provide vital and relevant information and evidence on the issue(s) under investigation. They may also seek submissions from government and non-governmental agencies known to have an interest in the matter under investigation, or invite persons and organizations with requisite experience and expertise to make submissions (Alabi 2017). Another vital aspect of the work of a committee is that members of a committee may decide to go out of their comfort zone (e.g., the Parliament) to other parts of the country and listen to witnesses and/or take physical evidence of a project or program of government. They may equally arrange informal briefings and conduct seminars to obtain more information on particular measures or issues (Alabi 2017).

Submissions made to the committee can then be carefully scrutinized and analyzed by members, sometimes with the assistance of professional advice by experts in that area. In the administrative aspect, a secretary, who is a non-legislator is appointed by the Clerk of the National Assembly to work closely with the chairman of the committee in the handling of administrative procedures. The secretariat staff on behalf of the members of the committee, arranges hearings, prepares questions to be asked witnesses, analyses and summarizes submissions and evidence, conducts research, prepares draft reports and monitors government and other responses to report (Ogbonnaya et al. 2014).

Powers of Legislative Committees

Another interesting thing to note concerning the committee system is that committees in the National Assembly of Nigeria lack final decision making powers on any matter placed before it. A committee of either the Senate or the House of Representatives do not have power of its own. Committees exercise powers delegated to them by the parent chamber and thus are expected to report back to the parent chamber after conclusion of its findings on investigative or law making issues. Therefore, reports are essential part of the work of a legislative committee. In the exercise of its functions, a committee lacks the power to kill a bill at the committee stage, but can carry out amendments on aspects of a bill. A committee has jurisdictions over matters the legislature has power to legislate on. Since different committees are set up to handle different aspects of government activities and its institutions, ministries, departments, and agencies, the power of a committee therefore, is limited to the specific matter (terms of reference) delegated to it by the parent chamber.

Working within the powers delegated to them, each standing committee and subcommittee is authorized to hold hearings, has power to require by subpoena or otherwise the attendance of such witnesses for the purpose of obtaining evidence from such witnesses, and each committee has the power to make investigations into any matter within its jurisdiction, and report such hearings to the parent chamber (PLAC 2016).

For the purpose of effectiveness and efficiency, each committee is authorized to adopt its own rules, but such rules must be consistent with the generally laid down rules of the House. Equally, each committee except the Committee on Appropriation is allowed to fix regular meeting days and make public announcement of the date, place, and subject matter of any hearing to be conducted by the committee, at least a week before the commencement of that hearing and also, as part of its procedures, each committee, except the Committee on Appropriation, may require a witness who is to appear before it to file with the clerk of the committee, at least one day before the date of appearance, a written statement of his proposed testimony (Roberts 2001).

Submission of Legislative Committee's Report

At the conclusion of its work either an investigation of an issue or the scrutinizing of a Bill submitted to it, House Rule 38(1) requires the chairman of the committee to prepare a draft report and submit it to the committee for consideration (Okechwukwu 2014). In practice, the chairman of the committee usually gives drafting instructions to the secretary, who prepares a draft with secretariat assistance. When a final report has been agreed to, committee members may add a minority or dissenting report or attach relevant conclusions and recommendations. While committees often attempt to reach consensus, dissenting reports are not uncommon (Richards 1972; Akhihiero 2009). The process of reporting is completed when a copy of the report signed by the chairman, is formally presented to the Senate or the House of Representatives. Until this is done, the report is kept under embargo and its content may not be made known to the public. Debate can take place after the report has been tabled. It should also be noted that the report of a given committee can as well be submitted to the President of the Senate or to the Speaker of the House of Representatives, or their deputies, when the chamber concern is not sitting, and it is deemed to have been presented to the Senate or to the House and can be authorized for publication.

Issues in the Committee System in the National Assembly

The Nigerian National Assembly and its committees both in the past and present have come under severe criticisms by the citizens of the country and other kin observers of Nigerian democracy outside the country. Quite a number of issues have been raised regarding the attitudes and operations of the members of the National Assemble and its committees, and its counterparts at the State level. This section of the work deals with a brief discussion of some fundamental issues that borders on the attitude of committee members and committee operational measures that has generated tension, confusion, and conflicts in the National Assembly.

First, members of committees of the National Assembly are been accused of pursuing personal interest at the expense of the generality of the masses who voted them to represent them at the Legislative arm of government. The perception among most Nigerians is that legislative members who constitute the various committees of the House often project their personal interests rather than the collective wellbeing of the people. Ewuim et al. (2014) stated that "a good number of members of the legislative houses at both federal and state levels pursue pure selfish interests that often inhibit them from combating the challenges of law making". Once elected into office, most of them concern themselves of what benefits they can achieve within the time period they stay in office, rather than make good laws that will alleviate the suffering of the masses. Thus, at the beginning of the life of the House, they scramble over allowances, improved salaries, furniture, cars loans, fuel allowances, toiletry allowances, accommodation allowances, and other petty regular and non-regular allowances. According to Umaru (2017), the group of Senators that resumed legislative business in 1999, asked for the sum of N3.5 million each as furniture allowances as soon as they started work, despite public outcry. Therefore, the average Nigerian legislator is usually interested, first and foremost, the monetary benefits accruing to him as a legislator. This wealth accumulation drive of our legislators has impacted negatively on the law making processes of nation. Okey (2017) observed that "a good number of Nigerian legislators are crazy for wealth acquisition as events and evidences over time have proven".

Many, therefore, usually jettison their primary responsibility of law making and chaste after government contracts and juicy appointments in the Assembly such as becoming chairmen and members of lucrative parliamentary committees with the intention of receiving bribes and other forms of gratifications. The issue of personal interest among legislative members at all levels has been a lingering issue, and it appears that, this phenomenon is likely to continue as no immediate solution is on sight.

Second, there is the issue of ambitious legislators whose concern is how he/she can utilize or maximize his/her present position to secure a more lucrative position in the future. Thus, many Nigerian legislators often see their present positions as a stepping stone to higher office (s) in the future. The practical implication here is that a member of a legislative committee with such ambition can easily compromise its duties in favor of whoever he/she feels can help him or her attain his desired goal in the future. It is not uncommon in Nigeria to see members of legislative committees' compromise with government officials, members of the Executive such as State Governors, Ministers, and other influential personalities in government. Thus, legislators ambition leading to unnecessary compromise, remain an issue in the committee system in democratic governance.

Third, there is the issue of slow passage of bills by law makers in the National Assembly. An observation made by Ewuim et al. (2014), shows that in 2011, after twelve years of the existence of the National Assembly in Nigeria, only 195 Acts were enacted into law, while over 189 bills were pending in the Senate, and over 1101 bills were also pending in the House of Representatives. Considering the number of bills unattended to by both Houses, it clearly shows lack of seriousness and commitment on the part of legislators. Appropriation Bills sometime stay in the National Assembly as long as six months or more before their passage into law. The delay of passage into law Appropriation Bills that serve as working document for the Executive arm in economic planning of the country indicates the inertia and lacklustre attitude that characterizes the behavior of the members of the law making body and its committees. Undoubtedly, this attitudinal trait of the National Assembly often generates intense debate and tension between the Executive and the Legislature in Nigeria.

Fourth, another issue that deserves mentioning is the issue of the cost of funding of the National Assembly and its committees. Nigeria practices a bicameral legislative system at the centre, while the States adopts a unicameral legislative system. Thus, the Nigerian National Assembly has two legislative chambers known as the Senate (also known as the Upper Chamber), and the House of Representatives (also called, the Lower Chambers or House). The Constitution of the Federal Republic of Nigeria, 1999 as amended, made it mandatory that the Senate be consisted of three Senators each from the thirty-six States of the Federation, and one Senator representing the Federal Capital Territory Abuja (FGN 1999). This figure amounts to 109 Senators, while the House of Representatives has a membership of three hundred and sixty (360) members. The National Assembly, therefore, is made up of a total number of 469 members drawn from different constituencies across the federation. It is these 469 representatives that are appointed into the various Senate and House of Representatives Committees. The fundamental issue associated with the size of the legislature is the cost of funding.

With regard to funding, Aluko (2010) argued that the actual recurrent expenditures on the 469 National Assembly members were N51.6 billion or N110 million per member in a year and this figure according to him is expected to increase to N118.9 billion or N253 million per member in 2010. In the same vein, a former Governor of Central Bank, Lamido Sanusi, Lamido lamented the high cost of funding the National Assembly. According to him, the Federal Government spend about 25% of its income on overheads for the National Assembly (Umaru 2017). He further revealed that in 2009, a Nigerian Senator earns as much as N240 million per annum, and a member of the lower chamber earns N203 million per annum (Umaru 2017). Despite the fact that Nigeria remains one of the poorest nations in the world, its lawmakers receive the highest salaries and allowances in the world (Edet and Attai 2014). On the other hand, countries with more stable and advanced economies like the United States, and Great Britain, among other law makers in these countries earn less than Nigerian law makers.

Fifth, there are issues of financial recklessness and corrupt practices of committee members of the Nigerian National Assembly. Since the beginning of this democratic regime, issues of financial recklessness and corrupt practices of members of the legislature have taken the front banner of reports in newspapers, magazines, periodicals, in the social media and electronic media as well. Okey (2017) posits that the legislature in Nigeria is bedeviled with multiplicity of corruption scandals and allegations from inception of self-rule in 1960. In the same vein, Ewuim et al. (2014) averred that bills in the National Assembly hardly sail through until members have had their hands greased. Dumoye (2005), cited in Okey (2017) also noted that members of the legislatures at the national and state levels lack decorum as their conduct have smeared the image of this great and important institution. The number of cases of alleged financial scams against members of legislative committees both in the Senate and in the House of Representatives makes it invariably difficult for anyone to discard or discredit the potency of the above observations.

In Nigeria, there are no established cases of corruption among members of the National Assembly, but the body has not able to absolved itself from allegations of corruption and corrupt practices among its leadership and among committee members of the various committees. Areas where perceived corruption and corrupt activities often take place include areas such as clearance of nominees, constituency projects, and bill passage, inflation of contracts, exercise of oversight functions and so on. For example, Mallam Nuhu Ribadu was nominated by the then President, Chief Olusegun Obasanjo as the chairman of the Economic and Financial Crime Commission (EFCC). Ribadu later claimed that Senator Ibrahim Mantu and Senator Jonathan Zwingina requested him to pay the sum of N54 million bribery to facilitate his clearance at the Senate (Okey 2017). Also, Funke Adedoyi and Professor Babalola Borishade claimed alleged bribery scam against the Senate to facilitate their clearance as nominees of the Executive arm. The alleged $10 million bribe of the National Assembly by Multinational Oil Companies to stall the passage of the Petroleum Industrial Bill, the alleged demand for the sum of N600 million by members of the National Assembly before they could pass into law the Sovereign Wealth Bill (SWB), the alleged $3 million bribery allegations against House of Representatives' ad hoc Committee Chairman on Oil Subsidy Investigation, Honourable Farouk Lawan and Mr. Emenalo Boniface, are just few examples of bribery incidences leveled against members of legislative committees in the National Assembly. Though, there is no record of prima facie case of judicial indictment of any member of the National Assembly, the issue of corruption and corrupt practices has tarnished the image of the institution and has severely diminished its integrity.

Sixth, there is the issue of interference on the functions of the executive, especially on the area of exercising legislative oversight and the scrutinizing of appropriations bills by committees of the National Assembly. The investigative powers of the National Assembly remain a potent source of conflict between the executive arm and the legislature in Nigeria. Often times the executive has claimed breach of functions by the legislature by usurping its functions in the name of performing its oversight functions. The legislature, though, have the rights to scrutinize and approve the Appropriation Bill submitted to it by the Executive. The area the executive is not often comfortable with the actions of legislative committee on Appropriation is its powers to either add or deduct appropriations on any of the items in the budget. Here come the issues of "Budget Padding", a phenomenon that has to do with the inclusion and or increase of the budget value from its initial value as passed by the House. According to Umaru (2017), "budget padding means making the budget proposal larger than the actual estimates for the project". The underlining goal is either to increase or decrease the total estimate of the budget, through the addition or subtraction of the estimate for a particular project or its expected revenue (Umaru 2017). Budget padding became an issue and a serious face-off between the members of the National Assembly and the Executive in 2016, when President Muhammadu Buhari accused the National Assembly of padding the 2016 budget in excess of N500 billion (Williams 2016).

Another area of reference is in the area of screening and confirmation or non-confirmation of nominees of the Executive. The Magu (the present acting Chairman, EFCC) case is still fresh in the minds of Nigerians, the invitation of the Inspector General of Police, Idris (now retired) who refused to appear before the floor of the House and was consequently described as an "enemy of democracy" by the Senate did go down well with the Executive arm. Apart from all these, other investigative activities on executive appointees by the National Assembly usually generate conflicts between them.

Seventh, another issue confronting the committee system in Nigeria is the lack of transparency in the performance of their duties. Transparency has to do with the adherence to laid down procedure in arriving at desired result. It emphasizes on the use of due process in handling problems. The goal of transparency is to ensure just and fair handling of issues and problems. Therefore, it is geared toward eliminating or reducing to the barest minimum sentiments, emotions and bias in the perception and thinking of those who are involved either directly or indirectly in an issue. Transparency in handling issues of investigation, exercise of oversight functions, screening of bills, screening of nominees, and other related dealings by legislative committees has been a subject of worry over the years.

Yet, another issue bordering on the attitude and operational mechanisms of the committees of the National Assembly include frequent changes in its leadership (e.g. the removal of Senator Ali Ndume) by the Senate President, Bukola Saraki in what appears to be an internal coup d' etat for having contrary view with the decision of the Senate on the screening of the present acting chairman of EFCC Ibrahim Magu. He had claimed that the Senate did not reject Ibrahim Magu, prompting a counter reaction by Senate spokesperson Aliyu Abdullahi. He was removed as Senate Majority Leader at the prerogative of the leadership of Senate and was replaced by Senator Ahmed Lawan through a letter read to members on the floor of the House by the Senate President Bukola Saraki, said to have been signed by caucus of the ruling All Progressive Congress (APC).

Lack of competent and professionals or experts in handling issues where it has to do with high level of expertise and specialization, the issue of first timers and seniority as criteria for the appointment of committee members in the assembly, and political party influence on appointment are some other issues confronting the operations of the committee system in the Nigerian National Assembly. No doubt that these issues have thrown up challenges the committee system needs to overcome.

Challenges of the Committee System in Nigeria's National Assembly

The first challenge before the committee system in Nigeria's National Assembly is the lack of public trust and confidence. With respect to the issues raised in the section preceding this section, there is no doubt that the genuine intentions of the members of the National Assembly in giving Nigerian citizens the desired goals in life through enduring legislations are greatly contestable. The lack of public trust and confidence in the committee system by majority of the citizens has wane the legitimacy of the democratic system in Nigeria. Rather than concentrate efforts toward addressing the fundamental issues of development, committee members are interested in fighting for their own selfish goals and not concerned with the plight of the average Nigerian. This has made the Nigerian public to lose trust and confidence in their ability to address the issues that impact negatively on the citizens.

A second challenge facing the committee system is lack of adequate funding. As a system that relies information gathering through visits, interviews, attending of seminars, conference (both in the country and abroad), purchasing of newspapers and magazines, committees need to be funded adequately to be able to perform their task effectively. Inadequate funding may sometimes be responsible to self-help efforts that may result to receiving bribes from individuals and organizations. It is not uncommon in Nigeria were legislative committees cry out for lack of funding which invariably hinder them from carrying out their work.

The third challenge is Executive interference on the constitutional responsibilities of the legislative committees, especially, in the appointment of committee members, and the exercise of its oversight functions. Often times, the Executive ensures that their cronies are selected for appointment into lucrative and preferred legislative committees. This is done often time to safeguard their personal interest and to protect against any hash decisions that may be taken against the executive arm of government. They also influence appointments of their supports into very important committees with the hope of getting critical information of the decisions and intentions of such committees to enable them prepare earlier response to such decisions and intentions.

On the other hand, political parties also want their interests to be protected and thus influence appointment of their members into some preferred committees. This usually involves unnecessary politicking and politicization in the appointment process. The obvious outcome is that, committees often lack the needed freedom and independence to discharge its statutory duties do to these unnecessary and undue influences from some external forces.

Another very critical challenge facing the effectiveness of legislative committees is the lack of competence colleagues in the different areas expertise. There are certain areas that are highly technical and therefore, need people with requisite professional knowledge and skills to handle issues concerning such areas. However, in most cases, committees usually lack such manpower to meet up such demands.

Conclusion and Recommendations

The legislature is the prime institution in any democracy as it represents all shade of opinions and believed to have clear understanding of the hopes and expectations of those they represent. The efficiency and effectiveness of the different committees in the Legislature are even more crucial owing to the fact that the bulk of the work of the legislature is carried out by the different committees. However, when this crucial institution is challenged by daunting issues bordering on morality, it becomes worrisome on how the hopes and expectations of the citizenry can be achieved in that society. One of the greatest problems facing Nigeria's democratic government today is the lack of commitment on the part of our legislator to address, in practical terms, those fundamental issues bordering the common man through the making of good laws. Nigeria's legislators at the national and state levels are known for their selfish-centeredness and their parochial chase of personal benefits and personal aggrandizements, leaving the poor masses at the mercy of God. The same committee system that has performed abysmally in Nigeria has been very successful in other parts of the world, especially, in the advance democracies. Their actions and inactions have had grave impacts on the growth and development of stable democratic in the country and have impacted negatively on the socio-economic wellbeing of the citizens of the nation. It is against this backdrop that the following suggestions are made and if implemented will no doubt go a long way in strengthening the operations of the committee system in the National Assembly.

First, there should be an internal mechanism aimed at checking the issue of corruption in the National and State Houses of Assembly. This can be achieved through the setting up of alarm team made up of non-legislators, but people with professional expertise in investigation and information gathering. Such body when established be made independent from the control of any of its committees, but should take directives and report findings directly to the presiding officer of the respective chambers.

Second, the issue of corruption has thrived in the legislature simply because, suspected individuals and organizations alleged to have given bribe or have taken one form of bribery or the other are usually not made to face prosecution. It is suggested here that, such organizations or individuals should be prosecuted and if found guilty, they should be made to face the full wrath of the law. This study believes study; if this carried out successfully it will serve as a deterrent measure for would culprits. Therefore, prosecution of those legislators guilty of corruption will go a long way in checking the incidence of corruption among committees in the Legislature.

Third, it is important that the electorates should exercise independence of mind in the selection of their representatives during election periods. Candidates, who do not have anything to offer if elected into election office, in spite of their wealth, such persons should not be given the privilege to represent us in the legislature. Experiences have shown in this country that over the years, wealthy individuals elected into elective positions are equally interested in their selfish interest and the protection of their massive investments with greater intentions for capital accumulation.

Finally, there should be a constitutional provision restricting registered political parties in the country on the asking price for nomination and expression forms of the various political parties. The high prices for nomination and expression forms of political parties are another technical way of depriving the poor and other persons of integrity from contested competitive elections with the wealthy in Nigeria. This should be frown at and should be discouraged seriously. If this is done, some men and women of integrity will have the privilege to contest and win election on the platform of the leading political parties. This will as well improve the quality of representation at the various levels of representative government.

References

Academy of Political Science [APS]. (2013). *The Origin of the Standing Committee System in American Legislative Bodies*. Academy of Political Science (APS). Available on https://www.jstor.org/stable/2140190. Accessed on December 25, 2018.

Akhihiero, P. A. (2009). *Governance at Great Cost: An Appraisal of the National Assembly*. Paper Presented at the NIALS Seminar for LL.M. Students in Legislative Drafting in the Nigerian Institute of Advance Legal Studies, Lagos.

Alabi, M. O. (2009). The Legislature in Africa: A Trajectory of Weakness. *African Journal of Political Science and International Relations, 3*(5), 233–241.

Alabi, O. (2017). *Parliament Within Parliament: The Commons System of the Legislature*. Lagos: The Nigerian Voice (Online). Accessed December 9, 2018.

Aluko, S. (2010, March 4). The Cost of Democracy in Nigeria. *The Nation*, Thursday, p. 15.

Anyebe, P. A. (2016). Rules and Procedures Governing Legislative Processes in Nigeria. *Journal of Law, Policy and Globalization, 48*(4), 71–83.

Deering, C. J., & Smith, S. S. (1997). *Committees in Congress*. Available at http://www.dx.doi.org. Accessed on November 13, 2018.

Dumoye, D. (2005). Senate Sets Up Ad Hoc Committee to Probe Special Intervention Fund. *This Day* (Online). Available at https://www.thisdaylive.com. Accessed on January 1, 2019.

Edet, J. T., & Attai, A. J. (2014). The Legislature and National Development: The Nigerian Experience. *Global Journal of Arts, Human and Social Sciences, 2*(9), 63–78.

Ewuim, N. C., Nnamani, D. O., & Eberinwa, O. M. (2014). Legislative Oversight and Good Governance in Nigeria National Assembly: An Analysis of Obasanjo and Jonathan's Administrations. *Review of Public Administration and Management, 3*(6), 140–153.

Ezeani, E. O. (2010). Integrity Issues in Legislative Oversight in Nigeria. *Nigerian Journal of Politics and Administration, 3*(1), 67–90.

Fashagbe, J. Y. (2009). The Role of the Committee System in Enhancing Legislative Efficiency in Nigeria: The Case of Kwara State House of Assembly. *Journal of Sustainable Development in Africa, 10*(4), 426–444.

Fawole, R. (2018). *The Oversight Powers of the National Assembly*. https://www.guardian.ng.com. Accessed January 6, 2019.

Federal Government of Nigeria. (1999). *Constitution of the Federal Republic of Nigeria*. Lagos: Federal Government Press (as amended).

Francis, W. L. (1989). *The Legislative Committee Game: A Comparative Analysis of Fifty States*. Columbus: Ohio State University Press.

Halchin, E. L., & Kaiser, F. M. (2012). *Oversight Is a Way for Congress to Check on the Executive Branch*. Washington, DC: Congressional Research Service. Available at https://www.crs.gov.com. Accessed December 28, 2018.

Manikyamba, P. (1995). *India's Little Legislatures*. Madras: T.R Publications Private Limited.

Mezey, M. (1979). *Comparative Legislatures*. Durham, NC: Duke University Press.

More, S. S. (1960). *Practice and Procedures of Indian Parliament*. Thacker and Co Ltd: Bombay.

Obiyo, R. E. (2007). *The South African Parliamentary Committee System: The Constitutional Parameters and Structures*. Available at https://www.wiredspace.wit.ac.za. Accessed on December 13, 2018.

Ogbonnaya, U. M., Ogujiuba, K., & Nancy, S. (2014). A Comparative Analysis of the Interplay of Administrative and Political Structures of the Legislature in the Legislative Procedures of Selected Federal Systems. *Journal of Social Science, 41*(1), 27–35.

Okechwukwu, N. O. (2014). The Legislature and Democracy in Nigeria (1960–2003): Historical, Constitutional Role and Prospects. *Journal of Research on Humanities and Social Sciences, 4*(15), 1–11.

Okey, L. E. (2017). A Critical Assessment of Corruption Within the Legislature in Nigeria. *International Journal of Scientific and Research Publications, 7*(1), 220–232.

Policy and Legal Advocacy Centre (PLAC). (2016). *Guide to Legislative Oversight in the National Assembly*. Abuja, Nigeria: Policy and Legal Advocacy Centre (PLAC).

Richards, P. (1972). *The Backbenchers*. London: Faber and Faber Press.

Roberts, J. C. (2001). Are Congressional Committees' Constitutional? Radical Textualism, Separation of Powers, and the Enactment Process. *Case Western Reserve Law Review, 52*(2), 1–85.

Russel, M., Morris, B., & Larkin, P. (2013). *Fitting the Bill: Bringing Commons Legislation Committees into Line with Best Practices*. London: University College London.

Shubhangi, R. (2017). *Committee System in Indian Parliament*. Available at https://www.politicalsciencenotes.com. Accessed on December 28, 2018.

Tripathi, M. (1980). Committee System in Indian Parliament. *Journal of Constitutional and Parliamentary Studies, 14*(4), 443–468.

Umaru, U. D. (2017). Corruption and Legislative Functions in Nigeria. *Journal of Economics and Finance, 8*(1), 1–8.

Vincent, C. H. (1992). *The Congressional Standing Committee System*. Congressional Research Services. The Library of Congress, USA. Available at http://pennyhill.com. Accessed January 2019.

Wikipedia. (2016). *List of Committees of the National Assembly of Nigeria*. http://www.wikipedia.com. Accessed on January 16, 2019.

Williams, D. (2016, May 15). What Manner of Senate? Abuja. *The Politico Magazine*, pp. 17–18.

Yamamoto, H. (2007). *Tools for Parliamentary Oversight: A Comparative Study of 88 National Parliaments*. Switzerland, Geneva: PCL Press.

CHAPTER 6

Evaluating the Nigerian National Assembly's Lawmaking Output and the Implications for Legislative Effectiveness

Adebola Rafiu Bakare

Introduction

Fish (2006) argued that the effectiveness status of the legislature determines the status of democracy. If the legislature of a country is strong, the democracy of that country is bound to be strong. The fundamental question is: how can we measure the effectiveness of a legislature in order to know how strong or weak such legislature is? Scholars, analysts, development partners, and legislative practitioners have come to realize the need to constantly and continuously evaluate the legislature in attempts to deepen democratic process. The motivating factor for this belief stems out of the centrality of the legislature to democratic experiences. In fact, it is arguable that democracy is inconceivable without the legislature, as the tenets of democracy are construed around the legislature. Perhaps, it

A. R. Bakare (✉)
Department of Political Science, University of Ilorin, Ilorin, Nigeria

F. A. Aremu and A. R. Bakare (eds.), *Two Decades of Legislative Politics and Governance in Nigeria's National Assembly*,
https://doi.org/10.1007/978-981-33-4455-6_6

is in light of this that Bello-Imam (2004) asserted that any attack against the legislature is a blow against democracy.

The essence of evaluating the legislature is to establish the level at which the institution fosters democratic sustenance or its extent at exposing democratic rule to threat of truncation especially in the developing countries. In all democracies, citizens are always interested in the performance level of their legislators in advancing the interests of the constituencies on the floor of the House and the number of developmental benefits the legislators is able to attract to the constituencies. Premised on this, the legislators began to give priority to serving the interests of their constituents in order to win their sympathy for the legislators' re-election bids. This coherent trajectory stimulated scholarship interests in evaluating the legislature thus leading to the emergence of the concept of "legislative effectiveness."

Since 1970s when the concept of "legislative effectiveness" gained momentum, different approaches, indicators, benchmarks, and assessment toolkits for evaluating the legislature have been put forward by scholars. These range from self-assessment guide to minimum criteria for legislative performance. Legislatures across the globe especially in the developed democracies have institutionalized these assessment toolkits and periodic evaluations have become more of tradition. However, the reverse is the case in developing democracies as most legislatures especially in Africa detest evaluation and the legislators are most willing to frustrate any attempt at evaluating them. More worrisome is the fact that most of the developed assessment toolkits are not applicable in these developing democracies given the differences that exist across the legislatures and the specificity of the political environment where the legislatures operate.

In view of these disheartening experiences in Africa, several efforts have been put into the development of workable assessment toolkits to evaluate legislatures in Africa. While these efforts are yielding fruitful outcomes, there are enormous gaps in the process. For instance, the developers of most of the African-specified assessment toolkits in picking their case studies usually snub Nigeria despite having the biggest legislature in the continent. The underlying assumptions and variables of the assessment toolkits are usually not applicable given the country's socio-political specificity. One will expects that Nigeria should have been the adorable bride to the developers as any toolkit developed on the specification of the country is likely to work in most (if not all) developing democracies.

It is against this backdrop that this paper attempts to examine a number of these assessment toolkits and identify the causal factors responsible for the difficulty or impossibility of their adoption in evaluating the legislature in Nigeria. The main objective therefore is to tap from these toolkits to develop an applicable assessment toolkit suitable for evaluating the legislature in Nigeria (and other developing democracies) especially in the aspect of the performance of its lawmaking function. In doing these, the chapter is divided into six sections. The first section being the introductory section is succeeded by the literature review and theoretical framework. In the third section, the chapter examines a number of global legislative effectiveness measuring toolkits, benchmarks, and indicators in the wake of the problematic of their adoptability in Nigeria. The fourth section attempts to bridge the gaps in evaluating the legislature in Nigeria by highlighting the utility of the Institutional Legislative Effectiveness Score (ILES) as an alternative to externally developed indicators. The fifth section serves as the major thrust of the paper where the ILES model is adopted to evaluate the National Assembly on its lawmaking function between 1999 and 2011 covering three Assemblies. The chapter ends with conclusion and recommendations (section six).

A Review of the Concept of Legislative Effectiveness

Scholarly work on the "legislative effectiveness" has its origin in the United States and can be traced to the period around 1970s. In his classic work, Mayhew (1974) attempted to identify the factors that can guarantee an incumbent parliamentarian of his/her seat in the next election. He examined the electoral connection in Congress and discovered that incumbents Congressmen are extremely sensitive to the potential electoral implications of their votes, and as a result, behaves strategically when announcing a position on a roll-call vote. In essence, the electorate will only return a legislator if he/she is seen to be effective in the parliament; thus legislative performance is largely motivated by re-election.

Building on this, other scholars argued that the effectiveness of a legislator is largely seen from the standpoint of institutional power or good public policy. Legislators are expected to pass legislation to please their constituents and to advance their policy agenda in a manner that will make them better-off being a member of Congress. For example, Fenno (1978, p. 139) notes that legislators who want to be seen as effective "believe that their supporters want their representative to be influential in Congress, and that they take a certain pride in having an effective Congressman- the more so when he is effective on their behalf." These observations paved the way for scholars to embark on series of research related to the effectiveness of the parliament and the parliamentarians (Carson et al. 2010; Wiseman and Wright 2008; Weissert 1991a, b; Miquel and Snyder 2006; Bartels 1991, 2000; Rohde 1991; Krehbiel 1991; Cox and McCubbins 1993, 2005; Aldrich and Rohde 1997; Arnold 1990; Canes-Wrone et al. 2002; Erikson and Wright 2001; among others).

What is central to the conceptualization of the term by these scholars is the fact that legislative effectiveness depends crucially on the ability of elected representatives to take the issues that are important to their constituents and to translate them into public policy. Precisely speaking, Volden and Wiseman (2013, p. 6) argued that it is the varying abilities of legislators to advance their legislative agendas, based on their personal aptitude and on their institutional positions that determined their position in the legislative effectiveness ranking. From this analysis, it can be deduced that the systematic differences across members in advancing agenda items can help us to understand the internal workings of the legislature and subsequently venture into the inquiry on why some legislators are more "effective" than others.

The Problems of Measuring Legislative Effectiveness and the Methods Adopted

Having popularized the term in the global political analysis (by the above mentioned scholarship efforts), the consequence was the contested issue of focus on whether legislative effectiveness can be determined through assessment of the individual legislators or the parliament as a whole. This as earlier noted led to the proliferation of indicators and benchmark such as the Commonwealth Parliamentary Association's (CPA) Recommended Benchmarks for Democratic Legislatures; the National Democratic Institute for International Affairs' (NDI) Minimum Standards Assessment Survey; the Inter-parliamentary Union's (IPU) Self-Assessment Toolkit for Parliaments; the Parliamentary Centre's Parliamentary Report Cards; the International IDEA's State of Democracy Assessment Methodology, among others for measuring parliaments' effective.

The ones for measuring individual legislator's effectiveness include: PRS Legislative Research Service developed in India; Pakistan Institute of Legislative Development and Transparency (PILDAT) developed in Pakistan; Africa Leadership Institute—AFLI Parliamentary Scorecard developed in Uganda; Legislative Effectiveness Score (LES) developed in the United States by Craig Volden and Allan Wiseman, among others. Despite the effort of the World Bank Institute and the Griffith University through the organization of a workshop on September 21–24, 2008 in Brisbane, Australia with the theme: Workshop on Legislative Benchmark and Indicators, where participants shared approaches, methodologies and results, and discuss whether a new holistic framework to measure legislature's capacity or performance could (or should) be established. No breakthrough was achieved on a unified benchmark and indicator owing to the fact that there is no unified resemblance of the status, function, institutional framework, membership composition of the legislature and most importantly the system of government in all democracies. Consequently, there emerged the case studies difficulties in developing appropriate indicators that can fit into all case studies.

There are fundamental methodological problems facing scholars, practitioners, donors, and politicians in measuring legislative effectiveness globally. These methodological problems emerged out of varying epistemological standpoints. Scholars attempt to measure legislative effectiveness from different standpoints depending on the perception of individual scholar on what to measure, how to measure, what method and tool to adopt in measuring intangible variable such as legislative effectiveness. First and foremost, some scholars of comparative legislature argued that measuring legislative effectiveness is best done by measuring individual legislative effectiveness (notably Volden and Wiseman 2013; Adcock and Collier 2001; Cox and William 2008; Wiseman and Wright 2008 etc.) while others make case for measuring the effectiveness of the legislature as an institution (notably Fish 2006; Fish and Kroenig 2006 etc.).

Whichever standpoint is chosen, there is also the problem of how and what to measure which led to the emergence of five different approaches. These are: formal powers cum autonomy, functional delivery, component, number and content of Bills, and reputational approaches. The formal powers cum autonomy approach measures the degree of power constitutionally ascribed to the legislature and the extent of institutional autonomy it enjoys in its relations with the executive. The functional delivery approach measures the extent to which the legislature delivers in the performance of its four core functions earlier discussed. Component approach examines the quality of key components and actors in the legislative process such as the committee system. While the number and content of Bills approach emphasize the number and content of Bills passed by the legislature over a given period of time, the reputational approach assesses the way the public perceives the legislature as a crucial institution by its performance and whether there is a high level of public trust or not in it (Fish and Kroenig 2009; Barkan 2010; Omotola 2014).

One of the most prominent and ground breaking analyses is the research work carried out by Volden and Wiseman in 2009 and revalidated in 2013 (which served as inspiration for this study to develop a peculiar benchmark for evaluating Nigerian legislature). They concisely defined legislative effectiveness as the proven ability to advance a member's agenda items through the legislative process and into law. They inferred that this definition has four key components. First, it discusses the "proven ability" of members on the ground that while many lawmakers may have great potential to bring about policy change, unless they use that potential to actually advance agenda items, they are not considered effective. Second, it laid emphasis on "advancing" legislation in view of the ability of a lawmaker to bring about positive change even in the face of daunting obstacles from proposals blockage by others. However, they recognized the fact that placing obstacles in an opponent's path is also an important aspect of legislative politics which consequently affected effectiveness status.

Third, the definition focuses on the "member's agenda items"; rather than the agenda items of the political party, the president, or the member's constituents. They argued that lawmakers have a great deal of choice and flexibility in deciding which issues to act upon and which to set aside. That it is these choices that form the basis for evaluation of a member's effectiveness. Fourth and finally, it focused on movement "through the legislative process and into law." They argued that effectiveness can be demonstrated at multiple stages of the lawmaking process, not simply in the passage of new laws. While such laws may be the ultimate goal, members may be effective at moving their proposed legislation through key committees and to the floor of the House. Yet, even if they fail to gain passage of their Bills on the floor, such members have demonstrated a level of effectiveness. Though, members whose Bills are eventually signed into law are regarded to be more effective.

From the foregoing, one can infer that the definition of legislative effectiveness excludes various legislative activities and behaviors, especially those that extend well beyond an ability to advance legislation. For instance, one could speak of their "fundraising effectiveness" with campaign contributors, their "electoral effectiveness" with their constituents, or their "administrative effectiveness" in managing a large legislative staff. It also excludes any exploration of whether the laws proposed by these members are themselves effective and beneficial to the people, since important work in the field of public policy analysis is done on a daily basis to assess the impact of policies and laws in line with the argument that a good public policy must always be in the public interest (Olaniyi 2003, p. 39).

However, in the Nigerian context, scholarship efforts on the study of the effectiveness of the Nigerian legislature are highly appreciable. Before the emergence of the Fourth Republic, it is difficult to make any meaningful analysis of the lawmaking institution, owing to the fact that the history of Nigeria's legislature has been riddled with disruptions, re-establishments, and reforms, all of which left it without strong, deeply engrained legislative tradition, norms, practices, and procedures. The experience from the four times (First to Fourth Republic) it has sprung back into life is that, the process of setting down roots has had to begin afresh. However, for the first time in independent Nigeria, the National Assembly has witnessed about two decades of uninterrupted legislative activities from 1999 to 2003 (4th Assembly), 2003 to 2007 (5th Assembly), 2007 to 2011 (6th Assembly), 2011 to 2015 (7th Assembly) and the current 8th Assembly of 2015 till date. This has undoubtedly prepared the ground on which to base performance assessment. It is against this backdrop that scholars began to measure the progression of the legislative branch of Nigeria's evolving democratic government.

In view of this, scholars have since been exploring the institutional workings of the National Assembly toward identifying the factors responsible for its efficiency and otherwise. While some based their analyses on the symmetric and asymmetric relations with the executive arm of government (Davies 1996; Bello-Imam 2004; Aiyede 2006; Zwingina 2006), others tend to see it from the invaluable roles it is playing in the democratic governance (Okoosi-Simbine 2010; Ijaiya 2010; Egwu 2005; Ojagbohunmi 2006). In a different perspective, some other scholars explore it as an institution of governance analyzing its workings and pointing out the challenges hindering its effectiveness (Saliu and Muhammed 2010; Alabi and Fashagba 2010; Solomon 2016; Lafenwa 2009; Fashagba 2010; Ishaya 2010).

Despite these efforts, little attention is made to scientifically measure the effectiveness of the National Assembly as it is the case in most developed democracies. Ekor et al. (2014) attempted to fill this gap by domesticating the model of Volden and Wiseman (2009, 2013) to study individual legislative effectiveness of Senators in the 6th Assembly. They (Ekor et al. 2014) came up with a framework for legislative effectiveness and also modified the LES model retaining most of the LES components and weighting system. As novel as this effort was, two gaps were observed. First, the analysis is limited to the Senate leaving out the House of Representatives. Perhaps, they followed the style of Volden and Wiseman who also used the LES model to study the United States' House of Representatives leaving out the Senate. Second, we believe it may have been better if the entire 109 Senators of the 6th Assembly are studied over the four years span. Ekor et al. (2014) only studied 43 Senators between 2007 and 2008 which in our view may not be enough to generalize the effectiveness level of the Senate in particular and the National Assembly in general. This paper attempts to fill these gaps in the course of the analysis.

Theoretical Framework

Legislative study is becoming a world-wide topic of discussion as identified by WBI (2008, p. 1), therefore, the need to theorize it becomes a necessity. Political scientists have worked assiduously in developing theoretical frameworks, perspectives, and issues on legislative studies. The outcome of these continuous efforts has led to the propounding of grounded, traditional and empirical theories as well as epistemological standpoint orientations otherwise known as approaches. Prominent among these theories and approaches include, legislative organization theory, legislative theory otherwise called legislative drafting theory, institutional approach, theory of legislative intent, and theories of legislative committee among others. However, this study adopted institutional approach because it considers the aspects of social structures noting the rules, norms, and routine in establishing guidelines for social behavior of an institution (Scott 2004). The theory is considered to be most suitable for this research work premised on its epistemological kernel and utility to the study of legislative activities and performance on the premise of the causal factors of why, when, and how.

One of the earliest proponents of the institutional approach, Pareto (1935 [1916]) argued that an institution is an embodiment of a particular way of thinking that has direct impact on behaviors of the people that are operating such institution. Selznick (1949) disagreed with Pareto's position and offered a variation to the use of institutional analysis. He opined that studying the natural history of an organization will enable one to understand the reason(s) why such organization behave in a particular way because "the most important thing about organizations is that, though they are tools, each nevertheless has a life of its own" (Selznick 1949, p. 10). However, the direction of the approach has since expanded beyond Selznick's view. Scholars believe that the two opinions are mutually inclusive in studying why an institution functions in a particular way. For instance, Ostrom (1990) in his view argued that institutional approach now deals with how organization evolves, the legal framework and how the operators of the institution make economical and managerial decisions particularly by investigating the non-rational, non-economic, and non-psychological factors.

Premised on the above, the institutional approach becomes useful in assessing the performance of Nigeria's legislature because the historical circumstances that led to the creation of the institution have largely shaped the way the legislature is run. In addition, there is a standing rule and convention that guide the modus operandi of the institution which influences the behavior of the operators. This study acknowledged the fact that the theory is deficient on two grounds. First, it gives primacy to structure and operating procedure over individual and group behaviors of the institutional actors. Second, it erred in acknowledging the fact that the operators of the institution can manipulate the operating procedures to achieve their own end. In order not to render the choice of the approach baseless, this study attempted to bridge the gap by adopting the New Institutional Analysis (also referred to as neo-institutional approach) which is a variant of the institutional approach that is developed to consider the economic models based on theory of public choice. This will enable us recognize the fact that external forces and sociological circumstances such as godfatherism, constituency and personal needs, political parties' manifestoes and leaders, among others, do influence rational decision making and performance of the Nigeria's National Assembly.

Global Legislative Effectiveness Measuring Toolkits, Benchmarks, and Indicators: The Problematic of Adoptability in Nigeria

Staddon (2013) opined that the proliferation and variations in the legislative effectiveness benchmarks and assessment frameworks is unavoidable, chiefly as a result of the differences that exist across legislatures in terms of powers and institutional development. However, in order to appreciate the plurality and the novelty of assessing legislative effectiveness and the inherent gaps as identified above, it becomes a necessity to briefly discuss the kernel of some selected global legislative effectiveness measuring toolkits, benchmarks, and indicators as put forward by scholars, practitioners, and legislative inclined organizations. It is worthy to note that the plurality or proliferation of the measuring toolkits is also a product of the end target or objective of the initiators either to establish a self-assessment or minimum criteria. The legislators may initiate assessment toolkits to evaluate their own performance or be assessed by external bodies who mostly establish a minimum standard expected of the legislature.

Whichever way, the essence or benefit of assessing the legislature is enormous, which include (but not limited to): ability to identify significant issues for reform, raising awareness about legislative governance, strengthening inter-parliamentary cooperation (Hubli 2009), empowering the parliament to claim its institutional position in governance order, provide opportunity for the legislature to know its areas of strengths and weaknesses, assist in designing parliamentary strengthening programming (UNDP 2007), increase academic interest in legislative studies, to establish democratic norms and values that will guide legislative operations, to enhance legislative transparency and accountability, and encourage comparative assessment of legislatures using different frameworks (Staddon 2013).

There are many measuring toolkits, benchmarks, and indicators of legislative assessment designed by scholars, practitioners, parliamentary assistance donors, and civil society organizations. Some of which had been mentioned earlier. However, some selected ones that are practically implementable in the context of African specificity are briefly discussed below with a view to take a stand on their adoptability in studying Nigeria's National Assembly.

The IPU Self-Assessment Toolkit for Parliaments

In an attempt to establish a widely accepted assessment toolkit suitable for all parliaments across the globe, the Inter-Parliamentary Union (IPU) in 2008 introduced a self-assessment toolkit which was a product of the collection of about seventy five examples of good legislative practices among member parliaments (WBI 2008). The intent of the IPU is to put forward a viable toolkit that is based on universal democratic values and principles relevant to all parliaments regardless of the type of political system and their stage of development. The core objective of the blueprint is to allow each legislature to perform a self-assessment of its activities. The wisdom behind this is premised on the argument that the parliamentarians themselves are in best position to identify the challenges hindering their legislative effectiveness and efficiency. However, the self-assessment is with a caveat that the legislature should involve external actors such as the civil society organizations, media practitioners, and academics among others. The initiator (IPU) therefore believes that this self-assessment will enable the legislature to suggest implementable practical solutions to the problem. The Union recognizes the fact that all legislatures differ on the basis of history, social, and political context; yet, it is believed that the toolkit can situate a mid-point to all the characteristics and provide a universal template and common criteria for assessing themselves on how they perform.

The IPU Self-assessment toolkit is made up of fifty four (54) questions set under six (6) categories:

i. the representativeness of parliament;
ii. parliamentary oversight over the executive;
iii. parliament's legislative capacity;
iv. the transparency and accessibility of parliament;
v. the accountability of parliament; and
vi. parliament's involvement in international policy.

Methodologically, the legislators are expected to answer the set of questions annually (in early October) after they might have trained a group of facilitators who will assist them in using the toolkit. The outcome of the assessment will then be published for the legislators and public consumption. In view of these, the WBI (2008) described the toolkit as one that follows a best practice approach. We strongly opine that the outcome of the assessment may not be empirically valid given the fact that it opens the door for bias and value judgment. The average legislators may not rate themselves poor even when they knew they had performed poorly. This is why it is generally believed in the Latin legal parlance that "*nemo judex incausa sua*" (one cannot be a judge on his/her own case). Rotberg and Salahub (2013, p. 19) also criticized the IPU's Self-assessment toolkit as "brief and bland." To them, the toolkit is not only incomplete but also lacks objectivity. To this end, we find this toolkit good but not adoptable for the nature of the study.

The UNDP Parliamentary Assessment Strategies

As one of the major parliamentary assistance donors in Africa, the United Nations Development Programme (UNDP) in 1999 initiated two different guidelines for assessing African parliaments:

i. ***Parliamentary Needs Assessment:*** This assessment guideline is designed to be adopted during the development phase of a parliamentary strengthening program, and
ii. ***Parliamentary Strengthening Programs Assessment:*** This serves as a guide to developing indicators that are aimed at monitoring and evaluating existing parliamentary strengthening programs in Africa.

Though the frameworks did not propose a particular scorecard system of evaluating parliaments, they prepare the ground for the development of assessment framework for legislatures within or across countries. The major thesis of the two toolkits is the seven (7) key questions to be answered prior to developing a parliamentary strengthening program:

i. How much power do the laws grant to the parliament?
ii. How much political space does the system allow the parliament?
iii. How much do legislators want to do to advance the institution as a significant actor in the political system?
iv. How well does the parliament interact with society?
v. How well does the parliament perform its lawmaking and oversight functions?

vi. How well do systems of parliamentary management and infrastructure help the parliament perform its representation, lawmaking, and oversight functions?
vii. What are other donors doing?

As novel as these questions seem in assessing legislative effectiveness, Bosley (2007) opined that they do not address parliamentary performance, instead, the questions only focus on the political and institutional contexts in which a parliament or parliamentary strengthening program operates and the issues confronting donors. However, we hold a contrasting opinion to that of Bosley. A close examination of the questions shows that they not only cover all the cardinal functions of the legislature but also take care of the relationship between the legislature and the wider democratic setting. By answering the questions in relation to a specific legislature, one will have been done with an assessment of the effectiveness of such legislature. However, we admit that the UNDP guidelines only prepare the ground for assessment but fail to provide the methodology of evaluating the legislature.

In what seems as a step to address the shortfall of the organization's input in legislative needs assessment, it also provides indicators necessary for legislative development. The UNDP (2001) provides a methodological procedure in evaluating the legislature. It noted in clear terms that for any meaningful assessment of the legislature to be done, the assessor must settle for quantitative research design over qualitative method and also avoid the use of *yes/no* questions that do not facilitate tracking incremental change. Though the organization supports the combination of the two research designs by arguing that secondary data sourced from government official publications and extant literatures are required to supplement key stakeholder interviews.

Conclusively, the second attempt also abdicates in providing a direct toolkit. It only gives methodological directions to the prospective assessors. However, both models note the challenges of developing universally applicable standards against which to evaluate parliament. Perhaps, this gap may not be unconnected with the difficulty in providing a one-size-fits-all assessment toolkit. Staddon (2013, p. 130) recognized this notion on the ground that "assessment frameworks need to be flexible in order to be relevant across the range of parliamentary and democratic models, but this flexibility inherently leads to complications." To this end, despite the significance and relevance of the UNDP's models, it is not suffice to be adopted as measuring toolkit for the assessment of the effectiveness of the Nigerian National Assembly. Thus, the need for a specific toolkit arises.

The PC's Parliamentary Report Card and Related Indicators of Parliamentary Performance in the Budget Process

The Parliamentary Centre provides a comprehensive assessment toolkit in the form of Parliamentary Report Card which assesses parliamentary performance in four cardinal functions: legislation, oversight, representation, and the budget. The novelty of this toolkit can be seen from the perspective that it takes cognizance of all the duties of the legislature and evaluate them against five performance tests: the level and range of activity; openness and transparency; participation; accountability; and policy and program impact. The report card showing the indexes is shown in Table 6.1.

To adopt the report card assessment toolkit, the Parliamentary Centre developed a number of questions (that serves as indicators) on each of the four cardinal functions of the legislature against the performance tests indexes. The indicators are phrased in questions form with response scale of 0–5. The 0 scale shows that the performance indicator is not present at all, and 5 shows it is very strongly present with 2.5 showing it is somewhat present. The respondents are required to choose scale answers to all indicators while the assessor then tally the responses into the report card to come up with the effectiveness result. This according to WBI (2008) makes it to be a results-based management approach. However, this toolkit has been criticized on the ground that it is "too detailed and

Table 6.1 Parliamentary Report Card

Performance tests	*Legislation*	*Oversight*	*Representation*	*Budget*
Level and range of activity				
Openness and transparency				
Participation				
Accountability				
Policy and program impact				

Source WBI (2008)

too imprecise" thereby losing out on the major concerns of legislative effectiveness (Rotberg and Salahub 2013, p. 19).

Rotberg and Salahub's African Legislative Effectiveness Score Card

In the process of measuring democratic institutions' effectiveness in Africa, Rotberg and Salahub (2013) argued that most studies focused on the roles of the executive and political parties with less attention given to the legislature. Weak democracy is the major reason attributed to this trajectory. In view of this, the North-South Institute situated in Ottawa at its meeting in December, 2012 initiated the need to develop a simple score card capable of being adopted as a tool for measuring legislative effectiveness in Africa; thus, Rotberg and Salahub were commissioned for the task. The outcome of the research is the development of what we termed "Rotberg and Salahub's African Legislative Effectiveness Score Card."

The score card has three criteria used to design questions on the oversight functions of the legislature. These criteria are:

i. Level of Legislature's ability to interrogate the executive, compelling them to explain and justify their actions and inactions with the intent of enhancing accountability and transparency of governance.
ii. The extents at which the legislatures use their constitutional power of executive appointments confirmation to influence executive's actions, and to pass, delay, reject, or improve executive Bills.
iii. The audacity of the legislature to exercise the "power of the purse" to maintain oversight of governmental activities.

In pilot testing the score card, Rotberg and Salahub (2013) chose four African legislatures as cases: Ghana, Malawi, South Africa, and Zimbabwe. They asked legislators, journalists, academics, and observers in all the four countries how they perceived the effectiveness of their legislators using the three criteria. Premised on this, they developed a simple score card on "Measuring Legislative Effectiveness" which seeks to assess the legislature on the extent to which it performs its cardinal functions of oversight. As novel as this toolkit seems, it is not appropriate for our study largely because it is chiefly designed to assess legislative effectiveness on oversight functions; whereas, this study is strictly based on lawmaking function of the legislature.

Identifying the Gaps in Evaluating the Legislature in Nigeria

From the foregoing, this paper identified some gaps which include contradictions among scholars as to how and what method is the most appropriate and efficient in measuring legislative effectiveness. It also found out that there is no agreement on whether to assess individual legislators or the parliament as a whole in the attempt to determine the legislative effectiveness. In the Nigerian context, while we acknowledged the lofty scholarship efforts on the subject matter, it however observed that there is dearth of studies on the scientific assessment of the National Assembly using indicators and benchmarks that are generally acceptable. The paper observed that most of the scholars and practitioners (whose works were reviewed) who are interested in engaging the subject matter more often than not resulted in the argument that the peculiarity of the nature and dynamics of Nigerian government and politics do not allow the adoption or domestication of most of the toolkits, benchmarks, and indicators of measuring legislative effectiveness in the Nigerian National Assembly. Prominent among these is Staddon (2013).

While the effort of Ekor et al. (2014) is duly acknowledged in this regard, this paper attempts to bridge these gaps and contradictions by designing a model suitable for the specificity of the Nigerian government and politics which is used to scientifically assess the level of effectiveness of the National Assembly in performing its lawmaking function. It is hoped that the model will be useful for research validation and further research on the National Assembly and sub-national legislatures in Nigeria in particular and Africa in general. To this end, this research becomes imperative in contributing to scholarship on legislative studies especially in Nigeria and also to prompt policy makers especially the legislators in waking up to their responsibility.

Bridging the Gaps in Evaluating the Legislature in Nigeria: The Institutional Legislative Effectiveness Score (ILES)

Having identified and examined a number of assessment toolkits, this paper found solace in Volden and Wiseman's (2009, 2013) Legislative Effectiveness Score (LES) model to evaluating the legislature in Nigeria. Volden and Wiseman (2013) used the model to assess individual legislative effectiveness in the United States House of Representatives over eighteen Congresses. However, three limitations to the model regarding its usage by the proponents were acknowledged, which makes it directly inapplicable in the context of Nigeria. First, the LES model is used to assess individual legislative effectiveness and second, it is limited to one chamber (House of Representatives). Third, there are variables and information used in the model that is not readily available and applicable in Nigeria; for example, classification of Bills by significance.

Minding these limitations, we modified the model to come up with a new version christened "Institutional Legislative Effectiveness Score (ILES)" which is capable of assessing institutional effectiveness of both chambers in Nigeria's National Assembly. The ILES aggregates the variables/information of all individual legislators to stand for the chamber as a unit (i.e., the study calculates the ILES for each chamber). In doing this, four indicators of effectiveness were combined to form the single measuring toolkit (i.e., ILES Model). The first indicator considers how many Bills were read the first time regardless of whether they are executive or members' Bills. This is premised on three factors. One, the paper adopts institutionalism approach and not individualism approach. Two, Bill sponsorship is overlooked because it may come either as a member, executive, or concurrent Bill. Three, there are some sponsored Bills submitted to the Committees on Rules and Business which the sponsor(s) have no intention of passing other than for record purpose that they sponsored such Bills. Such Bills were never followed up and the Committees on Rules and Business never slate them for first reading. The second indicator considers Bills that were read the second time, debated and successfully committed to appropriate Committee(s). The third indicator considers Bills that receive action in both Standing Committee and the Committee of the Whole House. Finally, the fourth indicator considers Bills that successfully get out of the Committee of the Whole and were passed at the third reading.

This paper acknowledged the fact that the legislative cycle is incomplete until the passed Bill is signed into law either by the Executive President or through legislative veto as provided by the constitution. We deliberately ignore this section which could have formed our fifth indicator for two reasons. First, all Bills passed by each chamber must be transmitted to the other chamber for concurrence passage. Two, all Bills identically passed by both chambers are recorded as "passed Bills" for the two chambers and are forwarded as single Bill to the executive for assent. If signed into law, such becomes double entry as both chambers are entitled to the glory of passing such Bill and will be recorded as such. This can be technically problematic using such as a measuring indicator. In future studies of single chamber or unicameral legislature, the ILES will have five indicators. The model is specifically drawn to assess institutional legislative effectiveness as against that of Volden and Wiseman that assess individual legislative effectiveness. This is shown in Eqs. 6.1 and 6.2:

ILES Model

$$\mathrm{ILES}_{it} = \frac{\delta}{N} \tag{6.1}$$

where:

$$\delta = \left(\frac{\alpha \, 1\mathrm{st}\, R_{it}}{\alpha \sum_{j=1}^{N} 1\mathrm{st}\, R_{ej}} + \frac{\beta \, 2\mathrm{nd}\, R_{it}}{\beta \sum_{j=1}^{N} 2\mathrm{nd}\, R_{ej}} + \frac{\gamma \, 3\mathrm{rd}\, R_{it}}{\gamma \sum_{j=1}^{N} 3\mathrm{rd}\, R_{ej}} + \frac{\lambda \mathrm{PASS}_{it}}{\lambda \sum_{j=1}^{N} \mathrm{PASS}_{ej}} \right) \left(\frac{x}{N} \right) \tag{6.2}$$

and where:

- δ: value of numerator of the ILES
- α: is the weight assigned to Bills read the first time, i.e., 1
- β: is the weight assigned to Bills read the second time, i.e., 2
- γ: is the weight assigned to Bills read the third time, i.e., 4
- Λ: is the weight assigned to Bills read the third time, i.e., 8
- i: each chamber (i.e., House of Representatives or Senate)
- t: each Assembly (i.e., 4th, 5th, or 6th Assembly)
- e: all chambers under review
- j: all Assemblies
- ej: all chambers in all Assemblies

it: each chamber in each Assembly
N: number of indicators
x: number of Assemblies
$\sum_{j=1}^{N}$: the sum of Bills taking all variables into consideration.
1st$R$: Bills read the first time
2nd$R$: Bills read the second time
3rd$R$: Bills read the third time
PASS: Bills passed by the parliament for presidential assent.
Source Author's conception

The ILES for each chamber is calculated by dividing the cumulative value of δ with number of indicators. The wisdom behind this is to make the model flexible and amenable to change where the indicators are more than four (as used in this study). In addition, the overall weighting of $\frac{\delta}{N}$ will normalize the value of ILES to be greater than 0 but less than or equal to 1 as thus:

$$0 < \text{ILES} \leq 1$$

The assumption is that no matter the situation or circumstance prevailing in any democracy (where the legislature is under review), each indicator is a value greater or equal to 0 as thus:

$$n \geq 0$$

where n is one indicator and N is total number of indicators

The essence of this is to bring the model to situate under the basic rule of correlation co-efficient that the value of r is equal to or less than 1. This will make it possible for us to adopt "Measures of Agreement" to formulate standard and global benchmark to be used to ascertain the effectiveness level and interpretation of ILES result. On the other hand, δ is calculated by the four large fractioned terms, each representing one indicator. The value of δ represent the fraction of each chamber's (*it*) Bills read the first time (1), second time (2), third time (3) and passed (4) relative to x (all Assemblies) under review. The four terms (indicators) were weighted by $\alpha = 1, \beta = 2, \gamma = 4$ and $\lambda = 8$. These weights were chosen to reflect the view that advancing a Bill through the four stages becomes more difficult in progress from early stage to subsequent stages (as also done by Volden and Wiseman). The rule of weighting is premised on subsequent stage attracting twice value of previous stage. Thus, a chamber or Assembly that introduces large number of Bills but failed to push them through the legislative process will receive a relatively low ILES while the one that is able to advance its Bills to the last stage will receive high ILES.

There are number of features in the model that should be noted. First, the model is comparatively inclined with inverse relationship among the variables under comparison. The ILES of one Assembly is greatly determined by the output of other Assemblies in the fraction i.e., the higher the ILES of one Assembly the lower the ILES of others. The model reward hard-work especially at the later stage of the lawmaking process due to the weighting system. Second, the value of δ can be greater than 1 but the ILES value cannot be greater than 1 as a result of the normalizing factor. This makes the Measures of Agreement (benchmark) to be inevitable. Third, the model displays variation ranging from poorly ineffective to perfectly effective. The scores for the Assemblies under review can be situated within the measuring scale. Fourth, the ILES value can be subjected to a further large fraction especially when it is used to assess bicameral legislature. In this case, in order to be able to do a horizontal comparison i.e., comparing Assemblies by merging the two chambers of an Assembly as a single entity, Eq. 6.3 (which is a complementary model) is adopted:

Assembly Average ILES

$$x_i = \frac{\text{"HoR"ILES} + \text{"Sen"ILES}}{2} \tag{6.3}$$

where x_i is both chambers of an Assembly.

Source Author's conception

The ILES of the House of Representatives (depicted as "HoR"ILES) is summed up with the ILES of the Senate (depicted as "Sen"ILES) and the value is divided by 2 to find the average effectiveness score of the Assembly. The scores of all Assemblies are compared to know which is more effective than others. The average score is also used to plot line graph to see the effectiveness direction. Finally, whether the comparison is made horizontally or vertically, the variation in the scores can further be subjected to "*value of significance*" using t-test to examine the degree of significance. This will enable technical and in-depth understanding of the variation beyond the face values thereby assisting in easy identification of all variables that contribute to the effectiveness or otherwise of the legislature.

Legislative Effectiveness Benchmark (ILES's Measures of Agreement)

The significance of the ILES model will not be fully appreciated without a benchmark. The benchmark will enable us interpret both the ILES and its average to identify their places in the variation range. In light of this, an acceptable benchmark is inevitable. This paper drew its benchmark using "MeasureofAgreement." Historically, the first measure of agreement was proposed by Cohen (1960) known as "*kappa* measureofagreement." The *kappa* measures the proportion of agreement between two raters and serves as an adjustment for agreement by chance, as defined under independence. It employs the model of independence as a baseline to identify discrepancy if there is a significant difference between an observed cell count and corresponding expected cell count. k ranges from $-\infty \leq k \leq 1$. It equals 1 when there is complete agreement between raters but 0 when the observed and expected by chance alone amounts of agreement are equal. *Kappa* will be negative if the observed agreement is less than the chance agreement. However, it becomes positive if the observed agreement is greater than chance agreement. It is defined in terms of observed frequencies as:

***Kappa* Measure of Agreement**

$$k = \frac{N \sum fii - \sum ifi + f + i}{N^2 - \sum ifi + f + i} \tag{6.4}$$

Source Jolayemi (1990)

Over the years, scholars and statisticians such as Tanner and Young (1985) and Fleiss et al. (1969) have used and modified the *kappa* as a measure of agreement. Some also proposed other measures of agreement based on the specificity of their research (such as Jolayemi 1990). However, this paper need not build a new measure of agreement but rely on the one proposed by Jolayemi (1990) with a minor modification to its classification. Jolayemi (1990) denoted his measure of agreement by τ where $-1 < \tau < 1$ (i.e., τ is greater than -1 but less than 1) and defined as:

Jolayemi's Measure of Agreement

$$\tau = \frac{\sqrt{\lambda}}{(I-1)N} \tag{6.5}$$

where $\lambda = X^2$

Source Jolayemi (1990)

In his analysis, λ is an R^2-type statistic and X^2 is the value of Pearson's goodness-of-fit test statistic under the model of independence. His classification of agreement range from 'poor' to 'almost perfect' as follows:

$$|\tau| = \begin{cases} 0.00 - 0.20 & \text{Poor} \\ 0.21 - 0.40 & \text{Slight} \\ 0.41 - 0.60 & \text{Moderate} \\ 0.61 - 0.81 & \text{Substantial} \\ > 0.81 & \text{Almost perfect} \end{cases}$$

Relying on Jolayemi's (1990) R^2-type statistic and X^2 value of Pearson's goodness-of-fit test statistic under the model of independence, we modified the above classification to serve as our Legislative Effectiveness Benchmark as thus:

$$|\tau| = \begin{cases} 0.00 - 0.10 & \text{Poorly ineffective} \\ 0.11 - 0.20 & \text{Ineffective} \\ 0.21 - 0.40 & \text{Fairly effective} \\ 0.41 - 0.60 & \text{Effective} \\ 0.61 - 0.80 & \text{Substantially effective} \\ > 0.80 & \text{Perfectly effective} \end{cases}$$

Source Author's conception

The above benchmark is a result of several analyses. The ILES model is pilot-tested with numerous possible hypothetical data. The results were subjected to Jolayemi's model and the modification was done in line with the assumption of the ILES model and observed trajectory. The wisdom behind adopting Jolayemi's version among several others stems out of the fact that it suits the specificity of this research's design. For instance, the overall weighting of the value of ILES is greater than 0 but less than or equal to 1 (i.e. $0 < ILES \leq 1$) likewise that of Jolayemi where $-1 < \tau < 1$ (i.e., τ is greater than -1 but less than 1).

Adopting ILES to Evaluate the Legislative Effectiveness of the Nigerian National Assembly

In applying the ILES as an evaluating tool, information on all Bills between 1999 and 2011 spanning three legislative Assemblies were collected and all the Bills were tracked through the Bill progression report of the Committees on Rules and Business of the three Assemblies as well as the reports of the Clerks. A number of key issues were identified. First, a comparative analysis of the performances of the 4th, 5th, and 6th Assemblies in terms of Bills processing and passage was done. Second, using the ILES model, a directional graph (line chart) was plotted with the score to show the level and pattern of effectiveness of the three Assemblies. Finally, comparing both percentages on average over time (1999–2011) enables the research to identify the chamber that has more capacity in Bill pushing through the four stages (indicators). However, we recognized the fact that the indicator is not all-encompassing as it set aside other functions of the legislature that could have made up the assessment process. This will be tried in further studies.

Data Analysis

Evaluating the Lawmaking Effectiveness of the National Assembly: The ILES Model Approach

The ILES model is used to assess the lawmaking effectiveness of the 4th, 5th, and 6th National Assembly. It is pertinent to note that the model is not interested in the number of Bills received by each chamber, rather the number of Bills that passed through the legislative cycle. Hence, importance is attached to those Bills that go beyond mere receipt but were slated for legislative actions starting from the first reading stage to the final Bill passage stage. Table 6.2 shows the.

i. Senate

Out of the 250 Bills received by the 4th Senate, 227 Bills were read the first time. This shows that 23 Bills were never processed beyond receipt stage. In other words, the 23 Bills never made it to the floor of the Senate. However, out of the 227 Bills that passed through the first reading, 138 Bills scaled through and were read the second time. By implication, 89

Table 6.2 Summary presentation of Bills received and processed in the 4th, 5th, 6th, and 7th Senate

	Bills received	*Bills passed*	*% of Bills passed*	*Bills not passed*	*% of Bills not passed*
4th Assembly (1999–2003)	250	64	25.6	186	74.4
5th Assembly (2003–2007)	446	129	28.9	317	71.1
6th Assembly (2007–2011)	477	72	15.1	405	84.9
7th Assembly (2011–2015)	615	125	20.3	490	79.7

Source Author's computation with data from NILS, 2016

Bills were killed after the first reading and never made it beyond the first stage of the legislative cycle. During debates, Committee stage, public hearing (for controversial or of sufficient importance) and the Committee of the whole, 14 Bills were killed leaving 124 Bills to move to the third reading stage. However, only 64 Bills made it to the final stage and were passed by the 4th Senate. It is discovered that 3 Bills were voluntarily withdrawn by the sponsors out of all the 163 killed Bills. The assessment of the lawmaking effectiveness of the 5th Senate shows that 377 Bills were read the first time, out of the 446 Bills received. This shows that 69 Bills were never slated by the Senate Committee on Rules and Business for legislative actions. 270 Bills were read the second time and 222 Bills were read the third time signifying that 107 Bills and 48 Bills were killed during the second and third readings, respectively. Out of these, 11 Bills were withdrawn. However, only 129 Bills were passed out of the 222 Bills that made it to the final stage. This shows that 93 Bills were killed after the third reading.

The 6th Senate received 477 Bills and 463 Bills were read the first time. This shows that 14 Bills were not processed beyond the receipt stage. Almost half of the Bills read the first time never made it to the second stage as 228 Bills were killed after the first reading leaving the number of Bills read the second time to stand at 235 Bills. The same trend continued during the third reading as 140 Bills were read the third time. During these stages, 12 Bills were withdrawn by the sponsors and others were killed. The final stage was not exempted from the trend as only 72

Bills out of the 140 Bills were passed. This brings the total number of Bills killed to 379 Bills. Adding this to the 12 withdrawn Bills shows that 391 did not scale through the lawmaking cycle. The foregoing data is subjected to ILES analysis as shown in Fig. 6.1.

Subjecting these data to the ILES model as shown in Fig. 6.1, the 4th Senate scored 0.17 against the 0.32 effectiveness score of the 5th Senate, while the 6th Senate scored 0.26. The interpretation of the scores based on the modified Jolayemi's (1990) R^2-type statistic and X^2 value of Pearson's goodness-of-fit test (Measure of Agreement), shows that the 4th Senate was ineffective while both 5th and 6th Senate were fairly effective.

Senate

Assembly	4th	5th	6th
1st Reading	227	377	463
2nd Reading	138	270	235
3rd Reading	124	222	140
Passed	64	129	72

Assembly	**ILES (Effectiveness Score):**	**Interpretation:**
4th	0.17325348	*Ineffective*
5th	0.32190305	*Fairly Effective*
6th	0.2548435	*Fairly Effective*

Fig. 6.1 ILES analysis of the lawmaking effectiveness of the 4th, 5th, and 6th Senate (*Source* Author's computation with data from NILS, 2013, using ILES Model Application)

ii. House of Representatives

The 4th House of Representatives received 325 Bills, out of which 321 Bills were read the first time. This shows that only 4 Bills were never processed beyond receipt stage. However, out of the 321 Bills that passed through the first reading, 225 Bills scaled through and were read the second time, leaving the number of killed Bills at 96 Bills after the first reading. 248 Bills were read the third time showing that only 8 Bills were killed during debates, Committee stage, public hearing and the Committee of the Whole. However, more than half of the Bills read the third time were never passed as only 103 Bills made it to the final stage and were passed by the 4th House of Representatives. In all, 208 Bills were killed during the four stages and 10 Bills withdrawn by the sponsors totaling 218 Bills that never made it through the legislative cycle. The 5th House brought about a change in the lawmaking trajectory as all the 343 received Bills were read the first time. However, not all the Bills made it to the second stage as 256 Bills were read the second time making 87 Bills that were killed during the second reading. 248 Bills were read the third time showing that only 8 Bills were killed in the process. Out of the 248 Bills, only 168 Bills were passed signifying that 80 Bills were killed in during the final stage. From the 343 Bills received, 168 Bills were passed, 15 Bills withdrawn and 160 Bills killed. Therefore, 175 Bills were not passed during the 5th House of Representatives (Table 6.3).

Table 6.3 Summary presentation of Bills received and processed in the 4th, 5th, 6th, and 7th House of Representatives

	Bills received	*Bills passed*	*% of Bills passed*	*Bills not passed*	*% of Bills not passed*
4th Assembly (1999–2003)	325	103	31.7	222	68.3
5th Assembly (2003–2007)	343	168	49	175	51
6th Assembly (2007–2011)	503	152	30.2	351	69.8
7th Assembly (2011–2015)	792	192	24.2	600	75.8

Source Author's computation with data from NILS, 2016

The 6th House followed the same trend as obtained in the 5th House. All the 503 Bills received were slated for legislative actions by the House Committee on Business and Rules and were read the first time. Out of these Bills, only 377 Bills were read the second time. Some Bills were killed at the third stage as 301 Bills were read the third time. However, only 152 Bills were passed at the final stage. This shows that 351 Bills (comprising 7 withdrawn Bills and 344 killed Bills) were not passed during the lawmaking cycle of the 6th House. Figure 6.2 shows the ILES analysis of the lawmaking effectiveness of the House over the period under review:

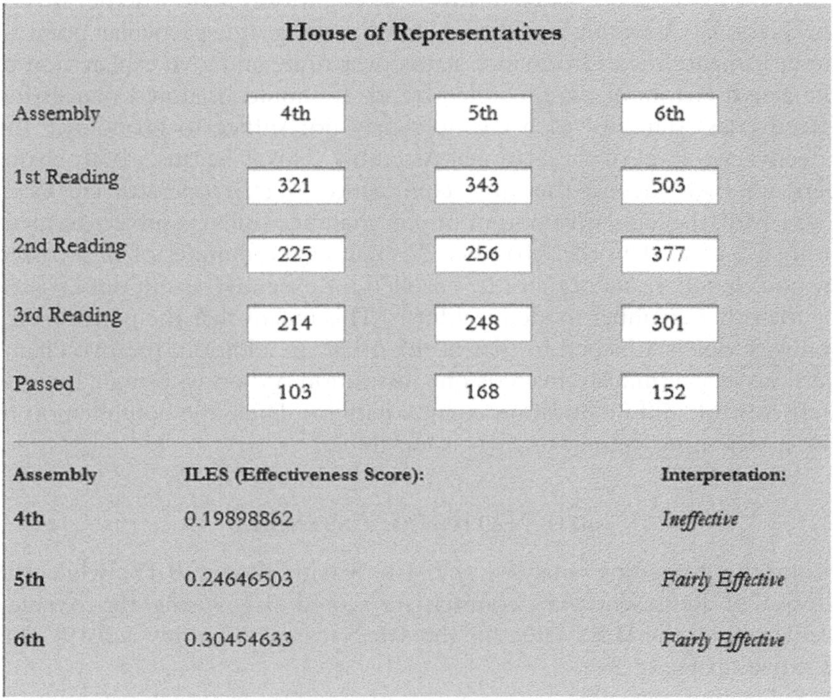

Fig. 6.2 ILES analysis of the lawmaking effectiveness of the 4th, 5th, and 6th House of Representatives (*Source* Author's computation with data from NILS, 2013, using ILES Model Application)

From Fig. 6.2, the 4th House scored 0.2 inferring that the Assembly was ineffective in lawmaking. The 5th House scored 0.25 and the 6th House earned 0.31, indicating that both Assemblies were fairly effective given the interpretation of the scores based Measure of Agreement.

Average ILES Analysis of the Lawmaking Effectiveness of the 4th, 5th, and 6th Assemblies

Having identified the effectiveness status of each chamber over the three Assemblies, we also need to find out the effectiveness status of each Assembly by combining the scores of the two chambers that made up each Assembly. The essence of this is to empirically state whether or not the National Assembly is effective in lawmaking at a particular point in time, compare the performance status over time; and give explanation of the causal factors of the identified trend. It should be noted that giving effectiveness status of each chamber may not suffice to pronounce the effectiveness level of the National Assembly. This is because, both chambers are two sides of the same coin. Since Nigeria operates bicameral legislature, the legislative output of one chamber (Bills) is subject to identical passage in the other chamber. No matter the number of Bills passed by one chamber, such cannot be enrolled for executive assent until passed by the other chamber in identical form. This means that the performance status of one is attached to that of the other. In addition, the two chambers are seen administratively as one institution operating a single budget, staff control, and identical procedural pattern. Thus, the combination of the scores using average analysis is inevitable.

4th National Assembly

From the foregoing analysis, the 4th Senate scored 0.17, while the House of Representatives counterpart scored 0.2. Using the Average ILES model, the ILES value for the 4th National Assembly is 0.19. This is shown in Fig. 6.3.

Subjecting the effectiveness score of the 4th National Assembly to our measure of agreement (benchmark) as can be seen from Fig. 6.3, we can empirically posit that the 4th National Assembly is ineffective in lawmaking.

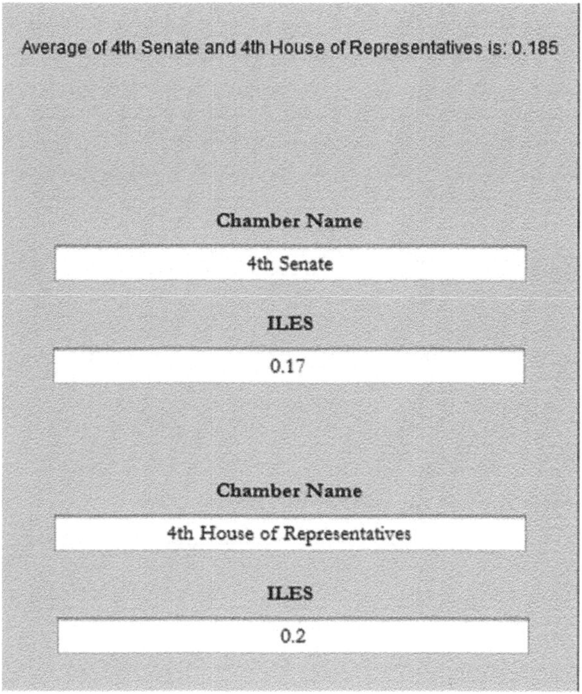

Fig. 6.3 Average ILES of 4th National Assembly (*Source* Author's computation with data from NILS, 2013, using ILES Model Application)

5th National Assembly

The Average ILES value of the 5th National Assembly is 0.29. While the Senate scored 0.32, the House of Representatives scored 0.25. This is shown in Fig. 6.4.

By interpretation based on our benchmark, we can empirically posit that the 5th National Assembly is fairly effective in lawmaking.

6th National Assembly

Going by the performances of the 6th Senate and House of Representatives, the 6th National Assembly earned 0.29 from the ILES of 0.26 and 0.31 of both chambers, respectively. This is shown in Fig. 6.5.

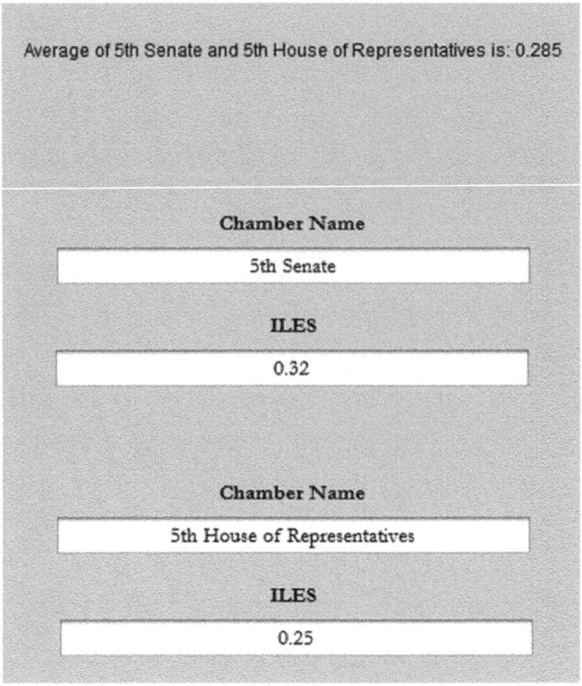

Fig. 6.4 Average ILES of 5th National Assembly (*Source* Author's computation with data from NILS, 2013, using ILES Model Application)

In view of the foregoing, the 6th National Assembly is fairly effective in lawmaking.

Aggregate Lawmaking Performance of the National Assembly (1999–2011)

In order to get the aggregate lawmaking performance of the National Assembly, the study finds the average score of the three Assemblies. This is shown below:

$$\frac{0.19 + 0.29 + 0.29}{3} = 0.27$$

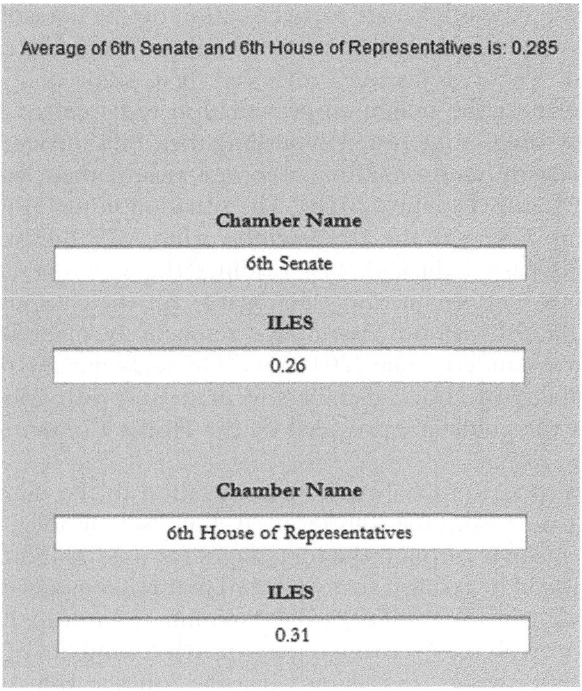

Fig. 6.5 Average ILES of 6th National Assembly (*Source* Author's computation with data from NILS, 2013, using ILES Model Application)

On a general perspective, we find the average effectiveness score of the National Assembly to be 0.27 for the period spanning 1999 to 2011. Situating this on the legislative effectiveness benchmark, the paper empirically posits that the National Assembly is ***fairly effective*** in lawmaking under the periods of study.

Discussion of Findings

Subjecting the gathered data to ILES analysis, the chapter discovered that not all received Bills were slated for legislative floor actions (which begin with first reading). For instance, the 4th Senate received 250 Bills out of which 227 Bills were read the first time. Out of the 446 Bills received by the 5th Senate, 377 Bills made it to the first reading and 463 out of 477

Bills received by the 6th Senate received action on the floor of the Senate. The study probed further with the lawmakers to identify the causal factors of this trend. Two reasons were advanced: first, some of the Bills initiated did not meet the minimum presentation requirement and second, some sponsors are not interested in pushing their Bills through the legislative cycle; only to have something recorded against their name to claim effectiveness status (Fadugba 2016). The situation in the House is somewhat different. Except in the 4th Assembly where 325 Bills were received and 321 Bills passed through first reading, the subsequent Assemblies recorded 100% performance in this regard. All the 343 and 503 Bills received in the 5th and 6th Assemblies, respectively, made it to the first reading stage. Akinderu-Fatai (2016) and Oritsegbumi (2016) attributed this to the ability of House members to draft Bills with good objectives and meeting the guidelines provided by the House Committee on Rules and Business.

The ILES model not only gives consideration to the number of Bills read the first time from the Bills received, but also considers the number of Bills that made it through the four stages (as used as indicators of the model). It should be recalled that we noted that ILES model reward hard-work with regard to the ability of the Assembly to push its Bills through the legislative cycle; thus, we found that the 4th Assemblies of both chambers were ineffective in lawmaking while the 5th and 6th Assemblies of both chambers were fairly effective. We also discovered that except in the 6th Senate, there is progressive increase in the ILES value from the 4th to 6th Assemblies of both chambers. The findings from the ILES model reveal that while there is progression in the lawmaking effectiveness of the House, the Senate recorded a different case. The 5th Assembly of the House is more effective than the 4th Assembly and the 6th Assembly out-performed the 5th Assembly. However, in the Senate, the 5th Assembly was more effective than the 4th Assembly but a decline in effectiveness was recorded as the 6th Assembly. Though, the number of Bills received is at an all time highest there was a geometric decline in lawmaking output which made the ILES to be lower. Figure 6.6 epitomizes these trajectories.

From Fig. 6.6, while there is a continuous ascension of lawmaking effectiveness of the House, the Senate increased from the 4th to 5th Assemblies before declining. This illustration shows that the House was more effective than the Senate in the 4th Assembly but the Senate was more effective in the 5th Assembly. The table was turned in the 6th

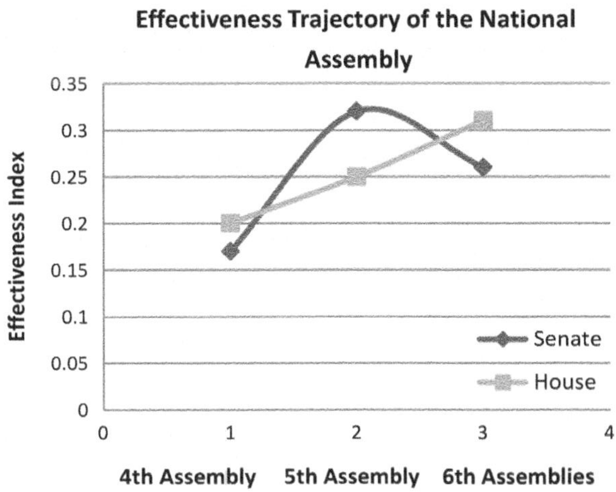

Fig. 6.6 Graphical presentation of the lawmaking effectiveness of the 4th, 5th, and 6th Assemblies by chambers (*Source* Author's computation with data from ILES calculation)

Assembly as the House reclaimed its spot at the top. In simple logic, this shows that the House is more effective than the Senate.

In addition, the second part of the ILES model which gives the average effectiveness status of the three National Assemblies shows that while the 4th National Assembly is ineffective in lawmaking, the 5th and 6th National Assemblies were fairly effective. This is graphically illustrated in Fig. 6.7.

From Fig. 6.7, the findings reveal that there is continuous growth in effectiveness status of the Nigerian legislature from the inception of the current republic. The effectiveness status increased from 0.2 to 0.25 and 0.31 for the three Assemblies, respectively.

Conclusion and Recommendations

The outcome of the assessment of the legislative effectiveness of the Nigerian National Assembly with reference to lawmaking function evidently shows that the performance output of the legislature is greatly influenced by the institutional framework and the political environment where the legislature is situated. In view of this, the study found that despite the

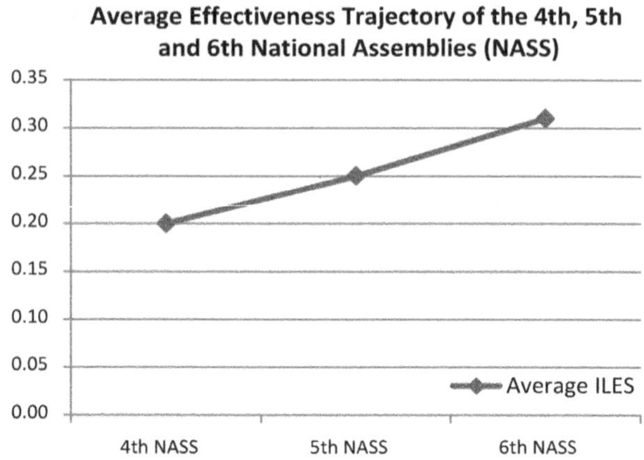

Fig. 6.7 Graphical illustration of the lawmaking effectiveness of the 4th, 5th, and 6th National Assemblies (*Source* Author's computation with data from Average ILES calculation)

myriad of challenges facing the legislature as identified in the work, it is fairly effective in lawmaking performance though with high prospects to perform better if certain steps are taken. There is need for more capacity building of the legislators through continuous training and re-orientation toward effective performance on Bill conceiving, legislative drafting and politics of Bill pushing. The necessity of this stems out of the gap between the number of Bills sponsored and number of Bills passed which shows that most legislators lack the ability and capacity to push through their Bills.

In addition, to solve the problem of the automatic death of Bills that are not passed at the end of the outgoing Assembly, we proposed that a mechanism should be put in place to ensure Bills continuity in the succeeding Assembly. For instance, if the sponsor(s) of a Bill does not return to the new Assembly, such Bill(s) should be collated and taken over by a designated personality created for that purpose. For example, a personality could be created to take charge perhaps, personified by the Majority Leader of the House/Senate who automatically becomes the sponsor of such Bills. However, such should not be counted for him/her as a person during assessment in order to prevent him from having undue advantage over others especially in ranking as suggested above. It should be recalled that we noted earlier that the outcome of this research cannot be generalized for overall assessment of the National Assembly. This is because the study only uses lawmaking function leaving out the other three cardinal functions (oversight, representation, and budgeting) for future research. Therefore, the conclusion that the Nigerian National Assembly is fairly effective is with regard to lawmaking function.

References

Adcock, R., & Collier, D. (2001). Measurement Validity: A Shared Standard for Qualitative and Quantitative Research. *American Political Science Review, 95*(3), 529–546.

Aiyede, E. R. (2006). Legislative Executive Relations in Nigeria's Democracy. In E. O. Ojo (Ed.), *Challenges of Sustainable Democracy in Nigeria*. Ibadan: John Archers Ltd.

Akinderu-Fatai, M. (2016). Interview with Hon. Moruf Akinderu-Fatai (Oshodi-Isolo Federal Constituency I, Lagos State), House Member (2007–2011) and Chairman, House Committee on Legislative Compliance (2011–2015) in his Oshodi, Lagos residence on February 18.

Alabi, M. O. A., & Fashagba, J. Y. (2010). The Legislature and Anti-corruption Crusade Under the Fourth Republic of Nigeria: Constitutional Imperatives and Practical Realities. *International Journal of Politics and Good Governance, 1*(1), 2 Quarter II.

Aldrich, J. H., & Rohde, D. W. (1997, April 10–13). *Balance of Power: Republican Party Leadership and the Committee System in the 104th House*. Paper Presented at the Annual Meeting of the Midwest Political Science Association, Chicago, IL.

Arnold, R. D. (1990). *The Logic of Congressional Action*. New Haven, CT: Yale University Press.

Barkan, J. D. (2010). Legislatures on the Rise? In L. Diamond & M. F. Plattner (Eds.), *Democratization in Africa: Progress and Retreat* (2nd ed., pp. 33–46). Baltimore: The John Hopkins University Press.

Bartels, L. M. (1991). Constituency Opinion and Congressional Policy Making: The Reagan Defense Build-Up. *The American Political Science Review, 85*(2), 457–474.

Bartels, L. M. (2000). Partisanship and Voting Behavior, 1952–1996. *American Journal of Political Science, 44*, 35–50.

Bello-Imam, I. B. (2004). The Legislature: Its Role, Performance, Problems and Prospect in Nigeria. In I. B. Bello-Imam & M. Obadan (Eds.), *Democratic Governance and Development Management in Nigeria's 4th republic, 1999-2003*. Ibadan: Centre for Local Government and Rural Development Studies.

Bosley, J. (2007, September). *A Review of Parliamentary Scorecards in Africa* (ACBF Working Paper No. 14). Available online at http://www.ansaafrica.net/uploads/documents/publications/ACBF_Working_Paper_14_Dec2007.pdf. Accessed on September 12, 2013.

Canes-Wrone, B., Brady, D. W., & Cogan, J. F. (2002). Out of Step, Out of Office: Electoral Accountability and House Members' Voting. *American Political Science Review, 96*(March), 127–140.

Carson, J. L., Koger, G., Lebo, M. J., & Young, E. (2010). The Electoral Costs of Party Loyalty in Congress. *American Journal of Political Science, 54*(3), 598–616.

Cohen, J. (1960). A Coefficient of Agreement for Nominal Scales. *Education Psychological Measurement, 20,* 37–46.

Cox, G., & McCubbins, M. (1993). *Legislative Leviathan: Party Government in the House*. Berkeley: University of California Press.

Cox, G., & McCubbins, M. (2005). *Setting the Agenda: Responsible Party Government in the US House of Representatives*. Cambridge: Cambridge University Press.

Cox, G. W., & William, C. T. (2008). Legislative Productivity in the 93rd-105th Congresses. *Legislative Studies Quarterly, 33*(4), 603–618.

Davies, A. E. (1996). Executive-Legislative Relations and Democratization During the Transition Programme. In A. Gboyega (Ed.), *Corruption and Democratization in Nigeria*. Ibadan: Agbo Areo Publishers.

Egwu, S. G. (2005). The Legislature in Nigeria's Fourth Republic. In A. T. Gana & Y. B. C. Omelle (Eds.), *Democratic Rebirth in Nigeria 1999-2003*. Princeton, NJ: Africa's Multimedia.

Ekor, M., Katz, M., & Iweala, O. (2014). Estimating Legislative Effectiveness in Nigeria. *Developing Country Studies, 4*(3), 69–77.

Erikson, R. S., & Wright, G. C. (2001). Voters, Candidates, and Issues in Congressional Elections. In L. C. Dodd & B. I. Oppenheimer (Eds.), *Congress Reconsidered* (7th ed., pp. 67–96). Washington, DC: CQ Press.

Fadugba, E. (2016). Interview with Ekundayo Fadugba, Senior Legislative Aide to Sen. Babajide Omoworare [Chairman, Senate Committee on Rules and Business (8th Assembly)] on July 25, 2016 at the Senate Wing of the National Assembly Complex, Abuja.

Fashagba, J. Y. (2010). The Committee System and Legislative Efficiency: The Case of Kwara State House of Assembly. *Nigeria Journal of Legislative Affairs, 3*(1& 2), 29–43.

Federal Republic of Nigeria. (1999). *Constitution of the Federal Republic of Nigeria*. Lagos: Federal Government Printer.

Fenno, R. F. (1978). *HomeStyle: House Members in Their Districts*. Boston: Little, Brown.

Fish, M. S. (2006). Stronger Legislatures, Stronger Democracies. *Journal of Democracy, 17*(1), 5–20. Available online at http://www.europarl.europa.eu/pdf/oppd/page_8/stronger_legislature_stronger_democracies.pdf. Accessed on March 13, 2014.

Fish, M. S., & Kroenig, M. (2006). *The Legislative Powers Survey and the Parliamentary Powers Index: A Global Study of the Powers of National Legislatures*. Berkeley: University of California.

Fish, S. M., & Kroenig, M. (2009). *The Handbook of National Legislatures: A Global Survey*. New York: Cambridge University Press.

Fleiss, J. L., Cohen, J., & Everitt, B. S. (1969). Large-sample Standard Errors of Kappa and Weighted Kappa. *Psychology Bulletin, 72*, 323–327.

Hubli, S. (2009). *Benchmarks and Standards for democratic Parliaments: An Emerging International Consensus?* A Paper delivered at the Joint IPU-ASGP meeting at Geneva, on October 22.

Ijaiya, G. (2010). Legislative Committees and Oversight Functions in Nigeria. *Nigerian Journal of Legislative Affairs, 3*(1&2), 159–169.

Inter-Parliamentary Union. (2011). *Legislative Principles for Development Effectiveness*. Available online at http://www.ipu.org/splz-e/busan11/principles.pdf. Accessed on July 14, 2013.

Inter-Parliamentary Union. (2016). *IPU PARLINE Database: Structure of Parliaments*. Available online at http://www.ipu.org. Accessed on October 25, 2015.

Ishaya, S. H. (2010). The Role and Challenges of Parliamentary Staff in a Nascent Democracy. *Nigerian Journal of Legislative Affairs, 3*(1&2), 170–180.

Jolayemi, E. T. (1990). On the Measure of Agreement Between Two Raters. *Biometrical Journal, 32*, 87–93.

Krehbiel, K. (1991). *Information and Legislative Organization*. Ann Arbor: University of Michigan Press.

Lafenwa, S. A. (2009, December 4–5). *The Legislature and the Challenges of Democratic Governance in Africa: The Nigerian Case*. A Draft Seminar Paper Prepared for Distribution at a Conference Organized by the Politics and International Studies (POLIS), Centre for African Studies, University of Leeds with assistance from EADI Working Group on Governance and Development on "Democratization in Africa: Retrospective and Future Prospects", at University of Leeds, Leeds, UK.

Mayhew, D. R. (1974). *Congress: The Electoral Connection*. New Haven: Yale University Press.

Miquel, G. P. I., & Snyder, J. M. (2006). Legislative Effectiveness and Legislative Careers. *Legislative Studies Quarterly, 31*(3), 347–381.

National Institute for Legislative Studies. (2013). *14 Years of Lawmaking in the Nigerian National Assembly, 1999-2013: An Analysis of Bills Processed*. Abuja: National Institute for Legislative Studies.

Ojagbohunmi, G. A. (2006, January 16–30). *Committees of the Legislature*. Paper Presented at a Training Workshop for Clerks-at-the-Table and Committee Clerks of the National Assembly held at Shiroro Hotel, Minna, Niger State.

Okoosi-Simbine, A. T. (2010). Understanding the Role and Challenges of the Legislature in the Fourth Republic: the Case of Oyo State House of Assembly. *Nigerian Journal of Legislative Affairs, 3*(1&2), 1–27.

Olaniyi, J. O. (2003). *Foundations of Public Policy Analysis*. Ibadan: Sunad Publishers Ltd.

Omotola, J. S. (2014). The Legislature in Democratic Theory: Nigeria in Comparative Perspective. In E. O. Ojo & J. S. Omotola (Eds.), *The Legislature and Governance in Nigeria*. Ibadan: John Archers Publishers Ltd.

Oritsegbumi, D. R. (2016). Interview with Hon. Daniel Reyenieju Oritsegbumi (5th, 6th, 7th and 8th House of Representatives, Warri South/Warri West Federal Constituency) on August 3, 2016 at his Official Office: Suite 0.16 House of Representative Wing, National Assembly Complex, Abuja.

Ostrom, E. (1990). *Governing the Commons: The Evolution of Institutions for Collective Action*. New York: Cambridge University.

Pareto, V. (1935 [1916]). *The Mind and Society*. New York: Harcourt.

Rohde, D. W. (1991). *Parties and Leaders in the Postreform House*. Chicago: University of Chicago Press.

Rotberg, R. I., & Salahub, J. E. (2013). *African Legislative Effectiveness*. The North-South Institute's Research Report. Available online at http://www.nsi-ins.ca/wp-content/uploads/2013/10/2013-African-Legislative-Effectiveness1.pdf. Accessed on December 13, 2017.

Saliu, H. A., & Muhammed, A. A. (2010). Exploring the Parliament. *Nigerian Journal of Legislative Affairs, 3*(1&2), 73–89.

Scott, W. R. (2004). Institutional Theory. In G. Ritzer (Ed.), *Encyclopedia of Social Theory*. Thousand Oaks, CA: Sage.

Selznick, P. (1949). *TVA and the Grass Roots: A Study in the Sociology of Formal Organization*. Berkeley: University of California Press.

Solomon, G. O. (2016). Interview with Sen. Ganiyu O. Solomon [Senate 6th and 7th (Minority Whip) Assemblies; House Member, 5th Assembly; Executive Chairman, Mushin Local Government, Lagos State (1999–2003)] in his Lagos residence on February 9.

Staddon, A. (2013). Benchmarking and Self-Assessment Frameworks for Democratic Parliaments. *Nigerian Journal of Legislative Affairs, 5*(2), 125–138.

Tanner, M. A., & Young, M. A. (1985). Modeling Agreement Among Raters. *Journal of American Statistics Association, 80*, 175–180.

UNDP. (2001). *Indicators for Legislative Development*. Available online at http://www.undp.org/governance/eventsites/LegislatureTechinques2001/indlegis.doc. Accessed on September 29, 2013.

UNDP. (2007). *Mid-Term Evaluation Report on Global Programme for Parliamentary Strengthening*. New York: UNDP.

UNDP. (1999). *How to Conduct a Legislative Needs Assessment*. Available online at http://magnet.undp.org/Docs/parliaments/How%20to%20conduct%20needs%20assessment.htm. Accessed on September 25, 2013.

USAID and SUNY-CLD. (2000). *Handbook on Legislative Strengthening*. Available online at http://www.usaid.gov/our_work/democracy_and_governance/publications/pdfs/pnacf632.pdf. Accessed on September 25, 2013.

Volden, C., & Wiseman, A. E. (2009). *Legislative Effectiveness in Congress*. Available online at https://my.vanderbilt.edu/alanwiseman/files/2011/08/LEP_webpage_090710.pdf. Accessed on July 13, 2013.

Volden, C., & Wiseman, A. E. (2013). *The Lawmakers*. Available online at http://polisci.emory.edu/home/cslpe/conference_2013/papers/Craig_Volden_Ch2_Ch4.pdf. Accessed on July 13, 2013.

Weissert, C. S. (1991a). Issue Salience and State Legislative Effectiveness. *Legislative Studies Quarterly, 16*(4), 509–520.

Weissert, C. S. (1991b). Determinants and Outcomes of State Legislative Effectiveness. *Social Science Quarterly, 72*(4), 797–806.

Wiseman, A. E., & Wright, J. R. (2008). The Legislative Median and Partisan Policy. *Journal of Theoretical Politics, 20*(1), 5–30.

World Bank Institute [WBI]. (2008). *Summary Report of Workshop on Legislative Benchmarks and Indicators*. Organized by WBI and Griffith University at Brisbane, Australia on September 21–24. Available online at https://www.agora-parl.org/sites/default/files/wbi_brisbane_workshop_on_legislative_benchmarks_and_indicators_-_summary_report.pdf. Accessed July November 1, 2017.

Zwingina, J. S. (2006). The Role of the Legislature in Democratic Governance: The Nigerian Experience. *Nigerian Journal of Legislative Affairs, 1*(1), 285–301.

CHAPTER 7

National Assembly as an Arena of Accountability Bargain: Issues, Challenges and Prospects

Gafar Idowu Ayodeji

Introduction

Globally, democratic political systems are typified by the presence of three separate arms of government—the legislature, the executive and the judiciary—whose existence is a *sine qua non* for the conduct of government business. This is because without legislative output the executive will be left with nothing to implement, while the judiciary will also virtually have nothing to interpret to guarantee the attainment of the rule of law (Jimoh 2015). Thus, the legislature as one of the basic structures of democratic political system is primarily charged with the functions of making laws, guaranteeing the maintenance of the political system and ensuring proper accountability in the conduct of government business.

G. I. Ayodeji (✉)
Department of Political Science, Tai Solarin University of Education, Ijagun, Ogun State, Nigeria
e-mail: ayodejigi@tasued.edu.ng

F. A. Aremu and A. R. Bakare (eds.), *Two Decades of Legislative Politics and Governance in Nigeria's National Assembly*,
https://doi.org/10.1007/978-981-33-4455-6_7

The regrettable military coup of 15 January 1966 truncated the civilian rule of the First Republic owing to political upheavals accentuated by unbridled corruption. Returning to civil rule in 1979, the leading political actors of the Nigerian state which comprised of the military and unrepentant political elites opted for the American presidential system over the previous British parliamentary model (Nyewusira and Nweke 2017). Notably, the presidential system of government is largely a function of meticulous adherence to the precepts of separation of power so it is no surprise that the legislature which at the federal level is referred to as the National Assembly (NASS) was first created in the 1979 Constitution and later duplicated in the succeeding 1987 and 1999 Constitutions (Nyewusira and Nweke 2017).

However, in spite of the accusation of corruption levied against the politicians in the First Republic, successive years of military rule were also characterised by poor economic management, rent-seeking tendencies and more importantly rampant corruption (Okonjo-Iweala 2007). Corruption, which is generally taken to mean the abuse of power or trust for self-interests (Akanbi 2004; Lipset and Lenz 2000) or deliberate distortion of standards of behaviour, legally, professionally and ethically either in private or public affairs (Oyebode 2002) remains a contemporary issue in the context of governance and attendant development.

Expectedly, since the rebirth of democracy in 1999 in Nigeria, one major focus of the National Assembly has been to provide necessary leadership in order to transform state institutions that have become decadent under past military regimes majorly due to corruption in government business and to put Nigeria on the path of democratic prosperity and good governance. This is so because the legislature is a vital arena which criss-crosses both vertical and horizontal accountability. This explains why the legislature or parliament of most nations has the constitutional mandate to watch over government and make it account for its actions and inactions (Stapenhurst et al. 2006). However, the performance of the Nigerian National Assembly in this direction has been a subject of intense debate, as claims and counterclaims continue to trail its performances, especially in the areas of acting as a watchdog which spans through accountability, legislations, investigations, oversights, appropriations and resolutions.

Thus, the main objective of this study is to ascertain the extent to which the Nigerian National Assembly has been able to perform one of its constitutionally assigned roles of ensuring accountability and curbing corruption in the Fourth Republic. This is with a view to identifying the factors responsible for the ineffectiveness of the National Assembly in curbing corruption the governance of Nigeria and determining if the National Assembly has prospects for improvement in the performance of its corruption fighting role in the governance of Nigeria.

The study is a mixed study which adopts a descriptive survey and relies on the thematic analysis of both primary and secondary data. Secondary data was gathered from journal articles, textbooks, newspapers and the internet. At the same time, a questionnaire was used as research instrument for sourcing primary data from a drawn sample size of 200 respondents among Ogun Central and Ogun East Senatorial Districts of Ogun state which were randomly selected. 200 copies of the questionnaire were distributed with the aid of 2 research assistants and 190 copies of the questionnaire were returned which represents 95% of the total responses generated. The research outcome is descriptively presented in the subsequent sections using statistical tools such as tables, frequency and percentage distribution.

Legislature as a Watchdog Against Corrupt Tendencies and Practices

The legislature is viewed as the branch of government with the outstanding purpose of the bringing into fruition the collective will of the people (Okoosi-Simbine 2010). In the opinion of Anyaebgunam (2000 cited in Oni 2013), the notion of legislature sums up the performance of the organ responsible for making, amending and repealing laws with a view to advance the interests of the citizenry. Stapenhurst, Ulrich and Strohal (2006, cited in Alabi and Fashagba 2010) ascertain that lawmaking, oversight function and representational roles are the three legislative tripods on which the legislative organ stands to fight against corruption in a democratic society. Furthermore, John Stuart Mill asserts that:

> The proper office of the legislature is to watch and control the government; to throw the light of publicity on its acts, to compel a full exposition and justification of all of them, which anyone considers questionable and; if the men who compose the government abuse their trust ... to expel them from office. (Anyaegbunam 2010, p. 25)

As reiterated by Muhammed (n.d) and Mathekga (2008), aside several functions performed by the legislature, two are most important and universal to all legislatures in all democracies of the world; these include the duty of lawmaking and that of acting as watchdog on behalf of the people they represent in order to ensure proper accountability.

The two positions or components of accountability enunciated by scholars like Bovens et al. (2010) and Ile and Makiva (2017) which are *active* accountability and *passive* accountability are relevant to this study. In the former case, accountability is conceived as a normative idea in which there are available set of standards for the assessment of the behaviour of public office holders, while in the latter case, accountability is viewed as an institutional relation or procedure whereby an actor or public office holder can be commanded to give account of his actions or conducts by a concerned authority.

As further noted by Pelizzo and Stapenhurst (2013) oversight cum watchdog efficacy and quality of democracy are interconnected. The degree of accountability of a political system signifies the extent to which the administration is responsible and can be penalised for its actions and inactions.

In the context of this study, there is a correlation between the level of watchdog role being played by the legislature and the extent to which the war against government's corrupt tendencies can be successfully fought. In most cases, legislatures, including the judiciary play crucial roles in keeping government accountable by capably performing their watchdog role. Where legislative bodies are more effectual watchdogs, especially in the areas of anti-corruption legislation and insistence on best practices, there are lesser tendencies for corrupt practices in governance and vice versa.

In the United States (US) where bicameral legislature reigns supreme like the Nigeria case, there are various standing committees and established bodies who serve as watchdogs to ensure probity and accountability in the conduct of government business. However, corruption appears to be inescapable in the US government's business, and this was evident in the results from the popular Gallup's Annual Governance poll conducted between 9 and 13 September 2015 and another survey (carried out by Transparency International (TI) in 2017. But in spite of the damning results of the foregoing surveys, facts from available literature indicate that the US Congress continuously make several efforts to fight corrupt practices. For instance, the establishment of Office of Congressional

Ethics, Committee on Oversight and Government Reform, Government Accountability Office (GAO) and the Office of Congressional Ethics (OCE) inter alia to serve as watchdogs and for accountability purposes to mention few (Georgetown University Library 2018).

In the same vein, the example of how the United Kingdom (UK) Parliament which comprises of House of Lords (Upper Chamber) and House of Commons (Lower Chamber) serve as watchdog is also relevant here. Although there is no formal written constitution or an organised single body formed for the purpose of serving as a watchdog over the affairs of the UK executive, there are numerous checks and balances that serve the exact purpose (Feikert-Ahalt 2017). For instance, ensuring the accountability of government ministers in United Kingdom started over the centuries through constitutional conventions, whereby, the primary convention allows for the watchdog of the executive by making government ministers accountable to the Parliament and the public for their actions (Feikert-Ahalt 2017). It must also be pointed out that at the heart of parliamentary watchdog of executive functions are select committees like the Public Accounts Committee of the British House of Commons (PAC) appointed by either Houses and assigned with a wide range of functions stated in the scope of the committee's review (Inter-Parliamentary Union 2007).

On the African experiences, the example of South Africa can also be relied on in depicting the impact of the role of the legislature as a watchdog. Manona (2015) stated that there is a widespread assumption in South Africa that Parliament is based on the ideals of democracy, accountability, transparency and accessibility even though there are still gaps and challenges as far as the oversight role of South African Parliament is concerned.

Constitutional Powers of the Nigerian National Assembly to Fight Corruption

It is edifying to note that Sections 4(2) and 3 of the 1999 Constitution of the Federal Republic of Nigeria (as amended) conferred the National Assembly with powers to make laws for the peace, order and good governance of the country regarding any matter included in the Exclusive legislative list and to make laws with respect to any matter in the Concurrent legislative list, and in respect of any other matter to which it is empowered to make laws in accordance with the provisions of the

Constitution (Alabi and Fashagba 2010; Faloore and Oyeleke 2016). The functions of legislators under the 1999 Constitution linked with curbing corruption and ensuring accountability are outlined as follows:

(i) making of law and formulation of policies;
(ii) oversight functions;
(iii) investigative functions, constituency responsibilities role; and
(iv) watchdog role over public funds (Faloore and Oyeleke 2016).

Aliu (2013) further emphasises that "the Nigerian legislature by virtue of its constitutional responsibilities is the principal institution of anti-corruption, accountability, and probity." Also, Chapter V of the 1999 Constitution of Nigeria (as amended) specifically makes provisions on legislative matters. Sections 52, 58, 59, 60, 62 and 63 deal with issues relating to the National Assembly powers, proper conducts and procedures to follow in ensuring accountability and serving as watchdog. Section 52 focuses on the declaration of assets, liabilities and oath of legislators. Section 58, on the other hand, stipulates the mode of exercising Federal Legislative power through lawmaking.

Also, by deliberate design, Chapter V, part E, Sections 80 to 89 deal generally with powers and control of the National Assembly over public funds. Section 88(2) (b) specifically empowers the National Assembly to "expose corruption, inefficiency or waste in the execution or administration of laws within its legislative competence and in the disbursement or administration of funds appropriated by it." In addition, Section 89 clearly empowers the National Assembly to summon, examine and investigate any person in Nigeria and cause evidence to be procured in the course of performing its legislative functions. From all indications, Sections 88 and 89 were promulgated to make the National Assembly the defender of anti-corruption fight. This was underscored in the verdict of the Supreme Court in A.G. Ondo State V. A.G. Federation and 35 others, where it was held that based on Sections 4(2) and 15(5) of the 1999 Constitution, as well as items 60a, 67 and 68 in the Exclusive legislative List of the said Constitution, the National Assembly is competent to legislate on corruption for the entire Federation (Onuigbo and Eme 2015).

As part of its efforts to curb corruption and enhance transparency and accountability in governance, the National Assembly has passed numerous anti-corruption Bills since the advent of the Fourth Republic—though not necessarily initiated by it. Some of the popular and major ones include the Independent Corrupt Practices (and other Related Offences) Commission (ICPC) Act, 2000, the Public Procurement Act 2007, the Economic and Financial Crimes Commission (EFCC) (Establishment) Act 2004, the Nigeria Extractive Industries Transparency Initiative Act 2007, The Fiscal Responsibility Act (FRA) 2007, Money Laundering (Prohibition) Act 2011 and Freedom of Information Act (FOIA) 2011, among others (Dan-Azumi 2012).

Summarily, and as shown in the views expressed by Ogbondah (2004), the watchdog function of the Nigerian National Assembly involves "investigating and unearthing the quantum levels of corruption, bribery, embezzlement, ineptitude, lack of accountability, graft and other nefarious practices inherent within the factions and fractions of the ruling civilian bourgeoisie."

An Assessment of the Performance of the National Assembly in Anti-corruption War in Nigeria's Fourth Republic

The prevalence of corruption in the governance of Nigeria despite the passage of the aforementioned anti-corruption Bills and their assent into law is raising some concerns among scholars and stakeholders. As noted by Ayoade (2011, cited in Onu 2014), corruption in Nigeria's governance has developed from an art and has reached the point of doctrine. Thus, the country has been weighed down by the challenge of prevailing corruption for decades to the extent that it has become institutionalised (Daloz 2002; Lewis 1996; Enweremadu 2012; Nyewusira and Nweke 2017).

Established cases of corruption under Obasanjo administration (1999–2007), who initiated and signed many anti-corruption Bills into law, were so numerous that some foreign diplomats submitted that Nigeria lost between $4 billion and $8 billion per annum to corruption during his eight-year reign as Nigerian president (Human Rights Watch 2007, cited in Ijewereme 2015).

The United Kingdom once disclosed that about $32 billion was looted through corruption during the six-year administration of Goodluck Jonathan (Oguntola and Earnest 2017). That is why Page (2018,

p. 1) asserted that corruption remains a singular impediment preventing the country from reaching its great potential and submitted that "the scope and complexity of corruption in Nigeria is immense."

Also, there have been startling revelations of corruption in the present Buhari administration. For instance the case of Abdulrasheed Maina, the presiding officer of the Pension Reform Task Team (PRTT) who in the process of carrying out a major reform of corrupted pension scheme looted N195 billion and accrued N100 million monthly from illegal transactions (Ojo 2016). Also, the arms deal scandal exposed top military officers and politicians who allegedly diverted about $2.1 billion earmarked for the purchase of arms to tackle Boko Haram and other insurgencies under former President Goodluck Jonathan's administration (Aondover 2018). Again, former petroleum minister, Mrs. Diezani Alison-Madueke bribed INEC officials with $115 million to secure victory for the PDP in the 2015 election (Page 2018) and supposedly diverted over $6 billion (N1.2 trillion) with the help of her allies (Ibekwe 2017; Stolen Asset Recovery Initiative 2018).

In the same vein, two Speakers of the House of Representatives were removed or forced to resign—Salisu Buhari was removed for certificate doctoring and forgery in 2000, while Patricia Etteh and her deputy Babangida Nguroje were removed for misappropriation of funds meant for the renovation of official residence and purchase of official cars in the tune of N628 million in 2007 (Lawrence 2017). Likewise, in 2000, two Senate Presidents, Pius Chuba Okadigbo and his Deputy, Haruna Abubakar were impeached for inflating an awarded contract and embezzling substantial funds purportedly expended on Christmas and Sallah gifts; ditto for the then Senate President, Adolphus Wabara, in 2005, who was also indicted for conspiring with Committee Chairmen of Senate and House of Representatives on Education to collect bribe totaling $458,333 from the representatives of Education Ministry.

The Former Federal Capital Territory Minister, Malam Nasir el-Rufai, in 2003 disclosed that some senators requested N54 million to pave way for his clearance for a ministerial position. Similarly, the former Central Bank Governor, Lamido Sanusi in 2010 claimed that NASS members consistently demanded bribes from Ministries, Departments and Agencies (MDAs) (Faloore and Oyeleke 2016).

Unlike in the past where acts of corruption were committed with impunity in the NASS and little was achieved in curbing it, the current Buhari administration appears not to be disposed to accepting any act of corruption from any government institution, including the National Assembly without the intervention of the EFCC and ICPC, and as a result it appears as if the corruption scandals in the 8th NASS have drastically reduced. However, the body language and disposition of the 8th National Assembly suggest that it does not only condone corruption in governance to some extent, but also wants to shield its members from prosecution for past and future misdeeds. For instance, the special court bill and other anti-corruption bills sent to it by the executive are lying unattended to fading away in the National Assembly.

Aside the foregoing, the National Assembly on three occasions refused to confirm Ibrahim Magu as the substantive EFCC Chairman, citing security reasons. Yet, it is believed that Magu's rejection can be linked to the travails of a significant number of Senators such as Godswill Akpabio, Jonah Jang, Aliyu Wamako, Stella Oduah, Theodore A. Orji, Danjuma Goje, Bukola Saraki, among others under EFCC investigation for various corrupt acts (Egbe 2018). The amendment of the Code of Conduct Bureau Act (CCB) and the Code of Conduct Tribunal Act (CCT) by the 8th NASS was totally condemned by Trade Union Congress (TUC) and Conference of Nigerian Political Parties (CNPP). In the amendment, National Assembly now determines who should be exempted from asset declaration. This amendment has been generally viewed as a self-serving attempt to sabotage the ongoing war against corruption, and to safeguard themselves from prosecution (Akowe and Omokhunu 2018).

Some scholars such as Eme and Onyishi (2014) believe that the NASS in the current political era has not been thorough and exemplary in its numerous investigative probes on the activities of government agencies as they have marred their good works with scandals, different fraudulent accounts and vendetta underdone. Such marred investigative hearings and probes include the National Integrated Power Project probe, the Pension Scam probe, the Securities and Exchange Commission (SEC) probe, the Oil Subsidy probe, the Bureau of Public Enterprises (BPE) probe, the Bureau of Public Employment probe, Ministry of Aviation probe, among others.

Akindele et al. (2012) also acknowledged legislative indisposition in the areas of the passage of the Freedom of Information Bill (FOI Bill); Money Laundering (Prevention and Prohibition) Bill (2017); and recently, the Sovereign Wealth Bill, Whistleblowers' Protection Bill (2016), Public Interest Disclosure and Witness Protection Bill (2017); Mutual Assistance in Criminal Matters Bill (2016); Proceed of Crime Bill (2017);

and the Nigerian Financial Intelligence Unit (NFIU) Bill (Bakare 2018). The Senate President, Dr. Bukola Saraki, also reviewed the activities of the Senate under his leadership and revealed that it was able to unravel high-level corruption in government (Elumoye 2018).

In spite of the foregoing gains of the National Assembly, it is evident from the avalanche of inundated analysis, reports and studies that the general perception is that National Assembly has been ineffectual in curbing corruption and ensuring accountability in governance. These point to the fact that incidences and allegations of corruption in the Nigerian National Assembly are interwoven, complex, sometimes discovered and on some occasions swept under the carpet.

Explanatory Framework

Institutional approach was adopted for this study's discourse mainly because of its descriptive and analytical potentials, especially with regard to the operations of the National Assembly as a legislative institution. Institutional approach remains part of the classical approaches ascribed to the works of early political thinkers like Plato, Aristotle, Hobbes, Locke, Rousseau, Montesquieu, among others who examined political phenomena in ancient times (Paki and Inokoba 2006).

Institutional approach is still relevant to modern scholarly study of most formidable political institutions, as it emphasises both their formal and structural aspects in relation to their processes. Van Dyke (1967, cited in Enemuo 2005) views an institution as "any persistent system of activities, or any pattern of group behaviour," and as "offices and agencies arranged in a hierarchy, each agency having certain functions and powers."

In essence, institutional approach considers functional aspects of political structures and concentrates on several governmental institutions, explaining their structures, organisation, duties and expected functions (Dyke 1967, p. 7; Ezeani 2010).

As a corollary from the foregoing, it is believed that the comprehension of the *modus operandi* of the legislature, and in this context the Nigerian NASS, is crucial to underscoring its quest to ensure accountability in governance through its watchdog role against corrupt practices in the governance of the country in the Fourth Republic. Ayodele (2004) buttresses that more than any other institution the legislature is "a core determinant of the character of the state." In the same vein, Ogunbiyi

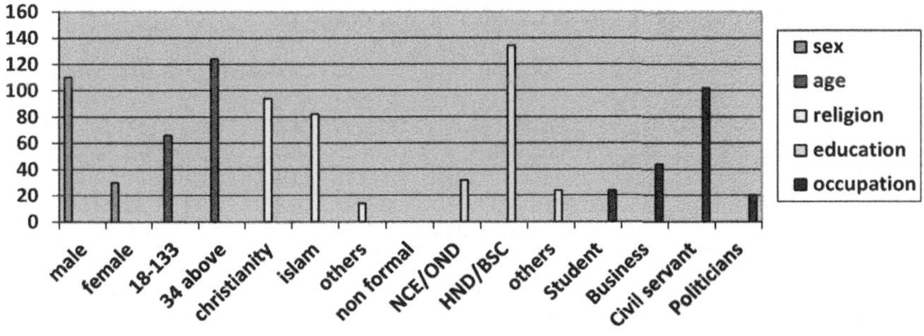

Fig. 7.1 Demographic characteristics of respondents

(2011) posits that "the state or level development of any country is strongly determined by capability of the legislature."

It is in this respect that the study adopts institutional approach to ascertain the extent to which the National Assembly has been able to carry out its watchdog role against corrupt tendencies and practices in governance in the Fourth Republic. However, the major drawback of the institutional approach has been identified to be its mere descriptive stance which on some occasions may appear unscientific. The study has, however, been able to make up for this shortcoming by combining it with survey research method so as to make its findings more acceptable; institutional approach takes care of the constitutional powers of the National Assembly to fight corruption, while survey method assesses how well the National Assembly has been able to fight corruption in governance since the advent of the Fourth Republic (Fig. 7.1).

Methodology Data Presentation and Analysis

Data displayed in Table 7.1, showed that 58% of the respondents were males while 42% of the respondents were females. Also, 35% of the respondents were between the age-bracket of 18–33 while 65% were 35 years and above. The religion spread of the respondents showed 49.5% as Christians and 43.2% as Muslims, while 14% of the respondents indicated no specific religion. Additionally, 0% of the respondents indicated no formal education, 16.9% of the respondents indicated that they possess NCE/OND and 70.5% reached the education level of HND/BSC, while 12.6% of the respondents claimed other higher levels of education. Lastly,

Table 7.1 Demographic characteristics of respondents

S/N	*Variables*	*Options*	*Frequencies*	*Percentage (%)*
1.	Sex	Male	110	58
		Female	80	42
			190	
2.	Age (in years)	18–33	66	35
		34 and above	124	65
			190	
3.	Religion	Christianity	94	49.5
		Islam	82	43.2
		Others	14	7.3
			190	
4.	Educational background	No formal education	0	0
		NCE/OND	32	16.9
		HND/BSC	134	70.5
		Others	24	12.6
			190	
5.	Occupation	Student	24	12.6
		Businessman/woman	44	23.2
		Civil/public servants	102	53.7
		Politicians	20	10.5
			190	

Source Field Research, 2018

in terms of occupation, 12.6% of the respondents were students, 23.2% were businessman/woman, 3.7% of the respondents were civil/public servants while 10.5% were politicians.

Data Analysis and Discussion of Findings

Objective 1: Determining the Extent Which the National Assembly Has Been Able to Ensure Accountability and Curb Corruption in Governance in Nigeria

As depicted in Table 7.2, the responses to the first item in the questionnaire shows that 187 (98.4%) respondents agreed that there is prevalence of corruption in governance in Nigeria, while 3 (1.6%) respondents disagreed. The larger percentage (98.4%) of the respondents' views tally with the arguments of scholars like Akanbi (2004), Daloz (2002), Alabi and Fashagba (2010), Enweremadu (2012), Aliu (2013), Ayoade (2011, cited in Onu 2014), Ojo (2016), Nyewusira and Nweke (2017) and Page

Table 7.2 Respondents' views on extent NASS has ensured accountability and curbed corruption in Nigeria

S/n	*Items/options*		
1.	Is corruption prevalent in governance in Nigeria?	Frequency	Percentage
	Yes	187	98.4
	No	3	1.6
	Total	190	100
2.	Are there adequate anti-corruption laws to ensure accountability and curb corruption in Nigeria?	Frequency	Percentage
	Yes	159	83.7
	No	31	16.3
	Total	190	100
3.	Is Nigerian NASS empowered constitutionally enough to ensure accountability and curb corruption in governance?	Frequency	Percentage
	Yes	125	65.7
	No	65	34.3
	Total	190	100
4.	Has the Nigerian NASS been able to ensure accountability and curb corruption in governance via watchdog and oversight functions?	Frequency	Percentage
	Yes	15	7.9
	No	175	92.1
	Total	190	100
5.	Is corruption prevalent in the Nigerian NASS?	Frequency	Percentage
	Yes	188	98.9
	No	2	1.1
	Total	190	100
6.	Does the usage of the Nigerian NASS by wrongdoers and corrupt officeholders as a shelter make corruption prevalent in the institution?	Frequency	Percentage
	Yes	101	53.2
	No	89	46.8
	Total	190	100
7.	Are the defective electoral process and conception of politics in terms of investment the cause of corruption in the NASS?	Frequency	Percentage
	Yes	141	74.2
	No	49	25.8
	Total	190	100
8.	Does inability to address the structural foundations of corruption in the larger society is the cause of corruption in the NASS?	Frequency	Percentage
	Yes	145	76.3
	No	45	23.7
	Total	190	100

(continued)

Table 7.2 (continued)

S/n	*Items/options*		
9.	Does gap in the 1999 Constitution cause corruption in the NASS?	Frequency	Percentage
	Yes	98	51.6
	No	82	48.4
	Total	190	100
10.	Do wealth materialistic drive and personality influence cause corruption in the NASS?	Frequency	Percentage
	Yes	182	95.8
	No	9	4.2
	Total	190	100
11.	Is there any prospect for the NASS overcoming its challenges?	Frequency	Percentage
	Yes	121	63.7
	No	69	36.3
	Total	190	100
12.	Will curbing corruption in the larger society influence NASS's quest to ensure accountability and curb corruption in governance?	Frequency	Percentage
	Yes	158	83.2
	No	64	16.8
	Total	190	100
13.	Will thorough background check on the prospective national legislators assist in curbing corruption in the NASS?	Frequency	Percentage
	Yes	168	88.4
	No	22	11.6
	Total	190	100
14.	Will the correction of the defect in the Constitution which allows NASS to fix its own salary and emoluments curb prevalent corruption in the NASS?	Frequency	Percentage
	Yes	117	61.6
	No	73	38.4
	Total	190	100
15.	If accountability mandate of the NASS is strengthened by following the recommendations, its ability to ensure accountability and fight corruption in governance will improve significantly	Frequency	Percentage
	Yes	167	87.9
	No	23	12.1
	Total	190	100

Source Author's Field Study, 2018

(2018) that corruption practices in Nigeria is endemic and has become institutionalised, a recurring decimal in public administration, and a major governance crisis as well as an impediment to nation's progress.

Items 2 and 3 are interrelated, in the sense that, while item 2 probes the adequacy of anti-corruption laws to curb corruption in the governance of Nigeria, item 3 queries the depth and strength of the NASS constitutional backing towards curbing corruption in governance. Findings on item 2 reveals that 159 (83.7%) respondents answered in the affirmative while 31(16.3%) respondents were opposed. Furthermore, responses to item 3 shows that 125 (65.7%) respondents believe that the National Assembly is adequately constitutionally empowered to ensure accountability and curb corruption in governance, while 65 (34.3%) of the respondents felt otherwise. The affirmative responses in both questions tallied with the line of thoughts of Onuigbo and Eme (2015), Alabi and Fashagba (2010) as well as the other scholarly works, hitherto, extensively reviewed under the segment of this paper tagged: Constitutional Powers of the Nigerian National Assembly to Fight Corruption.

Responses on item 4 which examines whether Nigerian NASS has been able to ensure accountability and curb corruption in governance via watchdog and oversight functions show that 175 (92.1%) respondents emphatically affirm Nigerian NASS failure to ensure accountability and curb corruption, while 15 (7.9%) respondents contrarily felt the NASS has tried to ensure accountability and curb corruption in governance via playing the watchdog role. The opinions of the majority of the respondents correspond with those of many scholars who have carried out related studies. The likes of Aliu (2013), Abegunde (2016), Ojo (2016), Ibekwe (2017), Usman (2017) and Aondover (2018) posit that the manifestations of corruption in MDAs such as the oil sector, defence, pension scheme, electoral institution, among others, attest to the fact that the NASS has failed in its oversight function to ensure accountability and curb corruption.

Similarly, Nwagwu (2014), buttresses that the legislature only functions as a mere alarm mechanism used for blackmailing or witch-hunting political opponents, extorting money from parastatals, departments and ministries under its supervision for selfish or for personal aggrandisement. In addition, the Civil Society Legislative Advocacy Centre (CISLAC) (2016) submits that "it is common knowledge that conflict of interest has impeded effective performance of the (Federal) legislators to discharge their mandates and uphold democratic values."

Item 5 which sought to determine whether corruption is prevalent in the Nigerian NASS showed majority of the respondents (98.9%) overwhelmingly agreeing that corruption is prevalent in the NASS with only 2 (1.1%) disagreeing. There is avalanche of scholarly literature testifying to the views of the majority of the respondents on the prevalence of corruption in the NASS. Akindele et al. (2012), Aliu (2013), Nwagwu (2014), Faloore and Oyeleke (2016), Obasanjo (2016), Lawrence (2017), Ameh et al. (2018), Yusuf et al. (2018) among others, reiterate that the NASS is a rotten den of corruption and the most corrupt government institutions.

Objective 2: Identifying Factors Responsible for the Ineffectiveness of the NASS in Curbing Corruption in the Governance of Nigeria

Item 6 queries whether the use of the NASS by some wrongdoers and corrupt officeholders as a shelter to cover up their past misdeeds makes corruption prevalent in the institution. Out of the 190 respondents whose opinions were sampled, 145 (76.3%) respondents agreed that the use of the NASS as a cover up shelter by wrongdoers and corrupt officeholders is responsible for the prevalence of corruption in the NASS while 45 (23.7%) said went against this notion. It would be recalled that on many different occasions, former President Olusegun Obasanjo (cited in Ndiribe et al. 2012) has stated that the NASS comprises rogues and criminals and held no hope for the country (*The Cable Online* 2016). This coming from a major political actor like him calls for concern.

No doubt, members of the NASS usually use it as a cover up for criminal or corruption allegations. In 2004, it was reported that a member of House of Representatives, Maurice Ibekwe (now late), had in 1992 defrauded a German businessman of $30 million and 5,000 Deutschmarks. His accomplice, Augunous Okoro is still standing trial (Faloore and Oyeleke 2016; Onanuga 2016). Also in 2017, a United States (US) Appeal Court upheld a ruling against Senator Buruji Kashamu on drug charges of heading a heroin trafficking cartel in the 1990s. He is being expected in the United States to face trial while his alleged co-offenders have been sentenced (Omohomhion 2018).

According to Isah (2018), twenty one senators had one time or the other faced criminal charges in courts or under serious investigation for corruption-related allegations. These include Bukola Saraki (Senate President), Ike Ekweremadu (Deputy Senate President), Ahmed Sanni Sani Yerima, Danjuma Goje, Alhaji Abdullahi Adamu, Abdulaziz Murtala

Nyako, Kashamu Buruji, Godswill Obot Akpabio, Bassy Akpan, Peter Nwaboshi, Dino Melaye, Magatakarda Wamakko, Rabiu Musa and David Mark, among others.

Joshua Chibi Dariye who was recently jailed 14 years (later reduced to 10 years) for criminal breach of trust and diversion of N1.62 billion ecological funds of Plateau state while serving as governor was reportedly still being paid N750,000 salary and N13.5 million monthly running cost from the NASS (Akinkuotu 2018). Also, another former governor of Plateau state and current member of the Senate, Jonah Jang was once released on bail for the alleged diversion of N6.3 billion public funds before he left office in 2015 (*Premium Times*, October 30, 2018).

Item 7 probed whether the defective electoral process and conception of politics in terms of investment is the cause of corruption in the NASS. A majority of 141 respondents, (74.2%) said yes while 49 (25.8%) respondents disagreed. As espoused by Alabi and Fashagba (2010), many NASS members won their seats through fraudulent means. Indeed how many members of the NASS can honestly deny being beneficiaries of vote buying culture, whereby, voters sell their votes to the highest bidder? This partly explains why majority of the federal legislators usually justify their salaries and allowances in spite of public outrage; like it was the case when Senator Sheu Sanni (Kaduna Central) revealed that senators take home the sum of N13.5 million per month as running cost, aside N750,000 as the consolidated monthly salary (Saludeen 2018). Also, the constituency project has been regarded as a conduit pipe by legislators to siphon public funds via padding of budgets. Consequently, the already compromised posture of legislators puts them in a difficult position to successfully legislate on anti-social behaviours like corruption (Alabi and Fashagba 2010).

According to Alabi and Fashagba (2010), the end-means relationship of politics also has a lot to do with persistent national legislative corruption in Nigeria. Most public and political office holders in Nigeria appear to follow the military's corruptive footprints. Consequently, any opportunity to hold any public office is viewed as an opportunity to amass wealth, referred to as sharing the national cake, instead of making sacrifices.

Theoretically, renowned scholars like Richard Joseph (1987, cited in Aliu 2013) assert that, office holders see government offices as prebends to be appropriated and used in generating material benefits. This explains why since the inception of the NASS in 1999, corrupt senators and representatives assigned to the so-called juicy committees that supervise high-budget ministries usually misuse watchdog roles, and even threaten ministers and their officials to turn down their budget/appropriation authorisation as trade-offs for kickbacks in cash or kind (Ejikeme 2014; Page 2018).

Two critical instances will be cited here to buttress the foregoing, starting with the probe into the virtual collapse of the capital market for two years running by the House Committee on Capital Market and Institutions. Instead of addressing the issue, the former Director-General of the Securities and Exchange Commission (SEC), Ms. Aruma Oteh (currently a Senator), questioned the credibility of the then Chairman of the House Committee, Mr. Herman Hembe to preside over the probe by revealing that Mr. Hembe had embarked on a fictitious NASS sponsored conference in Dominican Republic, and undermined his capacity to preside over the Committee by asking the SEC to contribute N39 million for the public hearing, and by demanding N5 million for himself to avert justice (Ejikeme 2014). Another instance is a litigation involving Farouk Lawan—Chairman, House of Representatives Ad Hoc Committee on the Monitoring of Fuel Subsidy—who was alleged to have been involved with other members in a bribery scandal of US$620,000 in the course of executing the statutory legislative oversight function on the N1.3 trillion fuel subsidy probe (Ejikeme 2014).

The focus of item 8 is on determining if the inability to address the structural foundations of corruption in the larger society is the cause of corruption in the NASS. To this end, 156 (82.1%) respondents agreed with this notion while 34 (17.9%) respondents disagreed. According to Nyewusira and Nweke (2017), the NASS, as a decisive institution of democracy has not been able to genuinely tackle the structural foundations of corruption that has essentially sustained the so-called "Nigerian factor." The "Nigerian factor" signifies the symbol for official corruption and institutional failure. The brazen display of wealth by the political class in terms of massive investments, state of art automobiles, luxury houses and acquired properties within and outside Nigeria is the accepted trend (Nyewusira and Nweke 2017). For instance, it was reported that Senator Dino Melaye owns a fleet of at least 28 luxury and antiquated cars worth billions of naira (Adebayo 2018). No wonder Aboyade (2010, cited in Nyewusira and Nweke 2017) portrayed NASS members as vampire elite, due to their penchant for corrupt practices.

Item 9 addresses the likelihood of the gap in the 1999 Constitution being a major cause of corruption in the NASS. To this end, 98 (51.6%)

answered affirmatively, while 82 (48.4%) disagreed. It is generally believed among the populace that the lacuna in the 1999 Constitution which empowers NASS to fix its own salary and emoluments is also the cause of persistent legislative corruption. Section 70 of the Constitution empowers the Revenue Mobilisation Allocation and Fiscal Commission (RMFAC) to approve the salaries and allowances of the legislators. However, it appears that the Commission lacks the political will to question the payment of the unauthorised salaries and allowances of the national legislators. That was why senators approved jumbo salaries and allowances for themselves under Peoples Democratic Party successive governments and this practice has been sustained till today.

Item 10 queries whether materialistic drive and personality influence cause corruption in the NASS. 182 respondents (95.8%) said yes, while 9 respondents (4.2%) said no. According to Ethelbert (2016), the wealth acquisitive drive and the quest for personality influence in the Nigerian society have also infiltrated the ranks of the NASS members. There is no doubt that many NASS members acquire wealth which translates to influence, recognition, honourary awards and chieftaincy titles, to the point of eschewing integrity, honesty and transparency (Lawrence 2017). Lawrence (2017) also explains that many political commentators and scholars in Nigeria usually refer to them as *legislooters*, and Waive (2016, cited in Lawrence 2017) traces the super wealthy status of Nigerian federal legislators to their use of state power and state treasury to feather their nests, Likewise, Zi and Benard (2013, cited in Lawrence 2017) observe that "wealth glorification has become part of contemporary Nigeria's tradition."

Summarily, the extant literature reviewed and deductions from observations on the research objectives reveal that the difficulties faced by the NASS in fighting corruption are caused by mutually inclusive factors, best classified as external—[(i) legislature's institutional chequered history; (ii) inability to address the structural foundations of corruption; (iii) gaps in the 1999 Constitution; (iv) wealth acquisition drive and personality influence; (v) general conception of politics as investment; (vi) improper emergence of NASS members]—and internal factors [(i) organisational character of Nigeria's legislature; and (ii) convenience of NASS as fortress for wrongdoers and looters].

Objective 3: Determining if NASS Has Prospects for Improvement in the Fight Against Corruption

Item 11 examines whether there are prospect for the NASS's overcoming its challenges. 121 (63.7%) respondents showed optimism by responding in the affirmative, while 69 (36.3%) respondents were pessimistic. Also, item 12 focuses on whether curbing corruption in the larger society will make the NASS task of ensuring accountability and curbing corruption easy, and responses to the item reveals that 158 (83.2%) respondents believe there is a link between curbing corruption in the larger society and a possible improvement in the NASS ability to curb corruption, while 64 (16.8%) respondents believe otherwise.

Furthermore, item 13 determines whether conducting a thorough background check on prospective legislators would assist in curbing corruption in the NASS. 168 (88.4%) respondents agreed with this notion while 22 (11.6%) respondents disagreed. Finally, Item 14 sought to know if the correction of a perceived defect in the 1999 Constitution that allows NASS to fix its own salary and emoluments would curb the prevalent corruption in the NASS. 117 respondents (61.6%) said yes while 73 respondents (38.4) felt otherwise.

The Way Forward

The majority of the respondents who believed that there is prospect for the NASS to overcome its challenges may be correct after all. Hindsight and personal observation of unfolding trends, show that corruption scandals that usually rocked and disturbed past NASS in the performance of their constitutional roles appear to have subsided in the 8th NASS—aside the intra/inter leadership tussle for relevance that bedevilled it at the advent of its inauguration. Also, there are expressions of great optimism among scholars and public analysts such as Alabi and Fashagba (2010) and Jimoh (2015), as well as from the majority of the respondents, that if NASS shows serious commitment and palpable wherewithal to anti-corruption fight through its oversight role, its prospect for effective performance in ensuring accountability and curbing corruption in Nigeria's governance will be enhanced. For better accountability as canvassed by Akinrinmade et al. (2013), NASS must at all times decontaminate and purge itself of members who by their acts put its credibility under threat. Part of the NASS challenges identified in this study is the lacunae in the 1999 Constitution which allows the NASS to fix its own outrageous remuneration. This is part of the reasons why many politicians result to foul means by viewing NASS membership as a do or die affair and as an avenue for personal aggrandisement. The jumbo remuneration and allowances should be revisited with necessary amendments made to reflect this. Revenue Mobilisation and Fiscal Commission (RMAFC) should be allowed to fix commensurate remuneration for the NASS.

Conclusion

As shown in the foregoing section, in spite of the enormous laws promulgated to instill accountability into governance in Nigeria via NASS's watchdog role, its performance in this area has left much to be desired. Thus, conflict of interests, deformed membership, defective electoral process and conception of politics in terms of investment, the structural foundations of corruption in the larger society, wealth accumulation and materialist drive and personality influence, among others, continue to weigh down the performance of the NASS, thus, inhibiting the institution from achieving its assigned role.

References

Abegunde, O. (2016). Legislature and Democratic Sustainability in Nigeria. *International Journal of Humanities & Social Science Studies (IJHSSS), III*(III), 226–235.

Achebe, C. (2011, January 15). Nigeria's Promise, Africa's Hope. *New York Times*. Retrieved from https://www.nytimes.com/2011/01/16/opinion/16achebe.html.

Ackerman, J. M. (2005, April 16). *Social Accountability in the Public Sector: A Conceptual Discussion*. Retrieved from http://documents.worldbank.org/curated/en/514581468134386783/Social-accountability-in-the-public-sector-a-conceptual-discussion.

Adebayo, H. (2018, September 8). I'm Entitled to My Privacy. Dino Melaye Reacts to *Premium Times* Report on N180 Million Car. Retrieved from https://www.premiumtimesng.com/news/headlines/212317-dino-melaye-reacts-to-premium-times-report-on-n180-million-car.html.

Akindele, S. T., Adeyemi, O. O., & Aluko, O. A. (2012). Democracy, Governance, Legislative Challenges and Impediments in Nigeria, 1999–2011. *Journal of Politics and Law, 5*(2), 175–187.

Akinkuotu, E. (2018, December 11). *Senate Pays Dariye N85.5m Allowances in Prison*. Retrieved from https://punchng.com/senate-pays-dariye-N85-5m-allowances-in-prison/.

Akinrinmade, G. O., Osifeso, B. Y., Kolawole, A. A., Johnson-Odukoya, A. O., & Ayanleye, O. A. (2013). An Assessment of the Role of the National Assembly in the Fight Against Corruption in Nigeria. *Proceedings of the 46th Annual Conference of the Nigerian Association of Law Teachers*, pp. 429–447.

Akowe, T., & Omokhunu, G. (2018, October 31). *More Knocks for Senate on CCB/CCT Act Amendment*. Retrieved from http://thenationonlineng.net/more-knocks-for-senate-on-ccb-cctact-amendment/.

Alabi, M. O. A., & Fashagba, J. Y. (2010). The Legislative and Anti-corruption Crusade Under the Fourth Republic of Nigeria: Constitutional Imperatives and Practices Realities. *International Journal of Politics and Good Governance, 1*(1–2), 1–39.

Albert, I. O. (2005). Explaining 'Godfatherism' in Nigerian Politics. *African Sociological Review*, *9*(2), 79–105.

Akanbi, M. (2004). Corruption, Accountability and Good Governance. In H. A. Saliu (Ed.), *Nigeria Under Democratic Rule, 1999–2003*. Ibadan: University Press PLC.

Aliu, M. (2013). Legislative Corruption and Democratic Consolidation in the Nigerian Fourth Republic. *Journal of Sustainable Development in Africa, 15*(6), 101–112.

Ameh, J., Adetayo, O., & Baiyewu, L. (2018, May 29). National Assembly Members Notorious for Bribe Taking-Jega. *Punch* Online. Retrieved from https://www.punch.com/nassassembly-members-notorious-for-bribe-taking-jega/.

Anyaegbunam, E. O. (2010). *The Legislations Companion: A Handbook for the National Assembly, State House of Assembly and Local Government Legislative Council*. Ibadan: Bookbinders.

Aondover, M. E. (2018). A Comparative Content Analysis of the Coverage of Arms Deal Scandal in Three Nigerian Newspapers. *Journal of Communication and Media Research, 10*(1), 28–37.

Ayodele, B. (2004). Institutional Development and Democratic Consolidation in the Nigeria Fourth Republic. In K. Ajayi & B. Ayodele (Eds.), *Perspectives on Democracy and Development in Post-military Nigeria*. Ibadan: Julius & Julius Associates.

Bakare, W. (2018). Senate and the Anti-corruption Fight. *The Guardian* Online. Retrieved 33 March 2018, from https://guardian.ng/sunday-magazine/senate-and-the-anti-corruption-fight/.

Blind, P. K. (2011). Accountability in Public Service Delivery: A Multidisciplinary Review of the Concept. *Prepared for the Expert Group Meeting Engaging Citizens to Enhance Public Sector Accountability and Prevent Corruption in the*

Delivery of Public Services. Retrieved from http://unpan1.un.org/intradoc/groups/public/documents/un-dpadm/unpan046363.pdf.

Bovens, M. T., Schillemans, T., & Goodin, R. E. (2010). Public Accountability. In M. T. Bovens, R. E. Goodin & T. Schillemans (Eds.), *The Oxford Handbook of Public Management* (pp. 1–22). Oxford: Oxford University Press.

Clarke, R. (2018, October 15). The Citadel of Corruption is in NASS, Says Robert Clarke. *Channels Television Online*. Retrieved from www.channelstv.com/2018/10/15/the-citadel-of-corruption-is-in-nass-says-robert-clarke/.

Daloz, J. P. (2002). *Elites et représentations politiques: La culture de l' échange inégal au Nigeria*. Pessac: Presses Universitaires de Bordeaux.

Dan-Azumi, J. D. (2012). Keylegislations in Nigeria, 1999–2015: Potentials for Impact and Challenges. *Nigerian Journal of Legislative Affairs (NJLA), 7*(2), 1–20.

Dowdle, M. W. (2006). *Public Accountability: Designs and Dilemmas, and Experience*. Cambridge: Cambridge University Press.

Dugan, A. (2015). Majority of Americans See Congress as Out of Touch, Corrupt. *Gallup*. Retrieved from https://news.gallup.com/poll/185918/majority-americans-congress-touch-corrupt.aspx.

Dyke, V. V. (1967). *Political Science: A Philosophical Analysis*. Standford: Standford University Press.

Egbe, R. (2018). Magu's Confirmation Battle. *The Nation* Online. Retrieved from http://thenationonlineng.net/magus-confirmation-battle/.

Ejikeme, J. N. (2014). Legislative Oversight in Nigeria: A Watchdog or a Hunting Dog. *Journal of Law, Policy and Globalization, 22*, 16–24.

Elumoye, D. (2018). Saraki: Senate Exposed High Level Corruption in Govt. *This Day* Online. Retrieved from https://www.thisdaylive.com/index.php/2018/06/11/saraki-senate-exposed-high-level-corruption-in-govt/.

Eme, O. I., & Onyishi, T. A. (2014). The Legislature and Anti-corruption Crusade Under Nigeria's Fourth Republic, 1999–2013. *Mediterranean Journal of Social Sciences, 5*(15), 28–36.

Enemuo, F. (2005). Approaches and Methods to the Study of Politics. In R. Anifowose & F. Enemuo (Eds.), *Elements of politics*. Lagos: Sam Iroanusi Publication.

Enweremadu, D. U. (2012). Anti-corruption Campaign in Nigeria (1999–2007): The Politics of a Failed Reform. *West African Politics and Society Series, 1*, 1–218. Retrieved from https://openaccess.leidenuniv.nl/bitstream/handle/1887/.../asc-075287668-3254-01.pdf.

Ewuim, N. C., Nnamani, D. O., & Eberinwa, O. M. (2014). Legislative Oversight and Good Governance in Nigeria National Assembly: An Analysis of Obasanjo and Jonathan's Administration. *Review of Public Administration and Management, 3*(6), 140–153.

Ezea, S. (2011, May 21). How the National Assembly Members Squander Nigerian Resources. *The Guardian*, Saturday, p. 54.

Ezeani, E. (2010). *Political Science: An Introduction*. Abakaliki: Willy Rose & Appleseed Publishing co.

Faloore, O. O., & Oyeleke, I. O. (2016). Legislative Corruption and the Challenges of Democratic Consolidation in Nigeria. *Applied Scientific Reports, 14*(3), 230–236.

Feikert-Ahalt, C. (2017). *Parliamentary Oversight of the Executive Branch: United Kingdom*. The Library of Congress. Retrieved from https://www.loc.gov/law/help/parliamentary-oversight/unitedkingdom.php.

Frink, D. D., & Klimoski, R. J. (2004). *Advancing Accountability Theory and Practice: Introduction to the Human Resource Management Review Special Edition. Human Resource Management Review, 14*(1), 1–17.

Georgetown University Library. (2018). *Guides: Congressional Information: Government Accountability Office*. Retrieved from https://guides.library.georgetown.edu/c.php?g=75524&p=4847150.

Government Accountability Office (GAO). (2017, September 19). *About GAO*. Retrieved from https://www.gao.gov/mobile/about.

Ibekwe, N. (2017, November 17). *Alleged Corruption: I'm Ready to Go to Jail-Ex-Minister Diezani Alison-Madueke*. Retrieved from www.premiumtimesng.com/news/headlines237045-alleged-corruption-im-ready-to-go-to-jail-ex-minister-diezani-alison-madueke.html.

Ijewereme, O. B. (2015). Anatomy of Corruption in the Nigerian public Sector: Theoretical Perspectives and Some Empirical Explanations. *Sage Open*. https://doi.org/10.1177/2158244015581188.

Ile, I. U., & Makiva, M. (2017). Monitoring Legislative Oversight and Accountability for Sector Based Transformation in South Africa: A Petroleum Downstream Perspective. *African Journal of Public Affairs, 9*(6), 12–24.

Inter-Parliamentary Union. (2007). *Tools for Parliamentary Oversight: A Comparative Study of 88 National Parliaments*. Retrieved from http://www.ipu.org.

Isah, A. Y. (2018, May 17). *8th Senate and Harvest of Corruption Cases*. Retrieved from https://leadership.ng/2018/05/17/8th-senate-and-harvest-of-corruption-cases/.

Jimoh, A. (2015). *What the New Legislators Must Understand*. Civil Society and Legislative Advocacy Centre. Retrieved from http://cislacnigeria.net/what-the-new-legislators-must-understand/.

Jimoh, A. M. (2017). Retooling National Assembly for Probity, Accountability. *The Guardian*. Retrieved from https://guardian.ng/politics/retooling-national-assembly-for-probity-accountability/.

Joshua, S., & Oni, S. (2014). The Nigerian House of Representatives and Corruption (1999–2011). *Mediterranean Journal of Social Sciences, 5*(2), 561–567.

Kennedy, L. (2017). *Congress Tries to Kill Independent Ethics Watchdog, Americans Fight Back*. Centre for American Progress. Retrieved from https://www.americanprogress.org/issues/democracy/news/2017/01/04/295846/congress-tries-to-kill-independent-ethics-watchdog-americans-fight-back/.

Lawrence, E. O. (2017). A Critical Assessment of Corruption Within the Legislature in Nigeria. *International Journal of Scientific and Research Publications, 7*(1), 220–232.

Lewis, M. P. (1996). From Prebendalism to Predation: Political Economy of Decline in Nigeria. *Journal of Modern African Studies, 34*(1), 79–103.

Lipset, S. M., & Lenz, G. S. (Eds.). (2000). *Corruption, Culture and Markets*. New York: Basic Books.

Manona, W. W. (2015). Critical Analysis of the Oversight Role of the Education Portfolio Committee in Parliament of South Africa. *Africa's Public Service Delivery & Performance Review, 3*(3), 72–94.

Mathekga, R. (2008). The ANC "Leadership Crisis" and the Age of Population in Post-Apartheid South Africa. In J. Praetorian's (Ed.), *Africa Politics: Beyond the Third Wave of Democratization*. Cape Town: Juta and Co Ltd.

Mosher, F. C. (1979). *The GAO: The Quest for Accountability in American Government*. Boulder, CO: Westview Press, no p.

Mudasiru, S. O. (n.d). *The Legislature and the Political Economy of Corruption in Nigeria*. Retrieved from http://www.academix.ng/documents/papers/1449057569_5387.pdf.

Muhammad, A. (n.d.). *Legislative Corruption and the Challenge of Democratic Sustenance in Nigeria, 1999–2007*. Retrieved from http://docs.google.com/views/a:$9=cache:ixUMJAal8j:www.unilorin on 8 August 2012.

Ndiribe, O., Umoru, H., Shaibu, I., & Ovuakporie, E. (2012, May 24). Nigeria: Senators, Representatives Blast Obasanjo. Vanguard Newspaper Online. Retrieved from https://allafrica.com/stories/201205250076.html.

Nna, N. J., & Jacob, O. A. (2012). The Institutional Approach to Anti-graft Crusade: The Case of Independent Corrupt Practices Commission in Nigeria. *African Journal of Social Sciences, 2*(1), 116–129.

Nwagwu, E. J. (2014). Legislative Oversight in Nigeria: A Watchdog or a Hunting Dog? *Journal of Law, Policy and Globalisation, 22*, 16–24.

Nwaubani, O. O. (2014). The Legislature and Democracy in Nigeria, (1960–2003): History, Constitutional Role and Prospects. *Research on Humanities and Social Sciences, 4*(15), 81–90.

Nyewusira, V., & Nweke, K. (2017). Anti-corruption Crusade in Nigeria: An Assessment of the Disposition of the National Assembly (1999–2013). *Mediterranean Journal of Social Sciences, 8*(4 S1), 194–204.

Odinga, R. (1994). Parliamentarians and Corruption and Human Right in AFL Summary Report of Seminar Organised by Africa Leadership Forum in Entebbe Uganda December 12–14, pp. 119–124.

Ogbondah, C. W. (2004). State-Press Relations in Contemporary Nigeria. In I. B. Bello-Imam & M. I. Obadan (Eds.), *Democratic Governance and Development Management in Nigeria's Fourth Republic* (pp. 1999–2003). Ibadan: JODAD Publishers.

Ogunbiyi, K. (2011, April 16). A Divided Legislature. *Thisday*, p. 34.

Oguntola, T., & Earnest, N. (2017, December, 12). Nigeria Lost $32bn to Corruption Under Jonathan—UK. *Leadership Newspaper*. Retrieved from https://leadership.ng/2017/12/12/nigeria-lost-32bn-to-corruption-jonathan-uk.

Ojo, S. (2016). Looting the Looters: The Paradox of Anti-corruption Crusades in Nigeria's Fourth Republic (1999–2014). *Canadian Social Science, 12*(9), 1–20.

Okonjo-Iweala, N. (2007). The State of Economic Reforms in Nigeria. *Panel Discussion Proceeding*, 6. Washington, DC.

Okoosi-Simbine, A. T. (2010). Understanding the Role and Challenges of the Legislature in the Fourth Republic: The Case of Oyo State House of Assembly. *Nigeria Journal of Legislative Affairs, 3*(1–3), 1–27.

Omohomhion, F. (2018, December 22). NDLEA Insists Kashamu Wanted in America over Alleged Importation of 6.6 kg Heroin. *Business Day* Online. Retrieved from https://www.businessayonline.com/news/article/ndlea-insists-kashamu-wanted-in-america-over-alleged-importation-of-6-6kg-heroin/.

Onanuga, A. (2016, August 19). How Maurice Ibekwe Defrauded German of $30 m-Forensic Expert. *The Nation* Online. Retrieved from http://thenationonlineng.net/how-maurice-ibekwe-defrauded-german-of-$30m-forensic-expert/.

Oni, S. (2013) *Legislative-Executive Relations in Nigeria in the Presidential System: A Study of Lagos and Ogun States, Nigeria, (1999–2011)* (Unpublished PhD Thesis), Department of Political Science and International Relations, Covenant University, Ota.

Onu, F. O. (2014). The Socio-cultural Dimension of Corruption in Nigeria: A Managerial Reflection. *International Journal of Economics, Commerce and Management, 2*(2), 1–6.

Onuigbo, R. A., & Eme, O. I. (2015). Analyses of Legal Frameworks for Fighting Corruption in Nigeria: Problems and Challenges. *Kuwait Chapter of Arabian Journal of Business and Management Review, 5*(3), 1–33.

Onwe, S. O., Ibeogu, A. S., & Nkwede, J. O. (2015). Imperatives of Legislative Oversight Function in Nigerian Democratic System. *Research on Humanities and Social Sciences, 5*(4), 72–79.

Oyebode, A. (Ed.). (2002). *The Anti-corruption Act: A Necessary Instrument for Growth of Our Nascent Democracy*. Ilorin: The Law Society, University of Ilorin.

Page, M. T. (2018, May 15). *A New Taxonomy for Corruption in Nigeria*. Carnegie Endowment for International Peace. Retrieved from https://carnegieendowment.org/2018/07/17/new-taxonomy-for-corruption-in-nigeria-pub-76811r.

Paki, F., & Inokoba, P. (2006). *An Invitation to Political Science*. Port Harcourt: Kemuela Publishers.

Transparency International. (2017). *Survey: Corruption in the USA: The Difference a Year Makes. New Public Opinion Survey Compares 2017 with 2016*. Retrieved fromhttps://www.transparency.org/news/feature/corruption_in_the_usa_the_difference_a_year_makes.

Pelizzo, R. (2014). *Democracy, Accountability and Parliaments*. Retrieved from https://ssrn.com/abstract=2492938, 12 May 2018.

Pelizzo, R., & Stapenhurst, F. (2012). *Parliamentary Oversight Tools*. London: Routledge.

Pelizzo, R., & Stapenhurst, F. (2013). *Government Accountability and Legislative Oversight*. New York: Routledge.

Press Release Nigeria. (2018, August 16). *Leadership Crisis: Civil Society Groups Blast Presidency, National Assembly*. Retrieved from http://prnigeria.com/2018/08/18/leadership-crisis-civil-society-groups-blast-presidency-national-assembly/.

Saludeen, L. (2018, March 22). National Assembly's Integrity Under Attack. *The Nation* Online. Retrieved from http://thenationonlineng.net/national-assemblys-integrity-under-attack/.

Society Legislative Advocacy Centre (CISLAC). (2016). *Legislative Digest, 10*(50), 4, 6.

Stapenhurst, R., Johnston, N., & Pelizzo, R. (Eds.). (2006). *The Role of Parliament in Curbing Corruption*. Washington, DC: The International Bank for Reconstruction and Development/The World Bank, no pp.

Stolen Asset Recovery Initiative (STAR). (2018, November 19). *Diezani Alison-Madueke*. Retrieved from https://star.worldbank.org/corruption-cases/printpdf/20499.

The Cable. (2016). Obasanjo: National Assembly Is a Den of Corruption Occupied by Unarmed Robbers. *The Cable* Online. Retrieved from https://www.thecable.ng/Obasanjo-national-assembly-is-a-den-of-corruption-occupied-by-unarmed-robbers, 22 November 2017.

The Editor. (2016). Civil Society Groups Demand Investigation of Alleged Corruption in National Assembly. *This Day* Online. Retrieved from www.thisdaylive.com/index.php/2016/10/17/civil-society-groups-demand-investigation-of-alleged-corruption-in-national-assembly, 8 November 2017.

The Editor. (2017, November 2). National Assembly: Citadel of Corruption, Fraud. *National Daily Newspaper* Online. Retrieved from https://nationaldailyng.com/national-assembly-citadel-of-corruption-fraud/.

Umaru, U. D. (2017). Corruption and Legislative Functions in Nigeria. *Journal of Economics and Finance (IOSR-JEF), 8*(1), 01–08.

Yusuf, Y. A., Yusoff, K. Z., & Zengeni, K. T. (2018). National Assembly and Democratic Consolidation in Nigeria's Fourth Republic: Functions and Operations (1999–2015). *European Academic Journal, 5*(10), 5832–5846.

CHAPTER 8

An Assessment of the Oversight Role of the National Assembly, 1999–2019

Andrew Ariyo Tobi, Gafar Idowu Ayodeji, and Boris Happy Odalonu

Introduction

One of the basic principles of democracy is the participation of the people in the governance process through their elected representatives in the legislature. Thus, the legislature occupies a central role in any democratic

A. A. Tobi
Department of Public Administration, Olabisi Onabanjo University, Ago-Iwoye, Ogun State, Nigeria
e-mail: tobi.ariyo@oouagoiwoye.edu.ng

G. I. Ayodeji (✉)
Department of Political Science, Tai Solarin University of Education, Ijagun, Ogun State, Nigeria
e-mail: ayodejigi@tasued.edu.ng

B. H. Odalonu
Department of Political Science, Federal College of Education, Eha-Amufu, Enugu State, Nigeria

F. A. Aremu and A. R. Bakare (eds.), *Two Decades of Legislative Politics and Governance in Nigeria's National Assembly*,
https://doi.org/10.1007/978-981-33-4455-6_8

setting. A government may exist without the legislature; nevertheless, without the legislature, democracy is not possible (Obasa 2016). Nigeria operates bicameral legislature at the federal level. This consists of two chambers: the Upper and Lower chambers known as the Senate and House of Representatives, respectively. The two chambers are collectively called the National Assembly. The Senate comprises 109 members while the House of Representatives is made up of 360 members elected across the six geopolitical zones of Nigeria. The members of the House of Representatives are drawn from all federal constituencies based on the principle of population, while the members of the Senate are drawn from all states based on the principle of 'equality of states' (Alao 2015).

In every democratic nation, there exist three arms of government: the Legislature, the Executive and the Judiciary. Depending on the system of government in place, either presidential or parliamentary, these arms of government may be separated or fused. The concept of separation of power as propounded by Jean Bodin and popularised by Baron de Montesquieu posits that in order to prevent arbitrariness and tyranny in governance, there should be a division of powers among the three arms of government (Okoro 2017). Consequently, most constitutional democracies in the world enshrined this principle of separation of powers in the organic law of their land. The 1999 Constitution of Federal Republic of Nigeria (amended) in Section 4–6 provided for a division of powers among the legislative, executive and judicial arms of government which consequently provided the framework for institutional oversight among them (Ifiemi 2016; Okoro 2017; Ihedioha 2012; Edet and Amadu 2014).

Under the 1999 Constitution of Nigeria (as amended) each of the arms of government has its specific roles and functions to perform for the good governance of the nation. In theory, the 1999 constitution recognises and makes provisions for the smooth relationship among the legislature, executive and judiciary by prescribing their functions based on the principle of separation of powers and checks and balances (Anyim-Ben et al. 2016). Despite these provisions in the Constitution, due to the complex nature of governance, the organs of government at times do encroach on the activities of one another. Nonetheless, the principle of separation of powers and the doctrine of checks and balances are mechanisms meant to help and ensure that leaders and operators of various institutions of government do not allow their selfish interest to override public interest and the common good (Anyim-Ben et al. 2016). Premised on this, the legislature as the elected arm of government that represents the masses and various interests through the traditional power of oversight oversees the activities of the other two arms of government in order to curb their excesses (Okoro 2017).

Though the primary function of the legislature is lawmaking, in order to ensure good governance, accountability, transparency and efficiency in governance, it performs two other fundamental roles, namely: representation and oversight. Thus, the legislature makes laws for the good governance of the country, carries out the function of representation and exercises oversight on the activities of other arms of government particularly the executive arm. Such oversight functions include overseeing and monitoring the activities of the Ministries, Departments and Agencies (MDAs) and to ensure that the government is held accountable to the people from where it derives its powers (Ihedioha 2012; Dogara 2016).

The legislative oversight functions on the (MDAs) are designed to promote accountability in governance and ensure that funds allocated to the MDAs are utilised appropriately for the good of the society in accordance with the laws of the land (Obasa 2016). However, observations and available evidence in the scholarly literature regarding the effectiveness of the functions of Nigeria's legislature known as National Assembly show that there are still gaps and challenges regarding legislative oversight since the birth of the Fourth Republic in 1999. This should not be surprising given the avalanche of complaints and reports exposing the inadequate performance of the (MDAs) and haemorrhage in public finances (Ehigiamusoe and Umar 2013; Erunke 2017; Ezeamalu 2018; Eneanya 2018). Thus, there is a widespread perception of ineffectiveness on the part of the National Assembly in its bid to perform the constitutionally assigned oversight role for good governance in Nigeria.

Given the narratives on the oversight functions of the legislature since the commencement of Nigeria's current democratic project (the Fourth Republic) since 1999, it is pertinent to ask some salient questions at this juncture. These are: What are the oversight functions of the legislature in Nigeria? To what extent has the National Assembly performed its oversight functions since the commencement of the Fourth Republic in 1999? What are the challenges mitigating against National Assembly in exercising its oversight functions? How can the challenges be addressed? This chapter addresses the above questions. It assesses the oversight role of the National Assembly to ascertain the extent of its effectiveness, identify the attendant impediments and to suggest measures through which this role can be enhanced for the promotion of good governance in Nigeria.

Conceptualising Legislative Oversight

Conceptualising legislative oversight is a daunting task and has attracted divergent views from various scholars (Olson 2008, cited in Pelizzo and Stapenhurst 2011). Thus, it is little wonder that several definitions have been proffered for legislative oversight. Despite the multiplicity of definitions of oversight functions in the literature, there is the agreement that it is about the monitoring and reviewing of government activities by the legislative arm of government. Schick (1976, quoted in Pelizzo and Stapenhurst 2011, p. 14) contended that oversight comprises legislative regulation of policies and programmes authorised by the government.

Ogul (1976) and Maffio (2002) cited in Pelizzo and Stapenhurst (2011), advanced the view that legislative oversight goes beyond mere control of the executive's legislative requests but also signifies the chains of activities that a legislature embarks upon to assess the implementation of policies. In a similar vein, Lenos (2010) viewed oversight as one of the vital attributes of executive and legislative relations whereby the onus is on the executive arm to give legislative branch necessary information. Lenos (2010) specifically described oversight as a regulation of the actions of administration which involves hearings, ministerial summons, enquiry motions and Special Inventory Committees and confirmation procedures.

To the National Democratic Institute (NDI) (2000), legislative oversight is often a post-lawmaking endeavour aimed at determining whether laws are correctly applied and ensuring that they address and correct the problems as envisioned by their drafters. In essence, legislative oversight refers to the ability of the legislature to review, track and control the agencies of the executive branch of government, their operations and policy implementation strategies (Ndoma-Egba 2012, cited in Nwagwu 2014). The *logic behind legislative oversight is to ensure the administration of public policy is in accordance with legislative intent* (Dahlberg 2014).

The understanding of legislative oversight adopted in this chapter is drawn from the Constitution of the Republic of South Africa, 1996 Act 108 of 1996 cited in Manona (2015) which sees legislative oversight as primarily concerned with the 'evaluation, monitoring and regulation of government and public agencies, including the implementation of policy and legislation'. This conception of oversight emphasises its rationale and nature rather than its processes.

Following the path blazed by Yamamoto (2007, pp. 9–10) and supported by PLAC (2016, pp. 5–6), the primary functions of legislative oversight comprise the following:

(i) To discover and prevent abuse, reckless behaviour, or unlawful and unconstitutional demeanour that may arise from the government and public agencies. At the centre of this role is the safeguard of the rights and liberties of citizens.
(ii) Ensure accountability in government with regard to how the taxpayers' money is utilised. Parliamentary oversight discovers wastage in government and public agencies. In doing this, the performance, economy and efficiency of government activities can be improved;
(iii) Legislative oversight is also intended at making sure that public policies formulated. In this context, it involves monitoring the attainment of goals as set out in government's programmes, and in the various tools of Legislative oversight; and
(iv) Enhance transparency of government activities and increase the public's confidence in government, which is itself a prerequisite for effective policy delivery.

The legislature in different climes employs different tools in carrying out the above functions. Though in the constitutions of various countries, some of these instruments are specified, nevertheless they are parts of the rules that govern parliamentary procedures (Manona 2015). In Nigeria, the National Assembly when exercising its oversight functions, employs various strategies such as committee hearings (public/investigative), hearings in plenary sessions of the legislature, public petition and request for explanation from the MDAs, among others (Dogara 2016).

Theoretical Framework

The extant literature on oversight makes available diverse approaches applicable to assessing legislative oversight. Thus, Montesquieu theory of separation of powers and structural-functional approach are considered the most suitable for this paper. On the one hand, using the principle of the separation of powers as one of the frameworks of analysis captures the utility of explaining the foundation of the legislative oversight. This is because '…the constitutional structure shows that legislative oversight function naturally flows from matter in which constitution allocates and separates power among the three branches of government' (Amusa 2013, p. 79). On the other hand, regarding the adoption of the structural-functional approach, the structural elements of oversight are considered essential. Legislative oversight is a multifaceted and multidimensional activity. Thus, in order to capture its effectiveness, an appropriate way is to measure the extent it is performing a specific function (Kinyondo et al. 2015, p. 1).

Theory of Separation of Powers

As far as the theory of separation of powers is concerned, a series of theoretical standpoints have emerged. However, the foremost modern enunciation of its principles is attributed to Montesquieu, whose grasp of it is grounded in the study of Locke's writings (Amusa 2013). For Locke, the human being is weak and imperfect and his propensity to grab power and misuse it is very high. Hence, it is dangerous to allow the same persons possessing the power to make laws to execute the same. This may lead to absurdity, whereby they may choose to obey or not to obey specific laws, depending on which laws favour or disfavour them (Wade and Bradley 1970). As espoused by Montesquieu, the absence of an abuse of power reinforced political liberty and based on experience, every person vested with power and authority is prone to abusing it. Thus, to prevent abuse of power, there should be a counterbalance of power whereby one power should be employed to check on another. That is each organ of government to serve as a watchdog on one another.

In essence, the primary purpose of separation of powers is to stipulate powers boundaries and limitations of each organ of government, to prevent tyranny and usurpation of power by one organ at the expense of the other organs. Be that as it may, the major limitation of the separation of powers principle is that any attempt to interpret it strictly and generally usually leads to confusion rather than elucidation (Ball 1977). That is why Amusa (2013) contended that for effective government, complete separation of powers is not feasible and considered necessary. It is little wonder that successive Nigerian constitutions since 1979 have tried to infuse interaction rather than creating seclusion or real separation of powers among the three arms of government. For instance,

Section 58(4) of the Constitution of Nigeria 1999 accords the President a veto power over legislation; Sections 12 and 147(2) create a role for the Senate in the approval of treaties and the appointment of ministers, and Section 6(6)(b) authorises the judiciary to determine cases or controversies. Thus, the three branches of government may appear to be distinct in functions but integrated with goals via the system of checks and balances whereby each of the arms of government is authorised to protect its position as prescribed within the constitutional arrangement of government (Amusa 2013). It is within the context of the preceding framework that legislative constitutional oversight role surfaces. Thus, the oversight role is a stakeout instrument adopts by the legislature to scrutinise the executive performance within the context of the spirit of the doctrine of separation of powers. However, despite the utility of the separation of powers' theory in capturing the scenario that led to the emergence of legislative oversight, it fails to clearly explain the performance of these oversight functions usually undertaken by the legislature. This is where the structural-functional approach comes into fill the gap.

Structural-Functional Approach

The theory originated from Augustus Comte and developed and popularised by Talcott Parsons (Onwe et al. 2015). However, Almond later regurgitated the scheme so considerably to the extent that his exposition is independent of Parsons' influence (Charlesworth 1968). The structural-functionalist theory regards society as a system or set of interconnected parts which together form a whole (Haralambos and Heald 1980). The usage of functions by scholars in politics and administration relates to the inputs of an activity (legislature) or patterns of behaviour for the upkeep of a given society (Nwosu and Ofoegbu 1986, cited in Onwe et al. 2015).

Olaniyi (1997) posited that structural-functionalism is an instrument of enquiry. When linked to politics and administration, it depicts a mode of explicating essential functions of not only political but administrative structures. From one point of view, structural-functionalism attempts to describe the relationship between the parts (structures); from another view, it explains the relationship between parts and the whole. This relationship is made clear in the context of the essential functions of each, which are taken to be positive contributions that assist towards the system maintenance or the dysfunction which depicts the negative contributions leading to the breakdown of the system, or non-functional which depicts neither positive nor negative stimulus to the working of the whole political or administrative system (Onwe et al. 2015).

Therefore, the approach provides a framework for the analysis of legislative oversight of the Nigerian National Assembly in this study. Using this framework, the government is seen as a social system while the arms of government are taken as structural parts or units of the political system or government. These political institutions, for example, the legislature (also perceived as structures) performs particular essential functions like oversight role in order to curb executive wastage, autocracy, ensures accountability in governance which are of immense benefits to the political system by promoting its stability, continuity and survival. Given this, the legislature is viewed as the eye of the government and crucial in any democratic setting. Therefore, the application of this theory to the requirements of the legislative oversight function in the Nigerian democratic system cannot be overemphasised. Since the National Assembly serves as the watchdog to the other arms of government, failure to do the needful will negatively affect the entire system.

Legislative Oversight Role of the National Assembly: The Constitutional and Legal Foundation

The 1999 Constitution of the Federal Republic of Nigeria entrusts the National Assembly with oversight powers (Sections 88, 89, 128 & 129). The handling of oversight is also endorsed by the various Standing Orders of the National Assembly. The 1999 Constitution, specifically in Section 88, contains provisions that help the National Assembly to perform its oversight functions. These include the issuance of warrants, summons, investigations as well as the imposition of fines on those who violated its orders. As noted earlier, the tools or ways through which the National Assembly conducts oversight function include, asking the government agencies for information and clarification of policy; obtaining information from external sources, presenting its opinion to the government and the general public. It also holds meetings informally with government officials. The oversight function of the legislature equally covers, the confirmation of certain categories of appointment made by the president and the control and regulation of the financial activities of the government.

However, it has been legally emphasised that there is no absoluteness in the power of the legislature to embark on legislative oversight. In Nigeria, in Tony Momoh V. Senate of the National Assembly (1982) NCLR, 105, it was submitted that the legislature lacked the powers to take over the functions of the executive in respect of the general investigation. The legislature was equally exempted from usurping the adjudicative responsibility of the judiciary. The Nigerian legal content regarding the limits on the power of legislative oversight has also been established and found support in Chief Justice, Earl Warren, American Jurist and Politician adumbration, when he stated among other things that no enquiry is an end in itself and that investigation undertaken by the legislature must be related to and in furtherance of the legislative task of Congress and that investigation conducted solely for the personal aggrandisement of the investigators or to punish those investigated cannot be defended (PLAC 2016).

Purpose, Types and Mechanisms/Procedures of Legislative Oversight

The primary purpose of parliamentary oversight is to ensure that the actions of the government are transparent, by providing financial accountability and by complying with the laws passed by the legislature. Legislative oversight, therefore, facilitates checks and balances and inculcates in public offices fiscal responsibility, good governance, accountability and transparency (Okoro 2017). As noted by Oyewo (2007), Arowolo (2010), Ehigiamusoe and Umar (2013), Abah and Obiajulu (2017). Oversight functions serve a variety of objectives and purposes such as:

1. Regulation of the excesses of the executive in governance and supervision of the nation's resources.
2. Provide financial accountability via government budget approval and oversight by exposing excessive spending inside publicly funded programmes.
3. Make the executive branch answerable by reviewing whether the policies of the government have been executed and whether they have the desired effects.
4. Promoting prudence and productivity in public policy formulation and administration.

5. Collect information in order to create fresh legislative proposals or change existing laws.
6. To ensure administrative compliance with legislative intents and prevent executive infringement on legislative power and prerogatives.
7. Improve the efficacy, economy and quality of governmental activities.
8. Review of MDAs' programmes and results.
9. Discover and avoid bad management, wastage, unreasonable and erratic conduct or unlawful and unconstitutional behaviour.
10. Update the general public and ensure that executive policies represent the public interest.
11. Checking the excesses of the executive arm and government agencies, minimising waste in administration, corruption and despotism in the exercise of political power.
12. To expose corruption, inefficiency or waste in public expenditure management.

The National Assembly's oversight duties can be exercised in different ways. These are:

(a) **Investigative Oversight**: Depending on the resolution of the Legislative House, the National Assembly is empowered to carry out inquiries into the activities of government agencies, either in plenary or by standing or ad hoc committees. This power is provided for by the 1999 Constitution in sections 4, 88(1) and (2) and 89.
(b) **Appropriation Oversight**: The National Assembly is authorised to deliberate, examine and approve the budgets submitted to it by the executive (annual or supplementary) and permit the executive to withdraw the money thus appropriated. Usually, the main committee is the Appropriation Committee, while other standing committees become sub-committees to debate the Appropriation, Bill. This kind of oversight is carried out at the time of enactment of the law, which allows committees the power to check excesses and misconduct by misallocating funds. It is also carried out during the budget cycle implementation process.

(c) **Routine oversight**: This is the frequent scrutiny conducted either by committees or plenary by a legislative body. In order to ensure compliance with the laws of (MDAs) in performing governmental operations, regular supervision is carried out by committees under their jurisdiction, as provided for in the Standing Orders. It involves frequent visits to MDAs, screening and approval of executive appointments, committee hearings and probes or any casual meeting between members of the legislature and the executive to foster public interest (PLAC 2016).

(d) **Public Accounts Committee Oversight**: The Public Accounts Committee, in both the Senate and the House of Representatives, is a standing and special committee. Unlike other committees whose authority is limited to particular subjects and jurisdictions, the Public Accounts Committee has broad jurisdiction under Section 85(2)–(5) of the 1999 Constitution (as amended) to review the Auditor General's Report on audited accounts of MDAs in the federation.

Succinctly put, oversight revolves around the act of checking, verifying, examining, criticising, censuring, challenging, questioning and calling for an account. This is achieved through various oversight tools such as committees' activities, e.g. site visit or project visitation, parliamentary questions, correspondence with MDAs, etc. (Alao 2015). Many legislatures have established legislative frameworks and instruments designed to promote their executive branch oversight function. The effectiveness of this position is accomplished through a wide variety of networks, organisations and systems. This varies from formal Committee meetings to informal Member communications with the Executive Officer, ranging from specialised selected committee inquiries to annual hearing appropriations.

However, the number of oversight tools varies from one constitutional form of government to another (Hamalai 2015). In Nigeria, the National Assembly has an array of tools and mechanisms in the exercise of oversight functions. These tools include a committee of inquiry, hearings, interpellation, ombudsperson, questions, question time, and specialised committees. Other instruments include budgetary control mechanisms, impeachment mechanisms, and the possibility for parliament to set up ad hoc committees, commissions of inquiry or offices of the ombudsman. Other supervisory procedures used by the legislature include public hearings, motion motions, budget processes, project physical review, investigative hearings and approval, among others (Okoro 2017). Moreover, the method to be used in the conduct of oversight depends on the modes of oversight. Oversight exercise can conveniently be divided into the following three phases.

(i) **Pre-Oversight**: Development of an oversight agenda. This is debated and accepted before the exercise at committee meetings. Committee meetings to consider the oversight agenda (subject), the logistics needed the date, the details or records/documents required and any other issues to promote the exercise's successful conduct. Internal official messages to the President/Speaker and House Clerk; communications to the oversighted MDAs are generally taken into account. In this correspondence, any document or information required should be reflected with a specific timeline for the submission of such documents. Depending on form, design, place and time of oversight, security arrangements.

(ii) **During Oversight**: Arrival, check-in and first-meeting planning. MDAs management team and the subject of oversight; inspection, visit, record verification, interactive session; closing remarks (regularly in a short meeting or executive session). A formal meeting to introduce members of the committee.

(iii) **Post Oversight**: Development of the report by the secretariat of the committee; meetings of the committee to consider, deliberate and make further suggestions in the report; presentation and reporting on the table; House debates and resolutions that may include an investigative hearing, an interactive session or some other legislative activities requested by the legislature (PLAC 2016).

Nature, Dimensions and Effectiveness of Legislative Oversight Functions in Nigeria

The 1999 Constitution of the Federal Republic of Nigeria (as amended) as noted earlier in Section 88 empowers the National Assembly to conduct investigations into government affairs. This power covers (a) any matter or thing with respect to which it has the power to make laws; and (b) the conduct of any official, authority or government department's affairs charged with or intended to be charged with the duty or responsibility for (i) the enforcement and administration of legislation enacted by the National Assembly. (ii) Disbursement or administration of funds allocated or to be allocated by the National Assembly. Furthermore, the Constitution states that certain powers granted the National Assembly under the provisions of that section can only be exercised to allow it (a) to make laws on any matter within its legislative power and to amend any flaws in existing laws; and (b) to uncover corruption, inefficiency or wastage in the implementation or administration of laws within its legislative power (1999 Constitution, Section 88[2]).

The Constitution explicitly empowers the National Assembly in carrying outs its oversight function to procure evidence written or oral from all persons whose evidence may be relevant to the issue under consideration; summon any person to give evidence, issue a warrant to compel the attendance of any person who had failed to do so after being summoned and to impose fines for failure to appear (Section 89[1]). These provisions, without doubt, confer on the legislature the task of making laws and that of a watchdog over the other arms of government and their agencies. Hence, legislative oversight is, without a doubt, an instrument for good governance.

From the provisions of the Constitution, it is glaring that the functions of the legislature in Nigeria extend beyond lawmaking to oversight of the entire activities of the government. Consequently, legislative oversight, to a large extent, determines the effectiveness of governance. As stated earlier, legislative oversight is intended to foster good governance through the promotion of checks and balances, the strengthening of fiscal responsibility, accountability and transparency in public offices. Legislative oversight also helps to recognise and discourage maladministration, waste, corruption, arbitrary and capricious actions, or unlawful and unconstitutional behaviour (Nwagwu 2014). The oversight function of the Nigerian legislature covers a series of responsibilities such as the appointments and removal of key government functionaries which require the consent of the legislature, declaration of a state of emergency which needs the approval of the legislature, power of impeachment conferred on the legislature and power to ensure that the disbursement of funds in line with procedures approved by the legislature, among others.

Since the birth of Nigeria's Fourth Republic, the legislature has undertaken several oversight functions. Some of the oversight functions undertaken led to strained relations between the legislature and the executive. This did not only cripple the governance process (Momodu and Matudi 2013) but is seen to have led to the impeachment of three consecutive Senate Presidents, namely Senators Evans Enwerem, Chuka Okadigbo and Adolphus Wabara.

Some of the visible activities of the legislature that have attracted public attention and or spawned controversies included that of summons, investigations, control of public finance and confirmation of appointments. Examples of landmark investigation hearings since the birth of the Fourth Republic in 1999 include, the House of Representatives investigation of the $16 billion invested in the power sector during the Obasanjo led administration, the Petroleum Trust Development Fund (PTDF) which involved former President Olusegun Obasanjo and Vice-President Abubakar Atiku, the fuel subsidy probe during the President Jonathan administration and the investigation of the Director-General of the Nigerian Securities and Exchange Commission, among others. Other legislative oversights that have drawn the attention of the public included, the rejection of the extension of the state of emergency in Adamawa, Yobe and Borno States, the summon of the Comptroller General of the Nigerian Customs services, confirmation of Mr. Ibrahim Magu as the Economic and Financial Crimes Commission (EFCC) chairman and the subpoena of the Inspector General of Police (IGP), among others.

Legislative oversight has been an instrument for the promotion of good governance in Nigeria. The legislature has through the exercise of its oversight functions succeeded in drawing the attention of the public to infringement of laid down rules and regulations by the executive and some of its agencies and equally exposed questionable financial transactions by many government establishments. For example, in 2001, the Senate Committee on Public Accounts investigated various public agencies, such as the Nigerian National Petroleum (NNPC), the Central Bank of Nigeria (CBN) and the National Electric Power Authority (NEPA) and through public hearings, a series of revelations on diversion of public funds to private accounts and inflation of contracts, among others, were revealed. Similarly, the Senate investigation of the National Identity Card Scheme in 2001 also revealed similar corrupt practices (Amusa 2013).

Through legislative oversight, the executive on different occasions was forced to reverse some policies deemed not to be in the general interest of the Nigerian public and recovered funds found to have been inappropriately appropriated. For instance, the House of Representatives panel investigated dubious oil sector activities found that the government paid questionable large amount of money for fuel subsidies, some of which were found to be bogus and fluke transactions (Osagie 2017). Other instances in which legislative scrutiny has been useful in exposing corrupt activities included the purchase of Nigerian Airway Limited (NAL) assets involving Dr. (Mrs.) Kema Chikwe, former Minister of Aviation, and the then Director-General of the Bureau for Public Enterprise (BPE). These officials were summoned to appear before the Committee of the National Assembly on the Privatisation of Public Enterprises. The secret deals of the Ministry of Aviation were disclosed through the oversight mechanism of the legislature, and the plans to buy NAL properties were aborted (Arowolo 2010). Similarly, in 2013, the National Assembly queried the then Minister of Aviation, Mrs. Stella Oduah for spending more than what was approved for the purchase of operational vehicles in the 2013 budget. Mrs. Oduah allowed the Nigerian Civil Aviation Authority (NCAA) to purchase two bulletproof BMW cars for approximately N255 million and an additional N643 million to procure 54 vehicles instead of adhering to the N240 million budgeted for 25 operational vehicles (Osagie 2017). Succinctly put, through legislative oversight, the National Assembly has been able to monitor and scrutinise the activities of the executive arm of government and its agencies and to some extent check the excesses of the executive arm of government, control corruption and promote good governance during the period under consideration

There are different perspectives on the effectiveness of these oversight functions of the legislature. To some, the legislature has not been forceful in the exercise of these functions while others have contended that it has been not done poorly. For instance, the 7th National Assembly that came into being on 6 June 2011 was severally criticised regarding its oversight functions. Its oversight activities have been described as scandalous affairs which involved both the executive and legislators (Aliyu 2015). Despite the criticisms, during the 7th National Assembly, some high profile cases of alleged corruption and waste in government were investigated by its relevant committees, chief among which were the Maina Pensions Scam, Kerosene Subsidy Scam, Police Pension Fund Fraud, Aruma Oteh/Herman Hembe SEC scandal, Stella Oduah Armoured vehicles Scam, Missing 20 billion Naira Oil Proceeds, $15 million private jets/arms scandal, Abba Moro/Immigration Recruitment Scandal, Malabu Oil Scandal, *Ettegate* and Farouk Lawan Scandal, etc. (Olufemi et al. 2015; Alao 2015). Olufemi et al. (2015) believe that although the oversight powers of the legislature were exercised judiciously to guarantee dividends to Nigerians for the election of their representatives, there were apparent cover-ups and a lack of political will to bring several cases to a close. In essence, it failed to do enough in the area of performing its watchdog function over the executive arm of government.

The President of the 8th Senate and Chairman of the National Assembly, Senator Dr. Abubakar Bukola Saraki, however viewed the oversight effectiveness from another perspective. While delivering the valedictory speech in commemoration of the 7th National Assembly, he averred that the legislature had made far-reaching oversight investigations and that the legislative process was a marathon. His conclusion was that the 7th Assembly had not done too poorly in the area of performing its oversight function. He, however, noted that precious time was wasted in fighting political wars and playing partisan politics at the expense of delivering public good (Saraki 2015; Alao 2015).

The 8th Assembly has been characterised by conflicts and confrontations with the executive in the performance of their oversight functions. These confrontations stemmed from executive interference in the choice of legislative leadership, non-confirmation of presidential appointment, budget approval, implementation and evaluation processes, corruption probes and investigative public hearings. For instance, the 8th National Assembly rejected the confirmation of Ibrahim Magu as the substantive Chairman of EFCC two times mainly due to a damning report by the Department of State Security Service (DSS) of him lacking the integrity to continue as EFCC chairman, yet he was allowed to continue to function as the acting as Chairman of EFCC. Again, in terms of budgetary oversight, there have been controversies between the executive and the National Assembly. For instance, there was a face-off between the executive and legislature due to discrepancies of the 2016 appropriation bill as presented by the President to the National Assembly. These discrepancies were tagged budget padding by the National Assembly members in collaboration with MDAs. The discrepancies generated allegations and counter-allegations, and the possibility that the presidency presented two versions of the budget. The House of Representatives investigated the allegation and subsequently suspended the Chairman of the appropriation committee, Hon. Abdulmumin Jibrin, for 181 legislative days. Abdulmumin Jibrin had claimed that the Speaker and other principal officers of the house inserted constituency projects into the budget.

Despite the conflicts that have characterised the 8th National Assembly, Dr Bukola Saraki still believed that the legislature played a more significant role in policy formulation and that it engaged more robustly with the executive at the different stages of policy formulation. He averred that the role of the legislature was borne out of the conviction that the role of nation-building belongs to all and sundry. He said that since 2015, many of the legislative steps they had adopted were aimed at driving growth, easing access to finance, generating jobs and improving livelihoods (Ogbonna 2018).

The foregoing aptly shows that although the legislature had undertaken various oversights functions and succeeded in unravelling a series of malfeasance in governance, the belief in many quarters is that the legislature found itself incapacitated when it made recommendations and such were tossed in the dustbin of antiquity. This is due to the absence of a constitutional provision empowering the legislature to determine punishments for offenders creates a lacuna exploited by the executive and this hampers the ability of the legislature to see oversight to a logical end. Simply put, there exists a series of impediments to effective legislative oversight in Nigeria's Fourth Republic. These are discussed in the section below.

Impediments to Effective Legislative Oversight of the National Assembly

Ezeani, as quoted by Nwagwu (2014), acknowledged the value of legislative oversight in contemporary democratic governance, but noted that it has been very contentious in all corollaries and remained the primary source of executive and legislative conflicts in Nigeria. There is no doubt that the National Assembly over the years has been overburdened by so many impediments which are both internal and external. Some of these impediments to effective oversight functions are highlighted and discussed below.

1. **Inadequate Funding Leading to Shortage of Support Staff and Ineffective Oversight**: Inability to provide the needed support staff for the committees, for instance, to run through heaps of files and documents before field visits resulting in ineffective oversight is a major impediment. This is also applicable to funding. The

former Speaker of the House of Representatives, Aminu Tambuwal lamented the poor funding of the National Assembly and called for funding given the enormous responsibilities of the legislature (NAN 2018). According to the President of the 8th Senate, Dr Olusola Saraki, contrary to the public perception that the National Assembly was being overfunded, it is on the contrary as increase in the 8th legislative activities had revealed that one of its major challenges was paucity of fund in executing its legislative functions (Busari 2018). Thus, it has been observed that the National Assembly committees are usually insufficiently funded to conduct effective oversight. Referring to the past impediments to effective legislative oversight, the Draft Legislative Agenda for the 8th Senate (2016) pointed out that the impediments to problems relating to funding and efficient staffing of Committees would be addressed.

2. **Corruption and Fraudulent Practices**: As noted earlier, 'effective legislative oversight can help make government more accountable and effective' (United States Agency for International Development (USAID) 2000, p. 47). In the Nigerian context, it has been employed to discover fraudulent financial practices and as a watchdog on the activities of the executive arm of government and its agencies with the view to ensuring that such activities are not against the public interest. Despite its utility, the oversight functions of the National Assembly have generated a series of criticisms which centre mostly on its abuse by the parliamentarians. One major issue that has continued to reoccur is corruption. There have been a series of allegations against members of the legislature, particularly members of committees who often see legislative oversight function as a short-cut for personal enrichment and promotion of their political profile. Legislators have been accused of abandoning their statutory oversight duties and turning themselves to contractors. This has not only worsened the problems of Nigeria but also contributed to a conflict of interest between public interest and private concern.

   A large portion of the narrative on oversight functions of the legislature has identified corruption as one of its limiting factors. Members of the legislature involved in investigations have been accused of using the opportunity to enrich themselves. Instances of this included the case of Farouk Lawan vis-a-vis Otedola. Lawan was alleged to have demanded a bribe of $3 million to remove the name of Zenon Oil and Gas Company owned by Mr. Femi Otedola from the list of indicted firms (Nwagwu 2014). A similar issue bordering on corruption also came up at the public hearing of the House of Representatives Committee on Security Market. The then Director-General of the Nigerian Securities and Exchange Commission, Ms. Arunma Oteh was summoned in connection with the crash of the Stock Exchange Market and in the process queried for spending eight months in the hotels and alleged of spending the sum of N30 million for hotel bills and N850,000 for food daily. Ms. Oteh alleged that the Committee was demanding a bribe of N44 million as the SEC contribution to the public hearing. She also alleged that the Chairman of the Committee collected the sum of N30 million to travel to the Dominican Republic, a trip he did not make yet he failed to return the money (Amusa 2013: Nwagwu 2014). The allegations also included situations where ministries, parastatals, agencies and other organisations sponsor the well-being of members of the legislature and their families for their overseas trips (Nwagwu 2014; Osagie 2017). Still, on corruption; the exercise of legislative oversight, particularly on the budget, has been very controversial. Reports and allegations of budget padding, particularly in the 8th National Assembly, are some of the dangerous developments that have not created a right image for the National Assembly.

3. **Shallow Democratic Culture of the Legislature**: The series of impediments to the effectiveness of the legislative oversight of the National Assembly in Nigeria crystallised into two folds. First, those associated with the nature and functioning of the legislature and second, those exogenous to the legislature. Among those related to the National Assembly include the shallow democratic culture of the legislature. It has been argued that, though the legislature is the watchdog of democracy, it is perhaps the most nascent and underdeveloped of the three arms of government because of its abuse by successive military governments before 1999. The argument is that the essential democratic culture and ingredients are yet to develop fully; consequently, some members of the legislature have not fully internalised the rules and guidelines guiding the workings of the legislature including the exercise of legislative oversight (Arowolo 2010).

4. **Composition of the Legislative Arm of Government**: Another internal dynamic of the legislature that has impeded effective legislative oversight in Nigeria is the composition of the legislative arm of government. Osagie (2017) argues that regarding the composition of the legislature, some members of the legislature to a considerable extent, have no business to be in the National Assembly. Some of them found themselves there as a result of imposition by their godfathers and political leaders. When such members found themselves in the committees investigating the activities of the executive, they seldom deliver what is expected of them. This imposition has further created a communication gap between the lawmakers and the people they ought to represent. This poor communication has not allowed the majority of the electorate to appreciate the oversight functions of the legislature.
5. **The Undue Interference in the Activities of the Legislature by Powerful Individuals and Groups Outside the Legislature**: This has also been undermining the effectiveness of legislative oversight in Nigeria. Reasons adduced for this trend is that such influential people were instrumental in the elections of many of the legislators, hence they always find it difficult not to pursue their agenda of their principals or succumb to their demands. In another context, the executive in some cases has been interfering in the activities of the legislature, thereby undermining the propriety of its actions. Though in the going Fourth Republic, the National Assembly has not deployed the instrument of impeachment on the executive, it has nevertheless witnessed a series of rumours and threats of impeachment directed at the leadership of the executive arm of government. Impeachment, however, has been used at the state level. The Fourth Republic has witnessed the impeachment of some state governors and deputy governors on flimsy excuses and without following the due process of the law. The judiciary however quashed some of the impeachments such as that of Peter Obi of Anambra State, Rasheed Ladoja of Oyo State and Dariye of Plateau states for acting outside the requirements of the law.
6. **Non-Adherence to the Practice of Separation of Powers**: Non-adherence to the practice of separation of power has also been identified as one of the impediments to effective legislative oversight. The legislature in carrying out its responsibilities has often being accused of going beyond its bounds. It is usually alleged

under the guise of exercising oversight function; the legislature was assuming the role of the executive as well as that of the judiciary. The legislature is seen to be enjoying unlimited freedom in its oversight functions. It has continued the exercise of this constitutional power into all spheres of governance without regard to functions of other arms of government (Nwagwu 2014). This has spawned a series of conflicts particularly between the legislature and the executive.

7. **The Attitude of the Executive and Its Agencies**: The attitude of the executive and its agencies are also seen to have impeded effective oversight functions over the years. The executive and its agencies have been identified as parts of the obstacles to oversight functions of the legislature. When summoned, the response has been either ignoring the National Assembly or refusal to appear in person and in some cases seeking court injunctions to restrain the National Assembly from summoning them. This played out when an Abuja High Court on 19 June 2014, gave an order restraining the National Assembly from probing Minister of Petroleum Resources, Mrs. Diezani Allison Maduekwe for allegedly spending N10 billion on chartered aircraft (Osagie 2017). Similar resistance was exhibited by the former Inspector General of Police (IGP), Ibrahim Kpotun Idris who was summoned by the Senate to provide information among other things on the lingering state of insecurity in the country's middle belt. The IGP refused to appear in person before the Senate even though he was summoned several times. This led the Senate to declare that the IGP was an 'enemy of democracy and unfit for public office within and outside Nigeria' (Oyedele and Ezigbo 2018). Expressing how lack of cooperation on the part of the executive has been impacting negatively on legislative oversight in Nigeria, the Deputy President of the Senate, 8th National Assembly, Ekweremadu lamented among other things that in utilising its powers of oversight and investigation, the legislature regularly had cause to summon executive officers. Sadly, Nigerians have continued to note with absolute dismay that some executive officers disparaged not only legislative resolutions but also refused legislative invitations (Baiyewu 2018).
8. **The Personal Ambitions of Parliamentarians**: The personal ambitions of parliamentarians, particularly those involved in the

investigation, have been identified as an impediment to legislative oversight. It is mostly believed that members serving in investigating committees usually go beyond their mandates, and most of the times use the opportunity to amplify their political profile. It is alleged that the legislature has compromised and abdicated its responsibility regarding its oversight function and has, therefore become a tool for the parliamentarian to blackmail or witch-hunt as well as extort money from parastatals, agencies and ministries under their control for selfish or personal aggrandisement (Nwagwu 2014).

9. **Personal Interests of Legislators**: A good number of members of the National Assembly (including lawmakers at the level of the state) have also been said to follow pure selfish interests that often preclude them from combating the problems of lawmaking, representation and supervision. Many of them concentrate on securing contracts from both Houses leadership and the Chief Executives of the different MDAs they are to scrutinise. This personal interest serves as a threat to the discharge of their oversight duties and thus making them easily compromise when it comes to contributing meaningfully to debates on the floor of the House. For instance, some of the activities of the National Assembly regarding oversight functions show that the two chambers of the National Assembly have never hidden their desire to see that their interests prevail in budgetary allocations. The legislators have become experts in increasing the different subheads in the national budget over the years, taking advantage of their statutory duty as the approving authority for the annual Appropriation Act. As rightly observed by the Nation Newspaper in its editorial of 16 November 2016 (cited in Abah and Obiajulu 2017) the National Assembly had demonstrated in many ways that it did not share the yearnings of Nigerians for prudence, accountability and transformation and that all that it was doing was to boost the personal interests of members and oblivious of the state of the nation.
10. **Lack of solid legislative framework for oversight**: Whenever oversight functions are undertaken, they are sometimes backed up by legislature resolutions. It should, however, be noted that sometimes the executive does disregard such resolutions. Such disregard to resolution without consequences has made oversight functions

to be ineffective. It would be better therefore if legislative resolutions were made obligatory for the executive to respond and to give reasons for their failure in enforcing them.

11. **Ethnic loyalty**: Legislators who belong to a specific ethnic group usually find it difficult to indict executive members of their ethnic extraction. This is because many politicians in Nigeria often put their primordial interests above national interests.
12. **Inadequacy of facilities**: Another problem is the inadequacy of facilities, and these include vehicles, office space, meeting rooms, research tools, professional staff, consultants, etc. All these factors serve as major impediments to the oversight efforts of the National Assembly.

In summary, obstacles to the successful exercise of legislative oversight functions, particularly in Nigeria, can be summed up as follows: the absence of constitutional provisions to enforce resolutions of the two chambers; lack of political will or incentives for legislators to follow through all their powers of oversight; the degradation and pervasion of oversight work by the pervasive political corruption of the broader political system; inadequate resources (money, men, material) and overbearing influence of the executive arm and political parties; late budget submission; antagonism between the government and the legislature, with the latter, frequently unwilling to accommodate a powerful parliament that can keep it accountable; the antagonism between the majority and minority parties frequently leads to a stalemate in a politically charged atmosphere with competing interests; and lack of transparency on the part of the Public Accounts Committee.

Enhancing Legislative Oversight Role of the National Assembly for the Promotion of Good Governance

Effective legislative oversight is critical to good governance in contemporary society. In Nigeria, it is institutionalised, but controversies are surrounding the way members of the legislature go about carrying out this noble assignment. However, on some occasions, these assignments have been carried with zeal and patriotism. However, there is a need to strengthen the oversight functions of the legislature so that it can serve as an instrument for good governance. The following measures are needed to enhance the effectiveness of legislative oversight in Nigeria.

(i) There is a need to strengthen the committee system in the legislature. The committees should be allowed to work independently and be focused on the mandate given to them.
(ii) We have in the preceding section identified shallow democratic culture as one of the problems inhibiting the effectiveness of the legislature. To address this problem, regular training and orientation about parliamentary procedures should be given to legislators. Training would enable parliamentarians to know the limits of their assignments and mandate. It will guard against the constant accusation of usurpation of the powers of the executive and the judiciary.
(iii) There is a saying that he who seeks equity must come with clean hands. As long as corruption continues to thrive in the legislature, it will be challenging to have a productive legislative function. The legislators must realise that one of their principal functions is to curb corruption and promote good governance. Consequently, they should be conscious of their callings and refrain from corrupt practices. Situations, where those being investigated for corruption accuse those doing the investigations of corrupt practices cannot promote useful oversight functions of the legislature.
(iv) There is the need to sanitise the electoral process with the view to ensuring that credible and competent people are elected to public offices. When the incidence of money, godfathers and imposition are relegated to the background, and internal democracy is allowed to triumph in the internal dynamics of the political parties, the external influence from the executive, power groups and individuals on the legislature will reduce drastically, and the business of the legislature as an institution will be enhanced.
(v) Members of the National Assembly should assume the substantial role of representation. In this case, they must continuously be in touch with their constituencies, have town hall meetings with them and execute constituency projects that are beneficial to the people.
(vi) There is the need to pay attention to what happens to the outcome of legislative oversight such as a public hearing on the discovery of diversion of public funds and abuse of power. The executive should implement the recommendations of the legislature in such cases.

Conclusion and Recommendations

The narrative of the oversight function of the legislature is that it is being abused. The general perception of legislative oversight is that it is a mere alarm raising mechanism whose aftermath is hardly known. People believed that panels of inquiry are usually set up as a matter of routine to douse public outcry against unpopular policy or issue. What happens after the hearing and investigations (apart from a few cases) are usually unknown hence peoples' confidence in public hearing and investigations carried out by the legislative is low.

Despite the criticisms against legislative oversight since the birth of the Fourth Republic, the National Assembly to a considerable extent has used it as an instrument for checking the excesses of the executive and its agencies as well as monitoring the activities of government as a whole. The various investigations conducted in the legislature led to the recovery of public funds fraudulently diverted to private accounts by some agencies. Moreover, the mere fact that the legislature can invite any public officer to explain his or her actions and activities is a guard against impunity. Consequently, what needed to be done is to devise mechanisms that would make legislative oversight a formidable instrument for good governance. Some of them have been discussed in the preceding section of this paper but to recast as follows:

(i) The way and manner the legislators and executive see the legislative oversight is not encouraging. The executive usually considers the exercise as a means to bring the legislature down. That is why some heads of department and agencies typically refuse to honour invitations by the legislative. There is the need for a constitutional backing that must compel whosoever the legislature summons to appear irrespective of the status of such officers.

(ii) Similarly, most of the criticisms against the exercise of legislative oversight are mainly on the conduct of the parliamentarians. As the institution charged with the task of curbing corruption, legislators much live by examples by shunning all forms of corrupt practices. They should not see investigations as a means to showcase their political profile or for personal enrichment.

(iii) As highlighted earlier, there is a need to focus on the calibre of those elected into public offices in Nigeria. As long as people whose sole purpose in government is private accumulation continue to dominate critical political institutions such as the legislature, there is the tendency for the continuity of lapses in the way they carry out their functions. Thus, for the electorate, when the opportunity comes for them to determine those to lead them, they must endeavour to cast their votes for competent and honest individuals and should shun peanuts given to them during the electioneering campaign.

(iv) The strengthening of the effectiveness of legislative oversight in Nigeria also requires the active involvement of non-state actors and agencies, particularly civil society organisations. The monitoring role of the civil society groups apart from complementing that of the media as the watchdog of government and public policy has the capacity of enabling them to sensitise the National Assembly to investigate cases of malfeasance and also enact legislation capable of correcting observed defects or infractions in existing law. Civil society groups in Nigeria should not only stop at ensuring that investigations are carried out but where infractions are discovered they should do a follow-up to ensure that the appropriate government agencies implement recommendations of the public hearings and investigations.

References

Abah, C. N., & Obiajulu, O. A. (2017). Relevance of Legislative Oversight in the Fight Against Corruption in Nigeria. *Social Scientia Journal of the Social Sciences and Humanities, 2*(1), 1–14.

Alao, T. S. (2015). *Performance of Oversight Functions by the National Assembly: A Critical Assessment of Nigeria's 7th House of Representatives', 2011–2015* (A Master Dissertation Submitted to University of Benin), Benin City, Nigeria.

Aliyu, A. (2015, January 8). 7th National Assembly's Scorecard. *Leadership Newspaper*.

Amusa, K. O. (2013). Legislative Oversight Functions in Nigeria– Odyssey of Hunters Becoming the Hunted. *AUDJ, 9*(2), 79–95.

Anyim-Ben, F. O., Okereke, S. N., & Chijioke, N. (2016). The Doctrine of Separation of Powers and Checks and Balances in the Nigerian Executive-Legislative Relationship. *Nnamdi Azikiwe Journal of Philosophy, 9*(1), 77–84.

Arowolo, G. A. (2010) Oversight Functions of the Legislature: An Instrument for National Building. *Nnamdi Azikwe University International Journal of Law and Jurisprudence, 1*, 27–40.

Baiyewu L. (2018) Undermining National Assembly Is a Recipe for Anarchy-Ekweremadu. *The Punch*. Retrieved from https://punchng.com/undermining-national-assembly-is-a-recipe-for-anarchy-ekweremadu/.

Ball, A. R. (1977). *Modern Politics and Government* (2nd ed.). London: Macmillan Press Ltd.

Busari, K. (2018, January 25). National Assembly Needs More Money. *Premium Times*. Retrieved from https://www.premiumtimesng.com/news/top-news/256697-national-assembly-needs-money-saraki.html.

Charlesworth, J. C. (1968). *Contemporary Political Analysis*. New York: The Free Press.

Dahlberg, P. (2014, December 4). *After the Bills Pass: The Importance of Legislative Oversight*. Retrieved from https://legisource.net/2014/12/04/after-the-bills-pass-the-importance-of-legislative-oversight/.

Dogara, Y. (2016). *Legislative Oversight as a Critical Component of Good Governance*. Thing a Lecture Delivered at the 4th Convocation Ceremony of Achievers University, Owo, Ondo State, Nigeria. Retrieved from http://guardian.ng/features/legislative-oversight-as-a-criticalcomponent-of-good-governance.

Draft Legislative Agenda for the 8th Senate. (2016). Retrieved from http://placing.org/uploads/2016/06/draft-legislative-agenda-for-the-8th-senate.

Edet, J. T., & Amadu, J. A. (2014). The Legislature and National Development: The Nigerian experience. *Global Journal of Arts Humanities and Social Sciences, 2*(9), 63–78.

Ehigiamusoe, U. K., & Umar, A. (2013). Legislative Oversights and Budget Performance in Nigeria: Issues and Policy Options. *IOSR Journal of Economics and Finance, 1*(5), 1–12.

Eneanya, A. N. (2018). Performance Management System and Public Service Delivery in Nigeria: Impacts, Problems, Challenges and Prospects. *Africa's Public Service Delivery & Performance Review, 6*(1), 78–92.

Erunke, J. (2017, March 1). Poor Revenue Performance of 2016 Budget Condemned. *Vanguard* Online. Retrieved from https://www.vanguardngr.com/2017/03/poor-revenue-performance-of-2016-budget-condemned.

Ezeamalu, B. (2018, February 1). Poor Remittances: Nigerian Govt. Considers New Performance Framework for MDAs. *Premium Times* Online. Retrieved from https://www.premiumtimesng.com/news/top-news/257291-poor-remittances-nigerian-govt-considers-new-performance-framework–mdas.html/.

Federal Republic of Nigeria. (1999). *Constitution of the Federal Republic of Nigeria*. Lagos: Federal Government Press.

Hamalai, L. (2015). *Legislative Oversight: A Study of Performance in Nigeria National Assembly*. Abuja: A Publication of the National Institute for Legislative Studies, National Assembly.

Haralambos, M., & Heald, R. M. (1980). *Sociology: Themes and Perspectives*. Englewood Cliffs, NJ: Prentice-Hall.

Ifiemi, A. (2016, July 2). Role of the Legislature in Engendering Good Governance in Nigeria. *The Nigerian Voice*. Retrieved from https://www.thenigerianvoice.com/news/221692/role-of-the-legislature-in-engendering-good-governance-in-ni.html.

Ihedioha, E. (2012). *The Legislature: Roles, Misconceptions and Experience in Democratic Nigeria (1)*. Being extracts from a paper presented by the Deputy Speaker of the House of Representatives, Emeka Ihedioha, at a public lecture organised by the Department of Political Science, University of Lagos. Retrieved from https://www.vanguardngr.com/2012/07/the-legislature-roles-misconceptions-and-experience-in-democratic-nigeria-1/.

Kinyondo, A., Pelizzo, R., & Umar, A. (2015). A Functionalist Theory of Oversight. *African Politics & Policy, 1*(5), 1–25.

Lenos, L. B. (2010). *Legislative Oversight of the Executive Branch in Six Democracies in Latin America*. A paper delivered at the Oxford-Princeton Global Leaders Workshop, Princeton, NJ. London: Pluto Press.

Manona, W. W. (2015). Critical Analysis of the Oversight Role of the Education Portfolio Committee in Parliament of South Africa. *Africa's Public Service Delivery & Performance Review, 3*(3), 72–94.

Momodu, A. J., & Matudi, G. I. (2013). The Implications of Executive-Legislative Conflicts on Good Governance in Nigeria. *Public Policy and Administration Research, 3*(8), 31–42.

National Democratic Institute. (2000). *Legislative Research Series. Strengthening Legislative Capacity in Legislative-Executive Relations*. Washington, DC: National Democratic Institute.

News Agency of Nigeria (NAN). (2018, October 23). Aminu Tambuwal: National Assembly Needs More Funding. *Today.ng*. Retrieved from https://www.today.ng/news/nigeria/aminu-tambuwal-national-assembly-needs-more-funding-1650715.

Nwagwu, E. J. (2014). Legislative Oversight in Nigeria: A Watchdog or a Hunting Dog. *Journal of Law, Policy and Globalisation, 22*, 16–24.

Obasa, M. (2016, December 11). The Legislature and Good Governance. *The Nation*. Retrieved from http://thenationonlineng.net/legislature-good-governance/.

Ogbonna, A. (2018, October 22). Effective Legislature Essential to Democracy, Economic devpt. – Saraki. *Vanguard*. Retrieved from https://www.vanguardngr.com/2018/10/effective-legislature-essential-to-democracy-economic-devpt-saraki/.

Okoro, O. (2017). *The Concept of Legislative Oversight*. Retrieved from http://www.aronewsonline.com/?p=1947.

Olaniyi, J. O. (1997). *Introduction to Contemporary Political Analysis*. Ilorin: Timsal.

Olufemi, J., Akinwunmi, R., & Ugonna, C. (2015, April 26). Top 10 Corruption Scandals Nigeria's National Assembly Hasn't Resolved. *Premium Times*. Retrieved from https://www.premiumtimesng.com/news/182111-top-10-corruption-scandals-nigerias-national-assembly-hasnt-resolved.html.

Onwe, S. O., Ibeogu, A. S., & Nkwede, J. O. (2015). Imperatives of Legislative Oversight Function in Nigerian Democratic System. *Research on Humanities and Social Sciences, 5*(4), 72–79.

Osagie, S. (2017, March 24). *National Assembly Oversight Functions: Constitutional Provisions and Implications for National Development (Web log post)*. Retrieved from https://www.orderpaper.ng/national-assembly-oversight-functions-constitutional-provisions-implications-national-development/.

Oyedele, D., & Ezigbo, O. (2018, May 10). Senate Declares IG Enemy of Democracy, Unfit for Public Office. *This Day*. Retrieved from https://www.thisdaylive.com/index.php/2018/05/10/senate-declares-ig-enemy-of-democracy-unfit-for-public-office.

Oyewo, O. (2007, April 18–21). Constitutionalism and the Oversight Function of the Legislature in Nigeria. *Draft paper presented at African Network of Constitutional Law Conference on Fostering Constitutionalism in Africa*, Nairobi, Kenya.

Pelizzo, R., & Stapenhurst, F. (2011). *Parliamentary Oversight Tools: A Comparative Analysis*. London: Routledge.

Policy and Legal Advocacy Centre (PLAC). (2016). *Guide to Legislative Oversight in the National Assembly*. Abuja: PLAC.

Saraki, A. B. (2015). *Seventh Assembly Valedictory Speech*. Retrieved from http://www.abubakarbukolasaraki.com/.

United States Agency for International Development (USAID). (2000). *Handbook on Legislative Strengthening*. Technical Publication Series. Washington, DC: Centre for Democracy and Governance Bureau for Global Programs, Field Support, and Research.

Wade, E. C. S., Bradley, A. W., & Phillips, G. (1970). *Constitutional and Administrative Law*. London: Longman.

Yamamoto, H. (2007). *Tools for Parliamentary Oversight: A Comparative Study of 88 National Parliaments*. Switzerland: Inter-Parliamentary Union.

CHAPTER 9

Leadership Crisis in Nigeria's 8th Assembly: Implications for Institutional Efficiency and Intra-organ Stability

Adekunle Mojeed Animashaun

Introduction

One of the gains of the post-third wave democratic strengthening in Sub-Saharan Africa is the growing institutionalization of the legislature as one of the core democratic institutions. Africa's political past had been characterized by restricted role for the parliament in the governance sphere (Olukoshi 1998; Animashaun 2006) which saw the legislature beholden to the political executives (Rotberg and Salahub 2013). However, in spite of the emergent executive dominance that characterized early years of democratic opening or what Joseph (1999) calls 'abertura', African legislatures have over the last three decades become more assertive not only in protecting their institutional autonomy but also in exercising their constitutionally endowed powers (Salih 2005). While cross national

A. M. Animashaun (✉)
Department of Political Science, Fountain University, Osogbo, Nigeria

F. A. Aremu and A. R. Bakare (eds.), *Two Decades of Legislative Politics and Governance in Nigeria's National Assembly*,
https://doi.org/10.1007/978-981-33-4455-6_9

studies on African parliaments suggest varying degrees of legislative efficiency (Mattes et al. 2012), there is a sense in which it can be argued that the legislature in Africa is deepening the democratization process in spite of its very challenging operational context (Barkan 2008). Two major expectations accompanied renewed legislative institutionalization in African politics. First, African citizens nursed the hope that the emerging legislature would bring its new 'activist' status to bear on the governance architecture particularly in terms of generating developmental legislations that could impact on the material existence of African citizenry. Second, it was also hoped that the legislature would be able to curb executive rascality and making political executives to account through effective oversight of the executive branch and its agencies.

Restoration of full constitutional rule to Nigeria in 1999 after prolonged years of military dictatorship saw to the re-emergence of the parliament as a frontline operator in national politics as opposed to a secondary actor it was under successive authoritarian regimes. Quasi-legislative institutions that legislated for the country under dictatorial rule came with different names including Supreme Military Council (SMC), Armed Forces Ruling Council (AFRC), National Defence and Security Council (NDSC) and Provisional Ruling Council (PRC) which was the last law making organ under the military state before the democratic transition of 1999 (Best 1998). Thus, Nigerians not only welcomed the return of civilian rule, they also had high expectations that the legislature would play a vanguard role in transforming the oil-rich nation. Studies on the performance of post-transition legislature in Nigeria have however revealed that the Nigerian legislature has largely failed to meet the aspirations of the Nigerian citizens (Egwu 2005; Wasah 2000; Animashaun 2010; Baban' Umma and Abdul 2010).

The 8th Assembly of Nigeria's fourth democratic attempt emerged following the successful conclusion of the 2015 elections. The 2015 polls were historic given that they led to the alternation of party in power for the first time in the electoral history of Africa's largest electoral democracy (Animashaun 2015). Before the historic elections, the national mood had converged against the Goodluck Jonathan-led People's Democratic Party (PDP) federal administration ultimately resulting into crushing defeat for the ruling party at the polls. The Jonathan administration was generally perceived as the worst manifestation of impunity, corruption and patronage that the 16 years of PDP rule represented (Abdullahi 2017). It is within this context that the high expectations that accompanied the inauguration of the 8th National Assembly on 9 June 2015 are better appreciated. Nigerians nursed the hope that the new legislative body would hit the ground running by setting in motion effective machinery for the task of national reconstruction in tandem with the objectives of the 'Change Agenda' initiated by the Muhammadu Buhari presidency.

This chapter attempts to undertake an analysis of the parliamentary activities of the 8th National Assembly and how internal contradictions within its two chambers have impacted on the delivery of their constitutional mandate. The chapter is divided into six sections including the Introduction. Section two titled "The Legislature and Democratic Governance" undertakes a literature review of the place of the legislature in democratic governance while Sectinn three. "Nigeria's 8th Assembly: Emergence, Leadership Recruitment and Genesis of Crisis" examines the emergence of the 8th Assembly, its leadership selection processes and the descent into internal crisis. Section four "Symptoms and Drivers of the Crisis" of the chapter discusses the major symptoms and primary drivers of the crisis in the legislative assembly while Section five titled. "Consequences of Crisis on National Assembly Performance and Institutional Stability" outlines the net consequences of the crisis on the institutional efficiency of the national parliament and its internal stability in the period under review. Section six "Conclusion: Repositioning National Assembly for Enhanced Institutional Efficiency" of the chapter which concludes the study suggests measures aimed at re-positioning the legislature for greater efficiency. For methodology, the chapter basically adopts desk research method complemented with internet search and speeches of key actors in the crisis.

The Legislature and Democratic Governance

The legislature occupies the heart of representative liberal democracy and is generally recognized as the most representative institution of democratic governance. As a salient defining attribute of electoral democracy, the legislature is expected to strengthen democratic governance through, among others, shaping of the content of public policies and the character of governmental operations (Barkan 2009). Generally regarded as the institutional will of the people in a democratic context (Roseline and Gulbert 2014), the legislature is composed of representatives who are elected directly by the people to represent legally defined electoral constituencies in a democratic political system. The legislature assumes different names across representative democracies and these include Congress, Parliament, Assembly, Duma and Bundestag (Lowenberg 1971). Essentially a constitutional creation in all democracies, the legislature is a key ingredient 'underlining the representative character of modern democratic governance' (Animashaun 2014). The legislature offers societal diverse interests and tendencies an institutional forum to compete for expression and influence within the national polity. Indeed, Bogdanor (1991) has shown that the authority of the legislature as a democratic institution is derived from the fact that its membership is representative of all the constituents within the political community. Legislature exists in both British Westminster model and American presidential system of government but its existence is marked by different mode of emergence and varying degree of institutional influence. In the parliamentary system, the executive arm of government emerges from the elected legislature while the two branches of government are elected separately under the presidential system (Animashaun 2014). Westminster system was operated in Nigeria during the country's First Republic between 1960 and 1966. In the account of some scholars, this model was conflict-prone thereby exposing the newly independent state to instability that eventually culminated into the collapse of Nigeria's First Republic in January 1966 (Dudley 1982; Momoh 2000). In an apparent bid to escape from the inherent drawbacks of the parliamentary regime, Nigeria resorted to the presidential system during her second attempt at constitutional rule in 1979. The Constitution Drafting Committee (CDC) which was instituted by the Federal Military Government as part of its demilitarization programme was mandated to frame a constitution that would encourage consensual politics and inclusive governance that would be a radical departure from the institutionalized oppositional politics of the parliamentary genre (Aiyede 2005).

In all democratic countries, the legislature performs three basic functions namely, representation, law making and oversight, albeit the legislature has had to assume other functions in view of the increasing complexity of modern democratic governance. The basic rationale of oversight as a parliamentary tool or activity is to ensure that laws, policies or programmes 'are effectively implemented … and capture the intent of their drafters' (PLAC 2016). In the words of Barkan (2009), oversight 'is essential to any democracy because it ensures both the vertical accountability of rulers to the ruled as well as horizontal accountability of all other government agencies to the one branch-the legislature- whose primary function is to represent the citizens'.

Whereas unicameral (one-chamber) and bicameral (two-chamber) legislature types have been identified as the two major models of organizing the legislature in the dominant literature, Heywood (2007) has revealed that Yugoslavia and South Africa once operated a five-chamber and three-chamber legislature respectively. Nigeria currently operates bicameral legislature model patterned after the American type parliament comprising the Senate and the House of Representatives (Fashagba 2009). In bicameral legislature, one chamber may enjoy a pre-eminent status over the other in terms of institutional powers and influence. For instance, in Nigeria's presidentialist model, whereas the two chambers of the federal parliament make/amend laws and undertake oversight activities, only the upper chamber (the Senate) has the constitutional powers to screen and ratify presidential appointments.

Nigeria's 8th Assembly: Emergence, Leadership Recruitment and Genesis of Crisis

Section 4 (1) of the 1999 Constitution of the Federal Republic of Nigeria (as amended), provides for a federal legislature for the federation called the National Assembly made up of the House of Representatives and the Senate. The current National Assembly is the eighth to be inaugurated in the democratic history of Nigeria but the fifth since the democratic rebirth of 1999. The previous four Assemblies ran between 1999–2003; 2003–2007; 2007–2011; and 2011–2015. Inaugurated on 9 June 2015, the Assembly is dominated by two major political parties, the ruling All Progressives Congress (APC) and the largest opposition party, the People's Democratic Party (PDP). The National Assembly consists of 469 members with the Senate composed of 3 members each from the 36 states on the principle of equality with 1 from the Federal Capital Territory totaling 109 Senators. 6 out of the current 109 members of the Senate are women. They are: Stella Oduah (Anambra North), Uche Ekwunife (Anambra Central), Monsurat Sunmonu (Oyo Central), Fatimat Raji Rasaki (Ekiti Central), Oluremi Tinubu (Lagos Central) and Binta Garba (Adamawa North). The House of Representatives composed on the basis of population of the constituent states of the Nigerian federation has 360 members. At the end of the 2015 federal parliamentary elections, the APC won 60 (although 59 were eventually inaugurated following the death of Senator Ahmed Zanna representing Borno Central on 16 May 2015) and 214 seats in the Senate and the House of Representatives respectively while the PDP won 49 senatorial and 125 House seats. This initial parliamentary representation excludes 11 federal constituency seats in Jigawa state where elections were still pending at the time of inauguration. Labour Party, All Progressives Grand Alliance and Accord Party shared the remaining 10 seats in the House of Representatives to take the total to 360. However, recent internal wrangling that seized the two main parties (APC and PDP) in the aftermath of their nomination primaries for the 2019 elections led to a gale of defections across the two parties which have affected the current parliamentary strength of the two parties.

One significant component of inauguration ceremonies of legislative assemblies in democratic countries is the selection of principal officers of legislative institutions who will pilot the affairs of the law making bodies. Leadership selection in the legislature is crucial not only because the selection process must be inclusive but also because the leadership that emerges out of the process must enjoy the legitimacy of the membership of the legislature. The two chambers of the 8th Assembly chose its leadership on 9 June 2015, that exercise turned out to be its albatross and the crisis engendered by that event has refused to abate as the Assembly winds down its four-year tenure.

On the floor of the Senate on 9 June 2015 as part of the inauguration activities, the Clerk of the National Assembly (CNA), Salisu Maikasuwa, called for nominations into the Office of the Senate President. Senator Ahmed Sani Yerima (Zamfara Central) nominated Senator Bukola Saraki (Kwara Central) and the nomination was seconded by Senator Dino Melaye (Kogi West). The Clerk called for counter nominations but none came apparently because Senator Ahmed Lawan (Yobe North), APC anointed candidate for the office and several other APC Senators-elect were not in the chambers at that material time. At the time the CNA was inaugurating the Senate, Senator Lawan and others were at the International Conference Centre for a meeting purportedly convened by the presidency to interact with Senators-elect on the platform of APC. As it turned out, Senator Saraki with the informed cooperation of PDP Senators-elect was elected as the President of the 8th Senate without any challenger. After Saraki's election, Senator Ekweremadu (Enugu West) of PDP was elected the Deputy Senate President; same office he occupied in the 6th and 7th Senate presided over by Senator David Mark (Benue South). Senator Ekweremadu, like Senator Saraki, clinched the office ahead of the preferred APC candidate, Senator Ali Ndume (Borno South).

On the same day on the floor of the House of Representatives, the 8th House was also inaugurated with Hon. Yakubu Dogara (Bogoro/Dass/Tafawa Balewa constituency) elected the Speaker with 182 votes as against 174 polled by Hon. Femi Gbajabiamila (Surulere 1), the official APC candidate for the office. Thus, with the developments in both the Senate and the House, the ruling APC failed in installing its preferred candidates as presiding officers of the 8th Assembly. In its immediate reaction to these developments, the APC described the processes as 'a civilian coup' saying those that emerged were not candidates of the party with a threat to sanction all disloyal party members that participated in the processes that produced leadership of the two chambers of the 8th Assembly. However, President Muhammadu Buhari, apparently resigning to fate, conceded that the federal law makers acted within the ambit of the law. According to a statement by his Special Adviser, Media and Publicity, Mr. Femi Adesina, President Buhari would have preferred that the decision of the party on the selection of the leadership of the National Assembly was followed. The statement added that in spite of the turn of event, '...the president took the view that a constitutional process has somewhat occurred' with the affirmation that the president was ready to work with whoever was elected by the legislators. In its own reaction, the Goodluck Jonathan Campaign Organisation commended federal law makers for being assertive and courageous enough to resist the imposition of leadership by external forces. In a statement released on 9 June 2015 by its spokesman and former Aviation Minister, Femi Fani-Kayode, the campaign organization referred to the outcome of the selection of the leadership of the National Assembly as 'the destruction and demystification of Bola Tinubu and his Yoruba loyalists by his erstwhile northern allies in the APC' (Fani Kayode 2015).

The intrigues that produced the leadership of the 8th National Assembly was witnessed in the lower chamber of the federal legislature in 2011 when Hon. Aminu Waziri Tambuwal (Kebbi/Tambuwal federal constituency) emerged the Speaker of the 7th House with the cooperation of members of the opposition parties (particularly APC) in defiance to the ruling party's (PDP) official choice for the position, Hon. Mulikat Adeola Akande (Ogbomoso North/Ogbomoso South/Orire federal constituency). A pertinent question at this juncture is: In both events of 2011 and 2015, did the federal legislators breach the laws of the land? The answer is emphatic No! Their actions draw strength from relevant sections of the national constitution. Section 50 (1) of the 1999 constitution (as amended), regarding the selection of leadership of the National Assembly, provides for (a) a President and a Deputy Senate President 'who shall be elected by members of that House from among themselves'; (b) a Speaker and a Deputy Speaker of the House of Representatives 'who shall be elected by the members of that House among themselves'. Against the backdrop of these constitutional stipulations therefore, the legislators did not commit any sin as the intra-party mock elections conducted by APC to pick candidates for offices of presiding officers of the 8th National Assembly, though totally not unusual as it was the practice in all previous assemblies under the PDP administration, is not known to the constitution. But in terms of the supremacy of party organization, the law makers practically undermined their party's preference as they did in 2011. However, evidence across presidential democracies shows that weak party supremacy is a major drawback of the presidential model. In contrast to the parliamentary model where strong party supremacy and collective responsibility shape the legislative behaviour of legislators, the weak party supremacy and individual responsibility that are core attributes of the Washington model give incentives to party members to act in defiance of party position and still escape sanctions from the party.

Symptoms and Drivers of the Crisis

While the foregoing section gave an insight into the genesis of the lingering crisis in the two chambers of the National Assembly, several symptoms of this crisis have emerged as to make the impasse seemingly intractable. This section of the chapter will interrogate these symptoms and identify the major drivers of the festering crisis.

There are four immediate symptoms of the crisis in the 8th National Assembly that could be identified. These are: suspension of Senator Ali Ndume, suspension of Senator Ovie Omo-Agege; suspension of Hon. Jibrin Abdulmumuni; and the unusually long annual recess of the national parliament.

The suspension of Ali Ndume, Senate Majority Leader, for 6 months in March 2017 was widely believed to have been orchestrated by the leadership of the senate. Senator Ndume was suspended for filing a petition against Senate President over allegation that an armoured Range Rover car valued at N298 million seized by the Nigeria Customs Service was owned by Saraki. His suspension was also based on his call for Senate's probe of alleged certificate forgery involving Senator Dino Melaye. While Senator Ndume is a key member of the Parliamentary Support Group, made up of serving senators loyal to President Buhari, Senator Melaye is a key loyalist of Senator Saraki and both Saraki and Melaye are believed to be the arrow heads of opposition to President Buhari within the 8th Senate. This suspension seriously engendered crisis of confidence in the 8th senate. The suspension of Senator Ovie Omo-Agege (Delta Central) in April 2018 was to further deepen internal mistrust within the 8th Senate. The Delta law maker was suspended over his criticism of the intended amendment of Section 25 of the Electoral Act regarding sequence of elections which he alleged was targeted at President Buhari. It is interesting to note that it was Senator Melaye that made the recommendation for the matter to be referred to the Senate Ethics and Privileges Committee which recommended Omo-Agege's suspension. In the House of Representatives, the suspension of Hon. Abdulmumuni Jibrin (Kiru/Bebeji federal constituency) generated controversy within the lower chamber of the National Assembly. Hon. Jibrin, Chairman, House Committee on Finance and Appropriation, was suspended for 180 legislative days in September 2016 over allegations of budget padding he levelled against the leadership of the House. Outside of the legislature, his suspension was widely condemned as an act of highhandedness by the leadership of the lower chamber to silence a 'whistle blower'. The prolonged annual recess of the National Assembly particularly that of Senate was another indicator of crisis in the hallowed chambers. Whereas the leadership of the National Assembly justified the yearly recess as an opportunity by the law makers to spend summer holidays with their family members, the prolonged recess which lasted from July till October 2018 was widely perceived as a strategic move by the presiding officers of the two chambers to stave off an untoward reaction from members to the defection of the presiding officers from the ruling APC to opposition PDP particularly when there were pressing issues of national importance including INEC election budget and ratification of appointments into boards and agencies of government pending before the federal legislators. While Senator Saraki defected to the PDP on 31 July 2018, Hon. Dogara switched party on 13 September 2018. Apart from these immediate indicators of crisis in the 8th Assembly, there are other remote symptoms which include the siege by the operatives of Directorate of State Security to the National Assembly complex on 7 August 2018 with the speculation that the military raid was aimed at effecting a forced change of leadership in the National Assembly particularly in the upper legislative house; and perceived disdain by the presidency for the legislature which partly manifested in the rejection of some bills passed by the National Assembly including the Electoral Act Amendment bill 2018. There is a sense in which the refusal of the senate to confirm the appointment of Mr. Ibrahim Magu as substantive chairman of the Economic and Financial Crimes Commission (EFCC), the refusal to approve presidential request for virement of constituency project votes for election expenditure as well as the heckling that attended the budget presentation by the president on December 19, 2018 can be considered to be orchestrated by the law makers to pay back the president for not according the legislators the respect and honour they deserve in his dealings with them.

Among the major drivers of crisis in the National Assembly are political ambition of some principal officers of the federal legislature; corruption cases involving some members of the two chambers of the Assembly; party differences as well as battle of supremacy between the legislature and the executive. It is believed in many quarters that the desperation demonstrated by Senator Saraki to clinch senate presidency in 2015 was driven by his ambition to use the Office of the Senate President to advance his presidential ambition. Senator Saraki's presidential ambition had been on the drawing board since when he was the Chairman of Governor's Forum, an umbrella body of elected state governors in Nigeria (El-Rufai 2013). The fact that Senator Saraki eventually dumped the APC for PDP when it was clear that he could not secure presidential ticket in the former lends some credence to this belief. While several members of both chambers of the assembly including principal officers are being investigated for alleged corruption and forgery, the cases involving Senator Saraki and Senator Ekweremadu have provoked frictions in the Senate. Specifically, the celebrated trial of Saraki generated crisis of confidence in the Senate between core loyalists of Saraki (some of whom accompanied the Senate President to court during trial) and other senators in the chamber. Battle of supremacy between the legislature and the executive is another driver of crisis in the legislature. Both the legislature and executive under the current dispensation operate as contenders for space within the democratic system. Some of the measures taken by the National Assembly to assert its authority in the face of perceived executive dominance were perceived by some legislators in the two chambers as being too aggressive and this has caused division in the two legislative houses. One instance that readily comes to mind here was the decision of the Senate to stay action on some presidential appointments in reaction to President's Buhari's failure to remove Ibrahim Magu as the chairman of the Economic and Financial Crimes Commission (EFCC).

Consequences of Crisis on National Assembly Performance and Institutional Stability

Legislative institution is a creation of the constitution in all representative democracies. This institution exists at all levels of government under the current democratic dispensation in Nigeria. It is called National Assembly at the federal level, House of Assembly at the state level and Legislative arm at the local government level. The powers and functions of each of these legislative bodies are contained in the 1999 constitution of the Federal Republic, as amended.

Section 4 (1) of the 1999 Constitution (as amended), provides that the legislative powers of the Federal Republic of Nigeria are vested in a National Assembly consisting of the Senate and the House of Representatives. The Constitution further provides in Section 4 (2) that the National Assembly shall have powers to make laws for the peace, order and good government of the federation. Part 1 of the Second Schedule to the 1999 Constitution provides for the Exclusive Legislative List which deals with specific legislative items in which only the federal legislature has the exclusive prerogative to legislate upon. These 68 items include defence, aviation, insurance, currency, copyright, immigration, foreign affairs, citizenship, meteorology, customs and excise duties as well as drugs and prisons among others. Similarly, part 11 to the Second Schedule provides for the Concurrent Legislative List which contains 30 items in which both the National Assembly and State Assemblies are constitutionally empowered to legislate upon. These issues include agriculture, education, health, collection of taxes and antiquities and monuments. Residual list contains items or matters that are not included in the Exclusive list or Concurrent list with such matters reserved for the states (Ihedioha 2015).

On 4 August 2015, the House of Representatives released a Legislative Agenda designed to drive the legislative business of the lower chamber during the 8th Assembly of the legislative house. Among other objectives, the document aims 'to deliver legislations in aid of development and reforms aimed at improving conditions of living in Nigeria' (see

Legislative Agenda. 8th House of Representatives of the Federal Republic of Nigeria). Pledging to collaborate with other arms of government to engender responsive governance for the common good, the document further promises to generate requisite laws 'to achieve reforms in Nigeria's national economy and development, tackle poverty, unemployment, confront the scourge of corruption, terrorism and security challenges in the country'. Similarly, the 8th Senate of the Federal Republic after inauguration also released a Legislative Agenda which it said would help the legislative institution deliver on the expectations of Nigerians. Among others, the document pledges to make efforts aimed at 'reforming critical sectors of the Nigerian society, and the economy and will aim to deliver development, reforms, transparency and accountability in government'. Furthermore, the Senate through the Legislative Agenda promised to 'curtail every form of wastages in governance, entrench probity, accountability and transparency' even as the upper chamber made a commitment to combat poverty, tackle insecurity and reduce unemployment (see Legislative Agenda for the 8th Senate of the Federal Republic of Nigeria).

Less than six months to the end of the life of the 8th National Assembly, available evidence suggests that the two chambers of the federal legislature have not substantially met the expectations of Nigerians. Studies have shown that perennial internal conflicts within the National Assembly since 1999 have ensured that the legislative institution could not effectively perform its constitutional responsibilities of generating pro-active laws, representing the interests of its constituents and making the executive branch to account for its actions (Fashagba 2009; Aiyede 2006; Bassey 2006). Examples that readily come to mind here include the internal crisis that led to the removal of Senator Adolphus Wabara and Senator Chuba Okadigbo as Senate President; the crisis that saw to the removal of Hon. Patricia Olubunmi Etteh as Speaker of the House of Representatives leading to the emergence of Hon. Dimeji Bankole as Speaker; as well as mistrust and intrigues that characterized the tenure of Hon. Bankole as the presiding officer of the 6th House.

There is no denying the fact that the lingering crisis in the 8th National Assembly has impacted negatively on Nigeria's democratic governance. As observed by the Guardian (Nigeria) newspaper in its 24 August 2018 Editorial captioned 'This Crisis-Prone National Assembly', the crisis and its consequences represent a 'systemic failure that has cost the nation some benefits including good representation from the National Assembly'. Internal schisms within the two chambers of the National Assembly fuelled by mistrust, intrigues, mischief, abuse of powers and privileges, suspicions, selfish interest and inordinate ambition among members have distracted the law makers from the business of real governance even as they have engendered instability in the two chambers. This has affected the quality of democratic governance under the current dispensation. Whereas, the leadership of the two chambers scored the National Assembly high in the performance of its constitutional mandate, the verdict of this self-assessment is at variance with public perception on the performance and integrity of the 8th Assembly. For instance, the Senate in March 2018 released a long list of over 200 bills which it had passed into law since inauguration in 2015. In the same vein, the House of Representatives in June 2018 disclosed that it had passed a total of 222 bills since inauguration in June 2015. According to the Spokesman of the lower chamber, Hon. Abdulrazak Namdas, the House introduced a total of 1,473 bills with 90 of them on constitutional amendment. However, the dominant opinion within the polity is that the National Assembly has hugely failed in effectively performing its three core functions of representation, law making and oversight (Abati 2017). It has failed to meet the expectations of Nigerians on issues of national importance such as electoral reform, constitutional amendment, budget oversight, the economy, national security and anti-corruption. This performance deficit of the current federal parliament has left very grave consequences for democratization in Nigeria.

Conclusion: Repositioning National Assembly for Enhanced Institutional Efficiency

Nigeria requires an active and well-resourced legislature to build on the modest gains of the last two decades of democratization. The National Assembly needs to rise up to the challenge of rising expectations among Nigerians on the promises of democratic rule. The less than stellar performance that the National Assembly has posted in the last 42 months raises serious questions about the capacity of the legislature in Nigeria to deepen democratic governance and deliver tangible democracy dividends to the hapless Nigerian citizenry. Whereas internal squabble has been a defining element of the National Assembly since the return to civil rule in 1999 in some cases leading to the removal of principal officers (Nnamani 2006), the crisis rocking the 8th Assembly is arguably the most turbulent and the most enduring not only spawning institutional paralysis of the legislative body, but ultimately leading to switching of parties by the presiding officers of the two chambers of the federal parliament.

The Legislature constitutes one of the key institutional actors in a democratic setting endowed with formal powers to discharge its representative, law making and oversight responsibilities in order to achieve responsible and responsive governance. The extent to which the legislature in all democracies is able to perform these responsibilities largely depends on availability of sufficient parliamentary resources as well as internal cohesion and stability. Parliamentary resources would include adequate funding from the national budget, experienced and well trained parliamentary workers as well as functional Information and Communication Technology (ICT) infrastructure. Legislators should eschew mistrust, suspicion and inter-party hostility in order to create a congenial environment for development-centred law making business in the chambers. Without a stable environment devoid of mistrust and hostility, achieving legislative efficiency will be a mirage. Above all, law makers should demonstrate the spirit of give and take and develop the sense of public service by putting national interest above personal or group interest.

References

Abati, R. (2017, April 4). Dino Melaye: The Making of a Brand. *Thisday Newspaper*.

Abdullahi, B. (2017). *On a Platter of Gold: How Jonathan Won and Lost Nigeria*. Lagos: Kachifo Limited.

Aiyede, E. R. (2005). Executive-Legislature Relations in Nigeria's Presidential Democracy. *UNILAG Journal of Politics, 2*(1), 65–87.

Aiyede, E. R. (2006). Legislature-Executive Relations in Nigeria's Democracy. In E. Ojo (Ed.), *Challenges of Sustainable Democracy in Nigeria* (pp 140–154). Ibadan: John Archers (Publishers) Limited.

Animashaun, M. A. (2006). African Regimes and the Challenge of African Peer Review Mechanism. *UNILAG Journal of Politics., 3*(1), 112–128.

Animashaun, M. A. (2010). The Legislature and Fiscal Oversight in Nigeria: 1999–2010. *UNIOSUN Journal of Politics and Society., 1*(1), 33–54.

Animashaun, M. A. (2014). Nigerian Legislature and Parliamentary Aid. *Political Science Review, 6*(1), 8–24.

Animashaun, M. A. (2015). Nigeria 2015 Presidential Election: The Votes, the Fears and the Regime Change. *Journal of African Elections., 14*(2), 186–211.

Baban' Umma, M. B., & Abdul, S. (2010). Democratic Governance and the Challenges of Nation Building in Nigeria. *UNIOSUN Journal of Politics and Society, 1*(1), 19–32.

Barkan, J. (2008). Legislature on the Rise? *Journal of Democracy, XIX*, 124–137.

Barkan, J. (2009). *Legislative Power in Emerging African Democracies*. Boulder: Rienner Publishers.

Bassey, C. O. (2006) Legislature-Executive Relations and the Future of Democracy in Nigeria. In E. Ojo (Ed.), *Challenges of Sustainable Democracy in Nigeria* (pp 128–139). Ibadan: John Archers (Publishers) Limited.

Best, S. G. (1998). The Legislature in a Democratic Setting. In S. G. Tyoden (Ed.), *Legislators and the Legislature: A Critical Guide to Legislators in Nigeria*. Jos: Sikitse Consults.

Bogdanor, V. (1991). *The Blackwell Encyclopedia of Political Science*. Oxford: Blackwell Publishers.

Dudley, B. J. (1982). *An introduction to Nigerian Government and Politics*. London: Macmillan Press.

Egwu, S. G. (2005). The Legislature in Nigeria's Fourth Republic. In A. Gana & Y. Omelle (Eds.), *Democratic Rebirth in Nigeria: 1999–2003* (Vol. 1, pp. 19–40). New Jersey: Africarus Multimedia.

El-Rufai, N. A. (2013). The Accidental Public Servant. Ibadan: Safari Books.

Fani Kayode, F. (2015, July 8). We Warned Tinubu That 'Northern Allies' Will Betray Him. *Vanguard Newspaper*.

Fashagba, J. Y. (2009). Legislative Oversight Under the Nigerian Presidential System. *Journal of Legislative Studies, 15*(4), 439–459.

Heywood, A. (2007). *Politics* (3rd ed.). New York: Palgrave Macmillan.

Ihedioha, E. (2015, February 9). *Legislature as Instrument of Social Change*. Public Lecture delivered at Champion Newspaper's Better Society Lecture series. Owerri.

Joseph, R. (1999). Africa, 1990–1997: from Abertura to Closure. In L. Diamond & M. Plattner (Eds.), *Democratization in Africa*. Baltimore and London: Johns Hopkins University Press.

Lowenberg, G. (1971). *Modern Parliaments*. Chicago: Aldine Atherton Inc.

Mattes, R., Barkan, J., & Mozaffar, S. (2012). African legislatures: A glass half full? In Do Parliaments Matter? African Legislatures and the Advance of Democracy. *Perspectives, 2*(12). Heinrich Boll Stiftung.

Momoh, A. (2000). The History and Politics of Constitution making in Nigeria (1992–1999). In Jegede Segun, Ayodele Ale, & Eni Akinsola (Eds.), *Path to People's Constitution*. Lagos: Committee for the Defence of Human Rights.

Nnamani, K. (2006). The National Assembly in Perspectives: 1999 to 2005. *Nigerian Journal of Legislative Affairs, 1*(1), 1–89.

Olukoshi, A. (1998). *The Elusive Prince of Denmark: Structural Adjustment and the Crisis of Governance in Africa* (Research Report No 14). Uppsala: The Nordic Africa Institute.

Policy and Legal Advocacy Centre. (2016). *Guide to Legislative Oversight in the National Assembly*. Abuja: PLAC.

Roseline, F. M., & Gulbert, B. P. (2014). *The Handbook of National Legislatures: A Global Survey*. Cambridge: Cambridge University Press.

Rotberg, R. I., & Salahub, J. E. (2013). *African Legislative Effectiveness* (Research Report). The North-South Institute, Ontario, Canada.

Salih, M. A. E. (Ed.). (2005). *African Parliaments: Between Governance and Government* (p. 20). New York: Palgrave Macmillan.

Wasah, C. (2000). Low Capacity Impedes Law Making in the States. *Legislative Mandate, 2*(4), 11–14.

CHAPTER 10

Legislative-Constituency Relations in Nigeria: How Representative are the Representatives?

Michael C. Egwu

Introduction

Modern democracy is so germane in the formation of government where the people can be ruled and represented by their elected or appointed leaders. This provides a veritable platform for consultation, interaction and expression of views with the public. In a democratic state, both the legislators and constituents are expected to synergize in providing supportive decisions that would better their livelihoods. As a bi-cameral parliament, Nigeria's legislature consists of two houses: the upper and lower house (the Senate and the House of Representatives) modeled after the United State Congress. Legislative assemblies at the state and local government areas operate a unicameral system. Elections into national and state assemblies hold once in four years where the electorate elect 360 members of the House of Representatives—representing the 360 Federal Constituencies in Nigeria; 109 Senators—three Senators per state and one

M. C. Egwu (✉)
Department of Political Science, Federal University of Lafia, Lafia, Nasarawa State, Nigeria

F. A. Aremu and A. R. Bakare (eds.), *Two Decades of Legislative Politics and Governance in Nigeria's National Assembly*,
https://doi.org/10.1007/978-981-33-4455-6_10

from FCT. The President of the Nigerian Senate chairs the plenary while the Speaker of the House of Representatives chairs the House. The president of the Senate chairs any joint session of the parliament but the Speaker of the House presides the assembly in absence of the Senate President (Odeyemi & Abioro 2018; Okon 2004).

The legislative arm of government is saddled with the responsibility of law-making (though the primary function), enactment of laws, representing the constituents' interest, oversight on the executive actions among others. In executing legislative functions, the legislators as representatives of the people are expected to act and operate in a way that their constituencies would benefit (PLAC 2016). The legislature is a critical organ of government that guarantees and promotes good governance to the grassroots populace in a democratic setting. However, this can be achieved upon cordial relationships between the representative and the constituents. Legislators with strong ties to their constituents are more likely to have the mandate of the constituents to be reelected at the expiration of their tenure.

The workability of any democratic system depends on the power of the constituents in electing its representatives. Constituency remains the legislator's geographical district where an elected official represents the constituents (Gale 2008; Abbass 2007). Constituency office is established to enable the representatives to interface and synergize with the constituents. This synergy contributes to build a cordial legislative-constituency relations in any constituency the representatives represent. Ideally, both the representative and the represented are two-sides of a coin. This is underscored on the premise that they are all stakeholders in policy issues. The legislators are the lubricants that lubricate the constituents in providing them with dosage of information on national issues. However, this has not been the case in most developing democracies. This process has been hijacked by the political elite who are concerned about their selfish interest at the detriment of the people; thereby, marring the relationships between the legislators and the people.

Legislative-constituency relation is central to democratic governance; yet, evidence in extant literature has shown that the legislators have not performed quite creditably in this regard. There are 13 Local Government Areas (L.G.As) in Nasarawa State; but, the study is delimited to a five L.G.A in the study area. The principal aim of this study is to establish the impact of the representatives on their constituencies particularly in Nasarawa South Senatorial District/Federal Constituency of

Nasarawa State the study area; while the understated specific objectives are raised with a view to establishing the impact of the legislators in their constituencies. There are:

1. To determine who benefit from the legislative function of law-making in Nasarawa South Senatorial District/Federal Constituency.
2. To identify the impediments to effective representation of legislators in Nasarawa South Senatorial District/Federal Constituency.
3. To proffer policy measures in addressing the impediments to effective representation of legislators in Nasarawa South Senatorial District/Federal Constituency.

The study relies on primary and secondary sources of data. By using field survey, 400 copies of questionnaires are distributed across the study area. Secondary data are generated from textbooks, official documents, journals, unpublished works, newspapers, internet materials among others. Yaro Yameni's and Bowling's formulae of sample and allocation sizes cited in Odoziobodo and Amam (2007) are employed as shown in Equations 1 and 2. We use STATA for the descriptive statistics and multinominal logistic regression in the analysis of the inferential statistics.

Yameni's formula for sample determination

$$n = \frac{N}{1 + N(e)^2} \tag{1}$$

where n = Sample size; N = Research population; e = Level of significance; i or 1 =The constant; $N = 811{,}020$; $e = 0.05$; $1 = 1$

$$\frac{811,020}{1 + 811,020(0.05)^2} = 399.80 \quad \text{or} \quad 400.$$

Bowling's formula for allocation of sample size:

$$nh = \frac{nNa}{N} \tag{2}$$

where n = Total Sample; Na = No. of people in each L.G.A; N = Total number of people in the selected constituency.

Legislative-Constituency Representation: A Review of Literature

Concept of Political Representation

SEP (2018), sees political representation as the political activity where the voices, opinions and perspectives of the citizens are felt and recognized in the process of formulating public policy. The represented voices and opinions are felt when their representatives demonstrate the political will to speak, advocate and act on pursuing the collective good of the citizens in their legislative engagements. It is on this premise that effective political representation is populist driven and tends to be of great assistance to the citizens in any democratic clime. This offers an alternative approach with which political achievement through political activism, movements and representation occurs. Representation is an advocacy which should not be understood as interests' aggregation; but, the preservation of disagreements which makes it plausible for the preservation of liberty (Disch 2015; Urbinati 2000).

The concept of political representation can be seen from two contradictory standpoints i.e., representation by delegate and trustee. On delegate representation, the representatives are obliged to adhere to the needs and preferences of their constituency; then, trustee representation holds that the representatives should strictly adhere to their own judgement in the course of policy formulation (SEP 2018). It behooves on the representatives to act in a manner that can make them accountable to their constituencies. The essence of legislative representation is for the legislatures to ensure that the interest, needs and opinions of their constituencies are realized. For this, it is ideal that political representation under 'delegate' and 'trustee', the constituents' interests and priorities must override the interests of the legislators.

Plotke (1997) asserts that the understanding of political representation hinges on the political realities. This presupposes the fact that having a clear view of the concept is dependent on the contemporary understanding of the political realities and practices. He further stresses that the scope of political representation espouses interest representation. This corroborates with SEP's 'trustee' representation which then questions the role and functions of the representatives. In democratic governance, the function of the legislators cannot be underestimated. The legislators as representatives are expected to execute legislative functions that would be beneficial to their constituencies (PLAC 2016).

Williams (1998, p. 8) argues that political representation is "tied to three different dimensions of political life which is incumbent on the representatives to adhere on: the dynamics of legislative decision-making, the nature of legislator-constituent relations, and the basis for aggregating citizens into representable constituencies". She further explains that each aspect of the political life has a corresponding anchorage premised on voice, trust and memory. These make it possible for the views and opinions of the disadvantaged groups to be incorporated in the course of legislative decision-making. While the represented voices are fundamental, trust remains the cornerstone that makes democracy accountable in legislatives-constituents relations as well as memory serving as the boundaries with which groups can establish their past experiences. These are geared towards maintaining robust relations between the represented and their representatives. Robust relations is of the essence because, the absence of electoral connection between a represented group and their representative is mere surrogate and virtual representation (Rehfeld 2011).

Saward (2010) sees political representation as the representatives not only advancing the interests or preferences of the constituents, but to focus on the institutional and collective conditions where claim-making can take place. The represented should always interrogate the claims of their representatives while the representatives on the other hand, should make resounding claims that will elicit the constituents' attentions and responses. On this premise, political representation is adjudged by the quality of legislation in a polity where the legislators do not act base on the elite interests. This kind of legislation makes it amenable for robust representation and resonates the true essence of representative democracy. This is the way to make the represented present again in a democratic system of government (Abdulrahman 2018; Pitkin 1967).

From the foregoing, the concept of political representation is the political activity that allows for interest representation of two actors—the representative and the represented in a polity. In pursuance of this interest, these parties express their opinions on how to achieve their expectations through political actions.

Concept of Constituency

McLean and McMillan (2003, p. 117) opine that constituency is an "area whose electorate returns a representative to a national parliament". The supposition is that political activism is of the essence which makes the electorate to have the power to elect their representatives. The elected representatives make laws that would guarantee the sustenance and existence of the constituency. While the political parties are saddled with the tasks of organizing the process of nominating candidates that would represent the constituency, it does not change the representatives' obligation to the constituents they are representing upon being elected (Gándara-Sánchez 2014).

Abbass (2007, p. 1) posits that "constituency is the legislator's geographical reference point or district to whom an elected official is responsible.... This area is bound by shared structures, aspirations and interests which may be desirably and periodically reviewed". Implicitly, constituency is the political and electoral unit or district from which a legislator is elected by people of that electoral unit or district to represent them at the federal or state assembly. The essence of representation is to convey the demands of the represented to the government.

Fenno (1978) posits that constituency can be four types. A *geographic constituency* is the type that its boundaries are fixed by legislative or court action. It is characterized by the size of the district, the location, the industrial/business character or the socio-economic status, ethnicity among other characteristics of its population. A *re-election constituency* is the type that consists of people in a district that would always support the re-election of their representative. The representative considers them as his or her supporters. A *primary constituency* is the strongest supporter of the representative. In most cases, these supporters are group activists that are close allies to the candidate. A *personal constituency* is the representative's closest advisers and confidants. The decision-making of the representative is always influenced by the primary constituency.

Eulau and Karps (1977) assert that constituency can be represented in many ways. While Fenno provides four types of constituencies, they consider constituency in an order of responsiveness. These include: *Policy responsiveness* which occurs when a representative advocate and promote issues that would be beneficial to the majority of his or her constituents. *Service responsiveness* makes the representative to work in a manner that would provide benefits for individual constituents, groups and not majority of the constituents. The representative makes intervention on behalf of the individual or groups through government agency. *Allocation responsiveness* makes the representative serve the constituency by 'bringing home the bacon', like tangible projects. *Symbolic responsiveness* has fewer tangible efforts by the representative. The constituents hardly gain or have trust on the representative. A *mirror representation* is the type in which the representative shares salient characteristics with the constituency, like race or gender. The essence of mirror representation is premised on the presumption that, an African-American legislator quite understands and speaks the needs of his/her African-American constituents than how a white legislator can (Pitkin 1967).

Gale (2008) argues that the workability of any democratic system is dependent on the power of the constituents to elect their representatives. This, being fundamental to the represented, offers them the potentiality of having popular control over government. The prevalence of this control may be limited by several factors. However, the constituents with the little information they have on public policies and the behaviour of their representatives can convey their specific concerns and lobby their representatives to press home their demands. This can be achieved through letters and e-mails, protests, party activism, interest groups among others. The last two are to a large extent restrained and checked the power of government.

The concept of constituency is a geographically located unit with human population who elect people to represent them at the regional or national level. The constituents have the political power to reelect or withdraw a representative for effective or poor representation as the case may be. The people within a constituency have to make inputs in public policies particularly, in democratic legislature.

Examining the Roles of the Constituency Office in the Community

In a democratic setting, the roles of constituency office in any community are of essence. Though, Dovi (2007) stresses that a good democratic representative may not be appreciated by all the members of the constituency but the representative tries to advocate and promote the welfare of his/her constituents. Elected representatives in any constituency must have a functional constituency office as a legislator. This office must be structured in a way that it has a communication channel between the elected legislator and the constituents. So, in examining the roles of the constituency office in the community, effort is made here to critically probe how the representatives have performed in sustaining and maintaining constituency offices in their respective communities. The roles of constituency office can be examined from the people's expectations of the elected legislators and on the other hand, the legislators' expectations from the constituents.

Fundamentally, constituency office is established with the purpose of serving as a contact point between the representative and the represented. With this contact, the legislator knows the needs of the constituents. On the other hand, he/she gets them abreast of national issues with a view to elicit their opinions. Ideally, this office supposed to be open for all where the people can easily get some sort of help from their representatives; but on the contrary, this has been hijacked by the political elite. The elected representatives hardly report to the constituents what happens at national or state assembly. The high level of partisanship makes it difficult for common people to access the office being one of the places where they can ventilate their views on governance as well as use such mediums to appraise the performance of the representative. This is an aberration to democratic governance and this defines the nature and character most developing democracies particularly, Nigeria. Constituency office in most of the western democracies make the office open for all which enhances a robust relationship between the legislator and the constituents. There is also a strong feedback mechanism in the course of this relationship.

The role of the constituency office is to address some problems of the people. That is why people go there to present their problems like unemployment, admission into tertiary institutions, recruitments into the military and para-military forces among others. Some of the representatives have done well in addressing these problems in their constituencies while most of them have performed abysmally low in this regard. This is not unconnected to the prevalence cases of nepotism, prebendalism, tribalism as well as politicizing of the process where these representatives use their position to determine who gets employed, admitted in higher institutions and recruited into the military, police, among others in Nigeria. Most of the beneficiaries are the political thugs of these representatives. The qualified are disqualified; thereby, replacing merit with mediocre which the representatives do so on the pretext of maintaining their patron-client political relevance in their constituencies. In some cases, people get employed in government's institutions through paying for 'slots' exclusively reserved for the power that be.

Most people especially, the young ones get interested in politics as a result of regular contact and interaction with their representatives at the constituency offices. So, this office serves as a training ground in the art of governance. A lot of people into active politics owes to the knowledge they gained from interfacing with their legislators at the community level. Most legislators do not think of the legacy they can bequeath future generations hence, they keep recycling leadership at the detriment of the young people. Gerontocratic practice has been the norm and character of the political matrix in Nigeria. Youth being the future leaders is a mere rhetorics in the nation's political space. There is an ardent need to get the young people educated in politics. This would make them active in political activism and guarantee their vibrancy in political leadership role.

The transformation of campaign offices to constituency offices by the elected legislators is not only for their political gains, but for the people to use such platforms to reduce pressure on the representatives. It is a known fact in Nigeria's political landscape that political actors (elected or appointed) engage in corrupt practices in a bid to maintain patron–client relations and reseeking of election even when they failed in service delivery in their constituencies. The people should know that elected representatives are to serve the interest of the constituency and not any individual mounting pressure for their demand to be satisfied even at the detriment of the people. They should not expect all their problems to be solved by these offices. Still, this pressure is not unconnected to the endemic poverty that ravages the Nigerian state.

Constituency offices at various communities should operate in a manner that it takes into cognizance of promoting national interest against local or regional interest. Some legislators sponsor bills that are predetermined by their people at the national assembly. Some of the legislators out of pressure they received from their people and their re-election bid compromised the collective interests of the people. Any issue or opinion presented at the constituency office that is inimical to the corporate existence of the people should be discouraged. Constituency offices are located in the study area as shown in Tables 10.3 and 10.4.

How Do People Perceive Their Legislators?

In Nigeria's context, people's perceptions of their lawmakers are of polemic divides—the optimists and the pessimists. The optimists believe that the legislators are performing optimally in their legislative responsibilities. On the other hand, the pessimists negate the position of the optimists and aver that the legislators own interest and that of the elite interest supercede that of the constituents' interests.

For the optimists, Umoru (2016) quoted the chairman, Senate Committee on Information, Senator Abdullahi Sabi on a validation workshop of the Institutional and Capacity Needs Assessment of the National Assembly as saying that 'the image Nigerians paint about the institution is appalling and must be discouraged and jettisoned'. They hold that lawmakers discharge their legislative duties in an effective and efficient manner. Instead of condemning their actions, effort should be geared towards correcting the misperceptions the public have on legislature in Nigeria. They are rather to be commended on the prudent management of resources at its disposal as well as the existing interrelationship among various organs of the National Assembly. Adeniyi (2017) captures that statement made by Mr. Speaker, Right Hon Yakubu Dogara, the Chairman of this occasion of the second-year anniversary and the mid-term of the 8th session of the National Assembly. The speaker commended the 8th House of Representatives for performing their legislative tasks of lawmaking effectively and harmonious relationships with the executive arm of government.

Pitkin (1967) contends that political representation is to be present again. But for the pessimists, the legislators are seen as representing their interest and not being present to represent the citizens' interests. Political representation focuses on the institutional and collective conditions where claim-making can take place (Saward 2010). These conditions have been undermined by the representatives in an attempt to maintain their political relevance.

Conclusively, people's perception of the legislators can be likened to the verdict of blind men on how elephants looks like. This is because, from the standpoints of the optimists and the pessimists, the former appreciates the impact of the legislators (as inside actors) for the fact that they benefit from the system while the latter (as outside actors) appears to be on the disadvantageous position. This raises the concern of the beneficiaries of the legislative process.

Legislators and Democratic Representation: Whose Interest Is Protected?

The Lincolnian model of democracy presupposes a government of the people, by the people and for the people. And so, democratic representation must be rooted in the constitution where the representatives can truly represent and protect the interest of the people. Modern democracy however makes it easier for effective representation of the people. In the legislative's duties, the legislators make laws that are key elements to legislative and governance process. Democratic polity allows for citizens to debate with one another on public issues which with their perception and understanding, can see public action as action they licensed and supported from onset (Pettit n.d.; Larmore 2003).

In pursuance of public action, the lawmakers also take an active role (oversight) in monitoring how executive arm or/and its agencies perform so as to achieve efficient and accountable leadership. The essence of representing the interests of the constituents in a given political entity, calls for the articulation and aggregation of their interests in policy formulation. However, the assumption of citizens' interests being catered for does not hold sway as most policy issues reflect the interest of the elite. Majority of the legislators are drawn from individuals and groups from the elite background. Through the electoral process, the masses are incorporated only to elect leaders and the political party they can be identified with. Elections are crucial to democratic representation because with the casting of votes, the representatives have the consent of the constituents to represent them (Egwu 2017; Scully & Farell 2001).

Challenges to Cordial Legislative-Constituency Relations

There are issues that mitigate legislative-constituency relations in developing democracies of the world particularly, the Nigerian state. Among the many issues, the understated and explained issues are peculiar to the nature and character of Nigerian State.

Platform for Assisting Individuals

Most developing democracies of the world are faced with the challenges of the constituents relying solely on their legislators in getting help to solve their problems. This is the case of Nigerian state that instead of being supportive to the legislators in providing knowledge for policy inputs, the constituents consider the political representation of these lawmakers as means of having direct assistance to their needs. This has given room for perpetuating patron–client politics in the nation. Implicitly, this trend within the political matrix of the state makes the legislators engage in corrupt practices with a view to meeting the needs and demands of their constituencies; and make the legislators always avoid interfacing with their constituencies. These would inhibit robust relation and representation between the represented and their representatives. The legislators are obliged to employ staff in their constituency offices that would be saddled with the responsibility of dealing with the constituents' needs and demands so as to enable them to concentrate in their legislative duties.

Undue Influence of Party Leaders

Another challenge to legislative-constituency relations is the way and manner with which the party leaders interfere and influence the representatives. This is predicated on the prevalence on patron–client politics that has leveraged this trend as most legislators are elected through sponsorship and support of party leaders and political godfathers. Instead of having effective representation to the constituents, they play subservient and puppetry role to their benefactors. The activities of party leaders make the legislators to be left with no adequate fund which inhibit development of the constituency. To have effective representation, it is imperative for legislators to delink and insulate themselves from these party leaders that are concerned of their own interest at the detriment of the constituents. They should be concerned with policies that would better the lots of their constituencies on account that collective welfare of the people is the dividend of good governance. Also, with the constituents' support, they can perform optimally in their legislative engagements.

Personal Interests of Lawmakers

Legislative-constituency relation is impeded on account of the personal interests of the legislators. While resource constraint affects their representation, it is also true that this representation has a dosage of hiccups due to underutilization of public funds for the interest of the legislators themselves. Most of the legislators do not utilize their constituency allowances and project funds; hence, they end up using them for their own interest at the detriment of the constituents. This arm of government is expected to be accountable; but, the legislators of the Fourth Republic are more concerned with the primitive acquisition of material wealth through the offices they occupy and the power they hold. They use these positions to promote their selfish and parochial interest against the interest of the nation (Alabi & Fasagba 2009; Benjamin 2010; Lafenwa 2009). Even with the money they amassed for themselves, they hardly establish a channel of communication with the constituents as most of them do not run or have constituency offices that are functional. If the interests of the constituents are not catered for, it would be difficult to have effective legislative-constituency representation.

Poor Knowledge of Legislative Procedures

PLAC (2016) sees effective legislative representation as the successful execution of legislative functions as expected of legislators by the constituency member. So, a vibrant and knowledgeable legislator is the pride of the constituents while the one with little or no capacity to represent his/her constituency cannot be effective in representation. Apart from some lawmakers having inadequate knowledge in legislative matters, most people or groups in the society do not have the understanding of legislative procedure which mitigate their ability to articulate their needs to the legislature (Nwanolue & Ojukwu 2012). Poor legislative knowledge affects legislative-constituency relation and representation as the legislators with poor legislative knowledge can hardly make any contribution on the floor of the chamber (red and hallowed chamber in Nigerian's context). Having such representatives will make the constituents have little or no confidence in the capacity of lawmakers to represent them.

High Level of Illiteracy/Poor Understanding of the System

With over 180 million people in Nigeria, majority of the populace is not educated. This has blindfolded their perception on legislative functions. Because of the level of their education, they misconstrue and hardly differentiate the functions of the arms of government-legislature, judiciary and executive. Though the legislative arm can perform oversight function (actively understanding and monitoring how the executive arm and its agencies perform), they are not the executive arm that is responsible for implementing government policies and programmes. This poor understanding of the system poses a problem for the legislative-constituency relation in Nigeria.

The above issues are not exhaustive but have been the bane of legislative-constituency representation in Nigeria as a developing democracy. Overcoming these trends call for the political actors and citizens to have a new orientation of playing a pragmatic role that would guarantee a robust legislative-constituency representation.

The subject of study is anchored on the Principal–agent theory. This theory presupposes a practice in a democratic setting where the political actors use actions in providing incentives to the other actors (agents). The Principal–agent theory holds that responsiveness of the political actors is mediated by their actions (Gailmard, 2014).

Research Case Findings and Discussion

In seeking to establish the impact of the legislators on their constituencies in Nasarawa South Senatorial District/Federal Constituency, 400 copies of questionnaires were administered to elicit responses from the respondents. 390 out of the 400 distributed questionnaires were returned while 10 were not returned. In the analysis, descriptive (percentage) and inferential (multinomial logistic regression) statistics were used. In the rating, Tables 10.7 and 10.8 use '0' which stands for Yes while '1' is for No. Likert Scale rating is used in Tables 10.9, 10.10 and 10.11 of 10.1, 10.2, 10.3, 10.4 and 10.5. For Table 10.9, very high extent (VHE) 5, high extent (HE) 4, low extent (LE) 3, very low extent (VLE) and undecided (Und); Table 10.10, legislators 5, party leaders 4, political godfathers 3, political loyalists 2 and the constituents; and Table 10.11, undue influence of party leaders 5, personal interest of legislators 4, lack of contact with the constituents 3, poor knowledge of legislative procedures and constituents' high level of illiteracy/poor understanding of the system (Table 10.6).

The outcome in Table 10.6 shows that those for Yes, are aware of the existence of constituency offices in the area are 117 (30%) while those for No that is, not aware of the existence of constituency offices in the area are 273 (70%). This means that majority of the constituents are not aware that constituency offices exist in their areas. With this, it

Table 10.1 Population of selected constituents in Nasarawa South

S/N	*L.G.A*	*Population*	*Males*	*Females*
1	Awe	112,574	56,205	56,369
2	Doma	139,607	70,545	69,062
3	Keana	79,253	39,233	40,020
4	Lafia	330,712	169,398	161,314
5	Obi	148,874	74,412	74,462
Total		811,020	409,793	401,227

Source NPC (2006)

Table 10.2 Sample size of L.G.As in Nasarawa South

Selected L.G.As	*n*	*Na*	*N*	*nNa/N*
Awe	400	112,574	811,020	56
Doma	400	139,607	811,020	69
Keana	400	79,253	811,020	39
Lafia	400	330,712	811,020	163
Obi	400	148,874	811,020	73
Total		811,020		400

Source Field Survey, 2018

Table 10.3 Senatorial districts in Nasarawa State

S/N	*Senatorial districts*	*Code*	*Name/No. of LGA*	*No. of Ras*	*Collation center*	*Elected person*
1	Nasarawa North	SD/074/NW	Akwanga, Nasarawa Eggon&Wamba (3)	35	VIP Council Chamber, Akwanga LGA	Sen. Philip AruwaGyunka
2	Nasarawa West	SD/075/NW	Nasarawa, Keffi, Kokona, Karu&Toto (5)	59	University Auditorium Keffi, Keffi LGA	Sen. Abdullahi Adamu
3.	Nasarawa South	SD/076/NW	Lafia, Awe, Doma, Keana&Obi (5)	53	Ibrahim Abacha Youth Center Lafia, Lafia LGA	Sen. Suleiman S. Adokwe

Source INEC (2015)

Table 10.4 Federal constituencies in Nasarawa South of Nasarawa State

S/N	*Name of Federal constituency*	*Code*	*No. of LGA*	*No. of Ras*	*Collation center*	*Elected person*
1	Awe/Doma/Keana	FC/253/NW	3	30	Council Chamber Awe LGA	Hon. Moh'dOgoshiOnawo
2	Lafia/Obi	FC/255/NW	2	23	College of Agric. Lafia, Lafia LGA	Hon. Moh'dDahiruSarki

Source INEC (2015)

Table 10.5 State constituencies in Nasarawa South of Nasarawa State

S/N	*Name of state constituency*	*Code*	*No. of RAs*	*Collation center*	*Elected person*
1	Awe North	SC/674/NW	6	LGA Chamber Awe	Hon. TankoTunga
2	Awe South	SC/675/NW	4	Azara School Azara	Hon. Yahaya Rilwan
3	Doma North	SC/676/NW	6	Doma LGA Secretariat	Hon. Muhammed OkpedeDoma
4	Doma South	SC/677/NW	4	GSS Okpata	Hon. James DanganaAkoza
5	Keana	SC/680/NW	10	FGGC Keana	Hon. Yakubu Dodo Usman
6	Lafia Central	SC/685/NW	7	College of Agric. Lafia	Muhammmed Imam Abubakar
7	Lafia North	SC/686/NW	6	Ibrahim Abacha Youth Center Lafia	Hon. Mohammed Ibrahim Alkali
8	Obi I	SC/691/NW	5	Govt. College Obi	Hon. Muhammed Sani Audu
9	Obi II	SC/692/NW	5	GSS Duduguru	Hon. Amos Agya

Source INEC (2015)

Table 10.6 Responses on awareness of constituency offices in the area

tab aco			
ACO	*Freq.*	*Percent*	*Cum.*
0	117	30.00	30.00
1	273	70.00	100.00
Total	390	100.00	

Source Field Survey, 2018

Table 10.7 Responses on contact with the representative in the constituency area

tab crca			
CRCA	*Freq.*	*Percent*	*Cum.*
0	117	30.00	30.00
1	273	70.00	100.00

Source Field Survey, 2018

Table 10.8 Responses on the extent of the legislative function on democratic representation

tab elfdr			
ELFDR	*Freq.*	*Percent*	*Cum.*
1	39	10.00	10.00
2	32	8.21	18.21
3	38	9.74	27.95
4	79	20.26	48.21
5	202	51.79	100.00
Total	390	100.00	

Source Field Survey, 2018

Table 10.9 Responses on the beneficiary of legislative function

tab blf			
BLF	*Freq.*	*Percent*	*Cum.*
1	32	8.21	8.21
2	40	10.26	18.46
3	53	13.59	32.05
4	99	25.38	57.44
5	166	42.56	100.00
Total	390	100.00	

Source Field Survey, 2018

Table 10.10
Responses on the mitigating factor against effective representation

tab mfaer

MFAER	*Freq.*	*Percent*	*Cum.*
1	74	18.97	18.97
2	69	17.69	36.67
3	75	19.23	55.90
4	81	20.77	76.67
5	91	23.33	100.00
Total	390	100.00	

Source Field Survey, 2018

will be very difficult for the people to express their views and opinions on public issues since a good number of them do not know about the existence of constituency office. This office serves as a contact point with the represented.

The response in Table 10.7 shows that the constituents who say Yes that they have contact or meet with their representatives in their constituency are 117 (30%) while those that say No that they do not have any contact with their representatives are 273 (70%). This shows that the majority of the representatives hardly have time to meet with the constituents. This raises the question of whose interest is the representative representing since he/she does not have time to time with the people.

The findings show that: VHE is 202 (51.79%), HE 79 (20.26%), LE 38 (9.74%), VLE 32 (8.21%) and Und 39 (10%). With 202 being the highest response, it shows that the legislators meeting with their constituencies are very important to democratic representation. However, this has not been the case in the study area despite the high value of the impact. The legislators appear not to be meeting with the represented as the descriptive statistics indicated otherwise.

It is indicated that the most beneficiaries of legislative function in the study area are shown as: legislators 166 (42.56%), party leaders 99 (25.38%), political godfathers 53 (13.59%), political loyalists 40 (10.26%) and the constituents 32 (8.21%). The legislators have the highest in ranking followed by the party leaders and the political godfathers. This means that the legislators operate to maintain these interests. This affirms the positions of Alabi and Fasagba (2009), Benjamin (2010), and Lafenwa (2009) that the role of the Fourth Republic legislators is geared towards

Table 10.11 Impact of the representatives on their constituencies

reg aco crca elfdr

Source	*SS*	*df*	*MS*
Model	68.5204716	2	34.2602358
Residual	13.3795284	387	0.034572425
Total	81.9	389	0.210539846
Number of obs = 390			
F(2, 387) = 990.97			
Prob > F = 0.0000			
R^2 = 0.8366			
Adj. R^2 = 0.8358			
Root MSE = 0.18594			

aco	*Coef.*	*Std. Err.*	t	*P > |t|*	*[95% Coef. Interval]*	
crca	0.9145367	0.205458	44.51	0.000	0.8741413	0.9549321
elfdr	0.0055571	0.0069378	0.80	0.424	– 0.0080835	0.0191977

Source STATA Software Application, 2018

acquiring material wealth through the offices they occupy as well as using their positions to achieve their selfish and at the detriment of the nation. They seek for political offices in furtherance of their primitive accumulation of wealth and not for the collective good of the citizens.

It is revealed that the mitigating factors against effective representation and legislative-constituency relation in the study area are: undue influence of party leaders 91 (23.33%), personal interest of legislators 81 (20.77%), lack of contact with the constituents 75 (19.23%), poor knowledge of legislative procedures 69 (17.69%) and the constituents' high level of illiteracy/poor understanding of the system 74 (18.97%). It is indicative from the findings that the major challenge to effective representation in the focal area is undue influence of party leaders. This owes to patron-clientism and godfatherism that have permeated the nation's political space. Party leadres often decide who becomes their party's flag-bearer in election and upon winning election, they influence them in their legislative matters.

To establish the impact of the representatives on their constituencies, the finding shows that it is poor due to poor communication channel between the represntatives and the contituents. The multinomial regression analysis is used and it is found appropriate because while the sign of the coefficient suggests the nature of the impact, the size of the coefficient suggests the magnitude of the impact. In the multinomial regression, awareness of constituency office (ACO) is used as the dependent variable while contact with the representative in the constitutency (CRCA) and extent of legislative function on democratic representation (ELFDR) are used as the independent variables. In terms of the nature of the impact, all the independent variables appear positively signed; suggesting that both CRCA and ELFDR have a positive impact on ACO. However, CRCA has much impact as the coefficient appears larger (0.9145367). It means that 1% increase will lead to 91% increase in ACO. On the overall goodness of fit, the model appears robust enough as the f calculated at 990.97 > f tabulated at 3.00 with 2 and 387 degrees of freedom.

Conclusion and Recommendations

A cordial legislative-constituency relation is of the essence in democratic representation hence, modern democracy allows for the representatives to be elected by the constituents to represent them by pursuing populist agenda in the scheme of governance. In light of this, a robust synergy between the representative and the represented cannot be undermined in the course of representation. This study draws conclusion that the major beneficiaries of the legislative functions are the legislators themselves. This implies that it is their selfish drives that spur them into seeking elective positions and not to protect and promote the interest of the constituents. This equally accounts for financial abuse and diversion of constituency allowances for their private gains. It can also be drawn that the most mitigating factor against effective representation is the undue influence of the party leaders. This finds expression in the way and manner political godfathers and benefactors do not allow legislators especially, those they sponsored in elections to operate on their own without undue interference. Resultantly, the legislators are constrained and do not have the leverage to discharge their legislative functions without being subjected to acting according to the dictate of the party leaders. Finally, lack of the constituents' contact with the representative in their constituency is the most important factor affecting legislative-constituency relations in the study area. This is because most of the constituents are not aware of the existence of constituency office let alone one-on-one contact with the legislators. Based on the findings of this study, we make the understated recommendations:

i. That the constituents' interest should be prioritized by the legislators in their legislative engagements at the national assembly. The essence of representation is to protect and promote the interest of the people through policy actions that are people-oriented and not individual-oriented. However, the people can rely on the constitutional ground to recall any legislator that errs in the discharge of his legislative functions in Nigeria.

ii. There should be legislation prohibiting party leaders from undue influence on the legislators. This entails insulating them (party leaders) from legislative matters. Once a legislator is elected, he/she should work to ensure effective representation of the entire constituency and not on the party line.

iii. There should be advocacy on constituency-based communication channel in all the constituencies in the federation. This would make it easier for regular contact between the legislators and the constituents; and, the constituency offices will not function only on campaigns or electioneering period. This will equally go a long way to strengthening and consolidating legislative-constituency relations in Nigeria. This contact can be achieved through the following communication approaches:

(a) An outreach approach where the legislators can have quality consultation with the constituents on public policies and actions. Here, the people are at liberty to express their views and opinions on such policies;
(b) A visit approach which makes it plausible for the representatives to elicit responses (feedback) from the represented; and
(c) Media approach where the legislators can engage the media to inform, educate and sensitize the public on legislative programmes.

References

Abbass, I. M. (2007).*Constituency office: Meaning and importance*. Being a paper presented at Legislative Aides Training at Denis Hotel Abuja on Tuesday 13th November 2007. Retrieved from: https://test.abu.edu.ng/abu/publications/2011-06-13-105201_5712.doc On: 17th December, 2018; 4.20 pm.

Abdulrahman, K. (2018, September 23). FCT and competitive legislative representation. *The Guardian Sunday Magazine*.

Adeniyi, O. (2017, June 9). Image perception of the legislature: Causes and possible solutions. *The Cable*. Retrieved from: https://www.thecable.ng/image-perception-legislature-causes-possible-solutions On 24th December, 2018; 3.00 pm.

Alabi, M. O. A., & Fasagba, J. Y. (2009). The legislature and anti-corruption crusade under the Fourth Republic of Nigeria: Constitutional imperatives and practical realities. *International Journal of Politics and Good Governance, 1*(1–2), pp. 1–39.

Benjamin, S. A. (2010). National Assembly: The limit of party politics in legislative process. *Nigeria Journal of Legislative Affairs, 3*(1–2), pp. 44–72.

Disch, L. (2015). The constructivist turn in democratic representation: A normative dead-end. *Constellations, 22*(4), pp. 487–499.

Dovi, S. (2007). *The good representation*. Oxford: Blackwell Publishing.

Egwu, M. C. (2017). Political leadership: A desideratum for national development in Nigeria's Fourth Republic. *South East Political Science Review, 1*, pp. 83-97.

Eulau, H., & Karps, P. D. (1977). The puzzle of representation: Specifying components of responsiveness. *Legislative Studies Quarterly, 2*(3), pp. 233–254.

Fenno, R. F. (1978). *Home style: House members in their districts*. Boston: Little, Brown.

Gailmard, S. (2014). *The oxford handbook of public accountability [Ed.]*. Retrieved from: http://www.oxfordhandbooks.com/view/10.1093/oxfordhb/9780199641253.001.0001/oxfordhb9780199641253e016 On 23rd December, 2018; 2.56 pm.

Gale, T. (2008). *International Encyclopedia of the Social Sciences*. Retrieved from https://www.encyclopedia.com/social-sciences-and-law/sociology-and-social-reform/sociology-general-terms-and-concepts/constituency On 6th December, 2018; 4.57 pm.

Gándara-Sánchez, R. (2014). *Legislative representation, political culture*. Retrieved from https://enciclopediapr.org/en/encyclopedia/legislative-representation-political-culture/ On December, 2018; 4.50 pm.

Independent National Electoral Commission [INEC]. (2015). Nasarawa State Office, Lafia.

Lafenwa, S. A. (2009). *The legislature and the challenges of democratic governance in Africa: The Nigerian case*. A seminar paper delivered at a conference on Governance and Development on Democratization in Africa: Retrospective and future, prospects. Held on: December 4–5, at University of Leeds, United Kingdom.

Larmore, C. (2003). *Public reason: The Cambridge companion to rawls*. S. Freeman [Ed.]. Cambridge: Cambridge University Press.

McLean, I., & McMillan, A. (2003). *The concise of dictionary of politics [Eds.]*. New York: Oxford University Press.

National Population Census [NPC]. (2006). Nasarawa State Office, Lafia.

Nwanolue, B. O. G., & Ojukwu, U. G. (2012). Legislative efficiency and democratic stability in the Fourth Republic governance and politics of Nigeria: A re-appraisal of National Assembly. *Kuwait Chapter of Arabian Journal of Business and Management Review, 1*(9), pp. 116–131.

Odeyemi, T. I., & Abioro, T. (2018). Digital technologies: Online engagement and parliament-citizen relations in Nigeria and South Africa. *Advances in African Economic, Social and Political Development. Springer International Publishing*, pp. 217–232. https://doi.org/10.1007/978-3-319-93509-6_12. Retrieved from https://en.wikipedia.org/wiki/National_Assembly_%28Nigeria%29 On: 20th December, 2018; 3.35 pm.

Odoziobodo, S. I., & Amam, W. I. (2007). *Research methodology for social and management sciences*. Enugu: Ingenious Creations Services Ltd.

Okon, A. O. (2004). Nigeria and a people's constitution: The imperative of democracy and change. *Journal of Constitutional Development*, *4*(1), pp. 11–36. Centre for Constitutionalism and Demilitarisation (CENCOD).

Pettit, P. (n.d.). *Varieties of public representation*. Retrieved from www.lecre.umontreal.ca/wp.../Varieties_of_Public_RepresentationPettitSept08.doc. On: 20th December, 2018; 4.01 pm.

Pitkin, H. (1967). *The concept of representation*. Berkeley and Los Angeles: University of California Press. Retrieved from https://en.wikipedia.org/wiki/Representation_%28politics%29 On 7th December, 2018; 4.36 pm.

Plotke, D. (1997). Representation is democracy. *Constellations, 4*, pp. 19–34.

Policy and Legal Advocacy Centre [PLAC]. (2016).*Guide to effective representation in the National Assembly*. Abuja, Nigeria. Retrieved from http://placng.org/wp/wp-content/uploads/2017/06/Guide-to-Effective-Representatio-for-Lawmakers.pdf On: 7th December, 2018; 3.48 pm.

Rehfeld, A. (2011). The concepts of representation. *American Political Science Review* https://doi.org/10.1017/s0003055411000190. Retrieved from: https://polisci.wustl.edu/files/polisci/imce/apsr_concepts_of_representation_rehfeld.pdf On: 14th December, 2018; 2.59 pm.

Umoru, H. (2016, August 30). Negative perception about us by the public worrisome—Senate. *Vanguard*. Retrieved from: https://www.vanguardngr.com/2016/08/negative-perception-us-public-worrisome-senate/ On: 24th December, 2018; 2.39 pm.

Urbinati, N. (2000). Representation as advocacy: A study of democratic deliberation. *Political Theory, 28*, pp. 258–786.

Scully, R., & Farell, D. M. (2001, May 31–June 2).*Understanding constituency representation in the European Parliament*. Paper Presented to the Conference of the European Community Studies Association. Madison.

Saward, M. (2010). *The representative claim*. Oxford: Oxford University Press.

Stanford Encyclopedia of Philosophy [SEP]. (2018). *Political representation* (revised edition). Retrieved from: https://plato.stanford.edu/entries/political-representation/ On: 8th December, 2018; 10.30 am.

Williams, M. (1998). *Voice, trust, and memory: Marginalized groups and the failings of liberal representation*. Princeton, NJ: Princeton University.

CHAPTER 11

The Nigerian House of Representatives from 1999–2019: A Performance Assessment

Terfa W. Abraham

Introduction

The importance of the legislature in Nigeria's democratic governance cannot be overemphasized. From its representative function, to oversight and lawmaking, several studies have continued to examine the performance of the country's legislature to take stock on its performance and impact on governance. While several of this studies have provided a review of the nation's legislative arm of government from historic (Olusanya 1980; Osadolor 2014) and contemporary perspective (Egwu 2005; NILS 2010, 2014; Hamalai 2015), examining the performance of the legislature from either perspective of the Senate or the House of Representatives (HoR) has become increasingly important given the need to establish the effectiveness of each House (Miquel and Synder, Jr 2004; Ekor et al. 2014; Crosson et al. 2018). While there are existing studies on the performance of the Nigerian House of Representatives, extending the coverage

T. W. Abraham (✉)
National Institute for Legislative and Democratic Studies (NILDS), Abuja, Nigeria

F. A. Aremu and A. R. Bakare (eds.), *Two Decades of Legislative Politics and Governance in Nigeria's National Assembly*,
https://doi.org/10.1007/978-981-33-4455-6_11

from 1999 to 2019 and introducing new dimensions to the analysis of existing data, would be a valuable addition. Such a study will extend the work of Osadolor (2014) that examines the evolution of the central legislature from 1982 to 2014, but did not contextualize how the evolution should enforce the relevance of the lower chamber and possibly, the need to rethink the ratio of member to population in the House of Representatives.

Secondly, the application of Volden and Wiseman (2009) on legislative effectiveness has been applied in the study of the Nigerian legislature (see Ekor et al. 2014). While this methodology seeks to deduce the effectiveness of specific legislators on Bills passage, the technique turns the attention of analyst interested in evaluating the overall effectiveness of the legislature from the institution to individual legislators. As such, assessing the performance of the legislature from a perspective that allows for the identification of periods where the legislature (as an Institution) performed better, is important to allow analyst to take stock of lessons to learn and areas to strengthen.

Although Section 4 (1 and 2) of the 1999 constitution of the Federal Republic of Nigeria (as amended) provides that the legislative powers of the Federal Republic of Nigeria shall be vested in a National Assembly for the Federation, which shall consist of a Senate and a House of Representatives; Section 60 of the 1999 Constitution (as amended) further provides that the Senate or the House of Representatives shall have power to regulate its own procedure, including the procedure for summoning and recess of the House. Unfortunately, studies examining the performance of the Nigerian legislature have not paid attention to how the Standing Order of the House of Representatives have changed and the implication it has for the effectiveness of the National Assembly. Using the Standing Order of the House of Representatives reprinted in June 2007 and that reprinted in July 2014, examining how the Standing Order have changed and how it affected the operation of the House of Representatives within 1999–2019, would provide useful insight to understanding the performance of the House of Representatives.

The oversight function of the Nigerian National Assembly is another aspect that has gained the attention of researchers (NILS 2014). A review of some of these studies to identify the frequency of oversight activities conducted by the Senate and House of Representatives, is also important as it would point out the aspects of the economy and democracy governance that the oversight activities of the House of Representatives relative to that of the Senate have concentrated from the fourth to the eighth Assembly.

A study by Hamalai (2015) also highlights the importance of resource competence on the performance of the House of Representatives. This position is also corroborated by Volden and Wiseman (2009) who argued that the innate abilities and cultivated skills of Members of congress, has a potential influence on the overall effectiveness of the legislature. Using existing data from NILS (2014) and Hamalai (2015), this chapter also examines how the academic qualifications of Members of the House of Representatives have changed within the Fourth and the Eighth National Assembly. Political developments of the country within 1999–2019 have also been accompanied by change in membership of political affiliation. Examining how the party membership of the Speakership of the House of Representatives have changed within the study period, is therefore important as it would help to measure the party that has held leadership of the House within the study period.

The study employs secondary data on evolution and composition of the legislature in Nigeria from existing studies. Two versions of Standing Order of the House of Representatives were also reviewed for comparative analysis. Existing data on oversight of the National Assembly, academic qualification and political party association, were also collected from secondary sources such as NILS (2014), Hamalai (2015) and online sources such as statisense.com (2015). Lastly, while data on Bills presented and passed in the House were collected from NILS (2017), additional data on Bills presented and passed in the House of Representatives were collected by publication on Bills passed within 2015–2018 of the House of Representatives. Data on Bills presented and passed were collected from the website of PLAC (Policy and Legal Advocacy Centre).

The paper is structured into four sections. Contained in section one is the introduction and identification of gap in the literature the paper seeks to fill. The conceptual framework for the study is provided in section two, while section three provides the analytical framework for the analysis of secondary data used for the paper. The aspects of performance analysis of the House of Representatives within 1999–2019 discussed in the chapter are also identified in section three. This includes the assessment of the Representation Framework of the House of Representatives, the Standing Order of the House of Representatives, Oversight activities, level of Educational Qualification of Members, political party affiliation of the Speakers of the House of Representatives and assessment of Bills Received and Passed in the HoR from 1999 to 2019.

Framework for Assessing the Performance of the Legislature

There are a number of parliamentary assessment frameworks created by different organizations. LSE (2009) identify five of these organizations to include:

i. Commonwealth Parliamentary Association/World Bank Institute/United Nations Development Programme Benchmarks (CPA/WBI/UNDP Benchmarks);
ii. National Democratic Institute Standards (NDI Standards);
iii. Inter-Parliamentary Union Self-Assessment Toolkit for Parliamentarians (IPU Toolkit);
iv. Parliamentary Centre—Budget Process (PC-Budget); and
v. Parliamentary Centre—Parliamentary Audit (PC-Audit).

These institutional assessment frameworks basically involve the use of indicators to assess the performance of parliaments. According to Imlach et al. (2009), the CPA/WBI/UNDP Benchmarks are phrased as standards rather than as questions and no system to code/categorize responses to these benchmarks is provided by the document itself. Indicators are divided into four main topical headings, namely General, Organization of the Legislature, Functions of the Legislature and Values of the Legislature, and there are additional subcategories listed within these main headings.

Another framework for assessing the performance of the legislator as identified in Lute (2009) is the National Democratic Institute Standards (NDI Standards). The methodology entails allowing civil society groups to discuss with parliaments in order to determine how parliamentarians adhere to core democratic values and on that basis, makes an assessment of the performance of the legislature. The approach of the Inter-Parliamentary Union is premised on the consideration that parliamentary assessment should be motivated by members of parliaments themselves, such that, the parliamentarians serve as the main actors in any assessment conducted.

The view of the IPU is that the five core values presented by their Toolkit, namely representativeness, transparency, accessibility, accountability and effectiveness, can be achieved by parliaments in different ways. As such, the IPU views parliamentary assessment as an action-oriented, demand-driven process, whereby parliamentarians discuss their answers to the questions raised in the IPU framework.

Other approaches of assessing the performance of the legislature focus on the budget process and performance of parliamentary audit committees. Both of these approaches are used by the Parliamentary Centre (PC). According to Miller (2005), the PC also devised a Parliamentary Report Card, which examines parliamentary activity in four areas, namely Legislation, Budget, Oversight and Representation (Miller 2005). In this regard, the approach also narrows to assessing the performance of the function of the legislator. The London School of Economics and Political Science (LSE 2009), extends these aspects of assessment to include: lawmaking, representation, procedures, public engagement, oversight and resources.

Institutional websites such as Afrobarometer, also use the public trust of democratic institutions such the National Assembly as a means of assessing the performance of the legislature. Using the Afrobarometer database, NILDS (2018) in its social indicator publication argued that the proportion of respondents who do not trust the national assembly increased from 35.8% in the Afrobarometer survey conducted in 2014/2015 to 43.1% in the survey carried out in 2016/2018. Studies that examined the performance of the Nigerian legislature, studies such as Hamalai (2015), assessed the performance of the Nigerian National Assembly in terms of resource competence, while others like PARP (2010), focused on the aspects of lawmaking, representation and oversight. An important aspect identified in LSE (2009) is that of procedure. Following Miller (2005) and LSE (2009), this study adapts a multi-perspective approach for its analysis of secondary data (see Fig. 11.1).

Analysis and Discussion of Existing Data

To carry out the objectives of this chapter, the performance assessment of the House of Representatives (HoR) from 1999 to 2019 is examined in six perspectives:

- Assessing the Representation Framework of the House of Representatives,
- Assessing the Changes in the Standing Order of the House of Representatives. Three issues are examined in this subsection. They are: Provision for Number of Committees; Handling of Bills from

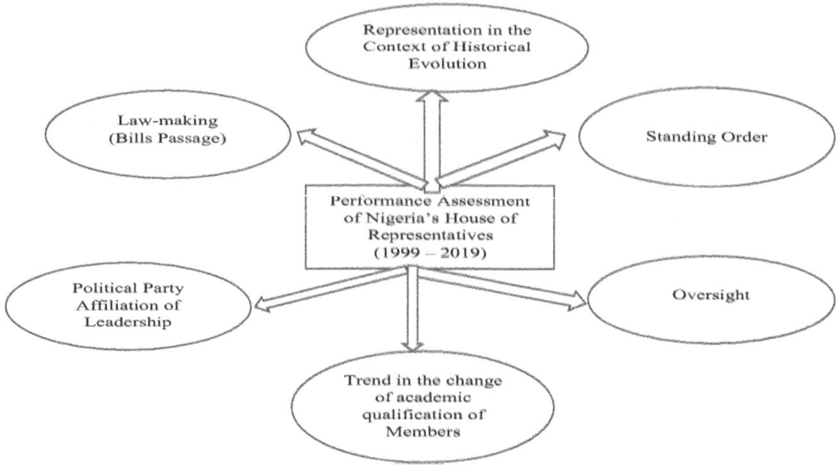

Fig. 11.1 A multi-dimensional framework for assessing the performance of the legislature (*Source* Author's Conceptualization)

Preceding Legislative Session and Nomination of Membership of Committees,
- Assessing the Oversight activities of the HoR,
- Assessing the Level of Educational Qualification in the HoR,
- Political Party affiliation of the Speakers of the House of Representatives and
- Assessment of Bills Received and Passed in the HoR.

Secondary data collected from existing literature, publications of the National Institute for Legislative and Democratic Studies and website of PLAC are examined using charts, tables, percentages and ratios. Rather than provide a separate section for the review of empirical and theoretical literature, the paper reviews existing literature in the context of each issue to be assessed. Although the scope of the study is 1999–2019, historical issues on the evolution of the House of Representatives were also visited. Also, the data for the 8th House of Representatives for 2019, were as of February.

Assessing the Representation Framework of the House of Representatives

The Section 4 (1 and 2) of the 1999 constitution of the Federal Republic of Nigeria (as amended) provides that:

> 4 (1) The legislative powers of the Federal Republic of Nigeria shall be vested in a National Assembly for the Federation, which shall consist of a Senate and a House of Representatives.
>
> 4 (2) The National Assembly shall have power to make laws for the peace, order and good government of the Federation or any part thereof with respect to any matter included in the Exclusive Legislative List set out in Part I of the Second Schedule to this Constitution.

The above provision shows that the powers to make laws rest with the both Houses of the National Assembly. Compared to the Senate where there are 109 Senators, the House of Representatives has 360 Members. A historic account would provide some insight on how Nigerian House of Representatives has evolved.

Nigeria has witnessed two phases in the evolution of its legislative arm of government. According to Osadolor (2014), the first phase was from 1952 to 1960, and the second phase is from 1960 to 1966. Within these periods, the central legislature developed from unicameral to bicameral legislature (Osadolor 2014). The major characteristics of the evolution of the legislature in Nigeria are presented in Tables 11.1, 11.2 and 11.3 (Figs. 11.2, 11.3, 11.4, 11.5).

Section 36 of the 1960 Independence Constitution introduced a bicameral legislature, and created the Senate as the upper chamber and the Federal House of Representatives as the lower chamber. An underlining consideration from the Lyttleton Constitution of 1954 that was sustained in the 1960 independence constitution as argued by Osadolor (2014) is the need for a lower chamber to give voice to all. It was also expected to facilitate representation for groups or interests that otherwise might be ignored (see Osadolor 2014). The number of senators in the upper chamber was provided for in the 1960 constitution to be 52, while the lower chamber provided for 320 Members (see Fig. 11.6). On Nigeria's return to democracy in 1999, however, the number of Senators increased to 109 and the number of Members in the lower chamber, to 360 (see Fig. 11.7).

Table 11.1 Evolution of the composition of the legislature in Nigeria: 1862–1913

Characteristics	*Type of Legislature in Place*
Following the British conquest and annexation of Lagos as a colony in 1861, a legislative council was established in June 1862 by Governor Stanhope Freeman, and functioned until 1906 From 1866 to 1874, Sierra Leone was the seat of the central administration of the British West African settlements in Sierra Leone, Lagos, The Gambia and Ghana (then Gold Coast). During this period, the legislative council of Lagos continued its separate existence under an Administrator In order to reduce administrative cost, within 1874–1885, the affairs of Lagos as a colony were transacted in Ghana (Gold Coast at the time). The task of administration of the legislative council revolved around the control of revenue and expenditure of the colony, with final powers residing with the Secretary of State; The second phase began in 1906 when the legislative council of southern Nigeria was established and functioned until 1913 In the Crown Colony system, the Governor as the representative of the Crown was the central institution of British colonial government and head of the executive government and was president of the legislature The legislature was not separate from the Executive Council but subordinated to it In May 1906, the Lagos Colony and protectorate was amalgamated with the protectorate of southern Nigeria. As such, the Legislative Council of Southern Nigeria was established as the central legislature for the territory until 1913	Central administration of Legislative Council for the four British colonies (Nigeria, Ghana, Sierra Leone and the Gambia) with Unicameral structure; indigenous membership was in the minority and could not form any formidable opposition to colonial policies

Source authors tabulation based on Osadolor (2014)

Table 11.2 Evolution of the composition of the legislature in Nigeria: 1914–1951

Characteristics	*Type of Legislature in Place*
Demand for separate legislative council for each of the British colonies The 1922 Clifford constitution established a legislative council with a maximum membership of 46 for which, 26 and the governor were officials and 19 were unofficial (see Fig. 11.2) The legislative council had the power to legislate on matters of colonial governance, peace order and good government in accordance with the usual practice in the Crown Colony for southern provinces In the Northern provinces, legislation was premised on the proclamation of the Governor-in-council, the lieutenant governor and with senior residents of the Northern provinces and representatives if the Kano chamber of commerce and the mining industry Richard Constitution of 1946 sought to provide a framework for greater interaction by bringing the North and the South into the same legislative authority. This necessitated the holding of sessional meetings outside Lagos After the general constitutional conference in January 1950, the Legislative Council held its sessional meeting in the Eastern region. It was during this meeting that the proposals for greatly enhanced regional autonomy within a united Nigeria was adopted A select committee was constituted to consider a possible position of a central legislature for all the regional legislative authorities The select committee of the legislative council considered the proposals for a bicameral legislature The select committee commenced a debate for bicameral legislature but settled for one chamber system The 1951 Macpherson Constitution established a unicameral legislature known as the House of Representatives, with 148[a] Members of which 136 were elected by and responsible to the regional legislature (see Olusanya 1980	Demand for separate legislative council for each of the British colonies; More seats were added to the Legislative Council within 1922–1946, but the legislative institution remained the same; North and the South came into the same legislative authority Regional legislative authorities; The legislative council remained central, increased in composition (see Fig. 11.3) but remained unicameral

[a]Northern House of Assembly = 68; Western House of Assembly = 34; Eastern House of Assembly = 34; Appointed Members to represent interests = 6; and Officials = 6

Source Authors tabulation based on Osadolor (2014)

Table 11.3 Evolution of the composition of the legislature in Nigeria: 1952–1966

Characteristics	*Kind of Legislature in Place*
The 1951 Macpherson constitution provided for regional inclusiveness in the membership to the parliament (see Fig. 11.3). However, it was not until 1954–1960 that officials and special Members were removed from the regional and federal legislatures, attributable to the legal provision of the Lyttleton constitution of 1954 The 1954 Lyttleton constitution increased the membership of the Federal House of Representatives to 184 (see Fig. 11.4) The central legislature during this period developed from unicameral to bicameral legislature. From 1952 to 1960, the parliament consisted of one chamber in which the executive and legislature were interconnected. From 1960 to 1966, the central legislature was structured into two chambers	The 1954 Lyttleton constitution increased the membership of the Federal House of Representatives to 184; The 1960 Constitution introduced a bicameral legislature; The lower chamber gave room for representation by groups or interests (*see* Fig. 11.5 *for composition of the Legislature as Provided by Lyttleton Constitution of 1954*)

Source authors tabulation based on Osadolor (2014)

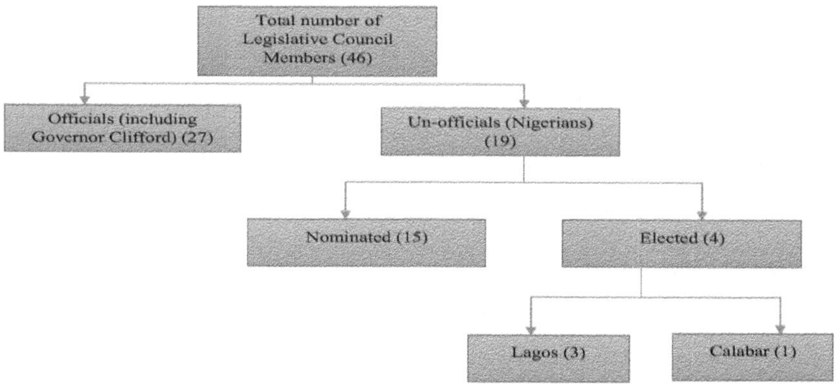

Fig. 11.2 Membership Composition of the Legislative Council in Colonial Nigeria (Unicameral Legislature as Provided by Clifford Constitution of 1922) (*Source* Authors Presentation)

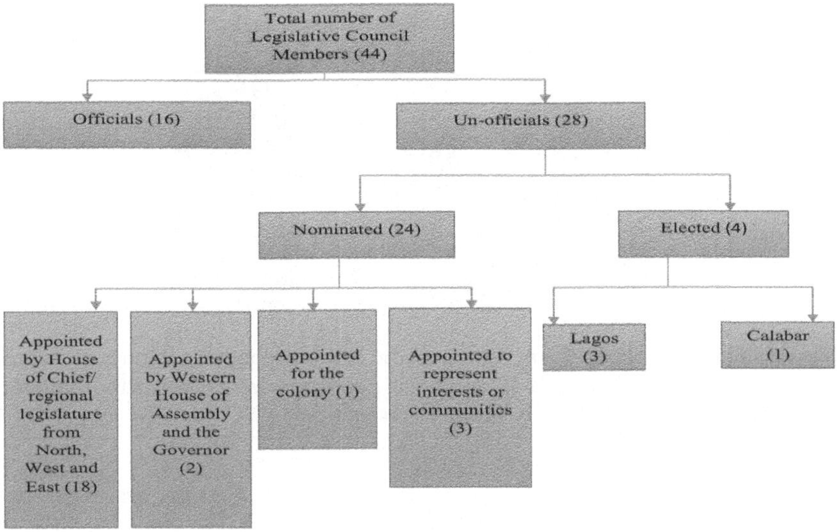

Fig. 11.3 Membership Composition of the Legislative Council in Colonial Nigeria (Unicameral Legislature as Provided by Richard Constitution of 1946) (*Source* Authors Presentation)

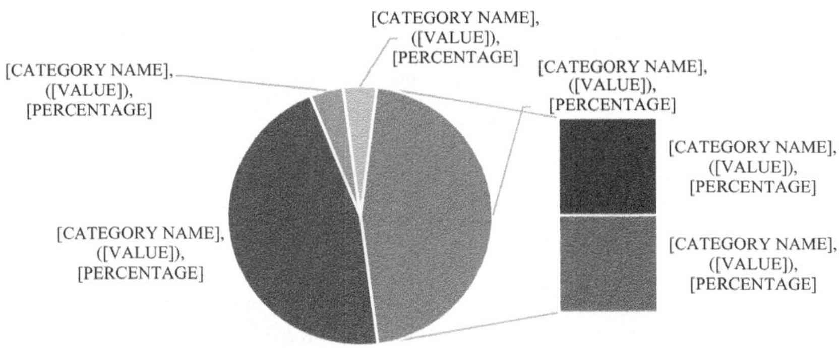

Fig. 11.4 Membership Composition of the Pre-independence House of Representatives in Colonial Nigeria (Unicameral Legislature as Provided by Macpherson Constitution of 1951) (*Source* Authors Presentation)

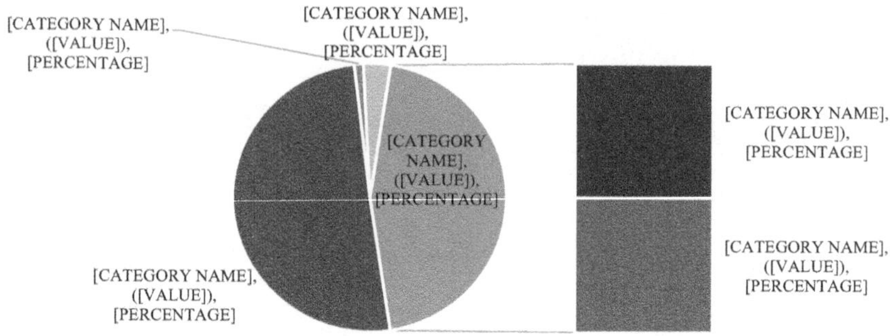

Fig. 11.5 Membership Composition of the Pre-independence House of Representatives in Colonial Nigeria (Unicameral Legislature as Provided by Lyttleton Constitution of 1954) (*Source* Authors Presentation)

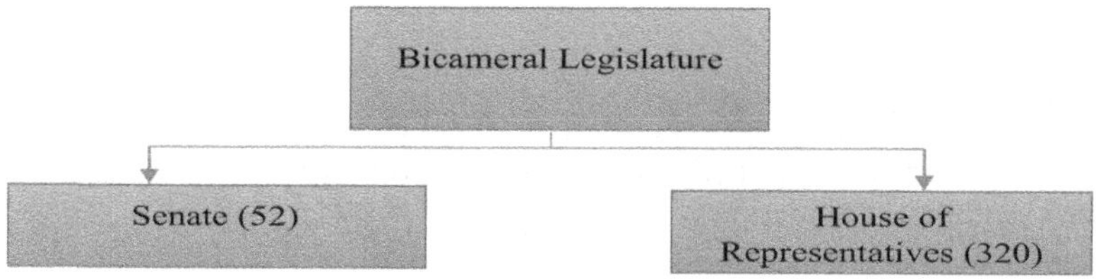

Fig. 11.6 Membership/Composition of Nigeria's Legislature as provided by the 1960 Independence Constitution (*Source* Authors Presentation)

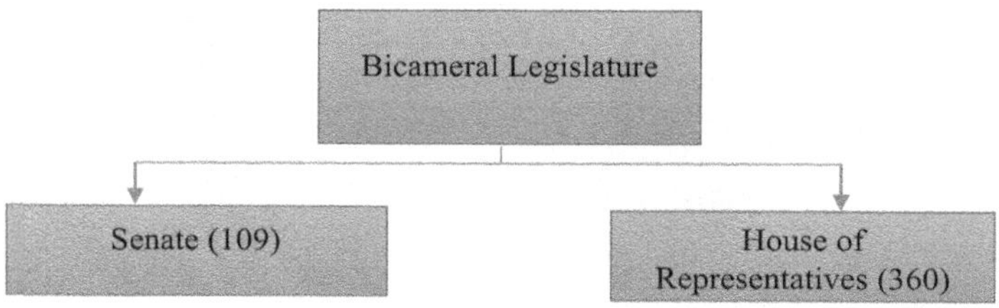

Fig. 11.7 Membership/Composition of Nigeria's Legislature as provided by the 1999 Constitution (as amended) (*Source* Authors Presentation)

Whereas Nigeria's population have changed from an average of 48,096,105 within 1960–1966 to 152,157,666 within 1999–2018, the total number of Members in the House of Representatives have only moved from 320 to 360 (a 12.5% change as against population that has recorded a percentage change of 216.36%). Within 1960–1966 the ratio of average number of people represented by a member of the House of Representatives was 1:150,300, it has increased to an average of 1:422,660 within 1999–2011, and to 1:516,720 within 2015–2019 (see Fig. 11.8). It is therefore not far-fetched while Members of the House of Representatives have continued to face mounting pressures and demands for financial assistance from their constituents. Restructuring the country towards a path that will increase the outcome of governance is therefore critical. This chapter demonstrates that National Assembly, in particular the House of Representatives through its lawmaking and representative functions, is positioned to contribute to the growth and development of the nation's democracy. Exploring how this can be achieved through continuous engagement with relevant stakeholders remains critical. This analysis is illustrated in Fig. 11.8.

One of the functions of the National Assembly is representation. As such, there should be a link between changing population and the number of representation especially in the House of Representatives where representation is hinged on the number of local governments and population. The 1999 constitution (as amended) provides for 360 Members of the House of Representatives. Whereas the population of the country has grown, reflecting this adjustment on the number of federal constituencies has not been commensurate. Table 11.2 shows the number of federal constituency in each geopolitical zone and the Federal Capital Territory (FCT) against the number of constituencies. Dividing the population in each zone by the number of federal constituencies shows that the ratio

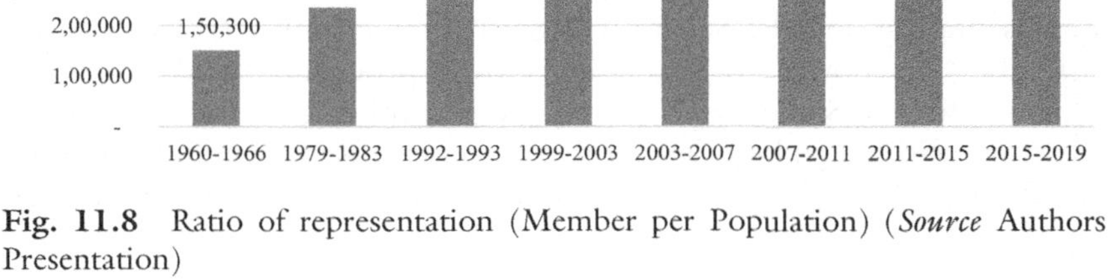

Fig. 11.8 Ratio of representation (Member per Population) (*Source* Authors Presentation)

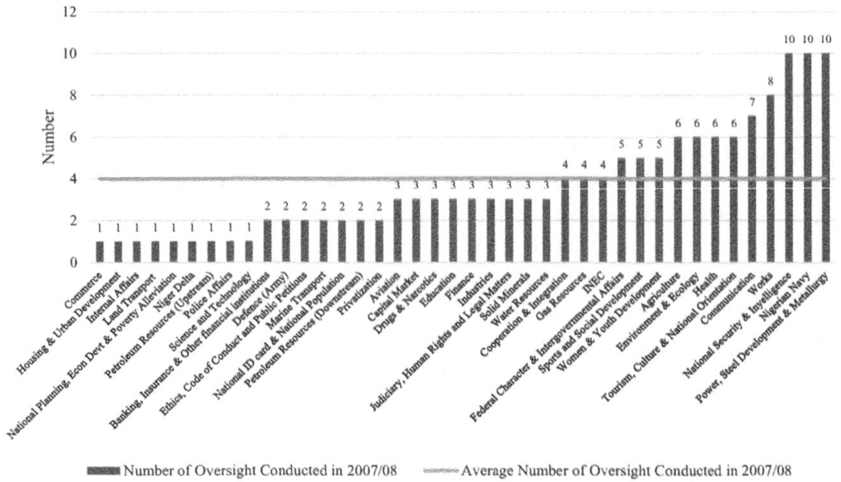

Fig. 11.9 Number of oversight activities conducted in the Senate in 2007/2008 (*Source* PARP; NASS [2010]; Authors Presentation)

of representative per population in the six geopolitical zones is about 1:500,000. The ratio for the FCT, however, shows huge concern as it yields 1:1,782,062. When this population is divided by three however, it yields a similar ratio with the rest of the zone which is 1: 594,020. The deduction from this analysis is that a constitutional alteration might be necessary to increase the number of House of Representatives members for FCT from 2 to 3. This is presented in Table 11.4.

Assessing the Changes in the Standing Order of the House of Representatives

Under the Nigerian 1999 Constitution (as amended), the power to legislate is vested in its National Assembly which is bicameral: the House of Representatives and the Senate. However, each chamber of the National Assembly has power to regulate its own procedure. Such rules are provided for the Standing Orders of each chamber. A comparison of the structure of the Standing Order of the House of Representatives in 2007 and 2014 shows that the contents reveal similarities and major differences.

Table 11.4 Number of federal constituency by geopolitical zone/fct and population

Zones	*No. of Federal Constituency*	*Regional Population*	*Rep Member per Population*
South East	43	21,955,414	510,591.01
South South	55	28,829,287	524,168.85
South West	71	38,257,261	538,834.66
North East	48	26,263,865	547,163.86
North Central	49	25,688,282	524,250.64
North West	92	48,942,307	531,981.59
FCT	2	3,564,126	1,782,062.83
National	360	193,500,540	537,501.50

Source statisense.com (2015; Appendix A), and National Population Commission (2016; Appendix B)

The Standing Order of the House of Representatives provides the rule upon which the operation of the Federal House of Representatives is premised. The basis for this rule is contained in Section 60 of the 1999 Constitution (as amended), which provides that: 'Subject to the provisions of this constitution, the Senate or the House of Representatives shall have power to regulate its own procedure, including the procedure for summoning and recess of the House'. This section reviews how the Standing Orders of the House of Representatives have changed within 1999–2019 and the implication it had for the operations of the lower chamber. To identify the changes in the House Rule, a reprint of the House Standing Order on 28 June 2007, is compared with a reprint version on 17 July 2014 (see Table 11.3). The issues raised in the Standing Order are discussed in three headings(Table 11.5).

- Provision for Number of Committees,
- Handling of Bills from Preceding Legislative Session and
- Nomination of Membership of Committees.

Table 11.5 Comparison of the standing order of the House of Representatives of 2007 and 2014

House of Reps Standing Order reprinted 28 June 2007	*House of Reps Standing Order reprinted 17 July 2014*
Order I—Rules for conduct of business Order II—Meeting of new Parliament —Election of presiding officers Order III—Quorum Order IV—Sittings of the House Order V—Privileges Order VI—Members Order VII—Duties and functions of officers of the House Order VIII—Arrangement of Business —Motions and Amendments Order IX—Rules of Debate —Behaviour of Members in the House Order X—Order in the House Order XI—Voting Order XII—Procedure on Bills Meeting of Conference Committee Procedure of Money Bills (Budget) Order XIII—**Annual reports and other sessional papers** Order XIV—Membership of Committees Order XV—Miscellaneous Business continued from session to session **Bills from the proceeding Assembly** Order XVI—Privileges on treaties Proceedings on proclamation of a state of emergency Order XVII—Committees of the House (Establishment and Jurisdiction of Committees) Special Committees (8) Standing Committees (66)	Order I—Rules for conduct of business Order II—Meeting of new Parliament Order III—Members Order IV—Quorum Order V—Sittings of the House Order VI—Privileges Order VII—Duties and functions of officers of the House Order VIII—Arrangement of Business —Motions and Amendments Order IX—Rules of Debate —Behaviour of Members in the House Order X—Order in the House Order XI—Voting Order XII—Procedure on Bills Meeting of Conference Committee **Bills Outstanding from the Preceding Assembly** Procedure of Money Bills (Budget) Order XIII—Procedure altering the Constitution Order XIV—Proceedings on Treaties Order XV—Proceedings of Proclamation of a State of Emergency Order XVI—**Annual reports and other sessional papers** Order XVII—Membership of Committees Order XVIII—Committees of the House Special Committees (8) Standing Committees (56) Order XIX—Miscellaneous Privileges of the Floor

Source Standing Orders of the Federal House of Representatives (HoR) 2007 and 2014 (Compiled by Author)

Provision for Number of Committees

In terms of similarities, all the seventeen orders contained in the Standing Order of 2007 were retained in the reprinted version of 2014. There were also no changes to the order stipulating the privileges enjoyed by Members. On the other hand, whereas the 2007 Standing Order of the

House of Representatives had eight (8) special committees and sixty-six (66) standing committees, the Standing Order of 2014 had eight (8) special committees and fifty-six standing (56) committees.

Secondly, the 2007 Standing Order made provision for how the business of the House shall continue from one seating to the next. However, this was not contained in the reprinted version of 2014. The advantage of that inclusion in 2007 is to allow the business of the House to continue in the next sitting as though there was no break. The disadvantage, however, is that, it may not allow for dynamism in the evolution of issues to discuss in the next seating, whether these issues are pertinent/urgent or not. In the 2014 reprint version, however, the advantage of the exclusion is that it will allow for issues discussed in the House to originate from topical issues of the day. Unfortunately, the disadvantage of such exclusion from the Standing Order in 2014 is that it does not provide for issues to be discussed in a sustained manner.

Handling of Bills from Preceding Legislative Session

The rules of the House of Representatives revised in July 2014 as with that of June 2007 allows for Bills outstanding from the preceding House of Representatives to be sustained in current House. This has the advantage of allowing the Bill to be re-considered in the present legislative session. Precisely, Section 94 of the Standing Order (reprinted in July 2014) provides that:

Bills passed by the preceding Assembly and forwarded to the Senate for concurrence for which no concurrence were made or negatived, or passed by the Senate and forwarded to the House for which no concurrence were made or negative or which were passed by the National Assembly and forwarded to the President for assent but for which assent or withholding thereof was not communicated before the end of the tenure of the Assembly, the House may resolve that such Bills upon being re-gazetted or clean copy circulated be re-considered in Committee of the Whole without being commenced de novo.

Source Standing Orders of the House of Representatives (8th Edition ordered to be reprinted 17 July 2014) and contained in page 82 Section 8 of the Standing Orders of the House of Representatives, ordered to be reprinted 28 June 2007

The Standing Orders of the House of Representatives reprinted in July 2014 provide in separate section of the procedure for altering the constitution. With the national confab that was held in 2014, the Standing Order of the Federal House of Representatives was revised to provide for clear procedures to altering the constitution (see Order XIII of the House of Representatives Standing Order). This provision was not contained in the Standing Order of the House Revised on the 28th of June 2007. This adjustment in the Standing Orders of the House of Representatives, project the lower chamber as progressive as efforts are sustained to ensure that legislative business is a continuum.

Nomination of Membership of Committees

In order to properly oversight the MDAs and to ensure that the operations of the MDAs are consistent with legislative requirements, Members of the House of Representatives are constituted into committees. An examination of the Standing Order of the House of Representatives shows that provision for the nominations of members into committees in the House of Representatives have changed within 1999–2019 to allow for nominations of membership of committees to be based on competence and relevance rather than on party affiliations.

Section 1 (1) of Order XIV of the Standing Rules of the House of Representatives (June, 2007) provides that: 'Members of Committees shall be nominated by the various political parties and appointed by the Committee on Selection in accordance with their strength in the House'. The clause that membership to committees will be based on nomination by various political parties weakened the composition of membership to committees as membership was tied to party affiliation rather than competence.

In the Standing Order of the House of Representatives (July 2014), this provision was revised to remove the clause that nomination to committees will be by political party. Section 107 (1) of Order XVII of the Standing Orders of the House of Representatives (July 2014), provides that, 'Members of Committees shall be nominated and appointed by Committee of selection'. Membership and composition of the Committee of Selection is structured in a manner that reflects leadership of the House and membership across geopolitical zone. This is contained in Section 118 (2) of Order XVII which provides that,

The Committee on Selection shall consist of the Speaker, the Deputy Speaker, House Leader, House Whip and Minority Leadership; provided that the Speaker if the need arises may co-opt other members into the Committee and shall in so doing reflect the equality of the geopolitical zones.

The Committee on Selection is one of the seven committees that should be constituted within the first thirty legislative days following the first sitting of the House.[1]

Assessing the Oversight Activities of the House of Representatives

The Policy Analysis and Research Project (PARP) in 2010, examined the performance of committees in the Nigerian National Assembly from 2003 to 2010. The study provides a review of how the committee system serves as workhorse of activities in the National Assembly. The study shows that committees in both chambers of the National Assembly have grown within the period. Factors responsible the growth of the number of committees identified in the study are: the need to position the National Assembly to respond to developments in the country; and need to effectively oversight the executive arm of government. The instrument employed by committees to carry out their functions include: Briefs received from MDAs, visits to MDAs, project inspection, engagement with Appropriation Bill/budgetary function, public/investigative hearings, public petitions, confirmation/screening of nominees, interactive sessions, interviews, Bills scrutiny/analysis and resolutions. To examine the application of these instruments to oversight activities in both the Senate and the House of Representatives, PARP (2010) drew a sample of 61 committees from the National Assembly for oversight activities conducted within 2008/2009. It was found that while committees in the Senate applied within 2–3 instruments of oversights, Committees in the House of Representatives apply within 4–5. Thus suggesting that the quality of oversight conducted by the House of Representatives is likely to be higher compared to what is obtained at the Senate. A major

[1]Others are: Committee on Rules and Business, Committee on House Services, Committee on Public Petitions, Committee on Public Accounts, Committee on Ethics and Privileges and Committee on Media and Public Affairs (see Section 117, Standing Order XVIII of the House of Representatives, July 2014).

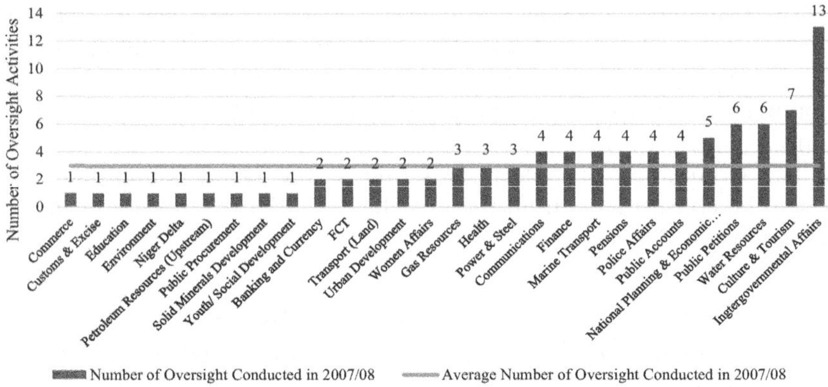

Fig. 11.10 Number of oversight activities conducted in the House of Representatives in 2007/2008 (*Source* PARP; NASS [2010]; Authors Presentation)

observation from the study is that, the number of oversight activities conducted in the National Assembly within 2007/2008 in the House of Representatives, is less than that carried out by the Senate. Whereas total number of oversight conducted in 2007/2008 in Senate is 146, it is 89 for the House of Representatives. The distribution of oversight activities conducted by the Senate within 2007/2008 shows that priority was given to infrastructural development and national security (see Fig. 11.10), while the House of Representatives gave priority to governance issues such as intergovernmental affairs, public petitions, public accounts, access to water resources, culture and tourism (see Fig. 11.9).

Assessing the Level of Educational Qualification in the House of Representatives

A review of existing studies on the educational qualification of Members elected into the House of Representatives within 1999–2019 also shows that the lower chamber has continued to attract persons with higher educational qualification as representatives (see Fig. 11.11). Although empirical evidence from Hamalai (2015) shows mix result on the effect of educational qualification of Members and Bills passage, public scrutiny of the legislature have continued to call for better representation at the National Assembly that is akin to higher levels of academic qualification.

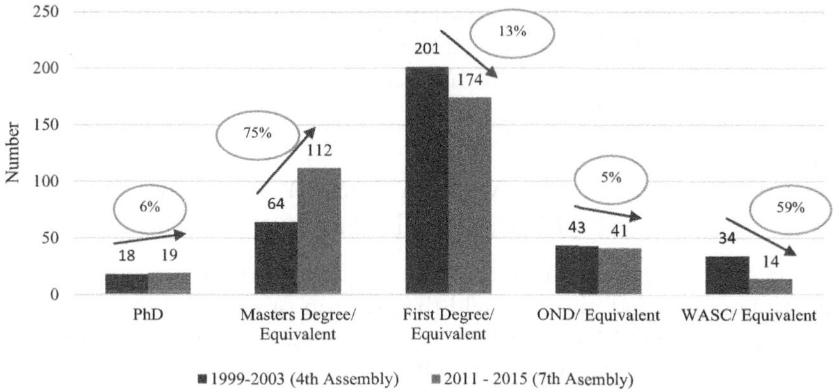

Fig. 11.11 Level of academic qualification in the House of Representatives 1999–2003 and 2011–2015 (*Source* Authors Presentation using data from Hamalai [2015]/Underlying Data from Personnel Management Department, NASS)

Within the 4th House of Representatives and the 7th House of Representatives, the number of PhD holders in the lower chamber increased from 18 to 19, while the Master's degree/equivalent increased from 64 to 112. As the number of Members with higher qualification increased, those with first degree/equivalent decreased from 201 to 174, with OND and WASC decreasing from 43 to 41, 34 to 14, respectively.

Figure 11.11 shows that the increase of Members with Master's degree/equivalent had the highest increase of 75% from the 4th House of Representatives to the 7th House of Representatives. On the other hand, the decline in the number of House of Representatives members with WASC/Equivalent recorded the largest decline. This implies that the quality of representation by the number of academic qualification in the House of Representatives has increased within 1999–2015. This argument is consistent with the argument that the innate abilities and cultivated skills of Members of congress, has a potential influence on the overall effectiveness of the legislature (see Volden and Wiseman 2009).

Besides the level of education, the level of experience of a legislator also matters in determining the level of Bills passage. This is demonstrated in Ekor et al. (2014), whose finding shows legislators with experience sponsored approximately 2.58 Bills per head compared to legislators without legislative experience, who sponsored approximately 2.32 Bills per head. Crosson et al. (2018) also argued that legislators become more effective in their legislative duties when they retain a more experienced legislative staff.

Political Party Affiliation of the Speakers of the House of Representatives

Analysis of the party affiliation of the House leadership is also vital in identifying the party that has held the position of speakership. Table 11.4 presents the name of and party affiliation of speakership at the House of Representatives. It shows that the PDP has maintained 80% (4 out of 5 times) of the leadership of the House Reps while the APC has held 20% (1 out of 5 times) (see Fig. 11.12). Statistically, the period for which the party leadership of the Aminu Tambuwal switched from PDP to APC, was cancelled by the period Yakubu Dogara switched from APC to PDP. Politically however, the move favoured both House Speakers as Aminu Tambuwal was able to win the governorship Ticket for Sokoto under the APC, while Yakubu Dogara, secure re-election to the House of Representatives during the 2019 Presidential and national Assembly elections that held on the 23rd of February 2019 (Table 11.6).

Other factors like party affiliation also affect legislative effectiveness. Miquel and Snyder, Jr (2004) in their study found that, while legislative effectiveness rises sharply with experience, the legislators' institutional positions and party affiliation also matters. More importantly, legislators

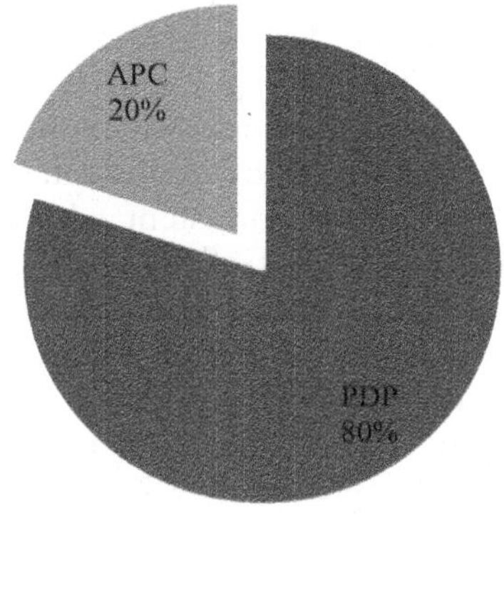

Fig. 11.12 Party of speaker of the HoR from 1999–2019

Table 11.6 Leadership of the House of Representatives and Party Affiliation

Assembly	*Name of Speaker*	*Year*	*Party*	*PDP*	*APC*
4th	Salisu Buhari/ Ghali Na'Abba	1999–2000/ 2000–2003	PDP	1	0
5th	Aminu B. Masari	2003–2007	PDP	1	0
6th	Patricia Etteh/ Oladimeji Bankole	2007–2007/ 2007–2011	PDP	1	0
7th	Aminu Tambuwal	2011–2015	PDP/APC	0.5	0.5
8th	Yakubu Dogara	2015–2019	APC/PDP	0.5	0.5
Party Control of the HoR within 1999–2019				**80%**	**20%**

Source statisense (2015) and Authors Computation

who are more willing to learn by doing, acquire larger capacity to become more effective. Similarly, Volden and Wiseman (2017) also found in the United States, that, legislators who were highly effective lawmakers in the U.S. House continue to be highly effective lawmakers in the Senate.

Assessment of Bills Received and Passed in the House of Representatives

Volden and Wiseman (2009) examined the effectiveness of lawmakers in the U.S. congress. They argue that, legislators become effective lawmakers through innate ability, by cultivating a crucial skill set over time, and by using the institutional structures of Congress to translate those abilities and learned skills into legislative accomplishments. To test this hypothesis, they developed Legislative Effectiveness Scores (LESs) for members of the U.S. House of Representatives and assessed the internal validity of the constructed measures.

Volden and Wiseman (2009) postulation generated different classification for Bills by weighting the relevance of Bill on the status of commemorative/symbolic (C), substantive (S) or substantively significant (SS). According to Volden and Wiseman (2009), a bill is deemed substantively significant if it had been the subject of an end of the year write-up in the Congressional Quarterly Almanac. Providing such a classification for the House of Representatives in Nigeria will be difficult as the significance of a Bill in Nigeria is not premised on classification based on Congressional Quarterly Almanac. Perhaps a modification to assess the performance of the House of Representatives from 1999 to 2019 by using the number of Bills introduced and passed, will provide some basis for value judgement.

Data on Bills received and passed were collected from NILS publication which contains data on Bills received and passed from 1999 to 2015 (i.e. the 4th–7th National Assembly). Additional data on Bills received and passed by the House of Representatives in the 8th National Assembly was collected from the House of Representatives publication on Bills and resolution from 2015–2018. Lastly, available data for Bills received and passed for 2019 was collected from PLAC. Although the legislature is vested with the power of lawmaking, oversight and representation, the effectiveness/performance of a legislature is best analysed using the number of Bills processed. It is contained in Section 4(2) of the 1999 constitution (as amended) that, the National Assembly shall have power to make laws for peace, order and good governance of the federation.

Table 11.7 presents the number of Bills received in the House of Representatives from 1999 to 2019. Several studies present the analysis of

Table 11.7 Number of bills presented and passed in the House of Representatives (1999–2019)

Year	*1999*	*2000*	*2001*	*2002*	*2003*	*2004*	*2005*	*2006*	*2007*	*2008*	*2009*
Number of Bills Presented	41	82	98	104	82	91	61	109	68	170	161
Number of Bills Passed	10	6	13	74	25	36	40	67	10	37	45
Proportion of Passage (%)	*24.4*	*7.3*	*13.3*	*71.2*	*30.5*	*39.6*	*65.6*	*61.5*	*14.7*	*21.8*	*28.0*
Year	2010	2011	2012	2013	2014	2015	2016	2017	2018	2019	Total
Number of Bills Presented	104	270	218	170	134	297	569	270	286	9	3,394
Number of Bills Passed	60	19	41	30	102	100	73	31	8	1	828
Proportion of Passage (%)	*57.69*	*7.037*	*18.81*	*17.65*	*76.12*	*33.67*	*12.83*	*11.48*	*2.797*	*11.11*	*24.4*

Source NILS, HoR, PLAC

the Bills received and passed by identifying whether the Bill was a private member or executive Bill. Since the Bills were passed by the House of Representatives, the focus of this study is to examine the proportion of Bills received and passed by the House of Representatives from 1999 to 2019.

Table 11.7 presents the number of Bills presented and passed in the House of Representatives from the 4th Assembly to the 8th Assembly. It shows that the fifth House of Representatives had the highest proportion of Bills passed as a percentage of Bills presented. Total number of Bills presented in the House of Representatives was 343, while the number of Bills passed by the House was 168, thus, yielding 48.98% as proportion of Bills passed. On the other hand, the eighth House of Representatives, had the lowest with 14.88%. Total number of Bills presented in this session of the House of Representatives was 1,431, while the number of Bills passed by the House was 213, hence, yielding 14.88% as proportion of Bills passed (Table 11.8).

Across legislative sessions, the number of Bills presented was highest in the 8th House of Representatives and lowest in the 4th Assembly (see Fig. 11.13). Contrary to expectation, the proportion of Bills passed was

Table 11.8 Bills presented and passed in the House of Representatives (4th to 8th National Assembly)

Legislative Session	*Statistically*	*No of Bills Received*	*No of Bills Passed*	*Proportion of Bills Passed (%)*	*Average proportion of Bills Passed (%)*	*Proportion Difference*
1999–2003	Fourth Assembly	325	103	31.69	29.85	+1.84
2003–2007	Fifth Assembly	343	168	48.98	29.85	+19.13
2007–2011	Sixth Assembly	503	152	30.22	29.85	+0.37
2011–2015	Seventh Assembly	792	192	24.24	29.85	−5.61
2015–2019	Eighth Assembly	1,431	213	14.88	29.85	−14.97
1999–2019	4th–8th HoR	3,394	828	24.40	29.85	−5.45

[a]As at February, 2019
Source NILS, HoR, PLAC and Authors Computation

Fig. 11.13 Trend of bills received and passed in the house of representatives: 1999–2019

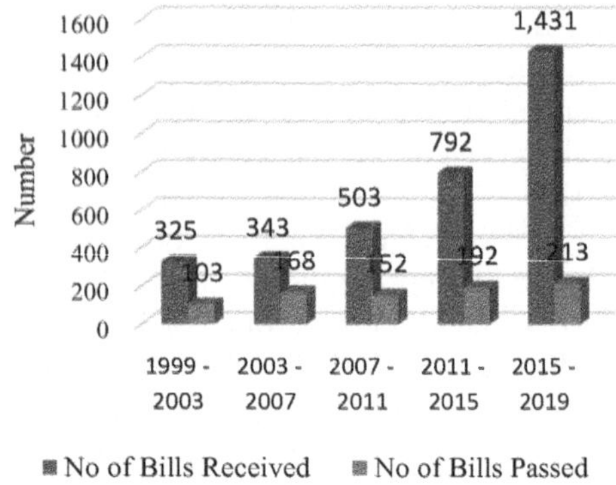

Fig. 11.14 Proportion of Bills Passed in the House of Representatives of total Bills Received within 1999–2019

lowest in the 8th Assembly and highest in the 5th Assembly. Furthermore, within 1999–2019, the total number of Bills presented was 3,394 while the number passed was 824, thus, yielding a 20% Bills passed proportion in the House of Representatives for the period (see Fig. 11.14).

Out of 1999–2019, it was found that within 2001–2006, the proportion of Bills passed out of the number received was higher than the average for the period under study (see Fig. 11.15). Proportion of Bills passed in 2010 was also higher than the average in 2010 and 2014, analysis for specific years shows that the proportion of Bills passed in the 8th House of Representatives was highest in 2015 and 2016 (i.e. 33.67% and

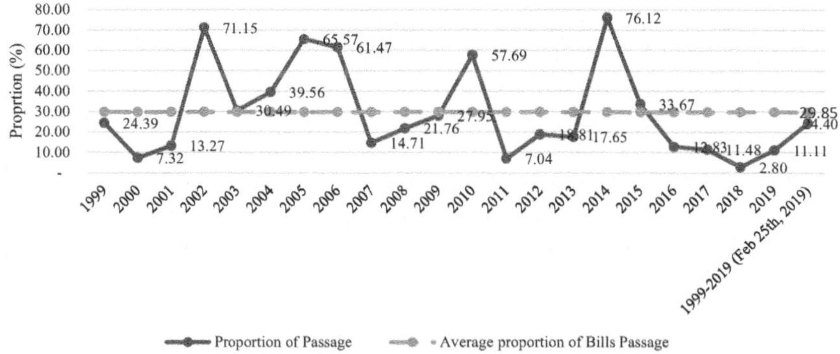

Fig. 11.15 Trend of Bills presented and passed as a proportion in the House of Representatives (1999–2019)

12.83%, respectively), and declined to 2.8% in 2018. The harmonious legislative-executive relationship that characterized executive-legislative relations in these years, explains why the performance was impressive as against the year 2018 when the proportion of Bills passage dropped. Available data for 2019 shows that while none Bills have been received in House of Representatives, only one has been passed. The passage of this bill by the House of Representatives is borne out of concern to pass the minimum wage Bill in order to enhance the welfare of the citizens. The political necessity of passing the Bill was also high as 2019 was a year of election. Despite the low proportion of Bills passed by the 8th House of Representatives, the effort to ensure sustained passage of Bills from 2017 to 2019, is commendable.

On yearly basis, it was found that the House of Representatives had an effective performance with the number of Bills introduced and passed in the following years: 2002–2006, 2010, 2014 and 2015 (see Fig. 11.14). The best years of Bills introduced and Bills passed were 2002 (with 41.3%), 2005 (with 35.72%), 2006 (with 31.62%), 2010 (with 27.84%) and 2014 (with 46.27%—the highest of them all). On the other hand, the worst years of the House of Representatives performance with Bills introduced and passed are: 2000 (with 22.53%), 2011 (with 22.81%) and 2018 (with 27.05%). In terms of growth rate in Bills presented and Bills passed from the 4th to the 8th House of Representatives, the number of Bills received grew by 5.54% in the 5th House of Representatives from the 4th, and by 46.65% from the 5th to the 6th House of Representatives (see Figs. 11.16 and 11.17). The highest grew rate was recorded in the 8th House of Representatives as the number of Bills received grew by 137.18% from the 7th House of Representatives. The increase in number of Bills received in the 8th House of Representatives shows that the 8th Assembly was really prepared to work and passage of Bills that will enhance the welfare of Nigerians. However, the number of Bills passed in the 8th House of Representatives was lower compared to the previous Houses.

The trend of the growth rate of Bills received and Bills passed by the HoR from 1999 to 2019 shows that while the number of Bills received in

Fig. 11.16 Growth rate of bills received

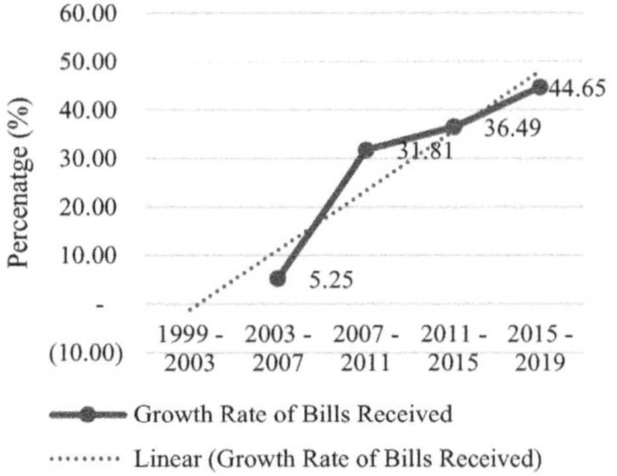

Fig. 11.17 Growth rate of bills passed

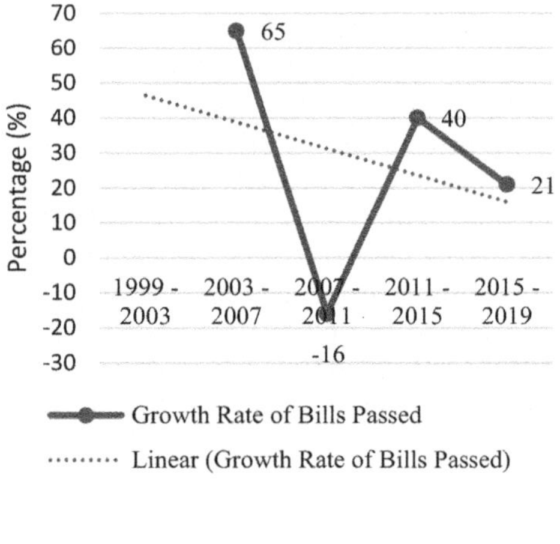

each legislative session has maintained a positive trend, the number of Bills passed has followed a staggered pattern/negative trend. This implies that the number of Bills passed in the House of Representatives within 1999–2019, has not been commensurate with the number of Bills received.

According to NILS (2017), whereas most Bills go through first and second readings, committees become overburdened when the Bills are referred to them after the second reading. Thus, while the high number of Bills presented may serve as an indicator of legislative performance, it could also lead to low number of Bills passed. More so, the high number of Bills to be processed could lead to poor quality in number of Bills passed. Another issue that have implication for the number of Bills passed is the high number of turnover of legislators (see NILS, 2017). As earlier pointed out, Section 94 of the Standing Order (reprinted in July 2014) provides for Bills considered in the previous House to be re-introduced in the current House. A situation where most Members of the House are new, will require training and capacity building in order for these Bills to get the required attention before passage.

Discussion of Findings

The findings from this section shows that, whereas within 1960–1966 the ratio of average number of people represented by a member of the House of Representatives was 1:150,300, it has increased to an average of 1:422,660 within 1999–2011 and to 1:516,720 within 2015–2019. With the unsettling adverse consequences of poverty in Nigeria, it is therefore not far-fetched while members of the House of Representatives have continue to face mounting pressure and demand for financial assistance from their constituents. Furthermore, whereas the number of federal constituencies in each geopolitical zone allows for representative ratio of 1:500,000; the ratio for the FCT is 1:1,782,062. Perhaps a constitutional alteration might be necessary to increase the number of House of Representatives members for FCT from 2 to 3.

There are major differences between the Standing Order of House of Representatives of 2007 and 2014. Whereas the 2007 Standing Order of the House of Representatives had eight (8) special committees and sixty six (66) standing committees, the Standing Order of 2014 had eight (8) special committees and fifty six standing (56) committees. However, the rules of the House of Representatives revised in July 2014 as with that of June 2007 allows for Bills outstanding from the preceding House of

Representatives to be sustained in current House. This has the advantage of allowing the Bill to be re-considered in the present legislative session.

Section 1 (1) of Order XIV of the Standing Rules of the House of Representatives (June, 2007) provides that: Members of Committees shall be nominated by the various political parties and appointed by the Committee on Selection in accordance with their strength in the House. In the Standing Order of the House of Representatives (July, 2014), this provision was revised to remove the clause that nomination to committees will be by political party (see Section 107 (1) of Order XVII). The distribution of oversight activities conducted by the House of Representatives shows that priority was given to governance issues such as intergovernmental affairs, public petitions, public accounts, access to water resources, culture and tourism, compared to the Senate where priority was on infrastructural development.

A review of existing studies on the educational qualification of Members elected into the House of Representatives within 1999–2019 also shows that the lower chamber has continued to attract persons with higher educational qualification as representatives. Although empirical evidence from Hamalai (2015) shows mix result on the effect of educational qualification of members and Bills passage, public scrutiny of the legislature have continued to call for better representation at the National Assembly that is akin to higher levels of academic qualification.

Analysis of the party affiliation of the House leadership shows that the PDP has maintained 80% (4 out of 5 times) of the leadership of the House of Representatives while the APC has held 20% (1 out of 5 times). Statistically, the period for which the party leadership of the Aminu Tambuwal switched from PDP to APC, was cancelled by the period Yakubu Dogara switched from APC to PDP. Politically however, the move favoured both House Speakers as Aminu Tambuwal was able to win governorship in Sokoto under the APC, while Yakubu Dogara, secured re-election to the House of Representatives during the 2019 Presidential and National Assembly elections that held on the 23rd of February 2019 (Table 11.6).

In terms of Bills, available data as at February 2019 shows that a total of 3,394 Bills have been received in the HoR since 1999, only 828 (24.4%), were passed. From the computation of the difference of proportion in Bills passed across the various House of Representatives Sessions from 1999 to 2019, it was found that the fifth House of Representatives had the highest level of effectiveness in Bills introduced and Bills passed. On the other hand, the eighth House of Representatives, had the worst performance in Bills introduced and Bills passed. When analysed on year by year basis, it was found that the House of Representatives had an effective performance with the number of Bills introduced and passed in the following years: 2002–2006, 2010, 2014 and 2015. The best years of Bills introduced and Bills passed were 2002 (with 41.3%), 2005 (with 35.72%), 2006 (with 31.62%), 2010 (with 27.84%) and 2014 (with 46.27%—the highest of them all). On the other hand, the worst years of the House of Representatives performance with Bills introduced and passed are: 2000 (with -22.53%), 2011 (with -22.81%) and 2018 (with −27.05%). The paper concludes that the situation of receiving large Bills with only few passed can be curtailed as Members develop higher capacity for Bill conceptualization, drafting, scrutiny and analysis. Public research and capacity building institutions such as the National Institute for Legislative and Democratic Studies (NILDS) and engagement of Members with private research institutions as well as engagement with Civil Society Organizations, will help enhance the capacity of members in this direction. However, because to consequence of Laws passed on private sector and civil society organizations members of House of Representatives through the committee system would be better off working with government think tank and capacity building institutions such as NILDS. Through public hearing, inputs from stakeholders in other to enhance the win–win chances from proposed laws, would be debated.

Summary and Conclusion

The representative, oversight and lawmaking function of the National Assembly plays an important role in sustaining Nigeria's democracy. Though these functions are carried out by both the Senate and the House of Representatives, structure of the House of Representatives allows for representation in the lower chamber in a manner that adjusts for number of local government and population. Periodic study on how the House of Representatives have performed over time, is therefore critical as it would enable stakeholders to take stock of development in the green chambers in order to come up with suggestions that can advance the nations experience with democratic governance. While there are several studies examining the performance of various sessions of the House of Representatives, a paper bringing these issues together for the period 1999–2019, would provide useful perspectives to the activities of the House of Representatives. Aspects of performance analysis of the House of Representatives within 1999–2019 discussed in the paper are: assessment of the representativeness of the House, changes in its Standing Order, frequency of oversight activities relative to the Senate, level of Educational Qualification of Members as well as political party affiliation of the Speakers of the House of Representatives. It also assesses the proportion of Bills presented and passed in the House of Representatives on a yearly basis and by legislative session. Using trend analysis, charts, frequency tables and percentage analysis, this paper provides a multi-perspective performance analysis of the House of Representatives from 1999 to 2019, the chapter found that:

i. Whereas Nigeria's population have changed from an average of 48,096,105 within 1960–1966 to 152,157,666 within 1999–2018, the total number of Members in the House of Representatives have only grown from 320 to 360: representing a 12.5% change as against population that has recorded a percentage change of 216.36%. likewise, the ratio of average number of people represented by a member of the House of Representatives was 1:150,300 as at 1960–1966, it has increased to an average of 1:422,660 within 1999–2011, and to 1:516,720 within 2015–2019;
ii. A comparative analysis of two versions of the Standing Order of the House of Representatives shows that the House have recorded significant feet in strengthening its internal rules to allow for effective selection of Members into committees unlike in the past where committee membership was based on party affiliation/nomination.
iii. Despite the numerically strengthen of the House, available data shows that the Senate within the period building up to the global economic crisis of 2007/2008, carried out more oversight activities than the House of Representatives.
iv. Whereas the oversight activities of the Senate within the 2007/2008 global economic crisis centred on infrastructural sectors and national security, that of the House of Representatives focused on governance issues such as intergovernmental affairs, public petitions, public accounts, access to water resources, culture and tourism.
v. A review of existing studies on the educational qualification of Members elected into the House of Representatives within 1999–2019 also shows that the lower chamber has continued to attract

persons with higher educational qualification as representatives. Within 1999–2003, and 2011–2015 for instance, the number of Members with Master's degree and its equivalent, grew from 64 to 112 (i.e. by 75%), while the number of members with WASC dropped from 34 to 14 (i.e. by 59%).

vi. Analysis of the party affiliation of speakers of the House also showed that the PDP has maintained 80% (4 out of 5 times) of the leadership of the House Representatives.

vii. Within 1999–2019, the total number of Bills presented in the House of Representatives was 3,394 while the number passed was 824, thus, yielding a proportion of 20% as Bills passed within the study period. Across legislative sessions, the number of Bills presented was highest in the 8th HoR and lowest in the 4th Assembly. Contrary to expectation, the proportion of Bills passed was lowest in the 8th Assembly and highest in the fifth Assembly.

The chapter concludes that, the Nigerian House of Representatives from 1999 to 2019 have a performance score of 20%, if measured by proportion of Bills passed. While the 8th House of Representatives came on board with high expectation as reflected by the number of Bills presented, it performed below expectation against this benchmark. Whereas there are variants of frameworks used to assess the performance of the Legislature, this chapter focused on analysing secondary data to assess the performance of the lower chamber. For further studies, the various aspects of these frameworks can be tested with primary data as well.

Appendix A: Number of Constituency by Geopolitical Zone in Nigeria

South East States	*No. of Constituency*	*South South States*	*No. of Constituency*	*South West States*	*No. of Constituency*
Abia	8	Akwa-Ibom	10	Ekiti	6
Anambra	11	Bayelsa	5	Lagos	24
Ebonyi	6	Cross River	8	Ogun	9
Enugu	8	Delta	10	Ondo	9
Imo	10	Edo	9	Osun	9
Total (5)	**43**	Rivers	13	Oyo	14
		Total (6)	**55**	**Total (6)**	**71**

(continued)

(continued)

South East States	*No. of Constituency*	*South South States*	*No. of Constituency*	*South West States*	*No. of Constituency*
North East States	*No. of Constituency*	*North Central Stats*	*No. of Constituency*	*North West States*	*No. of Constituency*
Adamawa	8	Benue	11	Jigawa	11
Bauchi	12	Kogi	9	Kaduna	16
Borno	10	Kwara	6	Kano	24
Gombe	6	Nasarawa	5	Katsina	15
Taraba	6	Niger	10	Kebbi	8
Yobe	6	Plateau	8	Sokoto	11
Total (6)	**48**	**Total (6)**	**49**	Zamfara	7
				Total (7)	**92**

Source statisense (2015)

Appendix B: Nigeria's population by states and geopolitical zone

Benue	5,741,815	Bauchi	6,537,314	Jigawa	5,828,163
Kogi	4,473,490	Borno	5,860,183	Kaduna	8,252,366
Kwara	3,192,893	Gombe	3,256,962	Kano	13,076,892
Nasarawa	2,523,395	Taraba	3,066,834	Katsina	7,831,319
Niger	5,556,247	Yobe	3,294,137	Kebbi	4,440,050
Plateau	4,200,442	Adamawa	4,248,436	Sokoto	4,998,090
North Central Population	21,487,840	North East Population	26,263,865	Zamfara	4,515,427
Akwa/Ibom	5,482,177	Ekiti	3,270,798	North West Population	48,942,307
Bayelsa	2,277,961	Lagos	12,550,598	Abia	3,727,347
Cross River	3,866,269	Ogun	5,217,716	Anambra	5,527,809
Delta	5,663,362	Ondo	4,671,695	Ebonyi	2,880,383
Edo	4,235,595	Osun	4,705,589	Enugu	4,411,119
Rivers	7,303,924	Oyo	7,840,864	Imo	5,408,756
South-South Population	28,829,287	South West Population	38,257,261	South East Population	21,955,414

(continued)

(continued)

FCT ABUJA	3,564,126	**Total Population (Nigeria, 2016 Estimate)**	**193,500,540**

Source National Population Commission (2016)

References

Crosson, J. M., Lorenz, G. M., Volden, C., & Wiseman, A. E. (2018). *How Experienced Legislative Staff Contribute to Effective Lawmaking*. CEL (Centre for Effective Law-making [Working Paper 2018-002]).

Egwu, S. (2005). The Legislature in Nigeria's Fourth Republic. In A. T. Gana, B. Yakubu, & C. Omelle (Eds.), *Democratic Rebirth in Nigeria: 1999–2003*. Abuja: The African Centre for Democratic Governance.

Ekor, M., Katz, M., & Iweala, O. (2014). Estimating Legislative Effectiveness in Nigeria. *Developing Country Studies, 4*(3), 69–77.

Hamalai, L. (2015). *Resource Competence and Legislative Performance in the National Assembly*. NILS (National Institute for Legislative Studies [Occasional Paper Series [OPS]] 5).

Imlach, A., Dhar, M., & Broom, D. (2009, February 27). *Commonwealth Parliamentary Association* [interview by the authors], London.

LSE. (2009). *Parliamentary Assessment: An Assessment of Existing Frameworks and Application to Selected Countries*. London School of Economics and Political Science (LSE) Report prepared for the World Bank Institute, Under the LSE- World Bank Capstone Project.

Lute, B. (2009, February 13). *National Democratic Institute* [interview by the authors] London and Washington, DC.

Miller, R. (2005). *The Development of Standards for Democratic Legislatures* (Provided to authors by Rick Stapenhurst, World Bank Institute).

Miquel, G. P., & Snyder, Jr, J. M. (2004, July). *Legislative Effectiveness and Legislative Careers*. A Publication of the Department of Economics and Departments of Political Science and Economics, Massachusetts Institute of Technology.

NILDS. (2018). *Nigeria's Macroeconomic and Social Indicators: 2015–2017*. A Publication of the National Institute for Legislative and Democratic Studies (NILDS), Abuja.

NILS. (2010). *10 Years of Law Making in the National Assembly: An Analysis of Bills Processed* (Vol. 4, L. Hamalai, Ed.). A Publication of the National Institute for Legislative Studies (NILS), National Assembly, Abuja.

NILS. (2014). *Committees in the Nigerian National Assembly: A Study of the Performance of Legislative Functions, 2003–2013* (Ladi Hamalai, Ed.). Published by the National Institute for Legislative Studies (NILS).

NILS. (2017). *16 Years of Law Making: 4th–7th National Assembly—An Analysis of Bills Processed* (Vol. 4, J. Dan-Azumi & T. Gbahabo, eds.). A Publication of the National Institute for Legislative Studies (NILS), National Assembly, Abuja.

Olusanya, G. O. (1980). Constitutional Development in Nigeria: 1861–1960. In O. Ikime (Ed.), *Groundwork of Nigerian History*. Ibadan: Heinemann.

Osadolor, O. E. (2014). *Evolution of the Central Legislature in Nigeria, 1862–2014* (Chapter three in 'The National Assembly and Democratic Governance in Nigeria' (L. Hamalai & R. Soberu, eds.). A publication of the National Institute of Legislative Studies (NILS).

Standing Orders of the House of Representatives (Ordered to be Reprinted 17 July 2014) (8th Ed.).

Standing Orders of the House of Representatives (Ordered to be reprinted 28 June 2007).

Statisense. (2015). *Nigeria Political Structure: Presidency: The States and the National Assembly* (1999–2015). https://www.slideshare.net/statisense/nigeria-political-structure-1999-2015?qid=578e68ba-572c-43b6-b730-b23a10050734&v=&b=&from_search=19.

Volden, C., & Wiseman, A. E. (2009). *Legislative Effectiveness in Congress*. Presented at the 2009 Annual Meeting of the Midwest Political Science Association.

Volden, C., & Wiseman, A. E. (2017, March). *Legislative Effectiveness in the United States Senate*. A Publication of the Centre for the Study of Democratic Institutions (CSDI) and Vanderbilt University (Working Paper: 4-2017).

CHAPTER 12

The Nigerian Senate, 1999–2019

Patrick Nnadozie Udefuna

Introduction

Parliaments are established across democracies as an important institution and ingredient of representative democracy and good governance. Thus, parliaments are primarily charged with responsibility to debate policy related issues and then process legislations that provide legal framework for good governance, development and the rule of law. Through the exercise of their three fundamental functions of law-making, representation and oversight functions, parliaments ensure transparency and accountability which fundamentally characterize modern day practice, to determine the trust of the citizenry. It has been argued that parliament is a law-making and policy influencing body in every democratic regime (Okoosi-Simbine 2010; Bogdanor 1991). Okoosi-Simbine (2010) and Bogdanor (1991) opined that legislators are the real custodians of state sovereignty. According to Awotokun (1998) this is because 'the will of the people' rest more with them than any other democratic institutions.

P. N. Udefuna (✉)
Department of Democratic Studies, National Assembly, National Institute for Legislative Studies (NILS), Abuja, Nigeria

F. A. Aremu and A. R. Bakare (eds.), *Two Decades of Legislative Politics and Governance in Nigeria's National Assembly*,
https://doi.org/10.1007/978-981-33-4455-6_12

Sequel to the enormous legislative responsibilities bestowed on the legislature by constitutional provisions, there is a need for a well-coordinated administrative process to bring the dreams of the legislative institutions to reality.

In Nigeria, the National Assembly is the highest law-making body of the Federation. It is a bicameral legislature with two (2) Houses (Senate and House of Representatives) with equal legislative powers in term s of law-making. However, the Senate is referred to as the 'Upper Chamber' while the House of Representatives is known as the 'Lower Chambers' protocol-wise (Hamalai 2015). Established under Section 4 of the Constitution of the Federal Republic of Nigeria 1999, the National Assembly consists of 109-member Sand 360-member House of Representatives. Modelled after the United States Congress, the National Assembly is patterned to ensure equal representation of the states regardless of size and population in the Senate and proportional representation of population in the House of Representations. Therefore, any bill introduced in either of the Houses must receive the concurrence of the other before it receives presidential assent. This book chapter therefore, undertakes a cursory look at the Senate of the Federal Republic of Nigeria from 1999 to 2019.

Composition of the Nigerian Senate

The Senate is the upper chamber of the National Assembly which is the supreme law-making organ of the government of Nigeria. Empowered by the 1999 Constitution to make laws for peace, order and good governance of the country. The President of Senate is statutorily empowered to preside over the affairs of Senate. Other principal officers of Senate include;

i. Deputy President of Senate
ii. Senate Majority Leader
iii. Senate Minority Leader
iv. Deputy MajorityLeader
v. Deputy Senate Minority Leader
vi. Senate Majority Whip
vii. Senate Minority Whip
viii. Deputy Majority Whip
ix. Deputy Minority Whip

The composition of the Senate in political party basis varied from 1999 to 2015. However, with the exception of the case of 2015 where the All Progressive Congress (APC) won the majority seats, the Peoples Democratic Party (PDP) has always dominated the Senate. Below is Table 12.1 which captures the composition.

Year	*PDP*	*APP*		*AD*		*Vacant*	
1999	59	29		20		1	
2003	76	27		6		Nil	
Year	*PDP*	*ANPP*		*AC/*		*PPA*	*Accord party*
2007	85	16		6		1	1
	PDP	CAN	ANPP	CPC	LP	APGA	DPP
2011	71	18	7	7	4	1	1
	PDP			*APC*			
2015	49			60			

Source Daily Trust, Tuesday, January 8, 2019, pp. 1 and 5

Duties and Functions of the Presiding Officers of the Senate

The presiding officer of the Senate of the Federal Republic of Nigeria is the *President of the Senate.* Elected alongside other 108 Senators and subsequently chosen by his colleagues by a simple majority of votes in the Chamber to preside over the Senate. He/she is assisted by the *Deputy*

Table 12.1 Relative stability in executive—Legislative leadership in Nigeria 1999–2013

President	*Tenure*	*Senate*	*Term*
OlusegunObasanjo	1999–2007	Evans Enwerem	June 1999–Nov 1999
		ChubaOkadigbo	November 1999— August 2000
		Anyim Pius Anyim	August 2000—May 2003
		AdolphusNwabara	2003–2005
		Ken Nnamani	April 2005–May 2007
UmaruYar'adua	2007–2010	David Mark	2007–2010
Goodluck Jonathan	2010–2015	David Mark	2010–2015
Muhammadu Buhari	2015–2019	Bukola Saraki	2015–2019

President of the Senate. The functions of the presiding officers according to chapter VI of the Senate Standing Order 2011 as Amended include:

i. Chairing the plenary sessions of the red Chamber and the committee of the whole Senate.
ii. The presiding officers sign the votes and proceedings of the *red chambers* after it has been confirmed by the Senate.
iii. It is his responsibility to ensure the observance of the Rules of Order both in Senate plenary and in committee sittings and activities.
iv. The President of Senate hall receive all correspondences addressed to the Senate;
v. Except as provided by rule of law, the presiding officer shall have general control of the Chamber of Senate, its passages and corridors;
vi. It is the duty of the President of the Senate to sign all acts enacted, addresses, resolutions, *subpoena*, etc, issued by order of the Senate;
vii. It is his duty to ensure the observance of the Rule of debate during legislature business. The presiding officer does this by giving rulings on Points of Order or of constitution raised by Senators during debate;
viii. The presiding officer also has a casting vote only to avoid a tie during voting one bills, etc.
ix. Final interpretation of the Chambers rules;
x. Shall chair the joint sessions of the two Chambers;
xi. Appointment of chairs and members of the committees in consultation with the committee on selection, which he chairs; and
xii. Represents the National Assembly at ceremonial occasion. The constitution of Nigeria makes him number 3 on the National Order of Precedence.

The Deputy President of the Senate is empowered by extant laws to perform all the duties and functions of the President of the Senate in the absence of his principal.

Election of Presiding Officers

Chapter II, Section 3 (2) VI of the Senate Standing Order 2011 as Amended provides that the nomination or selection of Presiding Officers, appointment of Senate Principal Officers, and other Officers of the Nigerian Senate or on any Parliamentary assignment must follow the ranking of Senators. In determining ranking, the following order apply:

a. Legislative Experience: this entails that returning Senators are considered based on number of times they have been re-elected to act as Presiding Officers, Principal Officers, etc.;
b. Senators with legislative experiences as former members of the House of Representatives or state houses of assembly; and
c. First-term Senators.

Therefore, in nominating senators for the election of presiding officers, a Senator-elect addressing the Clerk to the National Assembly, usually propose or nominate another Senator-elect to the Senate as candidate for the office of the President of the Senate. In doing this, the Senator-elect will move that his nominee 'Do take the chair of the Senate as President of the Senate' (Senate Standing Orders 2011 As Amended, p. 3). Thereafter, the nominee so nominated and seconded, rises to inform the Senate that he/she has accepted or declined his/her nomination and also addresses the Senate on his personality and policy road-map that will guide his government, if elected. The Clerk shall ask 'Are there any further nominations?' and in the absence of further nominations, the Clerk will then declare "I declare the nominations closed". The Clerk would then, proclaim the Senator-elect so nominated and seconded elected as President of Senate. The elected Senate President will be led to the Chair by the proposer and seconder of his nomination motion to properly assume officer and powers of the President of the Senate. However, election is conducted to determine the winner in a case where more than one nomination is made. During this process, the Clerk-at-the-Table is saddled with the conduct of voting using the Division List of the Senate with the Tellers in attendance. Furthermore, the Clerk-at-the-table is required to submit the result of the division to the Clerk of the National Assembly who will then declare the Senator-elect with the greater number of votes elected as the President of the Senate.

After the election processes, the President and Deputy are sworn-in. according to Chapter II, Section 5 of the Senate Standing Orders 2011 As Amended, are required to take and subscribe to the Oath/Affirmation of allegiance and membership captured in the Constitution under the watch of the Clerk to the National Assembly. It is after this that the President of the Senate returns his/her acknowledgement to the Senate expressing gratitude and readiness to discharge his/her duties as the President of Senate and thereafter the Mace (which prior to his/her election lay under the Table) is laid upon the Table as the elected President of Senate takes the chair.

Sittings of the Senate

In line with Chapter III, Section 11 (1) of the Senate Standing Order 2011 As Amended, the President of the Senate is saddled with the responsibility of allocating seat to every Senator. He/she also reserves the power to re-allocate these seats from time to time as the need arises.

The Senate of the Federal Republic of Nigeria sits for a minimum of 181 days per year (as does the Chamber of Representatives). It sits on Mondays to Fridays except the first and fourth Fridays of the Month and one-third of members constitute quorum.

Committees of the Senate

Agriculture, Air Force, Anti-Corruption & Financial Crimes, Appropriations, Army, Aviation, Banking, Insurance & Other Financial Institutions, Capital Market, Communications, Cooperation & Integration in Africa & NEPAD, Culture and Tourism and Customs, Excise &Tariff. Others include Defence, Diaspora & Civil Societies, Downstream Petroleum, Drugs &Narcotics, Ecology & Climate Change, Education (Basic & Secondary), Employment, Labour& Productivity, Environment, Establishment & Public Service, Ethics, Privileges and Public Petitions, Federal Capital Territory and Federal Character & Inter Governmental Affairs, FERMA, Finance, Foreign Affairs and Gas. These committees also include—Health, Housing, ICT & Cybercrime, Independent National Electoral Commission, Industry, Information & National Orientation, Inter-Parliamentary Affairs, Interior, Judiciary Human Rights & Legal Matters, Land Transport and Local & Foreign Debts. Marine Transport, Media & Public Affairs, National Identity & National Population,

National Planning & Economic Affairs, National Security and Intelligence, Navy, Niger Delta, Police Affairs, Poverty Alleviation & Social Welfare and Power. Others are Primary Health Care & Communicable Diseases, Privatization, Public Accounts, Public Procurement, Rules and Business, Science & Technology, Senate Services, Solid Minerals, Special Duties and Sports. They also include— States & Local Government, Sustainable Development Goals, Tertiary Institutions & TETFUND, Trade & Investment, Upstream Petroleum, Water Resources, Women Affairs and Works

Privileges

There are a plethora of privileges enjoyed by Senators as bestowed on them by the Legislative Houses (Powers and Privileges) Act CAP 208, Laws of the Federation of Nigeria 1990 and related statutes, etc. And Senators are empowered to rise and speak on matters bordering on breach of privileges uninterrupted.

Section 88(1) of the 1999 Constitution (as amended) empowers the two chambers of the National

Assembly to direct or cause to be directed an investigation into:

a. any matter or thing with respect to which it has power to make laws; and
b. the conduct of affairs of any person, authority, ministry or government department charged, or intended to be charged with the duty of or responsibility of:

    i. executing or administering laws enacted by the National Assembly, and
    ii. disbursing or administering of monies appropriated by the National Assembly.

Going by this constitutional provision, Order 97 (4) (a)(b) and (c) of the Senate Standing

Rules 2015 (as amended) made provisions for the establishment of the Senate Committee on Ethics, Privileges and Public Petitions with the mandate to investigate petitions from the public

(both private and corporate) on issues and matters of abuses especially the ones bordering on the conduct of affairs of government agencies.

Therefore, the Senate Committee on Ethics, Privileges and Public Petitions can be said to be an investigatory and/or fact-finding committee. It advises the Senate on such issues but does not impose on the *red chamber*.

The Senate Committee on Ethics, Privileges and Public Petitions has a secretariat supervised by the Clerk of the Committee. The responsibility of this committee secretariat is the effective day-to-day administration of the Committee. Thus, the Clerk of the Committee sends out and receives official communication for the committee and organizes committee meetings, oversight visits, investigative and public hearings.

The mandates of the Committee include:

i. to consider the subject matter of all petitions brought before it by the Senate.
ii. Recommending to the Senate of the Federal Republic of Nigeria administrative appropriate administrative actions necessary for establishing standards of official conduct for Senators
iii. Administer and monitor the activities of relevant parastatals considered to be within the purview of the Committee. They include:

    a. The Code of Conduct Bureau
    b. The Public Complaint Commission; and
    c. The Code of Conduct Tribunal

In situations where the Committee lacks jurisdiction, as it is in contractual issues between two citizens, it is expected that the Committee shall dismiss the petition or recommend that such matter be referred to appropriate body with the approval of the Senate.

Individuals and corporate organizations petition the Senate Committee on Ethics, Privileges and Public Petitions when the need arises either writing directly or by enlisting the services of a legal practitioner or any other form of representative. It is a fundamental requirement in such petitions that the petitioner or his representative attends the investigative hearing in order to defend the claims as contained in the petition.

Format for Drafting a Petition

Petition drafting does not have one universally accepted format. However, it is expected that a petition must be concise but detailing its objectives.

This entails that it must be comprehensible and lucid and embodies relevant information on the matter which the petitioner seeks to resolve. According to PLAC (2018), in conformity with the rules and practices of the Committee, a petition must:

i. Be expressly addressed through the Senator representing the petitioner to the Senate President, National Assembly, Abuja or through any Senator of petitioner's choice.
ii. Refer to a matter, which is within the jurisdiction of the Senate to intervene (e.g. matters before a competent court or those which are the responsibility of private entities may not be made the subject of a petition to be presented to the Senate).
iii. It must mention who the petitioner(s) are, outline the grievance or complaint for which the intervention of the Senate is being sought.
iv. Outline the request for action by clearly stating the course of action that the petitioner(s) wants the Senate to take in resolving his/her/their grievances.
v. It must be written in plain and respectful language devoid of any derogatory or insulting language.
vi. Must be accompanied by a certified translation if not written in English. The contact details of the translator must be attached for easy access.
vii. Must be neatly written and devoid cancellations.
viii. Must contain supporting documents and attachments such as letters, affidavits, photos, etc.
ix. Printed, photocopied, faxes or electronic signatures are not accepted in such petitions. Therefore, it must consist only of original, handwritten signatures.
x. Every page detailing at least the request for action must contain the signature of the petitioner (s) exactly as on the first page of the petition.

Submitting a Petition

The forgoing analysis indicates that every petition being addressed to the Nigerian Senate must be sponsored and presented at the Chamber by a serving Senator. However, this Senator sponsoring or presenting such petition must not be compelled to do so against his will. Therefore, a petitioner is expected to locate a senator to sponsor his/her/their petition once such petition has been drafted. However, a petitioner is required to submit his/her/their petition to the Chairman of the Senate Committee on Ethics, Privileges and Public Petitions, if he/she/they are unable to get a lawmaker to sponsor it. The Committee Chairman may be of immense help to the petitioner in getting a Senator to the petition in the Senate Chambers (Senate Standing Order 2011 As Amended). There are no costs for presentation or submission of a petition or filing of any other process.

Presentation of a Petition

Although Senators may accept to present petitions on behalf of their aggrieved constituents, it does not mean that they are in total support of the substance of such petition(s). The Senator is expected to make a brief statement while presenting such petitions on the floor of Senate. The Senator's brief statement states the petitioner, issues in the petition, requests and prayers.

It is noteworthy that only Petitions presented by Senator(s) can be processed and referred to the Senate Committee on Ethics, Privileges and Public Petitions. In such cases of urgent national importance, petitions emanating from the floor of the House of Representatives can be referred to the Senate Committee on Ethics, Privileges and Public Petitions. This Committee can only handle petitions that have been presented and considered in chamber.

Determination of a Petition

The Senate Standing Order 2011 As Amended expressly laid out the procedures for the determination of petitions by Senate Committee on Ethics, Privileges and Public Petitions. Therefore, the Committee is at liberty to choose any procedure which it considers expeditious and convenient in the handling any petition before it depending on the nature of the petition. However, the Committee is at the same time guided by the basic principles of natural justice. The general procedure for determination of petitions according to Senate Standing Orders 2011 as Amended is as follows:

i. Upon receipt of a petition, the Committee Chairman fixes a date for hearing and the Clerk communicates that date to the petitioner. The respondent is equally informed of the petition against him with a copy of same sent to him.
ii. The parties are mandated to file and exchange written briefs detailing their arguments/positions to the petition. Usually, the petitioner first writes his brief, files sufficient copies at the secretariat and also serves same on the respondent. The respondent does the same.
iii. The Committee may request the petitioner to provide any document(s) or material(s), which it deems necessary for the proper determination of the petitioner's case
iv. During the hearing of the petition, the petitioner is first given opportunity to present his case before the respondent presents his response.
v. The Committee may either elect to engage the parties as soon as each presents his/her brief or elect to interview both simultaneously after the presentations of their briefs.
vi. The parties are often given an opportunity to interview each other while the Committee observes.

Committee Recommendations and Reports

The Committee is required to write the report of its findings at the end of the hearing of a petition and lay it on the floor of the Senate during Plenary. Such reports must capture the committee's recommendations for consideration and adoption by the Senate in Plenary. The Senate in plenary reviews the report of the Committee and take decisions based on the recommendations contained in the report of the Committee. However, the Senate is not duty bound to accept any of the recommendation(s) of the report. Therefore, any decision taken by the Senate on the report will be treated as a resolution of the Senate.

Thus, the Clerk of the Committee will notify both the petitioner and the respondent of the Senate's resolution on the petition. However, any of the party (petitioner and respondent) who feels aggrieved or dissatisfied with the resolution of the Senate, has the right to approach the Court of law for judicial intervention if they so desire.

Lapse of Petitions

All legislative and sundry businesses before the Senate of the Federal Republic of Nigeria (this includes the Senate Committee on Ethics, Privileges and Public Petitions) lapses at the end of every session or term of the National Assembly. This means that all petitions pending at the Senate Committee on Ethics, Privileges and Public Petitions elapses too at the end of a legislative session. However, at the discretion of the new President of Senate, he/she choose to restore a petition pending in the last session. But in a situation whereby a petition is not reinstated, the petitioner is expected to re-present the petition to the newly constituted Senate Committee on Ethics, Privileges and Public Petitions.

Sitting Days

The Senate Committee on Ethics, Privileges and Public Petitions is at liberty to conduct investigative hearings on such petitions brought before it at any committee rooms of its choice in the National Assembly. One-Third (1/3) of its membership is needed in attendance to form quorum in any of its Committee sittings/hearings. Similarly, at least One-Third of members must sign the Committee's reports that make it valid. With the exception of hearings on sensitive national security matters, all other Committee hearings are always open for the public to get involved.

Comparative Analysis Comparing the Nigerian Senate with other Presidential systems

Comparison	*United States of America*	*Nigeria*	*Argentina*
Membership	The United States operate a Senate to Nigeria's version. Article I, Section 3, of the Constitution, outlines three fundamental requirements for somebody to become a Senator in the country. They include: i. The person must be at least 30 year ii. The candidate must have been citizens of the United States for the past nine years or longer; and iii. Candidate must be resident of the states that he/she desires to represent in the Senate as at the time of his/her election.	The first and most important is that you must be a citizen of Nigeria in order to be a Senator. Linked to this is that if you have acquired the citizenship of another country, you will not be able to run for the office of Senate. In order to be eligible for contesting an election for Senate, you must be at least 35 years of age. Any individual who wishes to run for the office of Senator in any constituency in Nigeria must be educated up to at least School Certificate level, which means all Senators must have completed at least secondary school education. In order to run for office of Senator, the individual must also be a member of a registered political party and sponsored by that political party to contest in the elections. The Nigerian Constitution and does not allow candidates to run as 'independents'	The National Senate of the Argentine Confederation came into being on July 29, 1854, in pursuant to Articles 46 to 54 of the country's 1853 Constitution. Section 55 of the constitution states that candidates for the country's Senate must: • "be at least 30 years old • "have been a citizen of Argentina for six years • "be native to the province of his office, or have been a resident of that province for two years"
Elections and term	In the United States a Senator is entitled to a term of 6 years and subject to renewal for as long as a Senator's constituents are satisfied with his stewardship.The 6-year terms are staggered so that approximately one-third of the seats are up for election every two years. This was brought about by sharing the senators of the 1st Congress into thirds (called classes). Sequel to this division, the terms of one-third *expires after two years, the terms of the* other third expires after four, and the terms of the last third expired after six years. This staggering of terms is done to ensure senatorial seat elections are not held at the same time general elections are contested. Eligible voters in a state elect their Senators. This means that the whole state is a senator's constituency as a whole.	In Nigeria, Senators are elected to serve a four-year term renewable as many time as possible based on the performance of the Senator and his/her acceptability within his constituency This means that they enjoy unlimited tenure and can remain in Senate for as long as they are re-elected in general elections. Senators are elected in a General Election in Nigeria and their tenure elapse uniformly irrespective of when a Senator joined the Senate. *The representation of each state in the Senate is* based on a proportional representation where each state has three Senators in the *Red Chambers* representing the three senatorial districts in each of the thirty-six states and one for the FCT. These Senators are directly elected by their constituents	In Argentina, Senators enjoy a six-year term by direct election on a provincial basis also renewable as many times as practicable. In this case, the political party with the highest votes is awarded two of the province's senate seats while the party with the second highest votes receives one senate seat. Like in the US, one-third of the senators are elected every two years. Sequel to this arrangement, one-third of the provinces hold senatorial elections every two years. *The 72 member Argentine Senate has three* Senators representing each province and three for the Autonomous City of Buenos Aires

(continued)

(continued)

Comparison	United States of America	Nigeria	Argentina
Seniority	The convention of Senate seniority in the US provides that the longest serving senator in each state is should be treated and referred to as the "senior senator" while the other is the "junior senator"	The Nigerian Senate copied the US example in recognising seniority and experience in legislative business when electing or choosing the presiding and principal officers. It even gave it some legal backing by ensuring the entrenchment of the ranking rule in the standing orders of the National Assembly. However, the enforcement remains weak as events have proven	In the Argentine Senate, seniority is based on the length of consecutive terms as a senator. There are several processes of determining seniority among senators who were inaugurated the same day. However, if after such processes no clear winner emerges, constituency population is adopted in determining the ranking
Expulsion and other disciplinary actions	The Senate may expel a senator by a two-thirds vote	The Senate Standing Orders 2011 As Amended which every Senator has sworn to abide withprovides that any Senators who steps out of the bound of what is interpreted to be proper conduct, should be disciplined. Such disciplinary measure is usually at the discretion of the Senate acting on the recommendation of the Ethics and Privileges Committee. Sections 60 and 101 of the 1999 Constitution (as amended) empowers the National Assembly to regulate its proceedings and procedures in accordance with the law	The Argentinian Senate also instil discipline to their members who may have been found wanting via its ethics committee, having considered the efficacy and substance of the allegations labelled against the senator in question, after which disciplinary actions are being taken in accordance to relevant Senate Convention. The rules governing discipline within Parliament are contained in Art. 66 of the Constitution, Rules 39, No. 4, and 165, and 167 to 173 of the Rules of Procedure of the Chamber of Deputies
Majority and Minority parties in Parliament.	In the US Congress, majority party connotes the political party that won the majority seats or enough seats to form a coalition with another or caucus with a majority of seats. However, the vice president's affiliation decides the majority party in a situation where there is a tie between or among two or three political parties. As it is the practices, the party with the second highest number of seats in Senate is known as the minority party. The majority party usually produces the president pro tempore, committee chairs, and some other officials	In Nigeria, the majority party in the Senate often produces the Senate President and other major principal officers like the Deputy Senate President, Majority Leader, and Chairmen of relevant committees. Although there is no law binding that the majority political party in the Senate must produce such principal officers, it is only reasonably implied by convention, subject to in-house political permutations	Just like in the US Congress, the majority party play pivotal roles in the Argentine Senate. Majority party has an advantage in agenda-setting because of the quorum requirement for opening floor sessions. Majority party enjoy more leadership positions in the Chamber of Deputies such as committee chairs, etc. The majority party maximises its numerical strength to push through legislations, resolution, etc. in parliament. Although the minority party get some committee chairs, such opportunities are minimal

(continued)

(continued)

Comparison	*United States of America*	*Nigeria*	*Argentina*
Presiding over the Senate	The US Vice President is constitutionally saddled with the responsibility of presiding of the Senate. He/she only votes can only vote in the Senate (ex officio, for he or she is not an elected directly into the legislature) when there is a tie. Presiding over the Senate is one of the main duties of the Vice President. One more important duty of the US Vice President is to receive from the states the tally of electoral ballots cast for the President and vice in Congress so that the total votes can be counted. His/her leadership in Senate is more of ceremonial as the President Pro Tempore (from the majority party) elected by Senators is empowered by the Constitution to preside over the Senate in the absence of the Vice President. The President Pro tempore usually delegates the power to preside over senate to a senator from the majority party	In Nigeria, the Senate is presided over by the President of the Senate. He/she is also the Chairman of the National Assembly. However, in the absence of the President of the Senate, the Deputy Senate President performs the functions of his/her principal. There are other functions ascribed to the office of the Deputy Senate President. Some of these functions include chairing the Constitution Review Committee of the Senate. Other leaders of the Nigerian Senate include: i. Majority Leader & Deputy ii. Minority Leader & Deputy iii. Majority Whip & Deputy iv. Minority Whip & Deputy	In Argentina, the Argentine Vice President is the President of Senate. However, the Provisional President is in charge of the daily leadership of the Senate
Filibuster and cloture	This is a tactic used by legislators to defeat bills and motions by prolonging debate. This usually takes the form of long speeches, dilatory motions, and an extensive series of proposed amendments. There are always filibusters in senate who adopt different tactic in defeating any legislation they are not in support of. Cloture is usually invoked by the Senate to end a filibuster in extreme cases. This requires the support of three-fifth of the Senators	The tactic of a filibuster is also prevalent in the Nigerian Senate, but differ from the United States Senate, in such a way that only the support of a simple majority can invoke a closure of a filibuster, following a point of order or a motion before the floor of the Senate chamber	This tactic is observed in the Argentinian Senate, when there is an attempt to defeat a debate before the floor, although this is regulated by the timing mechanism, to limit the duration of time to speak before the floor of the Senate chamber
Vacancy	In America, 36 states gave their Governors the power to make gubernatorial appointments to fill Senate vacancies	In Nigeria, vacancies in the Senate due to death, resignation or expulsion are filled through by-elections	Vacancy arising from expulsion, resignation, incapacitation or death in the senate is filled through a bye-election by the constituents

(continued)

(continued)

Comparison	*United States of America*	*Nigeria*	*Argentina*
Recall	The Constitution of the United States made no provision for the recall or removal of a US Senator nor any officer of government such as President, Vice President member of the House of Representative, etc.	There are three major steps in recalling a Nigerian senator, which are: **Stage 1: Petition** To recall a Nigerian Senator, a petition addressed to the Chairman of the Independent National Electoral Commission (INEC) and signed by more than half of the registered voters in the Senator's constituency declaring a vote of no confidence. The petition must reflect the polling units, wards, Local Government Areas, and constituency of the petitioners **Stage 2: Verification** The Commission notify the affected Senator after confirming the validity of the petition. Thereafter the INEC will issue a public notice announcing the time, date and location of the verification exercise. This exercise is to verify the signatures of the petitioners. These signatories must be dully registered voters. The Commission will then write to the petitioners stating that requirements for a referendum were not met should the number of verified signature fall below half of the voting population of the constituency INEC will then dismiss the petition based on its merit. **Stage 3: Referendum** INEC is required to conduct a referendum within 90 (counting from the day it received the petition) days if the number of signatures verified conforms to the minimum requirement. The referendum is a yes or no vote on whether the Senator should be recalled or not. The Senator losses his/her seat in Senate once a simple majority of his constituents votes yes. The Senator ceases to be a serving senator the moment the Chairman of the INEC sendsa **Certificate of Recall** to the Senate President to effect the recall	In Argentina, recall of a Senator is done after a petition is labelled against such a congressman by his constituents, followed by a referendum supporting the recall process of at least a minimum required percentage of the total number of the constituents

Compiled by the Author from https://lawpadi.com/recall-senator-nigeria/, http://archive.ipu.org/parline-e/reports/2012.htm, etc

Stylized Facts: Executive–Legislature Relationship (2010–2014)

Available evidence indicates that there has been relative cordiality in the relationship between the Legislature and the Executive under the Jonathan administration when compared with previous administrations before it. For instance, between 2010 and now, the legislature at the Federal level has witnessed stability in its leadership owing to the non-interference of the Executive in the affairs of the National Assembly. This was not the case in the period between 199 and at least 2007 (see Tables 12.1 and 12.2).

Tables 12.1 and 12.2 show a high degree of instability in the leadership of the National Assembly between 1999 and 2007 in comparison with executive leadership. This leadership instability in the Legislature had obvious implications for Legislative–Executive relations in terms of dominance and deference. However, there has been a relative stability in the leadership of the Legislature since 2010. This relative stability is attributable to a number of factors, especially the cordial relationship that has evolved between the Legislature and the Executive since 2007 and particularly within the period under consideration.

One of the consequences of this cordial Legislative-Executive relationship has been a relatively significant improvement in the execution of governmental functions such as early passage of appropriation Bills (see Table 12.3).

Table 12.2 House of Representatives

President	*Tenure*	*House of representatives*	*Term*
OlusegunObasanjo	1999–2007	Salisu Buhari	1999–2000
		Ghali Umar Na'Abba	2000–2003
		AminuMasari	2003–2007
UmaruYar'adua	2007–2010	Patricia Etteh	2007–2007
		OladimejiBankole	2007–2011
Goodluck Jonathan	2010–2015	AminuTambuwal	2011–2015
Muhammadu Buhari	2015–2019	Yakubu Dogara	2015–2019

Source Author's Compilation

Table 12.3 Time schedule in the preparation and enactment of federal government budget (2000–2019)

Fiscal year	*Date president present budget estimates to NASS*	*Date NASS transmit passed appropriation bill for president's assent*	*Date president assented to appropriation bill to become budget/appropriation act*	*Gestation period*
2000	November 24, 1999	April 14, 2000	May 5, 2000	5 months, 11 days
2001	November 9, 2000	December 21, 2000	December 21,2000	1 month, 12 days
2002	November 7, 2001	March 28, 2002	March 28, 2002	4 months, 21 days
2003	November 20, 2002	March 11, 2003	April 10, 2003	4 months, 21 days
2004	December 18, 2003	April 20, 2004	April 21, 2004	4 months, 3 days
2005	October 12, 2004	March 18, 2005	April 12, 2005	6 months
2006	December 6, 2005	February 21, 2006	April 22, 2006	4 months, 16 days
2007	October 6, 2006	December 22, 2006	December 22, 2006	2 months, 12 days
2008	November 8, 2007	March 27, 2008	April 14, 2008	5 months, 7 days
2009	December 2, 2008	February 3, 2009	March 10, 2009	3 months, 8 days
2010	November 23, 2009	March 25, 2010	April 22, 2010	4 months, 29 days
2011	December 15, 2010	May 25, 2011	May 26, 2011	5 months, 11 days
2012	December 15, 2011	March 15, 2012	April 13, 2012	4 months, 2 days
2013	October 10, 2012	January 30, 2013	February 26, 2013	3 months, 18 days
2014	December 19, 2013	April 22, 2014	May 21, 2014	5 months, 3 days
2015	December 17, 2014	May 6, 2015	May 6, 2015	4 months, 19 days
2016	December 22, 2015	March 23, 2016	May 6, 2016	4 months, 14 days

(continued)

Table 12.3 (continued)

Fiscal year	*Date president present budget estimates to NASS*	*Date NASS transmit passed appropriation bill for president's assent*	*Date president assented to appropriation bill to become budget/appropriation act*	*Gestation period*
2017	December 14, 2016	May 11, 2017	June 12, 2017	6 months
2018	November 7, 2017	May 16, 2018	June 20, 2018	6 months, 15 days
2019	December 18, 2018	April 30, 2019	May 27, 2019	5 months, 8 days

Source Bakare (2019)

Table 12.3 shows that since 2007 there has been a significant reduction in the number of days it takes for the Appropriation Bill sent to the National Assembly by the President to be passed and assented to.

Another outcome of this cordial Legislative–Executive relationship is the increase in the number of legislations or legislative bills passed by the National Assembly and assented to by the President. For instance, between May 2011 and May 2013, a total of 310 bills were presented for consideration at the Senate. Out of this number, 26 bills were passed, 2 rejected. 9 withdrawn and 273 at different stages of enactment. In the House of Representatives, a total of 435 bills were presented for consideration. 47 of this number were passed, 15 rejected, 5 withdrawn/stepped down and 368 at different stages of consideration (FGN 2013: 44). Thus, it can be asserted from the foregoing analysis that the evolving cordial Legislative–Executive relationship in Nigeria since 2010 has resulted to timely and speedy passage of bills and Appropriation Acts into law by the National Assembly.

Thirdly, this cordial working relationship has within the period under review resulted in the National Assembly achieving fiscal autonomy, institutional independence and greater participation in the management of the national economy. This institutional independence of the legislature is exemplified by the Jonathan's policy of non-interference in the internal affairs of the Legislature.

The foregoing submissions notwithstanding, there have been instances of conflictual Executive–Legislature relationships in Nigeria within the period under review. Specifically, issues of budget passage and implementation have remained contentious between the two arms of government. 2012, for example, was a year of serious conflictual relationship between the Executive and the Legislature especially over the proper implementation of the year's annual budget.

The two chambers of the National Assembly for the first time in many years set aside sentiment and self-aggrandizement and ensured that the national budget was passed in record time. Both Chambers harmonized the 2013 budget document and sent the harmonized version to the President for assent before the end of 2012 calendar year. However, President Jonathan delayed signing the budget into law for two months following a number of issues. The Executive was not comfortable with the $79 per barrel oil benchmark settled for by the National Assembly, the zero allocation budget to the Securities and Exchange Commission (SEC) and the National Assembly demand for 2012 constituency projects be rolled over into 2013 (*Vanguard* Newspaper, February 28, 2013). This misunderstanding was so pronounced that the opposition members of the National Assembly threatened that NASS would over-ride the President's assent.

Other instances in which rancorous and conflictual relationship between the Legislature and the Executive came to a tenors end within the period under study include the oil subsidy probe (the Hon. FaruokLawan-Femi Otedola saga), the Security and Exchange Commission probe (the Hon. Haman Hembe-Ote saga) and the Pension Commission probe and the drama that ensued. These issues and the allegation by the suspended Central Bank of Nigeria, Governor Mallam-SanusiLamidoSanusi that federal legislators gulp about 25% of federal government overheads annually drew the ire of the Legislature, which resulted in the botched attempt to amend the 2007 Central Bank of Nigeria Act.

Conclusion

The Senate of the Federal Republic of Nigeria has played a lead role in law-making, oversighting the various MDAs and representing the over 180 million Nigerians. The successes of the various administrations since 1999 benefited no less profoundly from the assiduous contributions of the First to the 8th Senate. However, these contributions were both cordial (co-ordinate) and conflictual in nature. It has in both 2011 and 2015 elected their preferred leaders in revolt to executive and party influence.

References

Awotokun, K. (1998). *Governance and legislative control in Nigeria: Lessons from the Second and Third Republics*. Bethesda: International Scholars Publications.

Bakare, A. R. (2019). *Strengthening or undermining democracy in Nigeria: An appraisal of the national assembly under the Fourth Republic*. Department of Political Science, University of Ilorin, Ilorin.

Baker, Richard A. *Traditions of the United States Senate* (PDF) (p. 4). politics.stackexchange.com/questions/2098/can-i-recall-my-us-senator-or-representatives-in-congress.

Bogdanor, V. (1991). *The Blackwell encyclopedia of political science*. Oxford: Blackwell.

Constitution of the Federal Republic of Nigeria, 1999 As Amended.

Daily Trust Newspaper. (2019, January 8).

FGN. (2013). *Mid-Term Report of the Transformation Agenda: Taking Stock, Moving Forward*. Available online at https://nigerianstat.gov.ng/pdfuploads/MID-TERM%20REPORT%20OF%20THE%20TRANSFORMATION%20AGENDA%20.pdf

Hamalai, L. (2015). *Legislative oversight: A study of performance in Nigeria national assembly*. A publication of NILS, National Assembly.

Jump up to:*"Direct Election of Senators". U.S. Senate official website*. Retrieved April 23, 2019.

Okoosi-Simbine, A. T. (2010). Understanding the role of the legislature in the Fourth Republic: The case of Oyo State House of Assembly. *Nigeria Journal of Legislative Affairs,* 3(1 & 2), 1–27.

Quinton, J. (2003, July 27). Thurmond's filibuster. *Backcountry Conservative*. Retrieved April 19, 2019.

Senate Standing Order, 2011 As Amended.

Senate Standing Order. (2015).

Vanguard Newspaper. (2013, February 28).

CHAPTER 13

Giving Voice to the Voiceless: The Challenges of Women Legislators in Nigeria's National Assembly

Angela Ajodo-Adebanjoko

Introduction

The need for more women in decision-making has gained prominence in recent years. Unlike in the past when women's representation was minimal in the public domain and mostly confined to individual families, in recent years scholars, decision makers, business organizations among others have come to recognize the fact that women's role in decision-making and is critical to the growth and development of a nation. Recognizing this, governments around the world are involving more women in governance and key areas of decision making such as the national parliaments. Despite this effort, women are under-represented in government and occupy less than one quarter of all seats in national parliaments which is about 23.8% of representatives in parliaments worldwide, an unequal

A. Ajodo-Adebanjoko (✉)
Department of Political Science, Federal University Lafia, Lafia, Nigeria

F. A. Aremu and A. R. Bakare (eds.), *Two Decades of Legislative Politics and Governance in Nigeria's National Assembly*,
https://doi.org/10.1007/978-981-33-4455-6_13

gender balance which has led to criticisms and the clamour for change (Apolitical 2017; Mikva 2015; Elgie 2008; BusinessDay 2018).

In Nigeria, women began to feature in the legislature after independence. Decades after, the number of female legislators vis-à-vis their male counterparts is still not desirable and a far cry from what is happening in most countries of the world, particularly in Africa. In countries like Rwanda, South Africa, Nambia and Senegal, women have high representation in parliament while Nigeria, the supposed giant of Africa still lags behind (Ajodo-Adebanjoko 2018a). As of 1st October 2018, Nigeria ranked 183 out of 193 countries in a data compiled by the Inter-Parliamentary Union (IPU 2018) on women in national parliament with Rwanda occupying the first position. Women's position as comprising almost half (49%) of Nigeria's population is considered an advantage to them in the electoral process (Ogbonna 2016) but despite the fact that politics is a game of numbers, women still constitute a minority in Nigeria's legislature in terms of elected representatives and leadership of the body. This may not be divorced from the fact that Nigeria has not yet accepted the leadership of women, a fact that is rooted in religion and culture. In addition to this, elections in Nigeria are based on the winner-take-all principle, a system which encourages the disenfranchisement of women and other minority groups. In a really equal democracy, every section or any section would be represented, not disproportionately, but proportionately (Ajodo-Adebanjoko 2018a). This is in line with Mill's (1861) argument in his popular treatise *'Representative Government'* that it is an essential part of democracy that minorities should be adequately represented as no real democracy is possible without it. According to him, unless minorities, of which women are a part (because of the lack of opportunity), are represented, we cannot talk of an equal government.

This chapter focuses on the need for increased representation and leadership of Nigerian women in the legislature. It brings to the fore the trend in women's representation in different parliaments across the world while comparing their performance. More importantly, the advantages of having more women in leadership positions in Nigeria's national legislature are discussed while the challenges to their representation and leadership role in the national parliament are identified and solutions suggested.

Women Parliamentarians in Representative Democracies: A Review

Historically, women were stuck in the '*Cult of Domesticity*'; in other words, they were restricted to domestic affairs, as the moral keepers for societies as well as the non-working house wives for families and considered unequal to their male companions legally and socially and as such were not allowed to hold public office (Bartleby Writing, nd). Across Europe, women could not vote, were strongly discouraged from owning a business and had fewer property rights than men (Bartleby Writing, nd). Women's groups such as the Suffragettes campaigned successfully for women to be granted the right to vote and on the 19th of September 1893 New Zealand became the first country to grant women the right to vote. This was followed years later when the 19th Amendment in 1920 gave women the right to vote. By the 1930s, women were granted franchise in most countries and after Saudi Arabia granted women franchise in 2015, Vatican City remains the only country where women are still denied the right to vote (Pearson 2015; Holter 2015; BBC 2015).

Despite the fact that franchise was granted to women to vote as early as 1893, Parliament was still male-dominated and women could only observe proceedings from a discreet distance from the ladies' gallery as was common in New Zealand (Ministry for Culture and Heritage 2018). It was not until the first half of the eighteenth century that this trend changed when in 1902 Australia became the first country to grant women the right to be elected into the parliament. However, it was not until nineteen years later, 1918 that a woman, Edith Cowan, was elected for the first time into the Legislative Assembly and in 1946 Dorothy Tangney became the first woman to be elected to the Senate while in the same year, 1946, Dame Enid Lyons became the first woman elected to the House of Representatives. In 1986, Joan Child became the first female Speaker of the House of Representatives and in 2007 Anna Bligh became Queensland's first female premier and Julia Gillard MP Deputy Prime Minister. In 2010, Gillard was elected the country's first female Prime Minister while Dame Quentin Bryce became the first and only woman appointed to Governor-General in 2008. Christine Milne also made history as the only woman to head a major political party with her election as leader of the Australian Greens in 2012 (Parliament of Australia 2018). However, Indigenous people or Aboriginal Australians were granted equal franchise with white Australians only in 1983 and following this, Carol Martin in

2001 became the first Indigenous woman elected to any Australian Parliament while Linda Burney became the first Aboriginal person elected to a State Parliament in 2003 and the first Aboriginal woman elected to the House of Representatives in 2016.

Although Australia was the first to grant women the right to stand for parliamentary elections, it was Finland that became the first country to elect women into parliament with the election of 19 women in 1907 after the national assembly in 1906 granted women the right to vote and stand for parliamentary elections. With 19 female parliamentarians, women's share of membership of the Finnish Parliament in 1907 was 9.5% (Korpela 2006). Parliamentary elections are held in the country every four years to elect representatives into 200 seats and from data made available by the Inter-Parliamentary Union (IPU) on 1 October 2018, with the election of a total of 84 (42.0%) female parliamentarians in 2015, the country ranks 11th in the ranking of female Members of Parliament (MPs) in national parliaments across the globe.

In the United States, the first female MP was Jeanette Rankin, member of the Republican Party who was elected into the House of Representatives on 29 August 1916 and was sworn in on 2 April 1917, serving from 1917 to 1919. Rankin's election came four years before the 19th Amendment gave women the right to vote. On 21 November 1922 Rebecca Latimer Felton, an 84-year old Democrat, became the first woman to be appointed to the Senate when she served for a single day during a special session of the 67th Congress, however, Hattie Caraway became the first female elected member of the Senate with her election in 1932 (Buchanan 2015). Despite being a champion of democracy women do not fare so well under the American democracy. For instance, apart from Nancy Pelosi who became the first female Speaker of the House of Representatives in 2007, no other woman has assumed this position so far and neither has any headed the Senate or served as deputy. America currently ranks a dismal 104 position with 87 (20.0%) of the 428 members of the House of Representatives and 23 (23.0%) of the 100 members of the Senate being women.

Like their counterparts in the United States, history was made in Russia in 1917 when nine women were elected as MPs on 25 November of that year. With 767 seats at the time, women constituted 1.17% in the legislative body. Russia currently has a bicameral legislature with women occupying 71 (15.8%) of the 450-member lower house, State Duma and 29 (17.1%) of 170 seats of the Federation Council or Council of the

Federation, the Senate and upper house of the Federal Assembly. In 2011, Valentina Matviyenko became the first female Speaker of Russia's upper house, the Federation Council while Natalia Poklonskaya became the first female Deputy of the State Duma on 5 October 2016. Despite this, the country ranks 132 among countries with female MPs.

The 1918 Act of Parliament in the United Kingdom was a landmark for women in the country as it allowed them to be elected into parliament. As a result, 17 women candidates emerged comprising 1 Conservative candidate, 4 Labour, 4 Liberal Democrat and 8 others. Constance Markievicz became the first woman to be elected to parliament in 1918 but being a Sinn Fein member she did not take her seat and this made Nancy Astor who took her seat in 1919 the first female MP. Since 1918, 489 women have been elected as Members of the House of Commons and of this, 283 (58%) were first elected as Labour MPs and 140 (29%) as Conservative (Keen et al. 2018). The proportion of women in the parliament before the late 1980s and 1997 was below 5% and 10% respectively but this rose to 18% after the 1997 General Election which saw the election of 120 women with the highest proportion, 208 (32%) recorded after the General Election of June 2017. The total number of women elected to the House since 1918 is more than the current number of men in the House of Commons, which is 442 (Keen et al. 2018). Margaret Thatcher, the first female Prime Minister, who served from 1979 to 1990, is renowned as the most influential female MP in British history. Becoming an MP in 1959, she was eventually elected as the leader of the Conservative Party in 1975. Theresa May, a Conservative, is the current Prime Minister. The United Kingdom currently ranks 38 in the globe with women occupying 209 (32.2%) of 650 seats in the House of Commons (lower house) and 208 (26.3%) of 791 seats in the House of Lords (upper house).

In Azerbaijan, Universal suffrage was introduced in 1918 making the country the first Muslim-majority country and Turk-majority country ever to grant franchise to women. Ayna Sultanova was the first female cabinet minister while Sakina Aliyeva was the first female head of parliament. In the October 2018 ranking of countries, the country ranked 123 with 21 of 125 (16.8%) of seats in the unicameral legislature occupied by women.

Women in Germany were granted the right to vote and stand for election into parliament for the first time on 19 January 1919 and this led to the initial election of 37 women, which later rose to 41, into the National Assembly. Germany ranks 46 on women in national parliaments with 218

(30.7%) of the 709 seats of the Bundestag (lower house) and 27 (39.1) of the 69 seats of the Bundesrat (upper house) occupied by women based on election conducted in 2017. In 2005, Angela Merkel was elected as the first woman to serve as Chancellor of the country and was re-elected in 2017 for a fourth term.

In spite of being the first country to grant voting rights to women, women in New Zealand only got the right to stand for parliamentary elections in 1919 and the first female Member of Parliament (MP) Elizabeth McCombs was elected in 1933 (Ministry for Culture and Heritage 2018). Based on the election conducted in 2017, the country ranks number 19 in the global index on female parliamentarians with 46 (38.3%) women in the parliament.

In Africa, the history of women in parliament began in South Africa in 1930 when the Women's Enfranchisement Act gave white women the right to stand for legislative election. In 1933, Leila Reitz became the first woman member of parliament and served till 1943 and 10 years later in 1953, Helen Suzman a daughter of Jewish immigrants was elected into the South African parliament. In 1994, Phumzile Mlambo-Ngcuka became the first black woman to be elected as MP while in 2011, Lindiwe Mazibuko became the first non-white person to lead the Democratic Alliance in parliament and in 2014, 24-year-old Hlomela Bucwa became the youngest MP in the country. South Africa is one of the countries that rank high in global comparison of women in parliament. It currently occupies the 10th position globally with 168 (42.%) out of 397 seats in the National Assembly (lower house) and 19 of the 54 seats (35.2%) in the National Council of Provinces (NCOP) (upper house) occupied by women.

Also in 1933 Carlota Pereira de Queirós, became the first woman elected to the National Congress in Brazil but despite this achievement, as of 1 October 2018, the country ranks 157 among countries with female parliamentarians following the result of the 2014 elections, where 51 of the 513 deputies (10.7%) in the Chamber of Deputies (lower house) and 11 of the 81 members of Senate (14.8%) are women. In 2010, the country elected Dilma Vana Rousseff, the former Chief of Staff (Ministra da Casa Civil) of the previous administration as its first female president. Rousseff who was elected with 56% of the votes and was re-elected for a second term in 2014 was however impeached in 2016 on the allegation of corruption, making her the first female elected president in history to be impeached. Despite this, her two terms in office showed that Brazil welcomed the leadership of a woman.

The journey to the parliament began for women in Turkey on 3 April 1930 when voting rights in local elections was granted by Act no. 1580, followed by the granting of full universal suffrage four years as a result of a legislation enacted on 5 December 1934. Two months later, on 8 February 1935, 17 women were elected as deputies to the Turkish parliament, the Grand National Assembly of Turkey (TBMM) and several years later in 1964, Mebrure Aksoley became the first woman to be elected to the Senate where she served till 1973. Turkey has had 4 female vice-speakers namely; Nermin Neftçi, first female vice-speaker, 1972; Meral Akşener and Güldal Mumcu of the Nationalist Movement Party and Republican People's Party, respectively who served concurrently from 2007 to 2015 and Ayşe Nur Bahçekapılı who served in 2011. Turkey's constitution allows political parties with more than twenty seats to form parliamentary groups each represented by a vice chairperson in parliament to perform general administrative duties as well as representing the party's president in his or her absence. In this regard, Oya Araslı of the Republican People's Party became the first female group vice chairperson between 1996 and 1999 while the other two are Emine Ülker Tarhan of the Republican People's Party and Pervin Buldan of the Peace and Democracy Party. Tansu Çiller who was elected party leader of the conservative True Path Party (DYP) on 13 June 1993 was appointed as the Prime Minister of a coalition government in June of the same year making her the first and only female Prime Minister in Turkey's history. Turkey currently (as of 1 October 2018) ranks 118 in the comparison of parliaments with 104 of 596 (17.4%) seats in parliament occupied by female MPs.

In France, 2 women, Marthe Simard and Lucie Aubrac, were nominated to the Provisional Consultative Assembly, an assembly of representatives of the different factions of the French during the Second World War in 1945 while that same year on 21 October, 33 women were elected to the National Constituent Assembly (Buchanan 2015). Occupying the 14th position of women in national parliament with 228 (29.3%) of 576 seats in the lower house and 102 out of 348 (25%) seats of the Senate occupied by women, France ranks as one of the 20 top countries that have more women in the parliament.

In Japan, women were elected to the House of Representatives as early as 1946 with about 8% of the 464 seats but despite this, the country currently ranks 162 as of 1 October 2018 with women occupying 47 (10.1%) of the 465 seats in the House of Representatives which is the lower house and 50 (20.7%) of the seats in the House of Councilors (upper house).

12 women were elected to the Israeli parliament in 1949 and from 1969 to 1974 Golda Meir became the first woman to be elected Prime Minister. In the 17th March 2015 election conducted in the country 33 women constituting 27.5% of the 120 members were elected to the parliament. Israel currently occupies the 57th position in the ranking of women in national parliaments. 1949 was also a watershed for women in the electoral history of Thailand as on June 5 that year Orapin Chaikarn became the first elected female MP. Several years later, in 2010 Yingluck Shinawatra became the Prime Minister, a first for Thai women in the political history of the country. Yingluck held this position till 2014. Thailand occupies the 184th position with 13 of 246 (5.3%) seats in the lower house held by women.

Women began to feature as MPs in Argentina in 1951 when Juanita Larrauri became the first woman Senator followed in 1952 by Seferina del Carmen Rodriguez de Copa who became the first female representative. The parliament comprises 257 seats in the Chamber of Deputies (lower house) and 7 seats in the Senate. In November 1991, Law 24,012 was passed in favour of legal and reserved seat quotas and requires that women candidates make up at least 30% of party lists in parliamentary elections (Buchanan 2015). This has no doubt increase the representation of women in the national parliament as the country currently occupies the 17th position in global ranking of countries with female MPs with 100 women representing (38.9%) occupying the seats in the Chamber of Deputies and 30 women representing (41.7)% occupying the Senate. The country made history in 2007 when Cristina Fernandez de Kirchner became the first woman to be elected as president. Before this time, Isabel Martinez de Perón became president (1974–1976) when as vice president she assumed the position following the death of her husband, President Juan Domingo Perón (Buchanan 2015).

Greece is renowned for being the country where democracy had its origin. However the country ranks low in terms of women in politics generally and in parliament, in particular, a fact that is not divorced from the fact that in early Athens, women were disenfranchised on the grounds that they were inferior to men (Ajodo-Adebanjoko 2018b). In 1952, Heleni Skoura became the first woman to be elected as a member of the

Greek parliament and Zoi Konstantopoulou as the speaker of the parliament. Greece ranks 108 in the comparison of female parliamentarians with women constituting 56 (18.7%) of the 300-member parliament.

In Mexico, Aurora Jiménez de Palacios became the first woman MP when she was elected to the House of Representatives in 1954 and in 1964 Alicia Arellano Tapia and María Lavalle Urbina were elected to the Senate. Mexico currently ranks 4th with 241 48.2(%) of 500 seats in the House of Representatives and 63 (49.2%) of 128 seats in the Senate occupied by women.

A year after Mexico's feat, in Indonesia, 17 women were elected to the national legislature (holding 6.5% of the seats). The country ranks 103 with women constituting 111 (19.8%) of the 560 members of the People's Representative Council (lower house) and 26% of the members of the Regional Representative Council, which is the upper house.

Indonesia has adopted legal quotas and under its electoral law, at least 30% of each party's candidate list must be comprised of women (Buchanan, 2018). In 2001, Megawati Sukarnoputri became the country's first female president following the removal of the president by parliament.

History was made in the Muslim world once again when In 1957, Begum Shaista Suhrawardy Ikramullah and Begum Jahanara Shahnawaz became the first female representatives in Pakistan with their election as members of the first Constituent Assembly and in 1988 Benazir Bhutto became the first woman to be elected as prime minister and by this she became the first woman to head the government of a Muslim country (Buchanan 2015).

Pakistan uses the reserve quota system with 60 reserved seats for women in the lower house and 17 reserved seats in the upper house. The country currently ranks 93 in the world with 68 (20.6%) of 330 seats in the National Assembly (lower house) and 20 (19.2%) of 104 seats in the Senate (upper house) held by women.

In the same year in 1957, Egypt elected her first female MP making history as the first in the Arab world. Egypt ranks 136 with women occupying 89 of 596 (14.9%) seats in the lower house according to data from election conducted on 17 October 2015.

For Nicaragua, Olga Nuñez de Saballos became the first woman to be elected as an MP in the country following her election into the House of

Representatives in 1957. The country currently ranks 8th in the comparison of women in national parliaments, with 42 of 92 (45.7%) seats in the lower house occupied by women.

Several other countries in the world have made gains in terms of female MPs so that today it is common to see female parliamentarians in all countries of the world. The history of women in Nigeria's parliament began in the immediate post-independence year in the first republic, when Nigeria became a sovereign nation.

Women in the National Assembly from 1960 to 2018

Nigeria's legislature dates back to the 10-member (2 Nigerians) Lagos Legislative Council of 1862 which was established in the colonial period as an advisory body without lawmaking powers. In 1914, a new legislative body, the Nigerian Council, with 36 members 6 of whom were Nigerians, was established for the rest of the Protectorate of Nigeria but like the Lagos Legislative Council before it, it had no legislative power. The Clifford Constitution in 1922 established a national legislative body, the Nigerian Council, with 46 members, 4 of whom were elected. The new body which replaced the Lagos Legislative Council had lawmaking power as members could introduce bills that were not finance-related. Although the jurisdiction of the Nigerian Council was limited to Lagos and the Southern Provinces, it nonetheless marked a watershed in the history of the legislature in Nigeria. Richards Constitution of 1946 laid the foundation of the country's current federal system when it established three regional legislative bodies: the Northern Regional Council (headquartered in Enugu), the Western House of Assembly (headquartered in Ibadan), and the Eastern House of Assembly (with Kaduna as its headquarters) with capacity to advise the central government on all proposed bills except finance bills but this however changed with the introduction of the 1951 Constitution, which gave the regional legislatures lawmaking powers on various regional issues and enhanced the representative nature of both the central and regional legislatures by increasing the seats of the bodies that needed to be filled through an election (Law Library of Congress 2017). In 1959 the Nigerian Senate, a 48 appointed member body was established and the Nigerian federal legislature, which was before this time a unicameral body, became bicameral.

The current National Assembly in Nigeria which is modelled after the United States Congress is the legislative arm of Nigeria's government and it has a bicameral legislature comprising the Senate which is the upper house and House of Representatives which is the lower house. The Senate is made up of 109 members and the House of Representatives, 360 members. Members of the Senate are elected periodically based on equal representation of the 36 states, that is, 3 members from each of the constituent states and 1 from Abuja, the Federal Capital Territory (FCT) while those of the House of Representatives are elected based on a four-year term. The Senate is presided over by a president who is usually from the ruling party and assisted by a deputy while the House of Representatives is headed by a Speaker and a Deputy speaker, all from the party with a majority in the house. The primary function of the National Assembly is to make laws although it performs oversight functions such as control over the spending of federal funds, the authority to provide advice and consent for appointments to key executive positions, the power to approve all treaties negotiated by the executive, and the power to impeach the President and his deputy (Law Library of Congress 2017).

Women's presence in the National Assembly in Nigeria dates back to the First Republic when Mrs. Esan Wuraola became the first female Senator. Esan, a member of the women's wing of the Action Group (AG) was appointed into the Senate to represent Ibadan West and in 1961 Margaret Ekpo became a member of the Eastern House of Assembly until 1966 while Janet Mokelu and Ekpo Young also won seats in the Eastern House of Assembly. In the Second Republic (1979–1983), there was only one female Senator out of 571 members, and 11 female members of the House of Representatives out of 445 members (Otu et al. 2015). Franca Afegbua was elected into the Senate to represent the old Bende state from 1979 to 1983 and by this, became the first female elected senator in Nigeria's history (Adenuga 2017) (Table 13.1).

With the return to democratic governance in 1999, 3 women were elected to the Senate and 12 to the House of Representatives and in 2003 this number increased to 4 and 21 respectively. In 2007 the number of women elected to the Senate increased to 9 while that of the House of Representatives increased to 25. Women also scored a first when Mrs. Patricia Olubunmi Etteh became the first Female Speaker of the House of Representatives in 2007. In 2011, the gains made by women in the Senate were lost when the number of women dropped to 7 while that of the House of Representatives increased to 26 and in 2015 7 women

Table 13.1 10 top African countries with the most women in the parliament as of 1 October 2018

Rank	*Country*	*Lower or single house*				*Upper house or Senate*			
		Last elections conducted	*No. of seats*	*No of women*	*% of women*	*Last elections conducted*	*No. of seats*	*No. of women*	*% of women*
1	Rwanda	3 September 2018	80	49	61%	3 September 2018	80	49	31.8%
2	Namibia	29 November 2014	104	48	46.2%	29 November 2014	104	48	23.8%
3	South Africa	7 May 2014	397	168	42.3%	7 May 2014	397	168	35.2%
4	Senegal	30 July 2017	165	69	41.8%	N/A	N/A	N/A	N/A
5	Mozambique	15 October 2014	250	99	39.6%	N/A	N/A	N/A	N/A
6	Ethiopia	24 May 2015	547	212	38.8%	5 October 2015	153	49	32.0%
7	Burundi	9 June 2015	121	44	36.4%	24 July 2015	39	18	46.2%
8	Uganda	18 February 2016	449	154	34.3%	N/A	N/A	N/A	N/A
9	Zimbabwe	30 July 2018	270	85	31.5%	30 July 2018	80	35	43.8%
10	Tunisia	26 October 2014	217	68	31.3%	N/A	N/A	N/A	N/A

Note N/A is used where a country has a unicameral legislature
Source Compiled by author with data from IPU (2018)

were once again elected to the Senate while the number of women in the House of Representatives dropped to 22. In fairness to leaders of both houses, some female lawmakers have been made to head certain committees or appointed as members of such committees. Despite this the number of female legislators in Nigeria is too small compared with what obtains globally. In Rwanda which currently ranks as the country with the highest number of female MP, women occupy 49% of representation compared to a world and regional averages of 23.8 and 22.4%, respectively(Mutume 2004; BusinessDay; 2018). The country has 64 women in parliament as against 36 for men (Frimpong 2017). Other countries such as South Africa, Senegal, Bolivia, Cuba and Sweden also rank high in the comparison of female MPs in national parliaments. For instance, Namibia and South Africa rank 6th and 10th globally (see Table 13.2 inset). Nigeria however ranks 183 with 22 women out of 360 (6.11%) members in the House of Representatives and 7 women out of 109 (6.42%) members of the Senate. Considering that the population of women in the country is almost half of the total population and majority of electorates, it means that the womenfolk and by extension children who are cared for more by women, do not have adequate representation. The business of legislation spans economic, social and political spheres and touches on areas where women have proved their mettle. To deny women more involvement in legislation is to deny the country the benefits of development.

From the data available from IPU, as of 1 October 2018, Nigeria ranks 43 among African countries, which is the last position for Africa according to the data. Smaller countries such as Niger, Benin, Mali, Gabon, Central African Republic and others such as Ghana and Cameroon were some of the countries that ranked higher.

From the table above, Rwanda takes the lead with women constituting 61% in the House of Representatives and 31. 8% in the Senate and is followed by Bolivia, Cuba and Sweden while the bottom five countries are Yemen, Vanuatu, Papua New Guinea, the Federated States of Micronesia and Oman. The world's largest economy, the United States, ranks low at No. 102 with women occupying 87 (20.0%) of the 428 seats in the House of Representatives and 23 (23.0%) of the 100 seats in the Senate while its economic competitor, China, ranks 70th, with around a quarter of its legislative seats occupied by women (Radu 2018).

Table 13.2 10 top countries with the most women in parliament, as of 1 October 2018

Rank	*Country*	*Lower or single house*				*Upper house or Senate*			
		Last elections conducted	*No. of seats*	*No. of women*	*% of women*	*Last election conducted*	*No. of seats*	*No. of women*	*% of women*
1	Rwanda	3 September 2018	80	49	61%	26 September 2011	26	10	38.5%
2	Cuba	11 March 2018	605	322	53.2%	N/A	N/A	N/A	N/A
3	Bolivia	12 October 2014	130	69	53.1%	12 October 2014	36	17	47.2%
4	Mexico	1 July 2018	500	241	48.2%	1 July 2018	128	63	49.2%
5	Grenada	13 March 2018	15	7	46.7%	27 April 2018	13	4	30.8%
6	Namibia	29 November 2014	104	48	46.2%	8 December 2015	42	10	23.8%
7	Sweden	9 September 2018	349	161	46.1%	N/A	N/A	N/A	N/A
8	Nicaragua	6 November 2016	92	42	45.7%	N/A	N/A	N/A	N/A
9	Costa Rica	4 February 2018	57	26	45.6%	N/A	N/A	N/A	N/A
10	South Africa	7 May 2014	397	168	42.3%	21 May 2014	54	19	35.2%

Note N/A is used where a country has a unicameral legislature
Source Compiled by author with data from IPU (2018)

Women Parliamentarians and the Struggle for Voice and Leadership in the National Assembly

Women in Nigeria have been struggling for recognition and a place in governance for decades. This is despite the fact that women played key roles in the pre-colonial period as warriors, spies, rulers and in the colonial period as activists as we saw in the case of the Aba Women riot of 1929, an action which resulted in putting an end to taxation of women and women's eventual appointment to serve in newly constituted Native Courts and hold positions in public affairs such as assisting to select new chiefs (Onyeji 2018). It was not until the first Republic that women began to take active part in politics and in this regard, Wuraola Esa, Margaret Ekpo and Funmilayo Ransome-Kuti set the pace as female politicians and activists in the immediate post-independence era. This activism was however stalled by the incursion of the military into Nigerian politics on 15 July 1966. While military decrees led to a lull in political activities, women's role in politics was enhanced through the office of the various First Ladies who took active part in governance through their various programmes and with the dawn of democracy in 1999, women began once again to play prominent roles in politics with a number of them given political appointments (BusinessDay 2018). Women have contested as governorship and senatorial as well as House of Representatives candidate while others such as Sarah Jubril and Josephine Sonaiya have vied for the number position in the land but despite this active push, women still lag behind in terms of representation and leadership particularly in the national legislature.

Leadership positions as it is with elective positions, seem to be purely the exclusive preserve of Nigerian male politicians or else how can one explain that 58 years after independence, the Senate is yet to produce a female President or Deputy President while the House of Representatives seems to be satisfied with the *once-in-a-life-time* opportunity given to women in 2007. As at 2018, the Senate had only one female principal officer, Sen. Abiodun Olujimi of the People's Democratic Party (PDP) who became the Senate Minority Leader after Godswill Akpabio who held the post, decamped to the All Progressives Congress (APC). From 2007 to 2011, the House of Representatives also had only one female principal officer, Hon. Mulikat Akande also of the PDP who was the House Leader (Gabriel 2015). Membership of committees is another area women are bereft of leaders. According to Erunke and Ndiribe (2013), "the committees of the National Assembly have been repeatedly identified as the engine room of the legislature, the pivot upon which the oversight, law-making and confirmatory processes rest upon." Given the primacy of these committees, it is expected and important that women feature prominently in them but this is not so. While women chair some committees, the number is not encouraging. Out of a total of 57 Senate Committees, women chair 5 of them which is a paltry 9% while out of 89 House of Representatives Committees, only 11 (12.3%) are chaired by women. Of the 4 Joint Committees of both houses, none is chaired by a woman. This scenario is made worse by the fact that women have low representation in the legislature, a situation which hampers their ability to push for more leadership positions for their gender.

Obstacles to Women's Representation and Leadership in the National Assembly

The obstacles to women's representation and leadership in the National Assembly are found in the pre-election and post-election period. While the factors that hinder women's representation are found in the pre-election period, the factors that hinder their appointment to leadership roles are a combination of both pre-election and post-election factors. These factors range from systemic, cultural to psychological factors

Nigeria's electoral system is a major obstacle to women's representation in the parliament. The First-Past-the-Post or plurality system which Nigeria practices is based on the winner takes all practice where a candidate who has the highest number of votes wins an election even when he or she doesn't have an absolute majority. This antiquated winner-take-all voting system that most major democracies have long since abandoned because of its unrepresentative and undemocratic nature still continues to be practiced in Nigeria and this gives room for marginalization of women (Hill 1995; Enyiuche 2017). Hill and Richie (nd) identified the shortcomings of the winner-takes-all system which include the underrepresentation of women, restriction of voters' choices to candidates within the two main parties and making most legislative elections effectively "no-choice" contests in districts dominated by a single party. Because of the "win at all cost" mentality of most politicians in the country, they are predisposed to wanton rigging of elections and violence which affect women candidates negatively with the end result being fewer women representatives (Ajodo-Adebanjoko 2018a).

The high cost of politics in Nigeria is another obstacle which women battle with. In Nigeria, most women are "*too-poor-to-run*" even when they have the ambition to run for elective office. The high cost of nomination forms discourages many women and even when such forms are given out for free, because of the stigma and humiliation that go with it, most women are discouraged from running until they can afford the cost. In preparation for the 2019 General elections, candidates vying for Senate or House of Representatives nomination were expected to pay as high as 7 million for the Senate and 3.8 million for the House of Representatives respectively. This is beside funds required for campaigns during the primary and main elections, if they succeed, as well as media coverage during electioneering which is often too high for women (Onyeji 2018). In most cases, female candidates do not attract donors who prefer to bet their wealth on male candidates whom they believe have the potentials to win. Even where women get donors, many do not accept the offer because of the strings that may be attached. The issue of the high cost of electioneering in Nigeria as well as such practices as vote buying has led to a monetized politics which is believed could impede the development of Nigerian politics and erode the core values of politics in the country (Okogba 2018).

Most political parties in Nigeria, particularly the major ones are characterized by an absence of internal democracy which encourages acts such as imposition of candidates, disqualification of women by zoning seats to an area where the female aspirant is not an indigene and lack of access to information by women. Since political parties are not the most transparent structures, women have to get used to this and figure their way in (Radu 2018). Imposition of candidates or consensus candidacy for instance has become a norm in Nigerian politics where since 2015 political parties impose candidates on their members. What we have is a situation where the female candidate is forced to step down for the male candidate even where she has a better chance of winning. While it may be argued that the constitution of the country or electoral law allows for this, we are yet to see a female candidate imposed as a consensus candidate. If it ever happens, it may be an exception to the rule.

Culture and religion, reinforced by ignorance are twin evils that continue to impede women's progress in the electoral process. The issue of culture and religion as obstacles has been a problem faced by many women in many societies across the globe but while the trend is changing, Nigeria seems to be more drawn to it as shown for the low number of women elected in every election. In 2018, women in the United States comprising those often viewed as minorities such as blacks, Africans, Latinos and Muslims among others broke barriers when they were elected into the US congress. For many like IIhan Omar a Muslim refugee from Sudan and Tlaib Rashida, a Muslim, Sylvia Garcia and Veronica Escobar, Latinas, it was a first. Their election was based on the recognition of what they could contribute to the development of the country despite their minority status. In African countries like Rwanda, South Africa, Namibia and Senegal to mention a few, culture and/or religion do/does not seem to have a place as many women are elected as representatives in their parliament. In the case of Nigeria, the future looks bleak politically for women as they continue to register low turn outs because of culture and religion which has not allowed men and women alike in the country to vote for them. The problem is made worse because many in Nigeria seem to be ignorant of the wave of achievements recorded by women in other countries as we continue to hold unto our traditional values of women should be seen and not heard in public.

Physical and psychological violence constitute another set of obstacles. Research shows that almost half of women in politics have faced serious abuse, including threats of murder, rape and assault with more than 44% of elected representatives threatened in office (Perkins 2018; Matfess 2017). Physical violence involving the use of thugs to harass, abduct and even in some instances kill female candidates discourages many women from politics. Several women who have been victims of the violence in Nigerian politics include Mary Omope, Women Leader in Ekiti State, Mrs. Igwe, wife of former Chairman Nigerian Bar Association, Onitsha, Janet Olapade in Ogun State, Kate Maimuna Commissioner for Women Affairs in Nasarawa State who were killed by assassins that were hired by their political opponents (Dike 2003). Psychologically, women are called names and vilified in the electoral process. Female candidates in Nigeria are in most cases viewed as women of easy virtues and *Iron Ladies*, those who seek to dominate men, as such their private lives are often exposed to the public in a bid to discredit them. Limo et al. (2005) linked Violence against women in politics to gender inequalities and harmful sociocultural norms, intimately linked to the existence of strong and negative conceptions of masculinity, the breakdown of traditional family and social structures and low economic empowerment which has the potential to negatively impact women's human rights. In addition, the violence and intimidation that women face while running for office, as well as after being elected, not only hurt the women themselves but the political process as a whole and threatens good governance (Matfess 2017). It is in recognition of this fact that a campaign and a programme of work were launched in 2008 to support parliaments in their efforts to end violence against women (IPU 2008).

The Queen Bee belief or the lack of cooperation from fellow women remains a problem in Nigerian politics. It is argued that women just can't get along (Cooper 2016). Women do not generally support each other either as a result of envy and jealousy, inferiority complex or because they do not see the need to do so. This reason makes it hard for many to believe that the problem of women's marginalization in politics is "*men-made*." Women are often allies of men when it comes to the oppression of their female counterpart as we see from cases of gender-based violence such as genital mutilation and widowhood practices which are often perpetrated on women by fellow women. If the problem of marginalization were the sole responsibility of men, one would have argued that women could use their number to elect their fellow women but this is not the case. In the 2011 presidential primaries, the only female presidential Aspirant Sarah Jubril got only one vote which she cast for herself despite the fact that some of the delegates were women.

Another major obstacle is the fact that many women do not begin from the lowest places such as local government areas, state House of Representatives etc. before vying for higher ones. Most women start their political career by wanting to be elected into the Federal legislature when at the local level they are not known. Some women sometimes bank on a few credentials such as the fact that their family is renowned or that they have a few followers. While the fact remains that some politicians in Nigeria have won elections at the national level despite not starting from the grassroots, it is a known fact that starting at the grassroots is key to electoral victory, especially for those who do not have godfathers. Aspiring female politicians must have a base at the grassroots where they must have been involved in politics at that level through community service to enhance their chances of being elected eventually when they vie for higher positions.

Most of the pre-election factors have been responsible for few women being elected into the parliament and this by extension has affected less of them being given leadership roles. With a total of 29 women as against 440 men, women currently constitute 6% of a total number of 469 law makers and it may not seem fair to make all the women leaders in the various committees of both arms of the legislature. Besides, women's fewer number does not place them in the position to shape decisions such as the choice of principal officers. What this means is that if the problem of few elected women is settled, the problem of fewer representations in leadership positions will be addressed.

Failure on the part of women has also affected their being considered for important leadership positions. For instance, while women are adjudged to be mostly free from corruption, the first and only female Speaker of the House of Representatives in Nigeria's history, Patricia Olubunmi Etteh served for only four months from July to October 2007 having been implicated in a corruption scandal having been found to have used 628 million naira for the renovation of her personal residence and that of her deputy, an issue which led to her hasty resignation to avoid impeachment. Others such as Stella Odua, a former Minister of Aviation Minister, Deziani Allison-Madueke, a former Minister of Petroleum, Olujumoke Akinjide a former Minister of the FCT have all been fingered in corruption scandals. This negative trend no doubt continues to affect women in their quest for leadership roles, even though it is argued that despite the fact that men are corrupt, they continue to assume leadership positions. The involvement of women in the crime of corruption as in other matters such as their being divorced, being single parents, etc., seems to be an unpardonable sin while men's can be overlooked.

The issue of culture and religion cannot be downplayed when we talk about women's few number in leadership positions. Just as this twin factor hinders their election, it also contributes to their being marginalized in leadership roles. Nigeria has not grown to the point where men, even those in the National Assembly that we assumed that are enlightened, have come to terms with women's leadership roles. Because of culture and religion which predisposes or requires that women should be submissive, it is often taken by men to mean that women cannot or should not lead where you have men. As such, what we have is fewer women in leadership positions and such positions are mostly where they can lead other women.

Another obstacle is the lack of focus on the part of women. Women have not really been able to define what they want and how they intend to achieve this. For instance, while many of them ask for increase in the number of elected representatives, they do not clearly define how they want this to be achieved. Besides, they seem to be concerned with only an increase in their number and do not press for more leadership roles.

Scholars and analysts are also guilty of this as we find that the focus is mainly on increasing the number of female representatives, not on leadership.

The Prospects of Female Lawmakers in the National Assembly: A Clarion Call

The advantages of having more women in the legislature are myriad. Inclusivity in political participation as a fundamental aspect of democracy leads to improved policy changes, economic growth, security and stability which results in a more prosperous economy (Policy and Legal Advocacy Centre 2016).

Women leaders are known to be effective in pressuring for amendment and initiation of national laws and local policies for improved infrastructure, constitutional and legislative reforms to repeal or abrogate repugnant laws and ratification of international resolutions for the protection of women's as well as children's rights while increasing awareness on social, cultural and traditional practices that affect women and girls such as female genital mutilation (FGM), child marriage, early marriage, domestic violence, gender-based violence (GBV) and human trafficking and support legislation to end them.. In Rwanda, Bolivia and other countries which rank high in female representation in parliament, women have used their legislative power to put forward bills on violence against women in politics, women's equality, child care, access to justice in addition to pushing forward for child rights among others (Radu 2018). Giving women more representation in legislation will aid in the realization of the Sustainable Development Goals (SDGs) 2030 which seek to the realization of human rights by all, and to achieve gender equality and the empowerment of all women and girls (Limo et al. 2005).

The presence of women in the legislature is also critical for pre-conflict, conflict and post-conflict policymaking. Women by their nature are peace lovers and they would favour legislations that promote peace. It is in recognition of this fact that gender is increasingly becoming an integral consideration in peace processes, as called for in the United Nations Security Council Resolution (UNSCR) 1325, adopted in 2000, the first ever formal women, peace and security resolution passed by the United Nations (UN) (Limo et al. 2005).

Women's increased presence in politics in general and in the legislature, in particular, is necessary for development. As a former Secretary-General of the UN, Kofi Anan posited, there is no development strategy in which women are not involved and when women are fully involved, the benefits are immediate and immense as families are healthier and better fed and their income, savings and investments go up, and what is true of families is true of communities and in the long run, of the whole country (Mutume 2004).

Strategies for Increasing the Voice and Leadership Opportunities for Women in the National Assembly

Changing the electoral system from plurality to proportional representation is necessary if Nigeria hopes to have gender balance in the legislature. Research has shown that countries with majority of women in their parliaments practice proportional representation (PR). As a system, PR gives opportunity for minorities to be voted in while it discourages violence which is the product of do-or-do mentality which emanates from the winner-take-all syndrome. As such, it has become imperative to replace the simple majority system which Nigerian has practiced for over five decades with a system that has been tested and proven to work in several countries in recent times.

Individual candidacy is also proposed. The fact that women have to belong to a political party to be eligible to be voted for undermines their ability to be elected because of factors such as absence of internal democracy, systemic disqualification, the practice of holding political meetings at night and money politics which continue to hamper their chances of being elected. After 58 years of independence, Nigeria has matured enough to have independent candidates and should be a trailblazer in this regard in Africa.

Capacity building initiatives which involve gender awareness training organized by Civil Society Organisations (CSOs), government and politicians are necessary. They should also be trained in the act of governance, leadership and this should be organized at the local and national levels, involving both men and women. It should also be carried out in schools and learning centres with the aim of reaching a wide range of participants.

Education of girls remains key to giving voice to the women. In some communities in Nigeria, it may be difficult to find a female representative where the women are uneducated. The lack of education is sometimes responsible for women holding the view of politics as a game only for men and for those who are morally deficient. When women are enlightened, they will see the benefit of representing their people and the need to have the right people in the right places. Education and economic empowerment will give women the necessary empowerment to make their mark in the political arena.

Gender equality in the political process is imperative to have a gender balance in the legislature. Gender equality is a prerequisite not only for development and growth, but for sustainable peace stability, faster economic growth, democratic inclusiveness and better human recovery. It is based on the fact that men and women are equal before and have both been endowed with leadership skills and abilities to better their society. Global statistics for gender parity showed that in 2015 out of 188 Nigeria was 152nd on the Human Development Index in gender inequality and 118th out of 192 countries in 2017 (Ayodele 2018). This is not a good report for a country which seeks to achieve the SDGs by 2030. Equal representation of women and men in leadership is therefore necessary.

Profiling women candidates would be necessary if women are to have more representation. The role of the media is very important in this regard as they can make or mar female candidates through their reportage. The media needs to shape election discourse with the aim of promoting women's political participation by way of enlightening the public on the role of Nigerian women in the past and also keeping them abreast of what is happening in different parts of the world in terms of women's representation and leadership abilities, while deemphasizing negative stereotypes or profiling (Onyeji 2018).

Civil Society Organisations (CSOs) have a role to play in ensuring that women are given leadership roles in the parliament. This will involve mounting pressure on the government to ensure that policies that promote gender parity are implemented so that more women are elected and stand the chance to assume leadership positions (Ogbonna 2016). The ratification of the Convention on the Elimination of Discrimination against Women in 1979 and the Beijing Platform for Action adopted at the Fourth Conference on Women in 1995 have not brought about gender equality and equity which will ensure more representation of women in the legislature. The 30% representation by women in governments recommended by the Beijing conference is yet to be strictly adhered to in the country as we have seen overtime. In 2003 for instance, only 3% of women were elected to public office, in 2007 the figure increased to about 7% but in 2015 dropped to 5.6% (Eniola 2018). Lawmakers must reverse this trend through their action. It is necessary to pressure the three arms of government to ensure that this is implemented.

The need for gender neutral or fifty-fifty quotas which will require equal number of seats to be allocated to both men and female candidates is imperative. Generally, quotas have been useful in increasing women's representation in governments across the globe. Evidence has shown that countries like Rwanda, South Africa, Argentina, and others that have large number of women in their parliaments today were able to achieve this feat through the allocation of quotas. Unlike the other types of quotas such as reserved seat quotas, legal candidate quotas and political party quotas which have generated criticisms on the grounds that they tend to negate the principle of equality which is a hallmark of democracy, gender neutral quotas give equal opportunities to men and women although that it is criticized for impinging on the choice of the electorate who ordinarily should vote for whomsoever he or she wants. However, for this system to be practicable in terms of appointment to leadership of the national legislature in Nigeria, the number of female representatives needs to be increased.

Conclusion

Women in position of power are still a rare find on the global political map despite the fact that closing the gender gap has long been a priority in many democracies (Radu, 2018). While there has been an improvement in several countries including countries in sub-Saharan Africa and other parts of Africa, Nigeria's case seems to worsen after every election as women continue to record poor outputs as representatives and leaders. With more female legislative candidates losing nomination bids in the prelude to the 2019 General elections, it shows that the country has a long way to go in achieving gender parity in the legislature. For a country which has assumed leadership of the African continent, demonstrating this in terms of giving women the pride of place in elective and leadership positions is a sine qua non if she hopes to continue to maintain a prominent place in the comity of nations.

References

Adenuga, A. (2017). *History throwback Thursday: First Nigerian women in politics*. https://connectnigeria.com/articles/2017/08/throwback-thursdaynigerian-first-women-politics/. Accessed 27 November 2018.

Ajodo-Adebanjoko, A. (2018a, June 28). *The quest for proportional representation in Nigeria*. Roundtable organized by Department of Political Science University of Abuja in Conjunction with Rosa Stiftung, Germany, held at the Parliamentary Building University of Abuja.

Ajodo-Adebanjoko, A. (2018b). *Gender-based violence and inequality in Nigerian politics*. Paper submitted for publication in Zaria Journal of Social Sciences. A publication of Faculty of Social Sciences, A.B.U Zaria.

Apolitical. (2017). Ranked and mapped: Which countries have the most women in parliament. http//:archive.ipu.org. Accessed 29 November 2018.

Ayodele, S. (2018). *Nigeria: General elections 2019, INEC seeks increased women's participation in electoral process*. INEC News http://www.inecnigeria.org/?inecnews=inec-seeks-increased-womens-participation-in-electoral-process. Accessed 2 December 2018.

Bartleby Writing. (nd). Essay on women's role in society in the 1800 s–728 Words/Bartleby. https://www.bartleby.com. Accessed 13 September 2018.

Bartleby Writing. (nd). *Essay on women's role in society: Throughout the years*. https://www.bartleby.com. Accessed 13 September 2018.

BBC News. (2015, December 12). *Saudi women cast their first votes*.

Buchanan, K. (2015). *Women in history: Elected representatives*. https://blogs.loc.gov/law/2015/03/women-in-history-elected-representatives/. Accessed 3 December 2018.

BusinessDay. (2018). *At 57, still a long walk to equal opportunity for Nigerian women*. www.businessdayonline.com. Accessed 13 September 2018.

Cooper, M. (2016). *Why women (Sometimes) don't help other women*. https://www.theatlantic.com/business/archive/2016/06/queen-bee/488144/. Accessed 30 November 2018.

Dike, V. (2003). *Nigeria and the politics of unreason: Political association, developments, money bags and public protests*. Sacramento: Centre for Social Justice and Human Development.

Elgie, C.D. R (2008, April 1). The effect of increased women's representation in parliament: The case of Rwanda. *Parliamentary Affairs, 61*(2), 237–254. https://doi.org/10.1093/pa/gsn007. Accessed 27 November 2018.

Eniola, T. (2018). *Where are all the women in Nigerian politics?* https://www.equaltimes.org/where-are-all-the-women-inaccessed. Accessed 2 December 2018.

Enyiuche. (2017). *Electoral voting process in Nigeria*. https://learnvercity.com/2456/electoral-voting-process-in-nigeria/. Accessed July 2018.

Erunke, J., & Ndiribe, O. (2013). *National Assembly committees: The bony and the juicy*. https://www.vanguardngr.com/2013/07/national-assembly-committees-the-bony-and-the-juicy/. Accessed 2 December 2018.

Frimpong, D. (2017). *The country with the most female politicians in the world is in Africa*. https://www.businessinsider.com/the-country-with-the-most-female-politicians-in-the-world-is-in-africa-2017-10. Accessed 29 November 2018.

Gabriel, C. (2015). *Elective positions: Why Nigeria records more women losers than winners*. https://www.vanguardngr.com/2015/05/elective-positions-why-nigeria-records-more-women-losers-than-winners/. Accessed 27 November 2018.

Hill, S. (1995). Political parties standing on the threshold of a third party dream, excerpt from a speech given to the annual national convention of the Green Party USA, July 29, 1995 and the annual national convention of the National Lawyers Guild, August 9, 1995.

Hill, S., & Richie, R. (nd). *The case for proportional representation*. http://www.fairvote.org/the_case_for_pr_. Accessed July 2018.

Holter, L. (2015, August 20). *There's 1 country where women can't vote & it's seriously time for it to break with tradition*. Bustle. Bryan Goldberg.

IPU (2008). *Taking action on violence against women*. http://archive.ipu.org/wmn-e/meeting.htm. Accessed 29 November 2018.

IPU. (2018). *Women in national parliaments: Situation as of 1st October 2018*. http://archive.ipu.org/wmn-e/classif.htm. Accessed 29 November 2018.

Keen, R., Cracknell, R., & Bolton, M. (2018, July 20). *Women in parliament and government* (Briefing Paper Number SN01250). House of Commons Library.

Korpela, S. (2006). *Finland's parliament: Pioneer of gender equality*. https://finland.fi/life-society/finlands-parliament-pioneer-of-gender-equality/. Accessed 3 December 2018.

Law Library of Congress. (2017). *National parliaments: Nigeria*. https://www.loc.gov/law/help/national-parliaments/nigeria.php. Accessed 2 December 2018.

Limo, I, Davies, V. O., & Bromley, J. (2005). *Protecting the rights of women through community focused approaches to strengthening gender in African peace support operations in the Democratic Republic of the Congo and Central African Republic*. Policy & Practice Brief, South Africa, ACCORD.

Matfess, H. (2017). *From Women and foreign policy program and women around the world violence against female politicians*. https://www.cfr.org/article/violence-against-female-politicians. Accessed 30 November 2018.

Mikva, K. (2015). *12 Sub-Saharan African countries with most women in parliament*. https://moguldom.com/90064/african-countries-women-parliament/. Accessed 29 November 2018.

Mill, J. S. (1861). *Considerations on representative government*. London, UK: Parker, Son and Bourn.

Ministry for Culture and Heritage. (2018). *Women MPs'*. https://nzhistory.govt.nz/politics/parliaments-people/women-mps. Accessed 3 December 2018.

Mutume, G. (2004). *Quota systems allow more women to gain elected office*. https://www.un.org/africarenewal/magazine/april-2004/women-break-african-politics. Accessed 29 November 2018.

Ogbonna, N. (2016). *Women in Nigeria make up 49 per cent of the population, but only four per cent of lawmakers*. http://blogs.lse.ac.uk/africaatlse/2016/03/08/women-in-nigeria-make-up-49-per-cent-of-the-population-but-only-four-per-cent-of-lawmakers/. Accessed 30 November 2018.

Okogba, E. (2017). *Monetisation of politics is eroding our political system- Bisi Akande*. https://www.vanguardngr.com/2017/07/monetisation-politics-eroding-political-system-bisi-akande/. Accessed 30 November 2018.

Okogba, E. (2018). *Monetisation of politics is eroding our political system- Bisi Akande*. https://www.vanguardngr.com/2017/07/monetisation-politicseroding-political-system-bisi-akande/. Accessed 27 November 2018.

Onyeji, E. (2018). *Profiling 2019 female aspirants: Why political space dwindles for Nigerian women*. https://www.premiumtimesng.com/news/headlines/277002-profiling-2019-female-aspirants-why-political-space-is-dwindling-for-nigerian-women.html. Accessed 2 December 2018.

Otu, E., Okechukwu, E. I., & Emmanuel, O. A. (2015, May). *Politics in Nigeria: To what extent has The gender agenda gained momentum? IOSR Journal of Humanities and Social Science (IOSR-JHSS)*, *20*(5), Ver. 1, 1–10. www.iosrjournals.org.

Parliament of Australia. (2018, November). *No. 3-Women in the Senate* (Senate Brief No. 3). http//:www.aph.gov.au. Accessed 3 December 2018.

Pearson, M. (2015, December 12). *Polls open in Saudi Arabia, first time women allowed to vote*. CNN.

Perkins, A. (2018). *Women in politics Almost half of women in politics have faced abuse or violence Global survey ahead of London summit finds 44% faced serious abuse, including threats of murder, rape and assault*. https://www.theguardian.com/politics/2018/mar/19/almost-half-of-women-in-politics-have-faced-abuse-or-violence. Accessed 30 November 2018.

Policy and Legal Advocacy Centre. (2016). *Women in politics*. https://www.premiumtimesng.com/news/top-news/183932-only-7-female-senators-in-8th-national-assembly.html. Accessed 2 December 2018.

Radu, S. (2018). *Women still a rare part of world's parliaments: Newer governments do more to include women in their legislatures than countries with older institutions*. https://www.usnews.com/news/best-countries/articles/2018-09-04/women-are-still-underrepresented-in-parliaments-around-the-world. Accessed 29 November 2018.

CHAPTER 14

The National Assembly and the Paradox of Defection Politics in Nigeria's Fourth Republic, 1999–2019

Muritala Babatunde Hassan

Introduction

From the 4th National Assembly in May June 1999 to the 8th National Assembly (2015–2019), Nigeria's Fourth Republic has witnessed a liturgical legislators' defection from the political parties through which they were elected to another. In both chambers of the National Assembly, i.e. the Senate and the House of Representatives, members have been moving from one political party to another at will, unmindful of the implication of their 'porting' on representative democracy. Representative democracy is hinged on the mandate of the citizens entrusted in their representatives elected through the platform of political parties. Except where constitution and electoral act of a state allow independent candidacy, political parties are usually the forums through which representatives are recruited

M. B. Hassan (✉)
Department of Political Science, Federal University Dutse, Dutse, Jigawa, Nigeria

F. A. Aremu and A. R. Bakare (eds.), *Two Decades of Legislative Politics and Governance in Nigeria's National Assembly*,
https://doi.org/10.1007/978-981-33-4455-6_14

in modern democracy. Political parties therefore represent a strong pillar of representative democracy as they, through their elected candidates, implement policies which reflect the wishes and interests of majority of the citizenry. A political party, according to Edmund Burke cited in Pulzer (1967), is a body of people united for promoting, by their joint endeavours, the national interest, upon some particular principles in which they are all agreed. Political parties gain support of the citizenry through the ideology and manifesto that they put forward and are expected to be implemented when voted to power. As such electorates identify contestants with particular parties and the broad political ideas and values they profess. It therefore means that any candidate elected on the platform of a political party is elected for the implementation of the party's ideas and values. However, when candidates defect from their sponsored party to another for unprincipled and non-ideologically inclined reasons, as the case in Nigeria, they not only confuse their constituencies, their action is undemocratic and destabilizes the political process (Okoosi-Simbine 2005).

In retrospect, politics of defection has been an incongruous part of the Nigerian political system right from the colonial period. The first celebrated parliamentarian defection dates back to 1951 in the Western Region's House of Assembly, when Chief Adeleke Adedoyin and other 19 members elected on the platform of the National Council of Nigerian and Cameroon (NCNC) (which won 42 out of 80 seats) defected to the Action Group (AG) thereby preventing the NCNC from producing the premier for the Western Region (Awefeso and Irabor 2017; Okoosi-Simbine 2005). Though there was no constitutional provision on defection during this period, but the action of the Yoruba members of the NCNC underscored the politics of ethnicity which culminated into the regional-based political parties that characterized the politics of the First Republic.

Since this scenario, defection has remained an indelible element of multiparty democracy in Nigeria. Most worrisome is the spate of legislators' defection in the Fourth Republic, which continues to cause tension, hostility and friction between the members of the National Assembly on one hand and the legislature and executive on the other. Though defection is a peculiar feature of party politics in any climes but the frequency and motive of occurrence in Nigeria, most especially in the National Assembly, make it a worrisome phenomenon. As Badejo et al. (2016) lament, '...the motive with which it [defection] is practiced in Nigeria by politicians and parliamentarians differs clearly from how it is practiced in most developed democracies like US, Britain and others' (p. 10). Unlike developed democracies where politicians defect for ideological reasons, Nigerian politicians decamp based on 'primordial interest and egoistic hedonism' (Badejo and Obah-Akpowoghaha 2015, p. 216). This form of political oscillation calls for concern most especially as regards the status of the National Assembly as the symbol of public representation.

The legislature, as observes by Igbokwe-Ibeto (2015), is the 'cynosure of the people' (p. 1) and is expected to act for the people as they would act for themselves. However, the gale of defection of the members of the National Assembly during the Fourth Republic questions the status of the institution as the symbol of representation. It is on the backdrop of this scenario that this chapter attempts a critical analysis of the politics of defection in the Nigerian National Assembly from 1999 to 2019. Relying heavily on documentary sources of data and anchoring analysis on the framework of political opportunism, the chapter critically interrogates the prevalent culture of defection among Nigerian legislators vis-à-vis the operation of representative democracy in the country. The chapter is structured into six sections. This introduction is followed by conceptual and theoretical framework. The third section is a review of the indispensability of the legislature for the practice of representative democracy. The fourth analyses the politics of legislative defection in relation to extant constitutional provisions and the controversy thereof. This is followed by an analysis of the implications of legislators' defection on representative democracy in Nigeria. The last section concludes the analysis and offers suggestions on how to tame the tide of politics of defection in Nigeria.

Conceptual and Theoretical Framework

The impracticability of direct democracy has made democracy synonymous with representative democracy worldwide. Representative democracy is hinged on the practice of electing, by majority vote at regular intervals, citizens who would rule on behalf of the people. By implication, it is expected that a representative government should be a replica of the larger society; a representative government is a microcosm of the larger interests of the people (Igbokwe-Ibeto 2015). It is based on the will or supremacy of the people through their representatives duly and credibly elected. The institution of democracy, in modern sense, is thus predicated on periodic elections to elect new representatives or renew the mandate given to the incumbents. Election, in the contemporary democracy is party-based. It is due to the centrality of political party in the electoral process that it has become a cardinal part of representative democracy. As bodies of like-minded people who have agreed upon ideal principles through which national interests can be achieved, political parties unify forces in the representational process. It is in recognition of the strategic position of political parties in a representative democracy that Mohammed (2017) argues that:

> Political parties are the linchpin of democracy. Parties serve as a conveyor belt between the electorate and their representatives... In short, the whole question of competition and representation in a democracy revolves around the existence of political parties and the inherent tradition of party competition for power... Essentially, it is within the context of people's choice offered by political parties that democracy today becomes the most cherished form of government... (p. 1).

Though political parties are assemblages of people with similar views on how best to govern a state, circumstances often warrant the dumping of a political party by a member for another party. When this occurs, such a member is said to have defected from his/her party to another.

This act has been tagged with different nomenclatures by analysts and commentators. For instance, Okoosi-Simbine (2005) calls it 'political vagrancy'; Badejo and Obah-Akpowoghaha (2015), Awofeso and Irabor (2016, 2017) see it as 'cross carpeting' while Ikechukwu (2015) tags it 'political normadism'. Others have described it as 'political port-de-port', 'political prostitution', 'canoe jumping', 'party hopping', 'party switching', 'political porting' among others (Jiddere 2017; Ogundiya 2011). Whatever the nomenclature, party defection entails the habit of politicians leaving political party they have been members for another, as new members. It is an act by politicians of changing loyalty and jettisoning a party and label which they have been identified with and aligning with another party and label for the purpose of continuing their career in politics or participating in election as candidates of the new party (Okoosi-Simbine 2005). Given the dynamic nature of human beings and their social conditions, party defection cannot be completely ruled out in any state with party politics. As such, the practice occurs in both developed and developing democracies; however, the frequency and motive of occurrence vary from one state to another.

It therefore follows that the habit of political defection is not always unethical, most especially when premised on philosophical and ideological justifications. It gains amoral colouration when ambition becomes the driving force behind it; 'when the principle has been left behind for geocentricism and self-aggrandizement' (Okoosi-Simbine 2005, p. 20). This, unfortunately, sums up the situation in Nigeria. The cases of defection recorded in the country so far show that Nigerian politicians do not change party for altruistic and ideological reasons; rather for selfish ends. The frequency of its occurrence, most especially after and prelude to general elections holds credence to the assertion that defection is an opportunistic tool in the Nigerian party politics. We therefore conceive politics of defection as front and back movement of Nigerian politicians from one political party to another based on calculated pay-offs. Most notably, the Fourth Republic has recorded many instances of National Assembly members defecting to another party. Such movement, in most instances, was prompted by feelings of personal dissatisfaction and discontent with the jettisoned party rather than on altruistic or ideological reason.

The intensity of the wave of defection politics in Nigeria can therefore be better understood if situated within the context of political opportunism. Given the fact that access to state power is a major source of capital accumulation in Nigeria, holding political office and consolidating it is seen as '*a must*' by the political elites. The socio-economic architecture of Nigeria has put the state "as the locus of the struggle for resources for personal advancement and group security" (Joseph, 1991 quoted in Okoli and Orinya 2014, p. 1478). As such, due to its attractiveness in terms of enabling quick personal enrichment, the capture of the state power is pursued in a 'do-or-die' manner. This is the mentality that guides the formation of political parties and the logic of electoral competition within and among them. Thus, rather than serving as platforms of actualizing national interests based on shared ideology, Nigerian political parties merely represent avenues of capturing power by political elite for self-survival. In this context, as Adejumobi poignantly puts it,

> ...the way of doing politics, in the words of Max Weber, is not to live for it, but to live from it. Politicians, therefore, assume the role of entrepreneurs who invest heavily in politics, with the aim of claiming super profits and dividends in the ruthless appropriation of state resources. In other words, politics is viewed only in terms of allocation of resources, that is, who

> gets what, when, how and, how much – a political game which inevitably assumes a consumerist dimension. Thus, political parties serve as nothing but political instruments for the continuation at all costs of an electoral warfare, in which the ends justifies the means, fair or foul. (Adejumobi 1997, p. 126)

It is within this context that one can plausibly analyse the litany of defection politics that characterized both chambers of the National Assembly since 1999 when the country transited from military to civil rule.

Legislature as a *Sine-qua-non* of Representative Democracy

That the legislature is the hallmark of representative democracy is well established in the literature (Alabi 2009; Akanle 2009; Bishin 2009; Okoosi-Simbine 2010; Omoweh 2006; Rechfeild 2005). This is not unconnected with the constituent representation symbolized by the legislature. As an institution with a broad outlook and composition, representing all facets of the society, the legislature is the 'most critical organ…of government in the development and crystallization of open and democratic societies' (Akanle 2009, p. 81). Being constituted by the largest number of elective representatives compared with executive organ, the legislature is the primary mechanism of popular sovereignty. For instance, while the president is the only member of the executive elected in Nigeria, 109 senators and 360 House of Representative members are elected. Likewise, as against one elected governor, each state of the federation has between 21 and 40 elected members of House of Assembly, depending on population strength. The legislature thus occupies a strategic place in democratic governance by aggregating collective interests of the people and galvanizing them through laws that protect people's interests and aspirations (Omoweh 2006).

It is due to the key position occupies by the legislative institution in a democratic political system that Okoosi-Simbine (2010) describes it as the 'First Estate of the Realm'; the embodiment of representation and location of popular sovereignty. The strategic position occupies by the legislature in a representative democracy also accounts for the crucial roles it plays in modern governance. Roles such as law making, constitutional amendment, oversight, impeachment of the executive heads, control of public purse, ratification of international treaties, etc., are some of the legislative function which makes the institution somehow sacred and honourable. As observes by Akanle (2009), the involvement of the legislature in most crucial aspects of governance processes— policy designing (effective law making), evaluation of results (oversight function) and appropriation of sanction (impeachment)—makes it a potent and lethal force in the practice of representative democracy. The appreciation of mechanisms and dynamics of the legislature, as opines further by Akanle, is therefore 'necessary and central to the legitimization of democracy as the government of the people, by the people and for the people, as the legislature identifies popular problems, negotiates consensus and set agenda for policy implementations through process of law making' (p. 81).

What is worth emphasizing here is that the honourable status of members of the legislature is earned by the institution being the cynosure of the people; their authority is derived from the people and should be exercised in accordance with the will of the people who they represent. It therefore follows that in a real representative democracy, a member of parliament is elected due to his/her membership of a political party, whose ideology and programmes majority members of the constituency prefer, rather than the personality of the legislator. Thus, if for any reason, the legislator decides to leave the party, it denotes that he/she has lost belief in the ideology and programmes accepted by his/her 'masters', i.e. the electorate. Though most legislators in Nigeria do justify their defection from the party through which they are elected on their constituencies' request, however, the circumstances of the defection prove otherwise. The experience in the country since 1999 shows that only in rare cases do legislators consult and rub minds with their constituents before defecting from the political platform through which the constituents elected them to another. This makes mockery of party politics and representative democracy.

The Politics of Legislator Defection in the Fourth Republic: Constitutional Provision and the Controversy Thereof

A telescopic view of party politics in Nigeria since 1999 would reveal that defection is a recurring phenomenon. As observed by Mohammed (2018), defection 'galore' has dotted the political landscape of the country in the Fourth Republic more than ever since the introduction of party politics in 1922. Countless politicians together with their supporters at the federal, state and local government levels have moved from one political party to another, in a front and back dimension. As regards the members of the National Assembly, though there is no certainty on the actual number of members who have defected from one party to another, however, the rate at which some of them change party affiliations, most especially in the build up to general elections shows that defection politics is a peculiar feature of Nigerian parliamentarians. Starting from the build up to the 2003 general elections, defection has been a strategy of politics of survival by most members of the National Assembly. It was during this period that Senators Wahab Dosunmu (Lagos West), Musiliu Obanikoro (Lagos Central) and Adeseye Ogunlewe (Lagos East) defected from the Alliance for Democracy (AD) to the ruling People's Democratic Party (PDP). This period also witnessed the defection of Senators Arthur Nzeribe (Orlu Zone, Imo), John Nwannunu (Abia Central) and Alex Usman kadiri (Kogi East) from the All Nigerian People's Party (ANPP) to the ruling PDP. The 6th National Assembly (2007–2011) also recorded the defection of no fewer than 13 senators and 15 House of Representative members from opposition parties to the ruling PDP (Ikechukwu 2015). Given the fledgling nature of democracy in the country then and coupled with the fact that the defection of these parliamentarians favoured the ruling PDP, their action generated less controversy.

The most pronounced and controversial cases of defection were those that happened in the build up to the 2015 and 2019 general elections. The intra-party crisis within the ruling PDP in 2013 led to the factionalization of the party and the subsequent defection of 5 out of the 7 aggrieved governors to the newly formed All Progressive Congress (APC) in November 2013. Their defection was trailed by the defection of 37 House of Representative members and 11 Senators in December 2013, premising their action on the factionalization of the PDP. The defected lawmakers in both chambers of the National Assembly are presented in Table 14.1.

Following this was the defection of the Speaker of House of Representative, Honourable Aminu Tambuwal, from the ruling PDP to the APC on 28 October 2014. His defection put an end to months of speculations that he would join the opposition party, having teamed up with the members of the defunct Action Congress of Nigeria (ACN) to

Table 14.1 National Assembly members who defected from the PDP to the APC in December 2013

House of Representatives			
S/N	*Name*	*State*	*Federal Constituency/Senatorial District*
1.	Abdullahi Balarabe	Sokoto	Gwadabawa/Illela
2.	Abdulmumin Jibrin	Kano	Bebeji/Kiru
3.	Abdullahi Wamakko Mohammed	Sokoto	Kware/Wamakko
4.	Ali Ahmad	Kwara	Ilorin East/Ilorin South
5.	Aliyu Bahago Ahman Pategi	Kwara	Edu/Moro/Pategi
6.	Ahmed Zerewa	Adamawa	Zerewa Karaye/Roga
7.	Aishatu Ahmed	Adamawa	Yola North/Yola South
8.	Aiyedun Olayinka	Kwara	Ekiti/Isin/Irepodun/Oke-ero
9.	Alhassan Ado Garba	Kano	Tudun-wada/Doguwa
10.	Aliyu Madaki Sani	Kano	Dala
11.	Aliyu Shehu	Sokoto	Bodinga/Dange-Shuni/Tureta
12.	Aminu Shagari Shehu	Sokoto	Shagari/Yabo
13.	Aminu Suleiman	Kano	Fagge
14.	Blessing Nsiegbe Ibiba	Rivers	Port Harcourt 2
15.	Dakuku Petersides Adol	Rivers	Andoni/Opobo/Nkoro
16.	Dawari George Ibietela	Rivers	Akuku-Toru/Asari-Toru
17.	Gibson Nathaniel Kauda	Adamawa	Guyuk/Shelleng
18.	Gogo Bright Tamuno	Rivers	Okrika/Ogu-Bolo
19.	Isa Bashir Salihu	Sokoto	Gudu/Tangaza
20.	Kabiru Achida Marafa	Sokoto	Wurno/Rabah
21.	Maurice Pronen	Rivers	Khana/Gokana
22.	Mohammed Sabo	Jigawa	Birni-Kudu/Buji
23.	Mpigi Barry	Rivers	Tai/Eleme/Oyigbo
24.	Mukhtar Muhammad Chiromawa	Kano	Kura/Madobi/Garun Malam
25.	Musa Ado	Kano	Gezawa/Gabasawa
26.	Musa Sarkin-Adar	Sokoto	Goronyo/Gada
27.	Mustapha Dawaki	Kano	Dawakin Kudu/Warawa
28.	Mustapha Moshood	Kwara	Asa/Ilorin West
29.	Ogbonna Nwuke	Rivers	Etche/Omuma
30.	Rafiu Ibrahim Adebayo	Kwara	Offa/Oyun/Ifelodun
31.	Sa'ad Nabunkari Mohammed	Sokoto	Binji/Silame
32.	Sani Aliyu Mohammed	Kano	Rano/Bunkure/Kibiya
33.	Shuaibu Gobir Gwandu	Sokoto	Isa/Sabon Birni
34.	Sokonto Davies Huttin	Rivers	Degema/Bonny

(continued)

Table 14.1 (continued)

House of Representatives			
S/N	*Name*	*State*	*Federal Constituency/Senatorial District*
35.	Umar Bature Mohammed	Sokoto	Sokoto North/Sokoto South
36.	Yusuf Danuri Sule	Jigawa	Mallam Madori/Kaugama
37.	Zakari Mohammed	Kwara	Baruten/Kaima
Senate			
1.	Abdullahi Adamu	Nasarawa	Nasarawa West
2.	Aisha Jummai Alhassan	Taraba	Taraba North
3.	Bindawa Muhammed Jibrilla	Adamawa	Adamawa North
4.	Bukola Saraki	Kwara	Kwara Central
5.	Ibrahim Abdullahi	Sokoto	Sokoto East
6.	Magnus Ngei Abe	Rivers	Rivers South
7.	Mohammed Ali Ndume	Borno	Borno South
8.	Mohammed Danjuma Goje	Gombe	Gombe Central
9.	Mohammad Shaba Lafiaji	Kwara	Kwara North
10.	Umaru Dahiru	Sokoto	Sokoto South
11	Wilson Asinobi Ake	Rivers	Rivers West

Source Compiled from *Vanguard* (January 29, 2014) and https://www.nass.ng/mp/assembly/7

emerge as speaker on 6 June 2011 against the PDP's favoured candidate, Alhaja Muikat Akande Adeola (Hassan and Lamidi 2017). The unprincipled nature of politics of defection as it concerns the members of the National Assembly and Nigerian politicians at large was further manifested in the defection of 51 APC members (14 Senators and 37 House of Representative members) to opposition parties, among which the PDP was the dominant recipient, on 24 July 2018. This was climaxed by the defection of Senator Bukola Saraki (Senate President), Senator Godswill Akpabio (Senate Minority Leader) and Hon. Yakubu Dogara (Speaker of House of Representatives) on 31 July 2018, 8 August 2018 and 13 September 2018 to the PDP, APC and PDP respectively. The post-2018 primary election also witnessed flock defection of members of the National Assembly from political parties (where they lost out) to others (which promised to field them as candidates). Some of these cases of defection are presented in Table 14.2.

It could be seen from Tables 14.1 and 14.2 that the culture of defection is endemic in the Nigerian body politics. This is in spite of the

Table 14.2 Major defections in the National Assembly in 2018

S/N	*Date*	*Name*	*State (Fed. Const./Sen.Dist.)*	*Chamber*	*Initial Party*	*New Party*
1.	July 24	Abdulrazak Atunwa	Kwara (Asa/Ilorin West)	HoRs	APC	PDP
2.	July 24	Abdulsamad Dasuki	Sokoto (Kebbe/Tambul)	HoRs	APC	PDP
3.	July 24	Abubakar Amuda Kanike	Kwara (Ilorin/South)	HoRs	APC	PDP
4.	July 24	Ahman Pategi	Kwara (Edu/Moro/Pategi)	HoRs	APC	PDP
5.	July 24	Ahmed Garba	Kano (Bichi)	HoRs	APC	PDP
6.	July 24	Akinola Taiwo Michael	Oyo (Ona-Ara/Egbeda)	HoRs	APC	ADC
7.	July 24	Ali Madaki	Kano (Dala)	HoRs	APC	PDP
8.	July 24	Aminu Shagari Shehu	Sokoto (Shagari/Yabo)	HoRs	APC	PDP
9.	July 24	Banabas Gemade	Benue (Benue North East)	Senate	APC	PDP
10.	July 24	Barry Mpigi	Rivers (Tai/Eleme/Oyigbo)	HoRs	APC	PDP
11.	July 24	Bashiru Salihu	Sokoto (Gudu/Tangaza)	HoRs	APC	PDP
12.	July 24	Benjamin Okolo	Kogi (Dekina/Bassa)	HoRs	APC	PDP
13.	July 24	Olabode Ayorinde	Ondo (Owo/Ose)	HoRs	APC	PDP
14.	July 24	Danbaba Ibrahim	Sokoto (Sokoto South)	Senate	APC	PDP
15.	July 24	Dickson Tarkighir	Benue (Makurdi/Guma)	HoRs	APC	PDP
16.	July 24	Dino Melaye	Kogi (Kogi West)	Senate	APC	PDP
17.	July 24	Emmanuel Orker-jev	Benue (Buruku)	HoRs	APC	[a]PDP
18.	July 24	Emmanuel Udende	Benue (Kastina-Ala/Ukum/Logo)	HoRs	APC	PDP

(continued)

Table 14.2 (continued)

S/N	*Date*	*Name*	*State (Fed. Const./Sen.Dist.)*	*Chamber*	*Initial Party*	*New Party*
19.	July 24	Funke Adedoyin (Late)	Kwara (Irepodun/Isin Ekiti/Oke Ero)	HoRs	APC	PDP
20.	July 24	Garba Umar	Kano (Sumaila/Takai)	HoRs	APC	PDP
21.	July 24	Hassan Omale	Kogi (Ankpa/Omala/Omalabor)	HoRs	APC	PDP
22.	July 24	Hassan Saleh	Benue (Ado/Obadigbo/Opkokwu)	HoRs	APC	PDP
23.	July 24	Isah Misau	Bauchi (Bauchi Central)	Senate	APC	PDP
24.	July 24	Kabiru Marafa	Sokoto (Wurno/Rabah)	HoRs	APC	PDP
25.	July 24	Lanre Tejuoso	Ogun (Ogun Central)	Senate	APC	PDP
26.	July 24	Lawal M. Rabiu	Kaduna (Lere)	HoRs	APC	PDP
27.	July 24	Mark Gbillah	Benue (Gwer East/Gwer West)	HoRs	APC	PDP
28.	July 24	Mohammad Shaba Lafiaji	Kwara (Kwara North)	Senate	APC	PDP
29.	July 24	Monsurat Sumonu	Oyo (Oyo Central)	Senate	APC	ADC
30.	July 24	Murtala Nyako	Adamawa (Adamawa Central)	Senate	APC	ADC
31.	July 24	Musa Ado Tsamiya	Kano (Gezawa/Gabasawa)	HoRs	APC	PDP
32.	July 24	Nasif Nafada	Bauchi (Bauchi North)	Senate	APC	PDP
33.	July 24	Nasiru Sule	Kano (Gwarzo/Ikabo)	HoRs	APC	PDP
34.	July 24	Nuhu Danburam	Kano (Kano Municipal)	HoRs	APC	PDP
35.	July 24	Olasupo Abiodun Adeola	Oyo (Iseyin/Itesiwaju/Kajola/Iwajowa)	HoRs	APC	ADC

(continued)

Table 14.2 (continued)

S/N	*Date*	*Name*	*State (Fed. Const./Sen.Dist.)*	*Chamber*	*Initial Party*	*New Party*
36.	July 24	Olayonu Tope Olarinoye	Kwara (Offa/Oyun/Ifelodun)	HoRs	APC	PDP
37.	July 24	Olugbemi Samson Sunbo	Oyo (Oluyole)	HoRs	APC	ADC
38.	July 24	Rabiu Muhammed	Kaduna (Tafa)	HoRs	APC	PDP
39.	July 24	Rabiu Musa Kwankwaso	Kano (Kano Central)	Senate	APC	PDP
40.	July 24	Rafiu Ibrahim Adebayo	Kwara (Kwara South)	Senate	APC	PDP
41.	July 24	Rufai Ahmed Chanchangi	Kaduna (Kaduna)	HoRs	APC	PDP
42.	July 24	Salisu Zakari	Bauchi (Ningi/Warji)	HoRs	APC	PDP
43.	July 24	Sani Aliyu Rano	Kano (Rano/Bunkure/Kibiya)	HoRs	APC	PDP
44.	July 24	Sani Zoro	Jigawa (Gumel/Maitagari/Tankarkar/Gaga.)	HoRs	APC	PDP
45.	July 24	Segun Ogunwuyi	Oyo (Ogbomosho North/South/Orire)	HoRs	APC	PDP
46.	July 24	Shehu Usman	Kano (Karaye/Rogo)	HoRs	APC	PDP
47.	July 24	Shitu Ubali	Jigawa (Jigawa North East)	Senate	APC	PDP
48.	July 24	Suleman Hunkuyi	Kaduna (Kaduna North)	Senate	APC	PDP
49.	July 24	Sunday Adepoju	Oyo (Ibarapa East/Ido)	HoRs	APC	ADC
50.	July 24	Usman Nafada	Gombe (Gombe North)	Senate	APC	PDP
51.	July 24	Zakari Mohammed	Kwara (Baruten/Kaima)	HoRs	APC	PDP
52.	July 31	Bukola Saraki	Kwara (Kwara Central)	[b]Senate	APC	PDP

(continued)

Table 14.2 (continued)

S/N	*Date*	*Name*	*State (Fed. Const./Sen.Dist.)*	*Chamber*	*Initial Party*	*New Party*
53.	August 8	Godswill Akpabio	Akwa Ibom (Akwa Ibom North West)	[c]Senate	PDP	APC
54.	September 13	Yakubu Dogara	Bauchi (Bogoro/Dass/Tafawa Balewa)	[d]HoRs	APC	PDP
55.	October 18	Akinlaja Joseph	Ondo (Ondo East/Ondo West)	HoRs	PDP	ZLP
56.	October 18	Olatoye Temitope	Oyo (Lagelu/Akinyele)	HoRs	APC	ADC
57.	October 19	Shehu Sani	Kaduna (Kaduna Central)	Senate	APC	PRP
58.	October 24	Hassan Omale	Kogi (Ankpa/Omala/Omalabor)	HoRs	PDP	ADC
59.	October 24	Mohammed Musa Soba	Kaduna (Soba)	HoRs	APC	–
60.	November 21	Babatunde Kolawole	Ondo(Akoko North East/West)	HoRs	APC	PDP
61.	November 21	Mukaila Kazzim	Ogun (Abeokuta North/Obafemi Owode/Odeda)	HoRs	APC	–
62.	November 22	Ahmed Abu	Niger (Lavun/Mokwa/Idati)	HoRs	APC	SDP
63.	November 22	Olemija Stephen	Ondo (Akoko North East/West)	HoRs	APC	AA

[a]No party was declared at the time of defection but later settled for PDP
[b]Senate President
[c]Speaker of House of Representatives
Source Nigerian Bulletin (July 24, 2018); *Punch* (October 21, 2018); Pulse.ng (July 24, 2018); *The Guardian* (August 8, 2018); *This Day* (August 1, 2018) and https://www.nass.gov.ng~profile

constitutional provision intended to reduce the instances of parliamentarian defection that weakens party politics and democracy in Nigeria. Section 68 (1g) of the 1999 Constitution (as amended) states that:

> A member of the Senate or of the House of Representatives shall vacate his seat in the House of which he is a member if- being a person whose election to the House was sponsored by a political party, he becomes a member of another political party before the expiration of the period for which that House was elected:
>
> Provided that his membership of the latter political party is not as a result of a division in the political party of which he was previously a

member or of a merger of two or more political parties or factions by one of which he was previously sponsored; (FRN 2011).

The conditional clause on the penalty for leaving a political party on whose sponsorship a member wins election into the legislature, has rendered this anti-defection law seemingly ineffective in curtailing the menace of defection. Recognition of 'division' in the defected party as a ground for defection without losing seat has created more problems than solutions. This is due to the ambiguity in the clause 'division in the political party of which he was previously a member'. The 'division' is not explicitly defined by the Constitution. The kind and nature of 'division' contemplated by the Section (organization or ideological) continues to be a controversial issue. Though the Constitution provides that a legislator must be sponsored by a political party (whose ideology he shares and intends to pursue) but is silent on what becomes of him/her if he/she defects from the party based on non-ideologically based division. This lacuna is being exploited by the legislators who orchestrate division in their political party as leverage for defection without losing seat. This was done in the prelude to the mass defection of the PDP members to the APC in December 2013 when the ruling PDP was deliberately factionalized leading to the emergence of the New-PDP, led by Alhaji Kawu Baraje. The July 2018 mass defection of the ruling APC members was also preceded by the emergence of the Reformed-APC, led by Alhaji Buba Galadima. This is only to create an impression of division in the about-to-be-dumped party to meet the constitutional condition of defection without losing seat.

However, the Supreme Court, in the case of Abegunde v Ondo State House of Assembly and others, has interpreted 'division' envisaged by Section 68 (1g) as division that makes it impossible or impracticable for a political party to function. Honourable Ifedayo Abegunde was elected on the platform of the Labour Party (LP) in 2011 as a member of the House of Representatives representing Akure North/South Federal Constituency of Ondo State. He defected to the defunct Action Congress of Nigeria (ACN) in 2012 citing a division in his state chapter of the LP and his seat was declared vacant as demanded by the Ondo State House of Assembly and LP. His attempt to retain his seat suffered loss at the Federal High Court, Appeal Court and Supreme Court. In its judgement on 17 April 2015, the Supreme Court asserts that:

> The principles enunciated by this court in the two cases of FEDECO v Goni supra and Attorney General of the Federation v Abubakar supra, are to the effect that only such factionalization, fragmentation, splintering or 'division' that makes it impossible or impracticable for a particular party to function as such will, by virtue of the proviso to Section 68 (1)(g), justify a person's defection to another party and the retention of his seat for the unexpired term in the House in spite of the defection. (*Vanguard News*, April 18, 2015)

Despite this interpretation, however, the application of Section 68 (1g) has in most cases been subject to the internal politics in the National Assembly and the whims of the Assembly's leadership. This explains the reason why the leadership of the 7th National Assembly (Senate President David Mark and Speaker Aminu Tambuwal) could not declare the seat of the PDP members who defected to the APC vacant despite the motion for that by the PDP. Similarly, it was due to political consideration that the Speaker of the House of Representative, Honourable Yakubu Dogara, refused to declare the seat of Honourables Zaphaniah Jisalo (representing Abuja Municipal Area Council/Bwari Federal Constituency of FCT) and Ahmed-Tijani Damisa (representing Okene/Ogori-Magongo Federal Constituency of Kogi State) vacant when the duo defected from the PDP to the ruling APC on 5 October 2017. In spite of the call by the PDP members on the Speaker to invoke Section 68 (1g) and declare their seats vacant, the Speaker declined to accede to the call. He argued that PDP members' reliance on Section 68 (1g) to demand for the declaration of the defectors' seat vacant was insufficient given that 'Division in a political party is not defined by the constitution. The constitution does not state whether it should be at the national, state or local government level' (Dogara, quoted by Ezea 2018). Ironically, the Speaker has also defected to the PDP. Consequent upon this, when some members of the ruling APC including the Senate President and Speaker of House of Representatives defected to PDP and other opposition parties, it was not only difficult for the APC members in the National Assembly to demand for the revocation of their seats but to also assume the leadership of both chamber in spite of the fact that it still controls majority seat.

Legislators' Defection and Representative Democracy in Nigeria: Matters Arising

It is incontestable from the foregoing that Nigerian legislators, and politicians at large, only see political parties as avenues for attaining power for personal political survival rather than serving the people through the programmes professed by the parties. The timing of most cases of defection, highlighted above, shows that they were mainly motivated by the inescapable need for retention of power. Unlike in most democracies where politicians defect for ideological reasons, politicians in Nigeria defect mostly for selfish ends in a bid to contest elections. Therefore some party members who foresee that they might not secure the ticket of their parties for the aspired posts or who are unable to get the ticket of their parties after primary election will immediately defect to another opposing parties for the actualization of their ambition. Ideally, political parties should be platforms through which the interests of the people are articulated, aggregated, promoted and actualized. However, most politicians in Nigeria, most especially during the Fourth Republic, have failed to appreciate the fact that in exchange for their trust, the electorates need to be constantly informed about their actions in government. What is of paramount importance to most politicians in Nigeria, as rightly observes by Babalola (2018), is how they will attain and consolidate political power. This desire for the actualization and consolidation of political power is therefore manifesting itself through ceaseless defection. With regard to the members of the National Assembly, politics of defection therefore means strategy of survival; an existential action motivated by an insatiable quest for power by the Nigerian legislators. However, in a 'representative democracy', where the focal point of members of the legislature is personal political survival and politics is seen from an opportunistic point of view rather than altruistic, adherence to the ideal norms of party politics becomes an aberration.

It is however worth emphasizing that litany of defection cases in Nigeria is intricately related to the issue of poverty of ideology in the party politics as being practiced in the country. Given that political parties attract people on the basis of some beliefs about governance around which they are focused and mobilized people, defection is thus related to the issue of ideological bases of parties. As defines by Scruton (1982) cited in Okoosi-Simbine (2005), "parties' ideology are moral systems that enshrine the sanctity of contract and promise between them and the electorate; they constitute the political doctrine from which a programme of political action emanates and on which basis citizens choose how they will like to be ruled" (p. 24). Hence, the most crucial selling point of a political party in a democracy is that it espouses and advances values and ideas that are relatively unique from those advocated by other political parties. Individuals join parties mainly because they share their espoused and advanced ideology and viewpoints on governance. It therefore follows that if politicians join parties based on principle and their agreement with their ideological bases, they are not expected to defect at the slightest provocation from such a party to another; defection should be based on those overarching issues that primarily bound members together (Okoosi-Simbine 2005). As such, legislators, as opines by Eme and Ogbochie (2014), 'are supposedly insightful and principled representatives deeply committed to the ideas and viewpoints of their parties' (p. 28). Since they joined their parties principally because they believe in their ideologies, the only thing that should warrant jettisoning of the parties is a change that runs contrary to the shared ideal values and viewpoints.

The situation in Nigeria is however contrary to this ideal situation. Primordial factors rather than shared values and ideology continue to determine political party affiliation. Right from independence, the country has had parties with ill-defined ideological bases, politicians are attracted to parties based on calculated opportunities and pay-offs. A cursory study of the manifestoes of the 91 registered political parties (as of August 2018) in Nigeria would show that their objectives and strategies are not remarkably different from one another. For instance, the APC and PDP manifestoes are almost a carbon copy of each other; the only difference discernible in them being the emphasis that they give to the programmes articulated, the strategies for implementation and the nomenclative slogans. This, in turn, is not unconnected with the nature of party formation in the country. Since colonial era, party formation has been driven by political necessity, protection of sectional interests and political opportunism rather than ideology. The first generation of political parties formed during the colonial administration was formed mainly as means of championing the demand for self-rule and were later driven by sectional interests as opposed to broad national issues. Likewise most of the dominant post-colonial political parties were hurriedly formed as a prerequisite for transfer of power from military rulers to the civilian rulers. This trend makes a caricature of democracy and bellies multiparty system as a system that enables politicians and electorates to choose from a variegated ideological options offered by different political parties in their competition for support.

Conclusion and Recommendations

There is an intricate relationship between party politics and representative democracy. This relationship is crucial in the sense that political parties are mostly concerned with the expression of policy preferences and choice by the citizens and serve as means of participating indirectly in the decision-making. Representative democracy is better practiced and the interests of the constituents are better served when parliamentarians are doggedly committed to their political parties. However, where legislators gyrate, on quarterly basis, around two or more political parties, representative democracy becomes a shadow of itself. The analysis in this chapter has painfully revealed the prevalence of the culture of opportunistically inclined party defection among the federal legislators in Nigeria, most especially from the 4th to the 8th National Assembly. The persistent cases of defection among the Nigerian legislators hold critical implications for the National Assembly as the symbol of representation, policy articulation and evaluation, strengthening of party politics and effective functioning of democracy in the country. For instance, the massive defection of the APC sponsored members in both chambers of the National Assembly to the PDP and other opposition parties in 2018 adversely affected the operations of the Assembly by diverting its attention from its core mandates to frivolous issues relating to party shifting. It electrified the political environment by further worsening the existing tensed relationship between the legislature and the executive and entrenched avoidable intra-parliamentary crises which ultimately affected the ability of the Assembly to reach consensus on some burning national issues.

In spite of the fact that Section 68 (1g) of the 1999 Constitution (as amended) tries to curtail this habit, there seems to be no end in sight to it as the invocation of the section is subject to the internal politics within the National Assembly and the whims of its leadership. To redress this ugly situation, Section 68 (1g) of the 1999 Constitution (as amended) needs to be amended in such a way that the nature of 'division' and the level of occurrence within a party are explicitly defined. A lawmaker who intends to defect based on 'division' in his party should be required to first obtain a court order recognizing the division in his party. In addition, Section 69 of the Constitution should be amended to ease the recall process. The proviso of the Section and the INEC guidelines are too cumbersome for a successive recall by a legislator's constituent.

References

Adejumobi, S. (1997). The Two Political Parties and the Electoral Process in Nigeria: 1989–1993. In G. Nzongola-Ntalaja (Ed.), *The State and Democracy in Africa*. Harare, Zimbabwe: The African Association of Political Science.

Akanle, O. (2009). Legislative Inputs and Good Governance in Nigeria: 1999–2009. In S. I. Ogundiya, O. A. Olutayo, & J. Hamza (Eds.), *A Decade of RE-DEMOCRATIZATION in Nigeria (1999–2009)*. Ibadan: Department of Political Science, Usmanu Danfodiyo University, Sokoto.

Alabi, M. O. A. (2009). The Legislatures in Africa: A Trajectory of Weakness. *African Journal of Political Science and International Relations, 3*(5), 233–241.

Awofeso, O., & Irabor, P. A. (2016). Party Cross-carpeting in Nigeria's Fourth Republic: Cases and Causes. *Journal of Public Administration and Governance, 6*(3), 31–40.

Awofeso, O., & Irabor, P. A. (2017). The Game Theory and the Politics of Cross-Carpeting in Nigeria's Fourth Republic. *Public Policy and Administration Research, 7*(7), 66–72.

Babalola, A. (2018, February 21). Nigeria Political Cross Carpeting: Danger to Democracy. *Vanguard News*. www.vanguardngr.com/2018/02/nigeria-political-cross-carpeting-danger-democracy/amp/.

Badejo, B. T., Agunyai, S. C., & Buraimo, S. O. (2016). The Politics of Defection and Power Game in Nigeria: Insights from the 7th Lower Legislative Chamber. *Public Policy and Administration Research, 6*(9), 6–14.

Badejo, B. T., & Obah-Akpowoghaha, N. G. (2015). The Impact of Cross Carpeting and Multiplicity of Political Parties in Nigerian Democratic Process. *Journal of African Studies and Development, 7*(8), 215–230.

Bishin, B. G. (2009). *Tyranny of the Minority: The Sub Constituency Politics Theory of Representation*. Philadelphia: Temple University Press.

Eme, O. I., & Ogbochie, A. (2014). The Legal/Constitution Basis of Political Party Defection in Nigeria. *Journal of Business and Management Review, 3*(11), 19–34.

Ezea, S. (2018, August 8). How National Assembly Lawmakers Sustain Unconstitutional Defection. *The Guardian*. www.guardian.ng/politics/how-national-assembly-lawmakers-sustain-unconstitutional-defection/amp/. Accessed on February 1, 2019.

Federal Republic of Nigeria. (2011). *Amended Constitution of the Federal Republic of Nigeria*.

Hassan, M. B., & Lamidi, K. O. (2017). The Ruling Party and Reactions to Opposition Parties in Nigerian Politics: Matters Arising. In M. Habu (Ed.), *The Patterns and Dynamics of Party Politics in Nigeria's Fourth Republic 1999–2015*. Kano: Department of Political Science, Federal University Dutse.

Igbokwe-Ibeto, J. C. (2015). Representative Democracy and Advocacy for the Poor in Nigeria: Finding the Missing Link. *Journal of Political Science and Public Affairs*. https://doi.org/10.4172/23310761SI:005. Accessed on January 16, 2019.

Ikechukwu, U. G. (2015). Political Nomadism and Its Implications on Political Development in Nigeria: A Critical Analysis. *International Journal of African and Asian Studies, 9*, 75–86.

Jiddere, A. J. (2017). The Politics of Party Defection, Cross-Carpeting and the Democratic Process in Nigeria. In H. Mohammed (Ed.), *The Patterns and Dynamics of Party Politics in Nigeria's Fourth Republic 1999–2015*. Kano: Department of Political Science, Federal University Dutse.

Mohammed, H. (2017). The Dilemmas of Political Parties in Nigeria. In H. Mohammed (Ed.), *The Patterns and Dynamics of Party Politics in Nigeria's Fourth Republic 1999–2015*. Kano: Department of Political Science, Federal University Dutse.

Mohammed, H. (2018, April 24). *Political Party Defection and the Future of Nigeria's Democracy Project*. A Paper Presented at the NAPP (FUD Chapter)'s Maiden Public Lecture.

Nigerian Bulletin. (2018, July 24). *Full List of 37 Reps Who Defected from APC for PDP, ADC*. www.nigerianbulletin.com/threads/full-list-of-37-reps-who-defected-from-apc-for-pdp-adc-today-ng.32964. Accessed on January 29, 2019.

Ogundiya, I. S. (2011). Party Switching and Defection in Nigeria: Implications for Democratic Consolidation. In I. S. Ogundiya (Ed.), *Political Parties and Democratic Consolidation in Nigeria*. Ibadan: Codat Publications.

Okoli, A. C., & Orinya, S. (2014). Political Opportunism and Crisis of Governance in Nigeria: Implications for Sustainable Statecraft and Development. *International Journal of Development and Sustainability, 3*(7), 1477–1487.

Okoosi-Simbine, A. T. (2005). Political Vagrancy and Democratic Consolidation in Nigeria. In G. Onu & A. Momoh (Eds.), *Election and Democratic Consolidation in Nigeria*. Lagos: A- Triad Associates.

Okoosi-Simbine, A. T. (2010). Understanding the Role of the Legislature in the Fourth Republic: The Case of Oyo State House of Assembly. *Nigeria Journal of Legislative Affairs*, 3(1 & 2), 1–27.

Omoweh, D. A. (2006). *The Parliament and the Crisis of Democratization in Nigeria*. Dakar, Senegal: CODESRIA Democratic Institute.

Pulse.ng. (2018, July 24). *15 Senators Dump Apc* [FULL LIST]. www.pulse.ng/news/politics/kwankwaso-melaye-15-senators-dump-apc-full-list/mg3y9zc. Accessed on January 29, 2019.

Pulzer, P. G. J. (1967). *Political Representation and Elections in Britain*. London: George Allen and Unwin Ltd.

Punch. (2018, October 21). *Shehu Sani Quits APC, Announces New Party Latest Tuesday*. www.punchng.com/shehu-sani-quits-apc-announces-new-party-latest-tuesday/amp/. Accessed on January 29, 2019.

Rehfeld, A. (2005). *The Concept of Constituency: Political Representation, Democratic Legitimacy, and Institutional Design*. Cambridge: Cambridge University Press.

The Guardian. (2018, August 8). *Godswill Akpabio: Why I Defected to APC*. www.guardian.ng/politics/godswill-akpabio-why-i-defected-to-apc/amp/. Accessed on January 29, 2019.

This Day. (2018, August 1). *Saraki, Ahmed, Ibeto Finally Defect to PDP*. www.thisdaylive.come/index.php/2018/08/01/saraki-ahmed-ibeto-finally-defect-to-pdp/%3famp/. Accessed on January 29, 2019.

Vanguard News. (2014, January 29). *Full list of PDP Senators that Defected to APC*. www.vanguardngr.com/2014/01/full-list-pdp-senators-defect-apc/amp/. Accessed on January 29, 2019.

Vanguard News. (2015, April 18). *Defection: S-Court Sacks House of Reps Members from Ondo State*. www.vanguardngr.com/2015/04/defection-s-court-sacks-house-of-reps-member-from-ondo-state/amp/. Accessed on February 1, 2019.

CHAPTER 15

Twenty Years of Legislative Politics and Governance in Nigeria: How Far, How Well?

Fatai Ayinde Aremu and Adebola Rafiu Bakare

Introduction: Unpacking Two Decades of Unbroken Legislative Practice in Nigeria

The legislature has intrinsic limitations. It is often polarized along ideological, ethno-religious, geopolitical, sectarian and other divisive interests. In developing countries, even in some advanced democracies, the legislature is confronted with the challenge of accessing real-time reliable, credible and robust information to enable it to play its watchdog role of holding the executive and private sector accountable. Often, the legislature depends on the same objects of oversight, such as the executive arm and private sector operatives, for information needed to conduct effective oversight. Information asymmetry tips the balance against the constitutional custodian of accountability and renders the legislature vulnerable to hijack and control by powerful vested interests. This challenge is more

F. A. Aremu · A. R. Bakare (✉)
Department of Political Science, University of Ilorin, Ilorin, Nigeria

F. A. Aremu and A. R. Bakare (eds.), *Two Decades of Legislative Politics and Governance in Nigeria's National Assembly*,
https://doi.org/10.1007/978-981-33-4455-6_15

acute when considering the security and defence matters where classified intelligence is sometimes withheld from the legislature, thus keeping it in the dark. By the time these endemic weaknesses are joined with poor public understanding of the workings of the legislature leading to unfavourable approval ratings, we have an institution embroiled in perpetual crisis of relevance in governance.

Nevertheless, the legislature continues to occupy a central position in the democratic governance and it is one of the institutions that drive the wheel of accountability. Indeed, the legislature epitomizes the existence of democracy such that no governance can be termed 'democratic' without the existence of the legislature. Scholars have continued to emphasize the inviolability of the legislature and the centrality of its role in advancing democratic practice (Volden and Wiseman 2013; Barkan 2010; Adetula 2009; Fish and Kroenig 2009; Cox and McCubbins 2005; Bello-Imam 2004; Mayhew 2000). The significance of the legislature also led to the argument of using its performance to rate the strength of democracy. Fish (2006) argued that the stronger a legislature is, the stronger the democracy of that country. In spite of these submissions, it may become worrisome, if the legislature of a country is observed to be engaging in acts that could truncate the democracy it is meant to protect.

Since 1999, Nigeria's legislative politics and governance has been characterized by activities that on the one hand, seem to engender good governance and on the other hand, pose threat to democratic survival in the country. The National Assembly as a key institution has become one of the most topical issues of discourse among practitioners, academia, public commentators and the citizens. While the institution strives to perform its legislative functions, it has been facing a lot of attacks from the people and the media. The efforts of the National Assembly in ensuring good governance can best be described with the avowal of 'beautiful in-self but ugly in the mirror'. As the federal legislators praise themselves for relentless efforts in the discharge of their duties, the people and media hardly celebrate the good actions of the legislature but are more prompt in picking faults in its actions and inactions that are perceived to be inimical to good governance and democratic survival. In view of this, hardly can one see a situation where the legislature is positively discussed in the country. Despite the inevitability and significance of the institution, it is widely tagged as an institution of extravagancy and assembly of 'rogues' better for nothing than seeking to milk the country dry.

This trajectory is unconnected with the issues that characterized the twenty years experience of legislative practice in the country. While one can agree that some of the actions taken by the National Assembly have help strengthening democracy, the perceived negative actions seem to override the positive actions. However, the fact that the country had witnessed two decades of democratic rule and still counting, points to the fact that one cannot totally condemn the legislature. From this standpoint, it seems difficult to place the National Assembly in either of the two sides, i.e. whether the institution is positively responsible for the long years of democratic sustenance or it is to be charged with the woes hindering good governance delivery in the country. It was on this basis that topical issues relating to the performance of the National Assembly were raised and discussed in this piece.

Dissecting the Major Arguments on Nigeria's Twenty Years of Legislative Politics and Governance

The book began by examining the major issues that characterized twenty years of legislative practice in Nigeria, noting the inadequacies of the legislators in addressing developmental challenges facing the institution in particular and the country in general. The issues raised in the introductory chapter include the controversial circumstances that surrounded the election, selection and appointment of the leadership and committees in the two chambers since the inception of the Fourth Republic in 1999. Excessive politicking and needless confrontations with the executive on matters of less importance to national development was also observed; which mostly led to impeachment attempts of the Presidents, notably President Olusegun Obasanjo in 2002. Other major issues range from instances of alleged corruption, insensitivity to people's needs leading to negative public perception of the institution, poor performance of oversight function, cold executive-legislative relations, effectiveness and efficiency debate, abuse of powers of summons and appointment ratification, poor legislative-constituency relations, the challenges of women legislators, emerging norm of defection politics in the legislature and scandalous salaries and allowances, among others. The major focus of the first chapter was to set the stage for critical evaluation of the twenty years of legislative practice in the country between 1999 and 2019.

From the historical perspective, the second chapter traced the origin of the legislature in Nigeria noting the significance of the institution and its relationship with other arms of government in the democratic process. The central argument is that the behaviour and performance of the National Assembly is heavily influenced by the circumstances that culminated in its emergence especially as an advisory institution during colonial rule. After independence, the executive finds it difficult to accede to the fact that the legislature has the power to set the governance template and monitors the activities of the executive and its agencies to avoid executive recklessness. On the one hand, the unwillingness of the executive to submit to the checks of the legislature and the attempt by the National Assembly to assert legislative authority is majorly responsible for the frictions between the two arms. On the other hand, the legislative relationship with the judiciary is limited to dispute adjudication between the legislature and the executive, except during ratification of judges' appointments. This submission correlates with the findings of Patterson (2002) that the major factor that shape the United States' presidential system is the relationship among the three arms of government with emphasis on the executive-legislative relations that mostly end up in conflict of interest and less interaction with the courts.

The third chapter examined the activities of the legislature in the country's governance in the period under review. The actions and inactions of the National Assembly were interrogated in line with its constitutional and institutional framework as provided in the 1999 constitution. The chapter argued that while one cannot denies the fact that the National Assembly do performed its constitutional roles as stipulated in the constitution; most of the legislative actions were geared towards the protection of the interests of the lawmakers at the expense of the general populace. The chapter submitted that the disconnection between the legislators and their constituents as a result of dormant constituency offices which ought to process communications between the two is responsible for the ineffectiveness of the National Assembly. This validated the classic arguments of Eulau and Karps (1977), Kornberg and Mishler (1976) and Hopkins (1970) that maintaining a good legislative-constituency relations are better and more important responsibility of a lawmaker than Bill and policy-related responsibilities. The significance of maintaining a good legislative-constituency relations stems out of the fact that all other responsibilities of a lawmaker are built on how well such lawmaker apprise his/her constituents of his/her activities and getting feedback from them which will shape his/her legislative agenda and more importantly avoid public misconception of the roles of the legislature in democratic governance (Murana and Bakare 2019).

One of the factors that determine the success of a lawmaker's re-election bid is the level of effectiveness as conceived by the constituent members in terms of how well the lawmaker represent their interest and pursue policies that will bring benefits to the constituency in a competitive scramble for scarce resources in the legislature (Miquel and Snyder 2006; Herrnson 1995; Mayhew 1974). However, the case in Nigeria seems deviant to this argument in the sense that some lawmakers perceived not effective still find their way to win their re-election bids. This contradictory trajectory formed the major preoccupation of the fourth chapter. Using the statistical review of successive legislative elections outcomes between 1999 and 2019, it was established that the country has witnessed a one-party dominated legislature since 1999 with the Peoples Democratic Party (PDP) dominating the institution since 1999 with an upset by the All Progressives Congress (APC) in 2015. The major argument is that most legislators were elected not based on their performances but majorly as a result of party sympathy by the electorates. The chapter submitted that one-party dominated legislature as experienced in Nigeria since 1999 is inimical to democratic advancement as a result of the consequence of legislative authoritarianism.

Studies have established that most of the work of legislature is conducted at the committee level (Fashagba 2010; Patterson 2002; Thompson 1995). This prompted some scholars to focus their attention on the activities of the committees in the attempt to assess legislative effectiveness (Russell et al. 2013; Akhihiero 2009). Chapter 5 of this study threads this path in a bid to examine issues and challenges facing the legislative committee system in the Nigerian context. Findings show that Nigeria is no exception to the centrality of the roles of committees in the legislative practice. Bills are scrutinized and put to shape at the committee level while almost all investigative and oversight functions are done through the relevant committees. Despite this, a number of challenges hinder the efficiency and effectiveness of the committee system which include but not limited to the use of committee apparatus to drive personal interest of members, inadequate funding which usually prompted some committees to request for operational support from agencies they are to oversee thereby depleting the integrity and moral justification for objective oversight, executive interference in the selection of members of committees to ensure their allies get selected in the committees of interest and external intervention of major political parties in the affairs and workings of the committee under the pretence of party supremacy, among others. The findings corroborated the submissions of Smith (1995), Frantzich and Schier (1995) and Rhode and Shepsle (1973); all in the United States context.

Out of the four cardinal functions of the legislature, lawmaking seems prominent. This is why it is often used to define the legislature as the lawmaking organ of government. One can contend with the fact that lawmaking is the only tangible function of the legislature that could be easily evaluated in measurable terms in form of number, content and impact. This accounted for high number of democratic scholars adopting the 'number and content of Bill' approach as propounded by Barkan (2010) to assess legislative effectiveness (Ekor et al. 2014; Volden and Wiseman 2013; Cox and William 2008; Miquel and Snyder 2006; Kruz 2005). Following this trend, the sixth chapter adopted the number and content of Bills approach to evaluate the lawmaking output of the National Assembly during the period under review. The methodology was hinged on ILES model to calculate the effectiveness score of each Assembly in a comparative perspective. Findings show that the Nigerian legislature was ineffective during the 4th Assembly and fairly effective during the 5th and 6th Assemblies. The chapter submitted that the National Assembly has capacity to sponsor higher number of Bills but lack the capacity to push most of the Bills into laws thus showing appreciable prospect of effectiveness if the capacity building of lawmakers is given adequate attention among other factors.

Chapter 7 of the book focused on the extent to which the National Assembly, during the two decades, was able to perform its constitutional roles in line with standard operating procedure. It probed the public perception of accountability and corruption index of the institution and found that wealth accumulation and materialist drive of most members of the National Assembly was responsible for perverting the legislative process which consequently resulted to higher level of corrupt-related behaviour in the institution. The alleged scandalous salaries and allowances and the refusal of the National Assembly authority to publicly declare the actual remuneration of members go a long way in undermining the accountability, credibility and integrity of the institution.

The assessment of the oversight function of the National Assembly which was done in Chapter 8 was indifferent to the findings of preceding chapters. Despite the significance of the legislative oversight as instrument for checking executive recklessness, evidences abound where lawmakers abuse the process. Findings show most committees see it as money-making venture, to the extent that lawmakers usually arm-twist heads of MDAs to take contract which in most cases are not executed, thus, denying the lawmakers the moral justification for probing financial improprieties of the executive. One instance in support of this finding is the July 2020 probe of financial misconduct of the Niger-Delta Development Commission where billions of naira were mismanaged, embezzled and misappropriated in flagrant disregard for the 2019 budget. During interrogation by the House of Representatives Committee on NDDC, the head of the agency, Daniel Kemebradikumo Pondei, publicly challenged the Chairman of the investigative Committee, Hon. Olubunmi Tunji-Ojo, to recuse himself as the lawmaker was a beneficiary of the slush fund through multiple contracts (Ayitogo 2020). Furthermore, the Minister of Niger-Delta, GodswillApkabio, also validated the allegation when he claimed that lawmakers from both chambers are greatest beneficiaries of the NDDC contracts (Vanguard, July 20 2020).

Chapter 9 singled out the leadership crisis that rocked the 8th Assembly and examined its implication for institutional efficiency and legislative stability. The chapter claimed that while leadership crisis has more or less becomes a norm in the Nigerian National Assembly, the case of Senator Bukola Saraki-led Senate and the Hon. Yakubu Dogara-led House of Representatives is exceptional as the crisis peaked to the extent that it threatened the stability of not only the National Assembly but democracy as a whole in the country. Chapter 10 examined the relationship between the legislators and their constituent members. It found that the relationship in most cases is not cordial as the lawmakers rarely meet their constituent members, thus seldom take legislative benefits to the people.

Furthermore, Chapters 11 and 12 were devoted to performance assessment of the House of Representatives and Senate, respectively. Using the three parameters (lawmaking, academic qualification and internal regulation), Chapter 12 of the book found that there were improvement in the number of Bills processed and the educational qualifications of members continued to increase in successive Assemblies. In addition, the House was able to manage its internal affairs through the strengthening of the Standing Order. However, the chapter submitted that the performance of the House fell below public expectation and the adopted benchmark.

In the same vein, the thirteenth chapter explored the institutional framework and internal workings of the Senate in a comparison with those of other presidential systems like United States and Argentina. The chapter's submission showed that the Senate seems to have recorded improvement between 1999 and 2019 but fell short of expectations.

We noted that the issue of gender mainstreaming is a global challenge facing the legislature. In view of this, Chapter 13 attempted to unravel the causal factors responsible for the low participation of women in Nigerian governance especially as legislators despite their huge political parties' membership strength. The chapter identified social factors mainly religion and perception of women as home-workers as the major factors inhibiting women's participation in legislative politics. It submitted that the low membership strength of women in the National Assembly is responsible for their inability to muster the courage to bid for leadership positions in the legislature, except positions given to them in the attempt to satisfy the thirty-five per cent affirmative action in gender balance. Chapter 14 focused on the defection politics that has over the years become a norm in the Nigerian legislative practice. The chapter found that the defection politics was borne out of self-survival rather than ideological considerations. The chapter submitted that the act is inimical to legislative development as it is mostly done in flagrance disregard for constitutional provisions in Section 68(1g) of the 1999 constitution (as amended).

A Discourse of the Basics

From the foregoing discussion, it can be inferred that an effective legislature is a prerequisite for the entrenchment of good governance and by extension, the sustenance of democratic values. The basic thesis of this book centred on the assessment of the effectiveness level of the National Assembly during the twenty years of legislative practice in Nigeria. From the discourse, one can describe the twenty years of legislative practice in the country as a situation of irregular atmospheric motion characterized by up-and-down motion. This is because the country witnessed a drifting legislative era where the National Assembly at one point is adjudged to be advancing democratic values and at other point seen to be retrograding in such a way that deplete people's interest in democratic rule. On the one hand for instance, Nigerians must have to be grateful to the National Assembly for saving democracy during the 2010 constitutional crisis that resulted to the passage of the 'doctrine of necessity' which made the then Vice-President, Goodluck Jonathan, to become the acting President when the President, Umaru Yar'Adua became medically incapacitated and failed to transmit a written declaration to the National Assembly as required in Section 145 of the 1999 constitution (as amended). On the other hand, the legislators engage in legislative actions and inactions that questioned the essentiality of the institution especially with regard to corruption allegations heightened by the refusal to make public their actual salaries and allowances and the circumstances that usually trail the purchase of official vehicles in each Assembly since 1999.

In the same vein, it is inferred that the myriads of challenges facing the National Assembly are the major clog in the wheel of the institution's effectiveness. As identified in the chapters, the factors militating against effectiveness of the National Assembly in the period under review include the consequences of the colonial legacies on the institution, inter-organ suspicion and excessive rivalry between executive and legislature, poor capacity of most legislators, poor funding, misconception of the roles of the legislature, high level of corruption allegations, excessive use of powers of summons, overambitious nature of some legislators in becoming principal officers leading to electoral tension, poor legislative-constituency relations, gender imbalance and incessant inter-party defections, among others.

It is pertinent to note that these challenges are not peculiar to Nigeria alone. Almost all legislatures across the world have their own challenges which are similar though in varying degrees. However, the Nigerian case seems disturbing among the developing democracies and the most provoking is the fact that little or nothing is done by the National Assembly to address these problems. While other challenges may be categorized as secondary, the primary challenge that ought to be tackled head-on is the issue of low capacity of lawmakers. We opine that if lawmakers are trained in standard operating procedures of a standard legislature, most of their legislative behaviours that give the institution negative image would be limited. As earlier noted, majority of the legislators are having capacity challenges hindering their effectiveness, however, despite the trainings to boost their legislative capacity, the productivity level is still very low as most of them are less effective in Bill engagement. The consequence of this is evident from the wide gap between the number of Bills processed and those actually passed and assented by the President, as discussed in Chapter 6. This situation of low legislative capacity is not only peculiar to Nigeria; rather it is a global issue of concern. To this end, legislators across the globe resorted to hiring support staff (legislative aides) from different relevant disciplines such as political science, law, sociology and economics, among others. The essence is to make up for the weakness of the legislators. While this works out in advanced climes, it is unfortunately not working in Nigeria as the lawmakers often jettison merit in the appointment. Rather than hiring experts that could support them, the lawmakers are in the habit of using the opportunity to settle political patronage. The National Assembly management provided the opportunity for each lawmaker to hire 5 legislative aides (NILS 2013), but in practice, most lawmakers hire their friends, family and political associates to the extent that some of the appointees failed to even show up in the National Assembly. This trajectory forced the lawmakers to resort to the engagement of legislative consultants which most of them could not financially afford, thus limiting their effectiveness.

The inability of the lawmakers to use the information and communications technology (ICT) equipment provided in the chamber is another challenge hindering their effectiveness. In spite of the training, the lawmakers are not inclined towards the use of the legislative support gadgets. For instance, we observed that the legislators still use voice voting despite the fact that electronic voting machine is long installed in the National Assembly gallery. Also, legislative businesses are still conducted in analogue form in the digital age. While most legislatures are resorting to paperless processes to save time and cost, the Nigerian lawmakers are not comfortable with this. They prefer Bills to be prepared in hard copy rather than soft copy to be sent to them through official email.

Despite the huge protest against the high cost of running the legislature in Nigeria, we opine that the National Assembly is grossly underfunded when compared to other countries such as South Africa, Kenya, Tanzania, India and United States, among others. The annual budget of the National Assembly hovers around N110–150 billion which is grossly inadequate for running the legislature as populated as Nigeria. The salaries and allowances of the lawmakers as well as their legislative aides in Abuja and their constituency offices are paid from the annual budget. In addition, the National Assembly management also funds the training, consultant engagement and the administration of the National

Institute for Legislative and Democratic Studies (NILDS), among others. In analyzing the budget for instance, out of the Nigerian 2013 budget of N4.9 trillion, the legislative budget was around N150 billion, which represents a paltry 3.1% of the entire budget. This is less than the annual budget of some government agencies such as the Central Bank of Nigeria with about N300 billion annual budget. Unfortunately, the public is misguided that National Assembly's annual budget gulps 25% of the countries budget. Consequently, this made the people to see the National Assembly as a wasteful venture for the country (Sumaila 2013). The Nigerian media outlets could be blamed for the misinformation as the then CBN Governor, Sanusi Lamido Sanusi, claimed that the National Assembly spending constituted 25% of overhead cost in the national budget (Agande and Shaibu 2010). However, the media reported the claim by removing 'overhead' from the statement, thus making it look as if the institution gulps 25% of the national budget.

While our argument should not be construed as been supportive of the National Assembly, we also note that the institution should be blamed for doing little to address the misinformation and misconception. The misconception of the role of lawmakers is the most daunting challenge facing the National Assembly. Majority of Nigerians regardless of their level of education could not identify the rudiments of separation of power and function among the arms of government especially the executive and the legislature. In addition, the executive's inability to provide the infrastructural facilities needed by the populace which resulted to the high incidences of poverty which necessitated the situation where the people approach the lawmakers based on their closeness to the grassroots to provide succor. This trajectory does distract the lawmakers from their primary function and prompted them to explore desperate means of making money to satisfy the needs of their constituencies.

On a final note, attention needs to be given to the wide gap between the executive and legislature as they often consider themselves as competitors leading to unnecessary superiority contest, thus heating the polity. Consequently, this necessitated the needless and excessive confrontations between the two arms of government. The legislature usually bears the brunt of the fallout of the confrontation. In the event of confrontation, the legislature is usually the condemned institution at most times. If there is confrontation as a result of meticulous oversight, the legislature is blamed for needless confrontation. Should the legislature go subtle on the executive, it will be regarded as a 'rubber stamp' institution. This contrasting condition induced the dilemma facing the National Assembly in Nigeria. It thus, precipitates the outcome of most research and assessment of the performance of the legislature.

The Future of Legislative Studies in Nigeria

We admit the fact that this book did not cover all aspects of the performance assessment of the National Assembly within the period under review. No single piece could do that given the enormous nature of legislative studies. This notwithstanding, it is our conviction that a greater part of the assessment has been done. Therefore, a number of gaps are identified for future research. First, individual study could be initiated to handle the assessment of each function of the legislature in the country. This will allow in-depth analysis of the situation at inception in comparison with current situation in order to identify the level of improvement or retrogradation. Second, there is need for a comparative study of the Nigerian experience with peer countries such as South Africa, Kenya, Ghana and Tanzania, among others to identify the exact performance status. One cannot win or lose a race against himself, thus, the need for comparison. There is also the need for future research to focus on inter-institutional interactions between the National Assembly and external institutions that have direct influence on legislative activities such as executive, judiciary, political parties, interest groups, development partners and the society. Assessing the legislature without recourse to the challenges inhibiting its effective performance may become efforts in futility, thus, there is need for future studies on the extent at which the challenges hinder the effectiveness and efficiency of the institution. Some of these challenges noted for examination include the difficulty in accessing data, high legislative turnover, negative public perception and the misconception of the roles and powers of the legislature and the specificity of the Nigerian political environment, among others.

References

Adetula, V. O. A. (2009). The Legislature and Nigeria's Development Process in the Era of Globalization. *Legislative Practice Review, 1*(1), 58–84.

Agande, B., & Shaibu, I. (2010, December 2). *N/Assembly Expenditure: Sanusi Insists, Says He's Ready to Quit If...* Vanguard. Available online at: https://www.vanguardngr.com/2010/12/nassembly-expenditure-sanusi-insists-says-hes-ready-to-quit-if/.

Akhihiero, P. A. (2009). *Governance at Great Cost: An Appraisal of the National Assembly*. Paper Presented at the NIALS Seminar for LL.M. Students in Legislative Drafting in the Nigerian Institute of Advance Legal Studies, Lagos.

Ayitogo, N. (2020, July 20). *Reps Committee Chairman Recuses Self from Panel Probing NDDC*. Premium Times. Available online at https://www.premiumtimesng.com/news/headlines/403973-breaking-reps-committee-chairman-recuses-self-from-panel-probing-nddc.html.

Barkan, J. D. (2010). Legislatures on the Rise? In L. Diamond & M. F. Plattner (Eds.), *Democratization in Africa: Progress and Retreat* (2nd ed., pp. 33–46). Baltimore: The John Hopkins University Press.

Bello-Imam, I. B. (2004). The Legislature: Its Role, Performance, Problems and Prospect in Nigeria. In I. B. Bello-Imam & M. Obadan (Eds.), *Democratic Governance and Development Management in Nigeria's 4th Republic, 1999–2003*. Centre for Local Government and Rural Development Studies, Ibadan.

Cox, G., & McCubbins, M. (2005). *Setting the Agenda: Responsible Party Government in the US House of Representatives*. Cambridge: Cambridge University Press.

Cox, G. W., & William, C. T. (2008). Legislative Productivity in the 93rd–105th Congresses. *Legislative Studies Quarterly, 33*(4), 603–618.

Ekor, M., Katz, M., & Iweala, O. (2014). Estimating Legislative Effectiveness in Nigeria. *Developing Country Studies, 4*(3), 69–77.

Eulau, H., & Karps, P. D. (1977). The Puzzle of Representation: Specifying Components of Responsiveness. *Legislative Studies Quarterly, 2*(3), 233–254.

Fashagba, J. Y. (2010). The Committee System and Legislative Efficiency: The Case of Kwara State House of Assembly. *Nigeria Journal of Legislative Affairs, 3*(1& 2), 29–43.

Federal Republic of Nigeria. (1999). *Constitution of the Federal Republic of Nigeria*. Lagos: Federal Government Printer.

Fish, M. S. (2006). Stronger Legislatures, Stronger Democracies. *Journal of Democracy, 17*(1), 5–20. Retrieved from: http://www.europarl.europa.eu/pdf/oppd/page_8/stronger_legislature_stronger_democracies.pdf. Accessed on March 13, 2014.

Fish, S. M., & Kroenig, M. (2009). *The Handbook of National Legislatures: A Global Survey*. New York: Cambridge University Press.

Frantzich, S. E., & Schier, S. E. (1995). *Congress: Games and Strategies*. Dubuque, IA: Brown & Benchmark.

Herrnson, P. S. (1995). *Congressional Elections: Campaigning at Home and in Washington*. Washington, DC: Congressional Quarterly Press.

Hopkins, R. F. (1970). The Role of the M.P. in Tanzania. *American Political Science Review, 64*, 754–771.

Kornberg, A., & Mishler, W. (1976). *Influence in Parliament: Canada*. Durham, NC: Duke University Press.

Krutz, G. (2005). Issues and Institutions: Winnowing in the US Congress. *American Journal of Political Science, 49*, 313–326.

Mayhew, D. R. (1974). *Congress: The Electoral Connection*. New Haven, CT: Yale University Press.

Mayhew, D. R. (2000). *America's Congress*. New Haven, CT: Yale University Press.

Miquel, G. P. I., & Snyder, J. M. (2006). Legislative Effectiveness and Legislative Careers. *Legislative Studies Quarterly, 31*(3), 347–381.

Murana, A. O., & Bakare, A. R. (2019). Constituency-Legislature Relations in Nigeria. In J. Y. Fashagba, O. M. Ajayi, & C. Nwankwor (Eds.), *The Nigerian National Assembly* (pp. 73–90). Switzerland: Springer. https://doi.org/10.1007/978-3-030-11905-8.

National Assembly. (2010). *Nigeria Legislature: 1861–2011*. Department of Information and Publications, National Assembly, Abuja.

National Institute for Legislative Studies [NILS]. (2013). *14 Years of Lawmaking in the Nigerian National Assembly, 1999–2013: An Analysis of Bills Processed*. Abuja: National Institute for Legislative Studies.

Patterson, T. E. (2002). *We the People: A Concise Introduction to American Politics*. New York: McGraw-Hill.

Rhode, D. W., & Shepsle, K. A. (1973, September). Domestic Committee Assignments in the House of Representatives. *American Political Science Review, 67*(3)889–905.

Russel, M., Morris, B., & Larkin, P. (2013). *Fitting the Bill: Bringing Commons Legislation Committees into Line with Best Practices*. London: University College.

Smith, S. S. (1995). *The American Congress*. Boston: Houghton Mifflin.

Sumaila, S. A. K. (2013, June 12). *Nigerian Parliament: Challenges and Prospects*. Being Text of a Paper Delivered on the Occasion of the Post Matriculation Lectures for Matriculating Students of Bayero University, Kano, Organized by the Student Union Government.

Thompson, D. F. (1995). *Ethics in Congress*. Washington, DC: Brookings Institution Press.

Vanguard. (July 20, 2020). *Senators, Reps Greatest Beneficiaries of NDDC Contracts-Akpabio*. Available on line at https://www.vanguardngr.com/2020/07/senators-reps-greatest-beneficiaries-of-nddc-contracts-akpabio/.

Volden, C., & Wiseman, A. E. (2013). *The Lawmakers*. Retrieved from: http://polisci.emory.edu/home/cslpe/conference_2013/papers/Craig_Volden_Ch2_Ch4.pdf. Accessed on July 13, 2013.

Index

F. A. Aremu and A. R. Bakare (eds.), *Two Decades of Legislative Politics and Governance in Nigeria's National Assembly*,
https://doi.org/10.1007/978-981-33-4455-6

O

Q

R

The manufacturer's authorised representative in the EU is Springer Nature Customer Service Centre GmbH, Europaplatz 3, 69115 Heidelberg, Germany. If you have any concerns regarding our products, please contact ProductSafety@springernature.com

Printed and bound by CPI Group (UK) Ltd, Croydon, CR0 4YY

30/09/2026

02225326-0019